✦ Scotland Is Not for the Squeamish ✦

Also by Bill Watkins
A Celtic Childhood

Scotland Is Not for the Squeamish

❧❧

Bill Watkins

Ruminator Books

ST. PAUL • MINNESOTA

Published by Ruminator Books
1648 Grand Avenue
St. Paul, MN 55105
www.ruminator.com

First Ruminator Books printing 2000

Cover design by Randall Heath
Drawing by Reg Watkins
Book design by Wendy Holdman
Typesetting by Stanton Publication Services
St. Paul, Minnesota

Printed in the United States of America

ISBN: 1-886913-42-0

Library of Congress Cataloging-in-Publication Data

Watkins, Bill, 1950–
    Scotland is not for the squeamish / Bill Watkins.
        p.   cm.
    ISBN 1-886913-42-0
    1. Scotland—Description and travel.   2. Scotland—
Social life and customs—20th century.   3. Watkins, Bill,
1950–   —Journeys—Scotland.   I. Title.

DA867.5.W38 2000
941.1085—dc21   00-042514

        10 9 8 7 6 5 4 3 2 1
                First Edition

To my wife Katie.

⚓

Preface

As a small child, in my grandparents house in Birmingham, I spent many hours thumbing through Robert Bain's book *The Clans and Tartans of Scotland*. One hundred and fifty richly colored plates depicted sets of plaid that dazzled my imagination. I knew little of Scotland, except what I had learned from comic books, where the kilted hero Rob Roy harried English redcoats in 1715, and Andrew Glenn, a quiet shepherd, outwitted bank robbers, sheep stealers, and Nazi spies, with the aid of his faithful dog, Black Bob.

Many people in England had grave misgivings about the Scots, whom they considered unruly and wild, but my Welsh granddad, Jim, was a self-confessed Scotophile, and my Irish grandda, Willie, had a best friend called Jock, from Ardrossan in Ayrshire.

Dr. Johnson is reputed to have said, "The finest aspect a Scotsman may behold, is the road that takes him to London." In my case, this sentiment can be reversed, but the method and means of my first excursion to Scotland were more by default than design.

I returned from adventuring in Ireland in the spring of 1967 and found myself immersed in the odd epoch known as the "Summer of Love." At first the radical trend looked promising—"flower power," "freedom," "make love, not war" were the watchwords of the day—but all too soon, what commercialism hadn't hijacked, wreaths of pot smoke had debilitated to the point where I lost interest. One scene that did benefit from the hippie movement was the folk club circuit. In the early summer of that year, I formed a guitar trio with Mack Tressler and Al Jones, playing at the Troubadour club in Bristol, along with Ian Anderson and "Spider" John Koerner. Later, I found myself in Liverpool, doing spots at the Green Moose café with the guitarist Gordon

Jones and the playwright Willie Russell. Some elements of "the Alternative Society" were fun. I enjoyed the music, but I didn't care for the drugs, and still I was restless. After a string of dead-end jobs and failed relationships, I decided to swim against the tide and turn off, tune out, and drop in. There were alternatives to being alternative, and I took one of the most time-honored routes for my escape. I went to sea.

Acknowledgments

My thanks go to the following: In Minneapolis, Kieran Folliard, Tim Fitzgerald, Kevin Finger, and all the crew at Kieran's Irish Pub; Liam Óg Watkins, Patrick O'Donnell and the Titanic Players, Randon Lund, Jane Davich and the Druid's Cauldron; Jon Bjornson, Tom Carrera, Matthew Lamphear, Cathy Cook, Tom Boland, and the staff, musicians, and regulars at Molly Quinn's; Lar Burke and Ethna McKieranan at Irish Books and Media; Tom Dahill, Anne and Charlie Heymann, Cheri Thompson, Jim Boyd, James Barri, and Stuart Reid Photography. In Duluth, Willowgreen, Ed Gleeson, and Northern Lights Books. Bill Holm in Minneota. In St. Paul, Msg. Jim Brooks, Mary Sue McFarland, and Seán T. Kelly at the *Irish Gazette*; Louise Duncan; John Ramsey; all at Irish on Grand; Sherry Ladig, Nick Potter, Gerry Brennan; Mary Byers, Pearl Kilbride, Alison Vandenberg, Rachel Osborne, and David Mezz at Ruminator Books; Casey Selix at the *St. Paul Pioneer Press*; Jackie Hesse, Nancy, and staff at Caravan Serai. Chris and Paula Dale in Los Angeles; Johnny Cunningham in New Bedford, Massachusetts; Cheryl and Jon Saunders; Cathy's Stage Door pub, Friends of the Library; LaDeDa Books; Suzanne Weiss at the *Herald Times* in Manitowoc, Wisconsin; Seán Hannon in Berlin. In Scotland, Andy M. Stewart, Mame Hadden, Phil Cunningham, Dougie Maclean, Dick Gaughan, Robbie Coltrane, Murray Grigor, Robbie Dinwoodie at the *Glasgow Herald*. John Dingley in Wales; Danny Watkins, Jer and Eithne O'Leary, Jim Sheridan, Manus Lunny, and Gerry O' Beirne in Ireland; Bob Thomas and Gordie Jones at Harbourtown Records; Uncle Walter Lloyd in Cumbria; Monica, Cara, and Amber Watkins in England; George Thompson; Dougie Ford; André Tammes in Australia; Nick Lethard, Dan Rein, and Marya Morstad at KFAI; Brad Walton and Patty Peterson at WCCO; Joe Skelly at KTCA-KTCI; Marshal at KAXE; Amy Gallagher in New York; and all of the Rambling Rovers, worldwide.

Glossary
of Unusual Words and Phrases and Their Derivation

Aen: one (Scots, from Gaelic, *aon*)

Afore: before (Scots)

Alba gu Brath! (Ala-puh goo braw!) Scotland forever! (Gaelic)

Amadawn: idiot (Gaelic: *amadan*, fool)

Aye (eye): yes (Scots; never confused with eye, which is pronounced *een*)

Balmpot: crazy person (British slang)

Banjaxed: surprise attack (Gaelic: *banaghaisge*, the surprising feats or exploits of a woman)

Barry: very good (Gypsy)

Barry gadgie: good lad (Gypsy)

Besom: awkward or spiteful woman (Scots: *besom*, a witch's broom)

Bint: woman (Arabic)

Black Watch: famous Highland regiment (Gaelic: *An Freiceadan dubh*)

Bloke: a man (Gaelic: *buachaill óg*, young man)

Bollix: hot ashes, used as a curse (Gaelic: *beolach*, live ashes)

Bollocks: testicles, or used to indicate nonsense (As above)

Breid (breed): bread (Scots)

Broch: a wide-based circular fortification with only one entrance (Pictish)

Brown breid (broon breid): dead (Rhyming slang)

Cailleach: an old woman, also a witch (Gaelic; perhaps from Hindu goddess Kali)

Cat-o'-nine-tails: a punishment lash with lead pieces on the whip ends (Nautical)

Chancer: a liar, or one who boasts of skills he doesn't possess (Tailor's slang)

Char: tea (Hindi)

Chorrie: to steal (Scots)

Cougar: wild cat (Gaelic: *cu gar*, garden hound)

Craic (krak): fun, also witty conversation (Gaelic)

Crikey: a contraction of "Christ help me"

Crivens: a contraction of "Christ in heavens"

Crofter: a subsistence farmer, usually in the Highlands and Islands

Deek: to look about (Doric)

Deid (deed): dead (Scots)

Dingle: a small copse of deciduous trees

Divil a thing: not much (Irish)

Divvy naw? Do you know? (Geordie and Lalland Scots)

Dreep: to slither, especially down a wall (Scots)

Dreich: overcast or rainy, bleak (Scots)

Dyke: a stone wall (Scots)

Eejit: idiot (Irish)

Fettle: to be in good health or spirits (Gaelic: *feudail,* a wealth of)

Fiddler's Green: the luxurious heaven reserved for dead sailors
    (Nautical)

Fit like? What are you like? How are you? (Doric)

Frowsty: stinky, mildewy

Gambol: to frolic about or cartwheel (French: *gambald,* to leap or
    spring)

Ged dear: a phrase used to show forbearance (Gaelic: *ged Dia,* although
    God)

Geordie: a native of Newcastle on Tyne and environs, so named for
    supporting King George during the Jacobite rebellion

Glasgow kiss: a head butt (Scots slang)

Glic: wise (Gaelic)

Golden elbow: to get fired, get the push; also known as the Spanish
    Archer, *el bow* (British slang)

Guzzunder: a chamber pot (Goes under the bed)

Gypsy's kiss: a piss, especially to put out a campfire (Rhyming slang)

Hame moot: home place (Norse)

Hank Marvin: starving (Rhyming slang)

Haukin (howkin): picking up or digging (Doric)

Havering: not getting to the point, useless talk (Scots)

Hawse pipe: the porthole through which an anchor chain runs (Nautical)

Jacobite: supporter of Bonnie Prince Charlie's and his father, King James Stuart's claim to the throne (Latin: *Jacobus,* James)

Japester: a practical joker, a wheeze wizard

Killick: an anchor (Nautical)

Kirk: the established Presbyterian Church (from *kirke,* a circle)

Knackered: tired out (from *nackers,* traders who buy and slaughter broken-down horses. ME: *nagge,* old horse)

Knackers: testicles (Gaelic: *cnag,* ball used in hurley games)

Knocking shop: brothel (British slang)

Langer: penis (Irish)

Langers: obviously drunk (Irish)

Lucrezia Borgia (1480–1519): daughter of Rodrigo, who became Pope Alexander VI; hobbies included incest with her father and brother and poisoning various relatives

Mickle: small (Scots)

Moich: mad, enraged. Moicher: a lunatic (Tinker cant)

Monkey's: not to give a damn (British slang)

Muckle: big (Scots)

Neb: nose (Scots, from *nub*)

Nicked: stolen (British slang)

Nudey-noddy: to be in an embarrassing situation (Gaelic: *niúidi neáidi*)

Och: but or however (Gaelic)

Oil tot: a favored place or occupation (perhaps from Gaelic: *ól tigh,* drinking house)

On the tear: out on the town, drinking (British slang)

Otter boards: large paddle-shaped boards that keep the mouth of a trawl net open (Nautical)

Paggering: a severe beating (Gypsy: probably from Spanish, *pagar,* to pay out)

Plus-fours: baggy tweed ankle breeches, equiv. U.S. knickerbockers plus four inches (Tailor's slang)

Poncing: living off a prostitute, pimping (British slang)

Raga: an impromptu tune played on the sitar (Hindi)

Rakes: lots of, an abundance (Irish)

Rob Roy: the famous MacGregor guerrilla warrior who fought against the British redcoats in the years leading up to the 1715 rebellion

Scallywags: petty criminals, jokers (Old Norse: *skjalla-weg,* a swaggering loudmouth)

Scouse: a native of Liverpool (from lobscouse, a seafarer's meat stew)

Scrapper: fighter, boxer (British slang)

Scunnered: bemused, bewildered (Scots)

Shagging: from shag, sexual intercourse (Gaelic: *seircín* [shac-*een*], a little lovemaking)

Shielings: huts or houses (Scots)

Shufti: look (Arabic)

Slacker: a lazy person (Gaelic: *salachar,* a filthy fellow)

Snacker: a deck boy on a trawler (Nautical)

Swithering: unable to make up one's mind (Scots)

Tadger: a penis (British slang probably from Taddler, a sausage)

Taen: taken (Scots)

Taking the piss: to mock, taking the mickey (Latin: *micturire,* to urinate)

Teuchter: country person (Gaelic: *tuathachdair*)

Thon: that (Scots)

Trews: trousers (Gaelic: *truis*)

Tumbrel: French farm cart used to take aristocrats to the guillotine

Victualers: store providing food and supplies for shipping (Nautical)

Wadi: dried-up river bed or depression (Arabic)

Walloch: penis (Scots)

Wanker: equivalent U.S. term: someone who jerks off

✦ Scotland Is Not for the Squeamish ✦

→ Chapter 1 ←

For honour's the sum of the mind.
James Hogg, *The Ettrick Shepherd*

TWO POINTS OFF THE STARBOARD BOW, AT THE END OF AN isthmus, a giant crag thrusts skyward like a decayed incisor. Mottled in dun and ocher, this fang of the faded British Empire roots deep into the jaw of General Franco's fascist Spain. The Arabs know this rock as Tariq's Mountain, which in their tongue carries the harmonious epithet *Jabal Tariq*. Defiantly, our imperial forebears, whether by linguistic choice or indifference to euphony, contracted the musical Arabic into the angular English nomen *Gibraltar*.

To port and some eight nautical miles away, across the lazy expanse of a languid azure sea, rises Mount Abyla, also called *Jabal Musa*, shimmering in the jaw of Morocco.

These two mighty eminences are the Pillars of Hercules, in legend forced apart by the Son of Zeus to let the rushing Atlantic waters slake the thirst of the arid Mediterranean. Now they quiver in the heat, tusks in a giant maw seemingly waiting for some tectonic tremor to overturn the Herculean feat and again clamp shut the gaping mouth.

Position: 36° 06′ N. 5° 21′ W.
The Straits of Gibraltar

The western end of the ancient world, beyond which, it was thought, fearsome sea monsters and sirens lay waiting to snatch the unwary into the torments of some unknown watery hell. They named it *Ne Plus Ultra*—"Nothing Lies Beyond."

The intrepid Phoenicians had no such qualms, and if they did, they kept them quiet. Even before the birth of the Roman Empire, these seafarers knew the straits as a portal to the riches found in the islands beyond where the great north wind blew. To assist their explorations, the ancient entrepreneurs established the great cities of Gadir (now Cádiz), in Spain, and Tangier, on the northernmost tip of the African continent.

Following the timeworn seaway from Barcelona, the sturdy freighter SS *Isle of May,* grinning with rust and rivets and loaded with barrels of green olives and red-tinned tomatoes, makes steady progress toward North Africa.

The wireless cabin aft of the bridge hums and crackles with the cacophony of shortwave whispers amid the static crashes of a thunderstorm ravaging the Bay of Biscay, five hundred miles to the north. Ethereal voices in a clamor of Greek, Portuguese, Spanish, and Arabic filter from the loudspeaker and are lost in a warm hiss of spray-ridden wind from the open portholes. In the corner of the radio shack, the old Creed teleprinter starts an erratic tap dance. An oblong of crisp white paper rises from its top as the carbon ribbon jigs out a message. As if typed by a ghostly hand, the message reads:

SS ISLE OF MAY STOP
CARGO 3278/CDZ
FROM CADIZ WILL BE SHIPPED BY
CONTAINER SHIP TODAY (24/8/69) STOP
AFTER OFF-LOAD TANGIER RETURN LONDON
STOP STOP *NNNN*

I tear off the paper and take it through to the Old Man, Captain Metcalf. He regards its contents with a noisy suck on his briar pipe.

"At this bloody rate we're working for bugger all. Bloody containers— they'll be the ruin of trampers like us!"

"Any reply, Captain?"

"No, no reply, Sparks, just acknowledge receipt. I think I know what this means." He taps the note with the stem of his pipe.

"What does it mean, sir?" The helmsman shifts his gaze to Captain Metcalf.

"It means . . . it means the old lady will be for the breaker's yard when we get back to London. Aye, and me along with her, no doubt. Two old dinosaurs ready to be fossilized. Is that not right, Mr. Mackenzie?"

The mate looks uneasy and little wonder: had the captain retired as he was due to, command of the vessel would surely pass to the mate, Mackenzie. A bit embarrassed by the directness of the question, the lugubrious Scotsman clears his throat before replying.

"Och, they'll tart the old doll up enough to get her through the Board of Trade inspection and she'll be fine and no mistake. Ye just see if she don't."

"Oh, ho! Well, now, Sparks, do we detect a note of optimism from the otherwise dour Scot?" The captain grins and pushes up the peak of his cap with his briar.

I take this as an invitation to comment.

"I'm sure it will be all right. The old girl just needs a bit of powder and paint and a working radar and she'll be grand!"

"H'm, yes, the radar. It hasn't worked properly since that dockside crane gave it a dunt yesterday. We may need to post extra lookouts, Mr. Mackenzie—and Sparks, see if you can at least make the scanner go round, so it looks like the bloody thing's working."

"Yes, sir."

We are closing on the port of Tangier, capital of the International Zone of Morocco. I peer at the headland through the bridge binoculars.

"I've never been to an Arab country. Any chance of a spell ashore, sir?"

"Well, I'll do you a deal. If you can fix that bloody radar, you can go ashore if you like. We'll need it working tomorrow night on the downhill run, and mind, we sail at dawn. So if you're off whoring, get the bint to wake you up!" He shares his laugh with Geordie Whittle, the helmsman, who doesn't miss the chance to needle me.

"You don't go wi' hoors, do ye, Billy boy? Aw, Jasus, look at him! He's gone all red!" Delighted at his own display of Geordie wit, he pulls sharp down on the steam whistle cord, sending busy flotillas of Arab lateen-rigged dhows scurrying for safety.

"No chance of steam giving way to sail here! Steady as she goes, number one!"

The bay area is thick with skiffs and lighters of every size and age. Only divine providence and a loud hooter avert disaster as we close on the harbor jetty. All around, brightly painted *dahabehas* pour gaggles of camera-clicking tourists onto the pierhead.

An eternity of verbal thrust and parry forms the negotiations between Arab dockers and the ship's master. Enticements and insults, in pidgin English, are flung to and fro on the warm spicy wind, until a bargain is struck.

We make fast alongside the white stone jetty. Before the mid-starboard companionway can be lowered, smiling stevedores climb over the side rails, sporting all the nimbleness of their Barbary ancestors. Some even have knives in their teeth.

Once on deck, the chattering throng assembles under the flapping arms of an elderly gentleman in long scarlet robes and a fez. Perched on top of an iron capstanhead, the gnarled old maestro conducts the ensuing performance with a bone-handled riding crop. Orchestrated by alternate curses and cajoling, his contingent's eager hands tear at the deck cargo, spurring crates and boxes aloft, soon to be spirited to the dockside by a forest of waving sunburned arms. Hundredweight bags of grain and burlap sacks full of chickpeas are scurried to the pier by sweat-soaked laborers who are nigh-on bandy-legged with the effort.

Despite their exertions, each manages a nod or a smile to the mate taking tally at the head of the gangway. Mr. Mackenzie ignores the gestures and stands aloof, stone-facedly ticking off items on the manifest sheets on his clipboard.

There's a sudden flurry of excitement as a case of ball bearings bursts open, sending cascades of the silver spheres hissing to the deck. The ancient red-cloaked gaffer launches into a new frenzy of invective, lashing the air above his subjects' heads with both his words and his whip. The once orderly disembarkation now dissolves into a scramble for the metal orbs.

Mackenzie shakes his head and looks up as if wondering why rain is falling onto his paperwork from the clear blue sky. Above the melee, the source dangles from the derrick of a dockside crane loading the next ship in line. Hanging like a giant tea bag, a terrified donkey brays pitifully from a swinging cargo net, its traverse from the dockside marked by a rainbow curve of urine droplets refracting in the sparkling sunlight.

Shadows shorten as the noonday sun climbs to its daily zenith. The deck is picked clean of cargo, and the porters retire to the shade of a stone archway to make their ritual ablutions and turn toward Mecca. All becomes still as, from mosque and minaret, electrically amplified voices call the faithful to prayer. Echoing from the lustrous mosaic of pastel stucco buildings rich in pink, red, ocher, and cream, the chanting soars into the heavens. I ascend with it, climbing the ship's signal mast to tend to the injured radar scanner, only to find that the problem is nothing more than a loose antenna connector. All it needs is a little jiggery-pokery and—there now! Coursing crisply in the florid air, the radar scanner turns, and I've earned my passport to adventure.

For a while I squat on the masthead, as in a crow's nest in the days of tall ships, surveying the view and musing on my good fortune to be in the *here and now*. On my left, North Africa beckons with an alluring intrigue. To my right, across the blue expanse of the Mediterranean, the Rock of Gibraltar, no longer looking so imposing, is dwarfed by the mountains of mainland Spain. At a distance of eighteen miles, this once impregnable British fortress seems strangely out of place in a world of free markets and international trade, but the garrison is still there, dwelling like trolls in the tunnel-riddled rock, training their guns on peaceful shipping and singing of the halcyon days when Britannia ruled the waves. The other creatures infesting the rock are the Barbary apes, Europe's only species of monkey. Legend has it that if these little monkeys ever leave the fortress, the great British Empire will fall. I wonder how many are left . . . Should Gibraltar be given back to Spain? Of course, but not while Franco and his fascist pals still rule the roost. My father fought for the Spanish Republic in the 1930s, and he told me how Britain, France, and other so-called democracies turned their backs on Spain, letting Hitler and Mussolini aid Franco in the overthrow of the legal government. That was all a long time ago. Dad was my age, just a wee laddie with a rifle and a noble cause. I don't think my father approves of trade with fascist dictators, but I had no say in the matter when we off-loaded in Barcelona. At the dockside, the Guardia Civil asked the names of all the ship's crewmen and looked them up in a big red book marked "Insurgentes y Criminales Internacionales." Like most volunteers at that time, Dad wasn't daft enough to enlist under his real name, but he will be pleased that the Spanish police are still looking for him and his comrades after all these years.

I chuckle my way down from the rigging. On entering the wheelhouse, I see that the beam sweeps the radar screen once more. The captain is pleased.

"Good man! You're a veritable Marconi, only he was Italian, wasn't he?"

"Half Italian, sir. His mother was Irish."

"No kidding? Did you know that, Mr. Whittle?"

"Micks, spicks, what's the difference?" mumbles the ghastly gargoyle, folding his toothless face in half, in a self-congratulatory grimace. Steering me away from the grisly apparition, the Old Man puts an avuncular arm on my shoulder.

"Well done, Billy. Now you're free to melt into the aromatic delights of this medieval metropolis! Beware of pickpockets, and don't go catching the clap!"

"I'm telling you, Capt'n, he doesn't go wi' the lassies. If we didn't know better, we'd think he's a poof! Divvy knaw, when we went to the cathouse in Barcelona, he went to the bloody cathedral!" Geordie Whittle twists his red-faced leer into a hideous version of a smile. He looks like a smashed pomegranate.

"Well, bully for you, Sparks! At least you'll have something nice to remember when the rest of these randy bastards are pissing razor blades and getting their spotty arses jabbed with penicillin! By the way, how old *are* you?"

"I'm nineteen, nearly twenty, Captain!"

"Ah, nineteen, d'ya know what I was doing when I was nineteen?" He looks to the mate and the quartermaster.

"Aye!" comes the chorus, "ye was the bo'sun's mate on Noah's fuckin' ark!"

I leave the three of them to their laughter and go below.

Captain Metcalf, forty years' service and still a spry old salt, leans on the bridge wing, pipe stuck fiercely into his white beard, a seagoing Santa Claus, always neat in his old double-breasted navy tunic and seldom a harsh word even in the foulest weather. He had "come up the hawse pipe," as they say, starting on square-riggers as a deckboy apprentice and learning every part of a ship, from the top gallants to the keel plate. He always exudes a quiet confidence that is infectious among the men, even a bridge crew as diverse as the saturnine mate Mr. Mackenzie and the giggling, Popeye-faced pisstank Geordie Whittle. Aye, he's a good old stick. It would be too bad if they beached him when we get back to blighty.

"Stepping ashore, sir!" I call from the well deck.

"Carry on, Sparks—have fun!" He returns my salute as I tread the white gangplank down to the limestone dock.

I can't believe my luck. A whole day to myself and a pocket full of Yankee dollars to blow. The language of the sea may be English, but the currency of the merchant marine is the U.S. dollar, acceptable everywhere at exchange rates legal and otherwise.

Tangier's catacombs of narrow, flagstoned alleys teem with kaftaned merchants. Against the press, I jostle my way toward the fortress walls of the old town. On every side, open-fronted shops and street bazaars spill their exotic goods out into the golden sunlight. Pungent smells of coffee, leather, and cooking spices issue from each portal, coalescing with the more delicate fragrance of sun-warmed fresh fruits.

Marijuana, being the ancient drug of choice, wreathes freely in the smoky air. I'm much taken by the sweet aroma of kif that fulminates from the hookahs of old worthies sitting stoically on their lush carpets. If you care to sit down with them, they will offer you the fuming silver mouthpiece of the bubbling apparatus as casually as a cucumber sandwich at a vicar's tea party. However, smoking pot has never been to my liking, as it gives me a sensation akin to toothache and bollocks to that.

The sound of a tinkling hammer draws me to the front of a metal-working shop where the proprietor effortlessly taps a lump of silver into a splendid drinking cup. The unassuming craftsmanship of these Moroccan artisans is breathtaking. His apprentice, a lad of maybe fifteen years, sits behind him turning out identical and beautifully intricate Islamic brass plates or wall plaques. There's a tug at my jacket sleeve. I look down.

Staring back up at me is a skinny barefoot laddie of eight or nine.

"Effendi, you American, yes? You want guide, yes?"

"No, not American!" I walk off up the street toward the seventeenth-century Great Mosque.

"Effendi, you English?" tries the waif.

"No!"

"¿Habla usted español?"

"¡No!"

"Sprechen Sie Deutsch?"

"Nein!" I toy with the boy's persistence.

"Parlez-vous français?

"Non!"

The small lad, nonplussed but determined, continues to skip along, rapidly firing barrages of multilingual questions at me.

"Ruskie?"

"Nyet!"

The boy is becoming a bit of a pest, and I've half a mind to tell him to bugger off.

The little bleeder tries several more languages that I don't even recognize. I shake my head in the negative. Crestfallen, he stops running and stands in puzzlement. Seemingly beaten, he shrugs his shoulders and shakes his head in a most forlorn fashion.

Shit! I've been a cad and now feel sorry for the street urchin. The poor little sod is only trying to make his way in the world by living on his wits, and I know what that's like.

"I'm Irish!" I smile at him. His face lights up.

"Conas atá tú?" the child blurts out in Gaelic.

Vindicated, the smiling youngster shakes my hand furiously. Any Moroccan mudlark who knows the Irish for "How are you?" has certainly gained my respect and earned his position as my guide.

The linguist's name is Mahmood, which is pronounced *Mach-mood*.

For a bit of fun, I call him Mack, which means *son* in Gaelic. He tugs and capers me through the labyrinthine guts of the old city's sprawl. His enthusiasm is tireless.

"Shufti! Shufti! Look, look here! Is beautiful, yes?" Without pausing for an answer, I'm snatched away to the next vista point.

Within the hour my poor brain, suffering from dehydration and kaleidoscopic contusion, threatens mutiny.

"Enough, Mack, I'm knackered!" I sink down onto the cool stone steps of a well hole.

"What is *knack-ka-red*, please?" inquires my walking lexicon, eager to add to his stock-in-trade.

"It means, very tired, exhausted, you have run the feet off me!" He looks at my shoes and mouths, "run the feet off me," then shakes his head.

"Ah!" He points skyward in heavenly inspiration. "You want drink beer, yes? I know place near, is good, not clip joint, savvy?"

"Yes, I savvy, but I thought there weren't any bars in Muslim countries? Drinking not allowed?"

"Is *okay* for you infidel, but not for Arab to drink *al-kho-hol*. Is Arabic word, savvy? Good to drink, but not for us—ha-ha-ha!"

He skips along the smooth stone slabs of a shady thoroughfare to the wonderful mirage of a Carlsberg lager sign. From the open window beneath, a ghastly rendition of Bob Dylan's "Where Are You Tonight, Sweet Marie?" is being battered out unmercifully on an excruciatingly out-of-tune piano.

"You Irish is same as Scotchman, yes?"

"Er, in a way, yes, I suppose."

"Come see crazy Scotchman . . . in here . . . he my friend Anxious, shufti!"

He vanishes into the yawning black portal. I pause for a minute on the doorstep, but when trepidation gives way to thirst, I follow.

The joint, copious with sundry ne'er-do-wells in crumpled cotton suits and smeary sunglasses, carries the expectation that any moment Joe Cairo will appear and say, "The Fatman wants to talk to you."

The low roof is hung with faded pink silk and dusty plastic palm leaves. The bar is a mess of old ship's timbers tied together with hemp rope, at the end of which stands a surly-looking stuffed camel with an ashtray stuck in its mouth and a device for opening beer bottles in its arse. The barman is obscured by a fury of French sailors roaring through their gesticulations at a shifty-looking gentleman, who periodically breaks away to consult a group of bar girls in the corner. The lassies take up the shouting and arm waving until the go-between, sweating pro-fusely and dabbing his head with a red damask handkerchief, makes his way back to the waiting matelots, who resume the tumult. In the up-roar, it's impossible to tell whether the sailors' display is negotiation or complaint. When not screaming, the miniskirted strumpets sit demurely sipping ice water. Surprisingly, these lovelies wouldn't look out of place on Sunset Boulevard or the Reeperbahn in Hamburg; their lives are a far cry from the traditional purdah of Islam.

As if the air weren't pungent enough with the lingering aroma of bhang and the more intimate fragrances of the prostitutes, the music, for want of a better word, would take the face off of you. The cause of the infernal din is a rubicund, copperwire-headed Scotsman with a smile like a boiled herring and a voice not unlike a cat caught in a mangle. He seems to have a vendetta against the ill-starred piano, which he is pul-verizing into submission with all the demonic relish of Vlad the Impaler. Most surprisingly, no one takes a blind bit of notice of him. He flails at the doomed instrument, sending pieces of stained ivory springing sky-ward from the aged keys. In accompaniment, his great sandaled foot pounds on the fortissimo pedal, while a sentinel glass of beer does a Highland jig along the defaced lid of the once-fine walnut upright. With a final tumultuous discord, he brings his concerto crashing to a halt. For a few seconds, he lies prostrate across the battered keyboard, then leaps to his feet, giving a great sweeping bow. To my amazement, the crowd gives him a hooting applause and me the growing idea that smok-ing kif does make you daft and they don't call it dope for nothing.

"Wha' have ye got wi' ye there, Mahmood? Who's this character?"

"He sailor Bill . . . nice man . . . drink beer . . . he my friend like you, Anxious!"

"Shut yer mouth, ye'll catch flies!" says the stranger, tapping me under the chin. "Ye have every right to be impressed. That piano has no been tuned since the Second World War! Onyway, my name's Rab, but folks call me Angus!" He thrusts out a long bony hand.

"Yes, shake hands with my friend Anxious . . . crazy Scotchman, yes!"

"Aye, I am, and I'll eat ye for dinner, wee laddie! Now away and get Seffri to bring us some beers. Tell him to put it on my account." The lad worms his way through the white bell-bottom-clad Frenchies, who are still arguing with the pimp.

"Listen," he says, "can ye get me on a ship fer Britain? I've been stuck here fer two months and I've got to get back to start university in September. I'm a geology student and I was doing my research in the Atlas Mountains until . . . em . . . until . . ."

"Until what?"

"Until I blew all my money on kif and got stranded here playing piano for handouts."

"You mean people pay you to play?"

"No, not at all. They pay me to shut up! Onyway, the owner's tone-deaf and the regulars don't like the Arabic music. Can ye help me? Could ye smuggle me on board yer ship?"

"No chance! Our ship's too small and there's nowhere to hide above decks."

"What about the hold?"

"It's refrigerated."

"Fuwk it! Jest my luck! Listen, Bill, I'm desperate. This is a British Post Office Savings Bank account book, showing a balance of thirty-four pounds seventeen shillings and sixpence. It's yours if ye can help me. If I give ye the book as security, would ye lend me ten pounds to get home? Give me yer address and I'll mail the money to ye. My folks are well off, so there's no problem there."

"Then why don't you ask your folks for the money?"

"I did and they sent it, but that was last month."

"Well, what happened to it?"

"He smoke it all away . . . bad man . . . smoke kif . . . money all gone . . . crazy Anxious, crazy Scotchman. Seffri say, 'No music, no beer, no account . . . all fucked up!'"

"Here, Bill, fer God's sake! Can ye no pay this little bugger, so he can piss off and bother somebody else?"

"Aye, I forgot, I've got some American dough here somewhere. What should I give him?"

"Gi' him a dollar and a kick up the arse for being a cheeky wee shite!"

"Here, Mack, here's a fiver and thanks a lot."

My guide's face beams.

"Allah be praised! You a good generous man—not like Anxious Scotchman. He mean bastard!" He ducks the swipe Angus fires at him and skips out into the blinding sunshine.

"Bye-bye, Bill, bye-bye, Anxious, fuck you!"

"He's got a great command of the language, that wee laddie. I'd no be surprised if he became the next president o' this kip! Onyway, can ye help me oot?"

I look him hard in the eye. He doesn't blink. I get the feeling he's telling the truth, and if he isn't, what the hell? The other guys were blowing their money in the brothel, and there is something about this rogue that I like. He seems to be, as my dad would say, "a man to ride the river with."

"Here, take this, it's thirty American dollars and keep your wee book. We'll just shake hands on it and have a few beers. I'll give you my folks' address in Birmingham. Let me know how you get on."

"Thanks, Bill. You're a pal and you'll never regret this! I'll gie ye the money back when I get hame, Scot's honor!"

"Is that Scout's honor or Scot's honor?"

"Scot's honor, ye Sassenach, *Scot's!*"

"I'm not a Sassenach! I'm an Éireannach!"

"What in the name o' Christ is that?"

"I'm not an Englishman. I'm an Irishman."

"That's almost as bad!"

"Thanks, Angus. If you don't spunk the money on hashish, I'll maybe see you in Scotland one day?"

"Aye, ye will, sure enough. I'll see you in God's ain country. God's ain country, Irishman!"

→ Chapter 2 ←

Here is the city of Gadir, formerly named Tartesses.
Himilco the Carthaginian

Position: 36° 5′ N. 7° 6′ W.
Heading NW. 315° magnetic
Making 12 knots
35 nautical miles off the ancient city of Cádiz

"COWBOY" COULSON HAS THE WATCH. THIS GANGLY GIANT, all boots and Stetson, is a walking encyclopedia of the old Wild West. His speech is delivered in a technicolor Texan drawl, which is all the more surprising because he comes from the northern English town of Sunderland. He calls everyone "partner," except the captain, whom he refers to as "the Marshal."

Sporting a Mexican bandit mustache, as bowed as his spindly legs, Cowboy is every inch the desperado of his dreams. He stuffs wads of Copenhagen chewing tobacco into his craggy cheeks and swills tarry coffee around it. As second mate, he's a fund of stories and a joy to be on watch with. Ashore, he has the greatest difficulty keeping his weather-beaten nose out of trouble and frequently requires rescuing from the clutches of the "Federales," as he refers to the various shore patrols and dockside police. Forever pulling out his imaginary six-gun fingers and *pow-powing* people, he's a real maverick. In Barcelona, he tried this nonsense on two Guardia Civil patrolling the ramblas and nearly ended up getting his noggin blown off.

Although this day we have a fair wind and a rolling sea, Cowboy's mind, unencumbered by reality, roams the western plains of Wyoming, where Indians attack the beleaguered wagon train of his thoughts. He mouths pistol shots while humming the theme from *The Big Country*. He's a card—a wild card.

"What ya reading there, partner? A good western is it? Zane Grey? J. T. Edson?"

"No, it's about the voyage of a guy called Himilco, who sailed these waters in 425 B.C. He was a Carthaginian."

"A Virginian, eh?"

"No, a Carthaginian, someone from Carthage."

"Is that Carthage, Illinois, or Carthage, Missouri?"

"What?"

"Well, ya must a heard of Belle Starr! She was a famous woman outlaw from Carthage, Missouri. Some say she fought with Quantrill's Raiders after the Civil War, and she ended up getting shot in—"

"No, no, not *that* Carthage, the other one in—"

"Oh yeah, *okay,* Illinois. Yeah, sure, that's where Joseph Smith, who founded the Mormon Church, got lynched in 1844. He was just about to—"

"NO! NO! NO! The other Carthage, the one in Africa!"

"Never heard of it!" He stands at the wheelhouse door, firing rifle shots from an imaginary Winchester at the puzzled crew of a Portuguese sardine boat wallowing, nets down, in the furrowed ocean.

What a head case he is. No matter how obscure the topic, how oblique the reference, how tangential the subject, Cowboy can always find a way to rope it in and brand it with some aspect of the Old West. It's a subliminal skill that he isn't even aware of, and my shoulders shake as I read him excerpts from the text of Avienus's account of Himilco's voyage, the *Orae Maritimae:*

> *Where the deep sea flows from the Ocean . . . is found the Atlantic Gulf. Here is the city of Gadir, formerly named Tartesses; here are the Columns of indomitable Hercules. They groan under the rigorous north wind but they stand undaunted. Here rises the head of the mountain chain, whose whole rocky mass runs chiefly towards the warm south wind.*

Under the head of this range, the Œstrymnis Gulf opens be-
fore the inhabitants, in which stand the Œstrymnides Islands,
widely scattered and rich in minerals, tin and lead. Here is a
vigorous people, proud in spirit, skilful at their work and in
their famous skiffs, they sail widely over the torpid gulf and
the abyss of the monster-infested ocean. These people have no
knowledge of making ships of pine, but a thing to marvel at;
they always construct their ships of skins, sewn together and
often in a hide, skim over the vast deep. From thence it is two
days' voyage to the Sacred Island, as the ancients call it. This
lies amid the waves, abounding and verdant and the race of
the Ierne, widespread live there. Next after it extends the
broad island of the Albiones.

"So, partner, who d'ya say wrote that?" Cowboy says, framing his lanky hulk in the wheelhouse doorway.

"The story was told by the Roman historian Rufus Festus Avienus."

"A roaming historian, eh? Festus, eh? D'ya know that was the name of Marshal Matt Dillon's sidekick in *Gunsmoke*?"

I run away screaming to the safety of the radio shack.

Scrambling up onto the top bunk in the little cabin aft of the radio room, I sprawl, arms folded behind my head, smiling at the ceiling. I am the luckiest bastard afloat. Since leaving school four years back, I have been a folk singer, an electrical apprentice in a contraceptive factory, a radio and television engineer, and now the best job in the world, a sea-going radio operator. Nothing can crush this moment. I feel the well-spring of joy bubbling up through the doubts and uncertainties of adolescence. In this one quintessential instant, the world about me seemed as perfect as I could wish for. Since my many childhood criss-crossings of the wild Irish Sea in the company of my mother, things maritime had always enticed me, and now I'm living the life I had dreamed about.

A ship at sea is like a floating village with all the trades, crafts, and social strata of its dryland counterpart. The captain, of course, is lord mayor and presides over his council of deck officers, like the burgo-master of a medieval walled town. All that exists within the plates, ribs, and stringers of the venerable vessel is his absolute domain. He is not above the law; he *is* the law and enjoys rights and privileges that land-lubbers could only dream of. As ship's master, it is within his ancient remit to have you clapped in irons, thrown in the brig, flogged, buried at sea, tried for mutiny, or joined in holy wedlock. He is the Almighty. So you wouldn't want to find yourself signed up with a lunatic like Captain Ahab in *Moby-Dick* or Captain Bligh of *Mutiny on the Bounty* fame.

The mate, the captain's first executive officer, is like the town clerk and is responsible for the running of the ship. He swaps shifts with the second mate. The navigation officer is, as the town planner, equipped with his sheaves of maps and charts. The bo'sun is the artificer, a cross between a carpenter and the keeper of the local hardware store; he's in charge of rigging, ropes, anchors, and the like, and he may carry a whistle to muster the crew. Like the many callings of a big town, a large merchant-man may carry several other officials, including a purser, a sort of banker who looks after the ship's accounts, or a shipping agent's representative known as the supercargo.

Below decks the chief engineer is "lord of the underworld" and rules his Hades in company with a demonic race of grease-begrimed acolytes called firemen, stokers, oilers, watermen, wipers, and donkeymen. He and his team of sweating stalwarts massage the hissing heart of the mighty steam turbine. Somehow, in the crashing noise of the plant room, the chief hears every unusual knock or tapping coming from the clanking contraption. To the music of the symphony of steam the mechanical maestro directs his fleet-footed fiends to anoint grease nipples and lubricate bearings with long-spouted oil cans.

The chief engineer is sovereign of all he beholds, and his subjects owe their fealty to him first and the captain second. There is a stereotype that all chief engineers are Scottish, and in my experience it's true, they are.

When not lurking in the fume-filled pit of the engine room, the black-handed gang climb blinking into the daylight to spit and curse from the aft fantail. Here they gaze astern, as if living their lives backward, for their memories are those of the bars and brothels in our wake, now sinking into the horizon. Seldom on deck at arrival, but usually congregating in twos or threes with the ordinary seamen after departure, they reminisce over the fights, fucks, and favors of the last port of call. These are the hard men of the ship's complement and not to be messed with, unless you want a hot steam hose stuck up your jerkin and the tap turned on.

Cooling in the half door of the galley hatchway, exhaling gunmetal-blue plumes of Capstan "Full Strength" Navy Cut cigarette smoke, is the cook, Leslie Beaton. He's butcher, baker, canapé maker, ship's "doctor," agony aunt, and resident homosexual. Known as "Ma" to the deck crew and Mrs. Beaton to the officers, the culinary queen struts the galley and mess room like the exotic host of a 1930s Berlin nightclub. He is well liked and a good cook, too, possessing a sharp wit and an even sharper tongue. You'd be ill-advised to get on his wrong side, as a tongue lashing from him is the modern-day equivalent of being keelhauled or getting a dose of the cat-o'-nine-tails. Mrs. Beaton has two assistants: "the Saucerer's Apprentice," who helps him with the cooking, and "the Crumb Bo'sun," who scrubs pots and waits tables. I always make a point of getting on well with the cook of any vessel I find myself on. You never know when you might need a sandwich at four in the morning.

In the hierarchy of the analogous township, the wireless operator, or radio officer, to be more precise, enjoys an unusual position. Universally known as Sparks, he (or she) is simultaneously herald, soothsayer, town crier, and communicator with unseen forces. We are regarded by the other members of the crew as odd, Druidlike recluses, who sit for hours in front of glowing dials and twitching meter needles. Seemingly doing nothing, but imbued with great and terrible powers, able, with the blue spark of a Morse key or the thrice-repeated word, *Mayday,* to summon fleets of ships, planes, helicopters, and lifeboats speeding to our rescue. Seafaring discerners of the arcane, our ilk is constantly tapping the ether for world news and events. We are privy to confidential company business, the most intimate secrets of the crew's conversations with loved ones at home, the football results, stock market prices, birthday linkups, Christmas greetings, and impending redundancy (layoff) notices. Our motto is simple: "Hear All and Say Nothing."

Although it might be thought that we spend most of our time keeping out of cold drafts and reading books, we are often the last off the ship when the shit hits the fan. Battery Park, in New York City, has a monument to the hundreds of radio operators who stayed at their posts and went down with the ship.

Apart from emergencies, radio officer is the cushiest job afloat. Shore stations provide traffic lists at regular intervals to be monitored by operators expecting messages. When you hear the name of your ship being called, you establish contact with the server and exchange what messages there are, using voice, teleprinter, or Morse code.

The radio distress frequency watch is based on a five-minute listening period every quarter hour, continuous. The ship's clock is marked in green and red segments to show watch periods. Although in reality, a continual watch is kept on 2182 kilocycles per second shortwave and channel 16 VHF, other frequencies throughout the spectrum can be used as conditions dictate. Most radio operators are self-employed or provided by agencies like Marconi International Marine. This enhances the mystique of the profession, since we are seldom working for the same bosses as the other officers and are usually answerable only to the captain. The ship's crew, above and below decks, considers us a race apart, and I like to think we are.

The bulk of the crew is made up of the ordinary seamen, who do the myriad of jobs that keep us prow to the wind and our feet dry. Like the population of the imaginary town, these chaps can turn a hand to many trades and, although sometimes living an almost monastic life, have just as many fights, feuds, and illicit love affairs as normal people. When off-duty in the mess room, I'll sometimes sing the odd stave of an old sea song just to entertain these lads:

> *There's Liverpool Pat, with his tarpaulin hat,*
> *Amelia where you bound to?*
> *And Yankee John the packet rat,*
> *All across the Western Ocean.*

Rumors of the captain's recall telegram have filtered down to the lads in the crew room, and when we fail to put into Cádiz their worst fears are compounded. The talk is all about the days of loose-cargo tramp steamers being over and done with and the industry killed off by the new modular land, sea, and air steel containers that require less handling. The thought of unemployment has never occurred to me. Britain still has the biggest merchant fleet in the world, and surely they will always need crewmen.

During dinner, the lewd-mouthed Geordie Whittle plonks himself down at my table and tries to get a rise out of me again.

"You wait, Billy boy, we'll all get the heave-ho when we dock in London. This old tub's for the scrap yard, and there'll be redundancy notices all round. You mark my words. Ye'll see more pink slips than a poof's pajama party. But you never naw . . . that might suit a wee shirt-tail lifter like you, eh, bonny lad?" He guffaws into his coffee mug.

I ignore his taunting. I'm used to it, and if you answer back, it only makes him worse. Mrs. Beaton, however, flutters to my defense.

"That lovely lad hasn't a queer thought in his head, more's the pity! But you, Geordie, I wonder about you. They say that people who are always going on about queers, poofs, and nancy boys are deep down a bit ripe themselves! What do you say, sweetie? Are you one of us? Do you follow the lavender banner?"

Geordie stares down at his chicken marsala. For once, he's at a loss for words. In the hiatus, I ask him if he's a homophobe.

"Naw! Not me, naw, naw never! I'm a married man, me! I can't stand the homo bastards, me!" Secure in his island of ignorance, Geordie nods assent to his inner thoughts as he tries to regain his composure. Mrs. Beaton returns with a flower in a glass of water and puts it down before him. Wrapping a dish towel around Geordie's head like a woman's scarf, Mrs. Beaton begins singing:

> *If you were the only girl in the world,*
> *And I was the only boy . . .*

Turning the heat up on Geordie for a change produces the desired effect. He splutters like a kettle on a hob, and everyone gets a good laugh at his expense. To aggravate matters, the crew pelt him with bread rolls and paper napkins and shout rude things about spanking his monkey.

"Yer all nowt but a bunch of fuckin' fairies!" shrieks the red-faced quartermaster, snatching up his dinner to eat alone, brooding, in his cabin.

"Well, thanks, Ma. That dirty-minded sod is always ragging on me."

"No problem, Sparky. That's put him in his place! Married man, indeed! Jesus! Who'd marry that? Could you imagine waking up with him in the morning? Gawdloveus! I'd rather go straight! Anyway, I owe you for helping me out at Tilbury!"

All heads turn to me.

"So, you old son of a gun! You helped out Mrs. Beaton at Tilbury, did you?" Cowboy's eyebrows raise in mock innuendo.

"Oh, don't you start! I just helped him get his meat ration from the victuallers."

I look up into a circle of sniggering faces.

"Well, he had a bad back!"

They nudge each other like schoolboys and giggle all the more.

Mrs. Beaton returns to the table with cheese, crackers, and sliced sausage.

"Now, now, girls, leave Sparky alone. That sainted soul helped me carry sixty pounds of frozen meat to feed you hungry lions, didn't you, Billy? And, I also needed him to keep me from ravishing that delicious boy in the butcher's department—you know, the blond curly one? I love the way he sucks his pencil while I'm inspecting his meat. I think he knows, you know? I says to him, 'Give me five pounds of sage-and-onion stuffing and one of those extralarge garlic sausages, and what I do with the sausage is nobody's business!' He says to me, 'Do you want it sliced?' I says, 'What do you think my arse is, a piggy-bank?'"

Laughter abruptly fades and Ma Beaton sweeps off into the galley, leaving the diners staring in horror at their half-eaten garlic sausage delicacies.

A good chef can be quite a rarity in the maritime service, so when you get one, you keep him. I've sailed with so-called cooks who could burn water and turn out meals that would grace the pages of a Lucrezia Borgia cookbook. The Royal Navy recruits Chinese cooks, both because their culinary prowess is legendary and because they tend to be small, so the navy can keep the galley size to a minimum.

I suppose, still using the township scenario, Geordie Whittle would be well suited to play the part of the village idiot or the town pervert. I don't care for the bullying way he likes to give it out but doesn't like to take it. It smacks of weakness. Mind you, when I first met him, I got off on the wrong foot.

Mackenzie told me that when I met Quartermaster Whittle to make sure I asked about his monkey. Being the innocent on board, when I was introduced over coffee in the galley, I promptly did.

"Pleased to meet you, Mr. Whittle. How's your pet monkey?"

"I'll monkey you, ya cheeky young bastard!" he shouts, storming out of the kitchen, slamming the door behind him. The crew have a great wheeze at my expense, but I'm bewildered.

"I don't understand. What was all that about?"

"He's from West Hartlepool," says the quartermaster's mate.

"So what?"

"Oh, well, if thee don't know, I'll tell thee. During the Napoleonic Wars, a French ship went down off the coast of Hartlepool and all the crew were lost, except for a half-drowned monkey that drifted ashore on some flotsam. The locals, being a bit backward like, had never seen a monkey, so they put 'im on trial and then hung 'im, thinking 'e wur a French spy. Anytime you mention 'hanging the monkey' to a bloke from West Hartlepool, 'e'll do 'is nut. What's even worse is, nine out of ten Hartlepudlians still think the monkey wur guilty!"

"That explains a lot," I confide to my coffee mug.

→ Chapter 3 ←

I sing the song to no one, save those who sail with me.

Anonymous eighteenth-century seaman

Position: 43° 00′ N. 9° 45′ W. Off the north coast of Galicia, Spain
Heading NNE. 20° magnetic
Making 12 knots
12 midnight–4 a.m., the graveyard watch

"THOSE LIGHTS ON THE HEADLAND, MR. MACKENZIE, IS THAT Cape Finisterre?"

"Aye, it is."

"Oh, good! That's the place the Romans thought was the end of the earth—*Finis Terrae!*" Hoping to pass the time by engaging my fellow Celt in some historical banter, I continue. "They also called it *Promuntorium Celticum,* 'the Celtic Promontory.'"

"H'mm, really?" The mate doesn't even look my way. He just answers abruptly, then stands there next to the dim outline of the helmsman, two black silhouettes in a wordless, inky pool, rippled only by the ghostly trace of the radar image.

Except for the wind-shrouded moan of the sea and the heart-timed thump of the engine, the only sound is the occasional creak from the ship's wheel. I begin to nod off. A safety match flares in the gloom, an acrid, spitting, spluttering arc, illuminating the mate's blue-jowled scowl with orange glow. He draws deeply on the cigarette before letting the smoke blow, dragonlike, from his distended nostrils to extinguish the match. The wheelhouse descends to darkness. I feel I must break the silence or die of boredom. It's not the done thing to carry on idle conversation with the man at the helm, so I try again with the mate.

"Mr. Mackenzie, you're a Scotsman, right?" I ask the shadow before me.

"Aye, what of it?" the specter replies.

"Well, what's Scotland like?" There's a long silence and I think that maybe he didn't hear the question. As I venture to repeat it, he speaks as if sensing the moment.

"Why do ye want to know?"

"Because when this trip is over, I'm going to go up there, get a job, and maybe stay for a while!"

The cigarette's red eye glimmers three feet from my face, a pinpoint of light, like the port lamp of a passing ship. The fiery end is sucked into a death pyre before an answer is forthcoming.

"Scotland's no place fer a wee laddie like you. Ye'd be eaten alive!"

"What makes you say that? What have you got up there, cannibals or something?" I try a laugh.

The black shape shifts nearer through the clammy darkness. A rough hand grasps my unwilling shoulder. I recoil from the tart stench of stale tobacco, but the iron grip holds fast.

"Did ye never hear tell of Sawney Bean, laddie?" the mate says menacingly in my face. "He lured young blokes like you to his sea cave at Bannane, on the Ayrshire coast. Then he hacked them into quarter joints, which he smoked in the fire of the chimney, so's he could feed his wife and ten kids wi' cuts of human ham!"

The hand slackens its hold, then grabs again.

"They sent out patrols, customs men, and troopers to try an' catch him, and d'ye know what?" The mate's blow-lamp breath is singeing my ear.

"Whaat?" My voice has gone all thin and wispy.

"He ate the lot of them! He did! Sooked the very marrow from their bones, and the wee ones feasted off the eyes and soft livers!"

He relaxes his grip and lights another smoke. The flaring lucifer briefly flickers a demonic projection of the mate's head and torso onto the wheelhouse ceiling, a dark, dancing shape, burned as an indelible afterimage into my night vision.

Oh dear God! I think I was happier when Mr. Mackenzie never said more than a few words to me. I stand in the murk resolved not to ask any more bloody stupid questions.

"North by northeast!" orders the taller of the two shapes.

"No' by no'theast it is, sir!" echoes the squat quartermaster.

After the watch, a few hours of turbulent sleep thrash around the unresolved questions. When did this Sawney Bean character live? Was he still alive? Had he been caught? In the insanity of near insomnia, all the foul phantoms of the night become attendant bedfellows. A fearful pageant of ghouls, kilted and kitted in blood-drenched tartan, beckons me to a savage land, where naked, blue-painted wildmen hunt haggis from the spiny backs of snarling Loch Ness monsters. Staring from the dark gape of stench-belching caverns, malefic matrons, nursing their malignant offspring, point scrawny, skull-white fingers at me.

"Look, babies—food!"

The cry is taken up by grotesque gaggles of half-starved, whisky-ravaged wretches, rising wraithlike from the thistle-ridden quagmire.

"Food! Food! Food!"

I make to run south, south to the English border, but my legs move only in slow-motion circles. Behind me, howling hordes of red-whiskered Anguses race through the purple heather, porridge and cabers spilling from their hairy sporrans. The plaid-clad clans wave blood-spattered claymores and amid roars of, *"Och aye the noo!"* First mate Mackenzie, wearing the horns of a Highland cow, tries to grab my arse as I scramble back over Hadrian's Wall. A great cheer drowns out my own cries of anguish, soon to be replaced by the primeval skirl of bagpipes and the strident screams of customs men being turned into garlic sausage. I awaken in a pool of liquid, which I hope to God is sweat.

In the galley mess, treacle-thick black coffee chases away the last tainted gossamer of spiderweb illusion from my nightmare-numbed brain. The starboard watch are tucking into their breakfasts, and even Mr. Mackenzie is in good spirits. He whispers something to his helmsman and they share the joke with impious laughter. Looking about, there seems to be more crew in the mess than is normal, and I wonder if the captain has had the bo'sun call a general muster. In the paranoia of the previous night's doings, I must be imagining things. Are people sneaking sideways glances at me? Mrs. Beaton arrives with a large, oval, silver-covered dish, usually reserved for the captain.

"Happy Birthday, Billy! Here's a special Scottish feast for you! Bon appétit!"

"But it's not my birthda—"

My words dissolve into meaningless windpuffs as he whisks off the plate cover with a flourish. Surrounded by a ring of sliced tomatoes and bright green parsley is a one-foot-long ham bone, wearing an old sea boot!

"Today's special, the Sawney Bean Breakfast!"

The old queen leads the assembled japesters in a jubilant circus of mockery. Realizing that Mackenzie has told everyone about putting the fear of Jasus into me, I surrender to the inevitable and join in, laughing at my own foolishness.

Fun over, men return to their business and my sausage, bacon, and eggs arrive, with Mrs. Beaton playing the capricious cook once again.

"They forced me to do it, so they did, wicked boys!" He throws his arm across his forehead and makes a Gloria Swanson exit though the galley door.

When I turn back round, Mr. Mackenzie has taken the seat opposite me.

"Sorry about that, Sparks, but I couldn't resist it, after last night when you nearly filled yer knickers wi' mince. So, are ye still wanting tae go tae bonny Scotland?"

"Aye, I am! More than ever—cannibals an' all!"

"Well, good fer you. If a fearsome-looking bugger like me doesn't put ye off, ye'll do just dandy. Here's a couple o' wee books fer ye tae read if ye like and dinnae be worried aboot Sawney Bean, he died years ago. Scotland's very civilized noo."

"Ah! I was wondering about him. What happened to him?"

"Och, they trapped him in his cave and dragged him in chains tae Edinburgh. Then doon in the Grassmarket, they tied him tae a stake and slit open his belly, an' pulled oot all his puddin's and burnt them afore his very eyes! Then they burnt the rest of him. They reckon his lard ran in rivers doon the street and blocked up all the drains!"

The mate stands up to leave and I stare into my breakfast plate. Somehow, my grease-soaked sausages have lost their allure. Mr. Mackenzie pats the history books on the table.

"God's ain country, Sparks, aye, God's ain country," he says, smiling.

A deep depression is sweeping in behind us from the storm center of the Atlantic, at latitude 45° North, longitude 45° West, the part of the ocean known as "the Devil's Blowhole." Before us, the weakening storm, which days ago had battered the Bay of Biscay, migrates northwest at a similar speed to ours, some thirteen knots. Riding the calm trough between these two fronts, the SS *Isle of May* makes steady progress toward the English Channel. Captain Metcalf takes a silver-mounted brass sextant from its plush-lined walnut box and strides to the bridge wing to "shoot the sun." He peers through the instrument's telescope and smoothly glides the tangent arm until the watery image of the sun's orb sits meekly on the horizon. He glances at the angle scale, with its finely incised graticule, and nods to himself. He doesn't need to calculate our position, he knows from experience. In fact, he didn't have to make the sighting at all; it had been done before he came onto the bridge. No one says anything. We all know he is using his beloved sextant for the last time. He cradles it in the crook of his arm, like a baby, as he gazes for'ard at the white, billowing bow-wave streaming from the biting prow. He seems pleased.

"She has the bone in her teeth. Mr. Coulson, making good way?"

"We sure are, Marshal, we sure are. We'll be in Dodge before sundown!"

The captain laughs and shakes his head. He walks to the chart table and replaces the antique instrument in its exquisite marquetry box. He produces a tiny key and turns it in the engraved brass escutcheon. Then, taking pains to hang the little key on his gold pocketwatch chain, he climbs into his captain's chair and in low tones sings:

> *I thought I heard the Old Man say,*
> *Leave her, Johnny, leave her*
> *It's one more pull and then belay*
> *And it's time for us to leave her,*

Leave her, Johnny, leave her
The sails are furled, our work is done
And it's time for us to leave her.

We are now, as the ancient Greeks would say, hyperborean, that is, beyond the north wind. The warm Mediterranean climate they knew is now far to the south and all but a distant dream. Turgid white mists flit through the English Channel like ghost ships, until they become lost in the swirling billows of dank drizzle. The chill air that has you diving into your locker for a woolen sweater bleeds moisture onto every cold surface, trickling rusty red tracery across the once white-painted bulkheads of the radio shack. Obscured by droplets, the inside face of the watch-keeping clock has become a milky blur, through which the incremental twitch of the second hand is almost indiscernible.

In the distance, to landward, flimsy curtains of cheerless gray vapor draw fleetingly apart, exposing dazzling chalk bluffs beyond, now incandescent against the threatening black skies. These are the famous white cliffs of southern England, gateway to the islands known to Himilco as the Œstrymnides Isles, to the Phoenicians as the Cassiterides or Tin Islands, and to the Romans as Britain, or Albion, the White Islands of the ancient Celts.

Turning northwest, off the fog-shrouded crags of the Isle of Sheppy, the loud clanging of a wreck buoy's bell marks the wartime grave of an ammunition ship, still full of unexploded shells and sodium amatol. Now, without the headlands to shelter us, scuds of wind-crazed rain lash like lunatics at the wheelhouse windows, obscuring sky and sea alike. Like a hoarse banshee, the ship's foghorn wails its warning. In the gaps between the somber blasts, she is answered by her distant cousins somewhere out in the gray gloom. Only the radar knows. One cyclopean eye in the maze of blips and dots sees the course of other vessels in our vicinity. We thread a wary path through the ferries, freighters, and pleasure craft plying the busy seaways around the mouth of the Thames.

"Christ Almighty—hard aport!" The wheel spins even as the order is shouted. The mast of a small sailing yacht tears along our starboard railing, spitting paint and wood splinters from its spars before vanishing into the clammy fog.

"Bloody idiot! Arsing around in weather like this—and not even a bloody radar reflector to let us know he's there! Amateur bloody sailors! Any tomfool who'd go to sea for fun, would go to hell for a holiday!"

As if summoned by the captain's diabolical allusion, a blinding flash of honey-fused sunlight floods the bridge, leaving the captain and crew as stunned and sightless as Saul on the road to Damascus. The Old Man's wrath subsides; he rubs his eyes and stares out of the window.

"I've sailed these waters, man and boy, for nigh on forty-five years and the weather here never ceases to amaze me—up an' down, like a bride's nightie!"

The nebulous labyrinth is behind us. From where the distant spires of London's skyline rise above the green-gray stream, the white wake of a pilot boat makes its choppy progression toward us.

"I'll take her in, Mr. Coulson."

"Of course, sir! Helmsman, make the wheel over to Captain Metcalf!" Even Cowboy is taken by the solemnity of the final watch and for once has forsaken his battered Stetson for the regular peaked cap worn by officers of the Merchant Marine.

"West by north, 280 magnetic, sir!" The helmsman waits until the captain's trusty hands have a firm grip on the wheel before standing back.

"West b' no'th, 280, it is! Thank you, Quartermaster."

The captain stands legs apart, shoulders squared to the wheel.

"You're a good old ship, aren't you, old girl?" he says to the tall brass binnacle before him. He feels the soul of his charge answering back through the helm and joins in, harmonizing with her last song:

> *It's growl you may, but go ye must*
> *Leave her Johnny, leave her,*
> *No matter if ye're last or fust*
> *For it's time for us to leave her,*
> *Leave her, Johnny, leave her,*
> *Our work is done, we'll rest or rust*
> *And it's time for us to leave her.*

✦ Chapter 4 ✦

The tide flows in, the tide flows out,
Twice every day returning.

Eighteenth-century folk song

Position: 51° 30′ N. 0° 00′ E/W.
The Pool of London
Beached

STANDING ON THE DOCKSIDE WATCHING THE *ISLE OF MAY* disgorge her final cargo, I feel like a baby bird that has fallen out of its nest. Although it pains me to admit it, Geordie Whittle was right and I have the pink slip to prove it. Men shuffle to the pubs, cursing their luck, and the more optimistic gaze in vain at the positions vacant notices on the shipping office board. I don't bother. With barely a couple of years' sea time I'm way down the pecking order when it comes to finding another ship. I had been lucky in the past, getting my first job on the *Scandinavian Sunset*, replacing another junior officer who developed appendicitis. Later, transferring as second radio operator on the *Isle of Thanet* and finally to her sister ship, the *Isle of May*. I'd had a good run, but as my mother would say, "Something will turn up—if it's only your toes!" I wander toward the dock gates, duffel bag on my shoulder. The nearest I have to a plan is to catch the bus into town and buy a bottle of rum and a train ticket to Birmingham to visit my folks. I cast a last backward glance toward the old ship, when a movement astern of her catches my eye.

An old tug boat is nosing around the tied-up vessels, like a dog sniffing trash cans. I recognize her. It's the *Olive Oyl,* owned by a big bear of a man called Martin, who says little and laughs a lot. The old tub is a scrapper, always on the lookout for ferrous metals and other forms of salvage to sell. I cup my hands to my mouth.

"Ahoy there, *Olive Oyl!* Ahoy there, Martin!" He hears me and comes alongside the jetty, all smiles. Heaving to, where a flight of stone steps descends to the lapping gray wave tops, the boat's lone crewman calls over.

"Hey there, Billy! How goes the struggle? Are you working?" he shouts, revving the boat's spluttering engine, to keep station against the strong tidal current.

"No, I just got paid off the *May,* over there. I'm beached. Any chance of a lift up town?" I roar toward his cupped ear.

"Sure, jump aboard, I've got some beers below."

Holding on to the wheel with one hand, he steps up on the side rail and stretches out his arm. I grab his hand and step into the well of the boat. *Toot! Toot!* He pulls down on the whistle and I steady myself as he puts about.

"Well, aren't you looking healthy. Where did you get the suntan? It certainly wasn't around here." Martin roots in an old army kit bag and hands me a can of MacEwan's Export beer from his carryout.

"No, I was off in the Med doing the Spanish-Portuguese run, but we got cut short on the contracts, so now I'm laid off."

"So, what now?" he asks, taking a long slug at his tin.

"Well, I don't know," I say, gulping down a sweet draft of the beer. "I'm thinking of going to see my folks, or maybe I'll go up to Scotland and try my luck there."

"You could do a lot worse. At least they make good beer. But, if you're sticking around, I need a hand here on the tug, and my mate Captain Johns is needing help refitting an old wooden patrol boat up at the tidal dock in Isleworth."

"What's the pay like?"

"Nothing, but you'd get food an' board and a share of whatever scrap metal we might salvage."

"Count me in!"

"You're on!" Martin smiles and opens the throttle, making further conversation difficult.

The ancient tugboat chews into the tide, biting jarring lumps out of every wave top and sending spray arcing high over the central cabin, to soak us both in the open cockpit, aft.

"She's a great old workhorse, eh?" the tug skipper shouts into my ear.

More like a three-legged mule going up a slippery ladder, I think to myself.

Martin starts up a song. His singing is deep and resonant, and although it certainly cuts through the engine noise, he has the sort of voice you'd have to train with a whip:

> *Old Father Thames keeps rolling along,*
> *Down to the mighty sea . . . eee,*
> *Down to the mighty sea . . . eeeee.*

London, the capital of the once mighty British Empire, was the seat of the tyranny that all true Irishmen had been brought up to despise, but I had no problem living in the belly of the beast. Sailing from these waters, I'd visited far-flung ports all over Europe and there sampled their fare; I had drank the finest of French wines, the tastiest of German beers, highly illegal akvavit in Norway, smooth yellow Advocaat in Holland, and some awful piss made of distilled pinecones in Finland. In my travels, I had seen the Little Mermaid in Copenhagen, escaped from jail in Wilhelmshaven, was almost coerced into joining the French Foreign Legion in Marseilles, and thrown out of a sex show in Sweden for not taking it seriously enough. It was good to be back in London. I hated John Bull—but I loved his daughters, whenever I got the chance, which wasn't often.

The wheel of the tugboat spins, first one way, then the other, following the curves of the ancient waterway twisting through the city like a contorted colon. Old Father Thames is in a sorry state, his grimy waters replete with foul sludge. As we cruise past Tower Bridge with the ebbing tide running out, the fetor of rising mud banks fills our nostrils until we are blissfully assuaged by the exotic scent of curry powder wafting across from Butler's spice-grinding mill. The aroma is rich and evocative. I am put in mind of India and the river Tamasa, "the dark river," a tributary of the Ganges dedicated to the mother goddess. The Thames, too, was once a female deity, bearing the similar Celtic name *Tamesis,* but the water goddess has lost her purity and seemingly undergone a sex change since the Roman occupation. Old Father Thames, my arse!

At Westminster Bridge, opposite the Houses of Parliament, another strange transformation has taken place. Queen Boudicca, leader of the British Celtic tribes against Rome's legions, stands defiantly in her war chariot, her back scarred by the Roman lash and her raped daughters by her side. Curiously, the statue, symbolizing both the violation of native peoples and the determined resistance to foreign invaders, was erected by the Victorian English, arguably the biggest invaders and violators in history. What's even stranger is that a Celtic warrior queen, who had sacked London in the Iceni revolt of A.D. 60, has been transmogrified by Londoners into an English heroine queen and, to complete the insult, given the Latinized name Boadicea.

"Hail, Boudicca!" I shout, clenched fist raised in Celtic salutation.

"Are you all right, mate?" Martin shouts in my ear, as we chug past Big Ben.

"Yes, I'm fine. I'm just setting my watch to Greenwich Mean Time."

"Don't hurt yourself." He laughs and returns to his singing.

Martin's a good geezer. He says he might be a Londoner, but he's glad he ain't a Cockney. I'd first met him last year in a dockside pub in Lewisham, where he asked me, "Since my dad was a paddy, could I get an Irish passport?" I told him he could, most certainly, and then spent the evening telling him everything about Ireland he wanted to know. He wasn't your typical Eastender, parochial and suspicious of foreigners. We got along great. The Cockneys can be an insular bunch and often think of themselves as a cut above the rest, an elite even among other Londoners. They claim that to be a true Cockney you must be born within the sound of the bells of St. Mary-le-Bow Church in Cheapside. Martin says *cockney* derives from *cocken-ey,* meaning an egg laid by a cockerel, or someone who thinks he's really bloody special!

In Victorian times, London was the hub of the vast empire, and the Cockneys were right there in the middle, ground down by poverty, but still grease on the shaft. With a loyalty that bordered on lunacy, they lived secure in the knowledge that, though the bones of their bare arses were showing through their rags, they still resided next door to the

Royal family. But for all their love of their queen ("Gawd bless 'er!"), they had scant regard for the Queen's English and were virtually unintelligible to their countrymen outside of their own neighborhood.

The rolling river snakes on in a generally westward direction, but going through all points of the compass to achieve it. From the bank opposite rises the massive square bastion of Battersea Power Station, its four huge chimneys spitting smoke skyward, like a battery of anti-aircraft guns. Behind this stands the Battersea Dogs Home, erected by Victorian gentlefolk for the care and well-being of London's stray pooches. The great white queen, Victoria herself, was so distressed by the plight of the capital's starving mutts that she gave five pounds toward their upkeep, and since her benevolence knew no bounds, she gave a further five pounds to aid the two million of her starving subjects in famine-ravaged Ireland.

> 'Tis not we begrudge, the poor old dogs a bite,
> But your callous indifference will cause to ignite,
> The fire of rebellion, that will burn you down,
> And Ireland be free from your hungry crown

"What's that you're muttering?"

"Oh, nothing, just a song about how much the English love their dogs."

"Yeah, they love their dogs all right—man's best friend, so they say."

It's evening when the *Olive Oyl* finally ties up at the wooden jetty near Apprentice Island. Several other boats are moored in the harbor, connected by pontoons and wooden walkways. Martin points to the vessel lying by the stone pierhead.

"That's the *Comanche* over there, on the tidal grid. She's an ex-naval warship, a submarine chaser, built in Canada, 1917, and in very good fettle for her age. She's got beautiful lines, hasn't she?"

"She does, Martin, kinda like a slim destroyer. Who d'ya say owns her?"

"Cap'n Johns. You'll meet him tomorrow after work—he's a good lad. Now go below and stow your gear. You can shack up in the rear cabin. There's a hammock already slung."

Swinging in a rope hammock, below decks, in the tar-scented interior of an old tugboat is the place to read Scottish history. I read until the oil lamp runs low and the raucous snores of the skipper set me dreaming of gigantic whales blowing and breaching in the vastness of the northern oceans. I have never before slept so snug, rocking gently in the sleeping net amid the aroma of old timbers, linseed oil, and kerosene.

The steady rise and fall of the great tidal river sets the clock for the working day. The next morning, I awaken to the sound of gurgling waters washing around the hull from the slapping wakes of the first of many pleasure boats coursing sightseers upstream to visit the famous botanical gardens at Kew. After a brew of strong black tea and bite of breakfast, Martin casts off, and as we begin our scavenging patrol, he fills me in on the job description.

"The whole of the river is ours to scout, from Teddington Lock to the Thames estuary. Salvage is fun, and scrap metal's easy enough to find. For some stupid reason, people prefer to dump their old cars, washing machines, refrigerators, and whatnot into the river rather than disposing of them legally. Our job is simple—find 'em, fish 'em out, and flog 'em to the scrap metal dealers. We'll never be rich, but we'll never be starving!"

Martin goes on to expound the theory that supermarket trolleys have a high suicide rate, and their preferred method of destruction is to jump from bridge parapets. This he proves by trawling a grapnel under the first river bridge we come to. Within minutes he has hooked one, and, with a little tugging, its scant wire skeleton looms up from the murky depths. By noon we have five more stacked on the afterdeck.

"You know, Martin, I reckon it's some atavistic impulse, buried deep in the genes of the Thames Valley dwellers, that causes the phenomenon. A thousand years ago, their forefathers threw bronze shields into the water as an offering to the river goddess, and now it's more likely to be a shagged-out Ford Escort."

"Yeah, it would be nice to pull up a Celtic shield or a sword or something—make a few bob and retire, eh, Billy?"

"Sure! What's the best haul you've ever made?"

"A couple of years ago, I helped the police raise a Daimler limousine that had a body in it. The car had no plates or identification numbers, and the dead geezer had no face or fingertips. Nothing to identify him at all."

"Who was he?"

"I don't know, but the cops said it was some kind of gangland killing, probably a rival gangster or a squealer."

"So what happened?"

"Well, the corpse was never claimed by anyone and neither was the car, so after three months, it became mine by right of salvage."

"What, the car?"

"No, the bloody corpse, you nincompoop!" Martin racks the wheel hard over and the tug turns full about under the overhanging willow trees.

"Let's head back up to the moorings and see if Johns has put in an appearance."

Captain Johns, lean and muscular, is standing on the foredeck of his beloved *Comanche*. Over handshakes and a cup of tea in the wheelhouse, he tells me how he found the vessel sunk in the river Medway with her aft section rotted out. Resurrected from the sticky gray mud, she showed herself to be carvel built and copper fastened with aromatic pitch pine planking on sturdy oak ribs. Once pumped dry, the *Olive Oyl* towed her out of the Medway and up to the Thames without mishap. Now, with the help of friends and family, Johns has the *Comanche* well on the way to being restored to her former glory. We get the grand tour of the vessel, Captain Johns presiding, neatly trimmed beard bristling with pride and eager brown eyes smiling.

"There's no greater satisfaction in life than using your hands to fashion things that last," says Johns, tapping the hard, rich walnut of a recently carved ship's stern post with a wood chisel. "A submarine chaser is a tough little fighting ship, usually about a hundred and twelve feet long and eighteen feet across the beam. They were powered by two bloody great Perkins diesels and could ram an enemy sub at twenty-five knots. I've got her engines out for refits at the moment and two ton of cast iron ingots left in their place to act as ballast."

He stands back to look at his handiwork.

"Did you know the *Comanche* was used back in 1940, for the evacuation of the British Army from Dunkirk? I had to patch up old bullet holes in her hull!"

Johns is rightly proud of his magnificent wooden wonder and takes me up on my offer to donate some time helping him fix her up.

"I can help you with installing the electrical wiring and any radio equipment you might have."

"Well, at the moment we have little to put in, but would you mind helping me with the woodworking side?"

"If you can show me what to do, Skipper. I don't know much about shipbuilding."

We shake on it.

"Welcome aboard," he says.

When not pulling garbage out of the river or towing disabled craft off mud banks, I labor under the skilled eye of Captain Johns. He's a natural teacher, exacting but patient. From this self-taught master, I learn the sweaty craft of steam-bending long timber stringers along the length of the hull interior and chamfering them with neat precision into the massive keel top. This process is followed by a deafening "Duet for Two Hammers and a Bucket of Four-Inch Copper Rivets." In this performance, one man outside the hull belts nails through the planking and ribs, while the other, on the inside, puts a copper washer on each emerging nail head and dollies the rivet ends over with great hammer blows. Row upon row of these glinting rivets mark the progress along the hull, until all the timbers are as one.

This work would be impossible without the aid of the tidal grid. This comprises an oblong lattice of massive square timbers set in a concrete base below the pier wall. Any vessel tied to the quayside above it drops with the ebbing tide onto the grid, where her dry bottom can be worked on, until the returning tide refloats her hours later. At each low tide we stand on the grid, hammering putty-soaked hemp caulking into the gaps between the timber planking to completely seal the hull.

Today with the tide falling, it's clear to Captain Johns that the *Comanche* is settling in an odd fashion on the grid; something is obviously wrong with the apparatus, and he runs across the wooden catwalks calling to us.

"Martin, Billy, are you there?"

"Aye, we are," says I, emerging with a half-eaten bacon sandwich in my hand.

"Do you want some breakfast?" says Martin, stirring rashers in an old cast iron skillet.

"No, lads—can you help? I think something is wrong with the boat. She's not—" Johns's words are stifled by the hideous crack of splintering timbers as the *Comanche* slips suddenly downward with an upsurge of hissing foam.

"Dear God!"

We scramble over the pontoons to the stricken vessel. Onboard all seems normal, except for a few spilled paint tins and a couple of broken coffee cups. It's only when the tide falls farther that we can begin to see the cause of the damage. Against all the odds, an almost totally waterlogged mooring pylon, leisurely drifting seaward with the tide, had been trapped under the keel of the *Comanche*. The sheer weight bearing down of the aft keel section has snapped over twenty feet of it clean away. This is a disaster. Massive timbers fit for keel work are hard to come by and very expensive. The fear is that if the integrity of the ship's hull has been compromised by the loss of the keel, the weakened aft section won't be able to support the two tons of cast iron ballast inside. With his beloved ship in danger of breaking apart, Captain Johns has the look of a man about to be hung. Desperate measures need to be taken, but we stand staring like cows at a juggler, until suddenly Johns takes command, ordering a three-inch-thick rope hawser to be slipped under the hull from the stern end. Martin and I jump to it.

"Tie the ends together in a reef knot and pass the loop over the iron bollard on the dockside!"

"Okay, now what?"

"Martin, grab a scaffolding pipe and twist it in the loop to take up the slack!"

"Right!" Martin turns the steel pipe in the hoop of rope, and the hawser tightens until it takes all three of us to make the final twist. Johns binds the scaffolding tube into place with lash line to stop it spinning back out.

"There, that should hold it for a while. That's what you call a Spanish windlass," he says to me with a wink. "The next bit is a little more tricky. We need to get into the water and jack up the aft end with blocks and stanchions to support the weight when the buoyancy's gone. Can you both swim?"

"Aye!" says Martin stripping off his shirt.

"Of course!" I say, lying, not wanting to be left out.

Before too long, I wish I had been left out. Standing up to my waist in murky water is not a pleasant feeling, and balancing precariously on the three-foot-high slippery piles of the tidal grid has my arse knitting an Aran sweater.

Splashing in the filthy current, we jack timber supports from the concrete riverbed to the bottom of the wooden hull. As the tide falls, the job becomes less terrifying; the tops of the grid frame can now be seen, lessening the danger of stepping off and vanishing into the tidal race. At full ebb, the luckless craft creaks and groans pitifully, but the fixings hold.

We all get cleaned up and Johns inspects the full length of the splintered keel, assessing the damage, running his hand along the hull planks like a trainer petting a horse's neck.

"The good news is that the keel snapped aft of the stern scarf joint, so we can marry a new piece on from there. The bad news is, I don't know where to get a twenty-one-foot piece of seasoned timber deep enough or broad enough."

Being the last dog on the dump, I had no idea, but Martin raises a finger in the air.

"Old man Comerford! He's got a warehouse full of ship's timbers and all sorts a couple of miles down the river."

"No, no, old Comerford is a cranky old sod. I tried to buy some Perspex off him once and he just about set the dogs on me."

"That's because you were looking for something man-made. He won't have any truck with fiberglass or plastic—he says it's the ruin of the industry. You stay here and keep an eye on the boat, and me an' Billy will pop down in the Land Rover to see if he can help."

Captain Johns nods and Martin grabs the keys to the old red jeep.

We arrive fifteen minutes later at Comerford's wood yard. After nervously passing the pen of snarling German shepherds at the gateway, we enter a high-walled courtyard stuffed with pallets of timbers, some green with creosote and others ancient with mold.

Apart from a desk drowning in a sea of sun-bleached paperwork, the timber merchant's office is empty. The old clock on the wall stopped so long ago that spiders have made generations of webs between its hands, while beneath, a faded Michelin calendar indicates that five years ago St. Patrick's Day was on a Wednesday.

"What the bloody hell do you want!" comes a raspish voice. We look around, but there's no one to be seen.

"Mr. Comerford, is that you?"

"Who else would it be, ya blithering idiot? What do ya want?"

The gruff, gravelly voice seems to be coming from outside, but stepping once more into the daylight, we can still see no sign of the owner.

"Are you daft beggars going to stand there rubbernecking all day, or do you want something?" growls a vicious-looking circular saw.

"Oh, there you are!" says Martin, peering into the brick-lined saw pit beneath the machine from which a moon-round face blazes crimson below a conical skullcap of white sawdust.

"So what d'ya want? Cat got your tongue, has he? Speak up or bugger off, I'm busy!"

The blue overalled sawyer ascends from the pit, wiping grease and sawdust from his hands. He views us with obvious distaste.

"We need a piece of timber, for a keel," Martin offers with a smile.

"Oh, do you now? Well, I only supply real shipbuilders, not trendy young upstarts building plastic toy yachts." He turns his back and begins walking away toward the warehouse.

"It's . . . it's a real ship!" I find myself stammering. "A warship, pitch pine on oak—carvel built!"

The old boy stops in his tracks.

"What kind o' warship?"

"She's a 1917 submarine chaser—ML class!"

"Is it that ML tied up at Isleworth?" he asks, shaking his head and sending wood chips and sawdust in all directions.

"Yes, that's her, the *Comanche*. She's broken the end off her keel."

"What you need is a piece of walnut, and I just so have one. The last cut in the store. Come with me." The old chap makes off, chuckling to himself.

We follow him into a hangar filled to the roof with seasoned timber beams. Mr. Comerford wanders about, tapping his front teeth with a pencil. Then he stops and points to a slab of wood straddling the rafters.

"Up there, a lovely lump of walnut I've had since the Second World

War. If you want it, get it down." With that he toddles off, pencil behind his ear.

We require no further invitation and, clambering up the swaying piles of lumber, with much grunting and cursing, wrestle the burdensome balk to the ground.

"By God, lads, you're keen and no mistake. I'm surprised you could lift it. Anyway, how long did you say it had to be?" he says, running a flexible ruler along the edge.

"Twenty-one feet."

"Well, you're in luck—it's twenty-one foot exactly!"

"How much is it?" says Martin pulling out his wallet.

"You can have it for free! I've seen the work you young lads are doing to that boat. You have heart and soul in it, and I'm glad to see it go to a good home. Now piss off, afore I change me mind!" He heads off to feed his whooping dogs.

We do as we're bidden, speeding away from the yard with the new keel timber jutting out dangerously from the back of the jeep and me sitting on the other end to balance it.

Johns stares at the walnut beam, his arms making silent circles in the air.

"It's . . . it's perfect!" he finally says. "All it needs is an angled cut to make the scarf joint and a little hand planing, and I'm sure it will fit. How much was it?"

"Oh, let's just say you owe us a beer—or two."

Captain Johns is a happy boy again and begins preparing the piece. Martin and I descend to the grid to make ready for the repair. Here we drill fixing holes from below and drop in long keel-securing bolts from above. With the aid of arc lights, we work far into the night, using the flotation of the rising tide to buoy the heavy new keel timber into place. At last, it is done and us with it. Back on the tug, a beer never tasted so good, nor rope hammock felt so comfortable.

"What a bloody day!" says Martin, quenching the oil lamp.

The following morning is clear and cloudless. After breakfast we remove the remains of the *Comanche*'s rotten transom. To her designer's eternal credit, even with her backside open to the sky, she hardly ships a thimble-ful of water from the wake of passing river craft. By evening a thunder-storm of cataclysmic proportions tears away the protective tarpaulin covering the open stern and fills the *Comanche* with two feet of rain-water. Johns fires up the ancient bilge pump, which promptly fails, leav-ing the water lying in great rusty puddles among the cast iron ingots. After the hardships involved in riveting and floating on keel sections, replanking the transom is a leisurely doddle, the last bolt being snugged down just before sunset on Friday evening.

At weekends, Martin often disappears, leaving me sole custodian of the *Olive Oyl*. Unlike myself, he has a girlfriend tucked away some-where. With nothing better to do I explore the riverbanks and sandbars, just as I did in my childhood along the shores of the river Shannon in Ireland. Each low tide reveals a different aspect of the ever-changing watercourse, and, when you know where to look, the glory holes of the great river give up treasures. Old clay pipes, brass military buttons, Victorian coins, and glass marbles all surrender to the prying eye, and pieces of terra-cotta Italian pottery are evidence that the Celtic town of Lugdunnum later became the Roman garrison town of Londinium.

This weekend, work on the *Comanche* has stopped; Johns and his girlfriend have gone up to London for the weekend and he's asked me to keep an eye on the boat. I make a tour of inspection to see if there are any odd jobs I might be doing, just as a courtesy like. Below decks, the bottom part of the hold still swims with several hundred gallons of gory-looking, rust water greasy with creosote and teak oil. Determined to be a hero and pump it out, I idle my time trying to manufacture a bilge pump from old washing machine parts. My efforts are met with failure, until it dawns on me that the vessel, being seated on a tidal grid, is for the next few hours, basically in dry dock. If I open the six seacocks along the ship's bottom, all of the water above the stems will spill out of the interior and I can mop up what's left. Splashing around in the hold, I locate each seacock and yank the levers to the open position. Soon, six whirlpool eddies form over the open valves, making a noise like an old man sucking his gums. I climb outside to take a look. The *Comanche* is sitting high and dry with her seacocks discharging steady streams of sanguine bilge onto the concrete slabs below, where it congeals like blood on a slaughterhouse floor.

Inside the hull, the water level begins to drop, revealing a tan tide mark of creosote stains around the timbers and the oxidizing ingots underneath.

A dark shadow flits across the piles of pig iron as Martin's great gape of a face appears over the hatchway.

"Billy? Ah, good! You're pumping her out, Cap'n Johns will be pleased . . . erm . . . bugger, I've forgotten what I had to tell you. Oh, yes—I ran into some of your old shipmates. They're meeting up in the Apprentice this afternoon for your skipper's retirement party. You'd better get yer skates on if you're going."

"Damn it, Martin! I'd forgotten all about it. I'd best get changed out of these overalls. Are you gone for the weekend?"

"Yeah, I'm going over to Thames Ditton to visit my old mum—it's her birthday. Keep your eye on things for me and I'll see you Monday!"

"Sure, no bother. Have a good time."

"You, too!"

Martin vanishes from whence he came. I climb out of the hold to blithely stroll back to the tugboat in a cloud of smug contentment. Getting the *Comanche* to drain herself was a stroke of sheer bloody genius. What a clever little cock I am!

Position: 51° 30′ N. 0° 03′ W.
The London Apprentice Tavern
Dead in the water

An odd-looking assembly takes place in the riverside tavern. Mate Mackenzie and Cowboy Coulson have reserved a room overlooking the Thames and the chief engineer, Geordie Whittle, the bo'sun, Mrs. Beaton, and myself are all in our best bib and tucker for the occasion.

An old Morris Minor motorcar, with a wheelchair sticking out of the boot, chugs into the pub carpark and grinds to a halt with a sonorous squeal of brakes.

"They're here!" says Mackenzie. Cowboy and Geordie Whittle are detailed to assist the captain and his invalid wife out of their vehicle. We line up either side of the door as Captain and Mrs. Metcalf enter. Bo'sun

Parry, whistle in his cupped hand, pipes the couple aboard into the company of applauding shipmates.

Mrs. Metcalf, an outgoing, pleasant lady with a merry eye and quick wit, is propelled by the master toward me.

"Sparks . . . er . . . sorry, Bill. I don't believe you've ever met my wife?"

"No, sir. I've never had the pleasure. I'm pleased to meet you, Mrs. Metcalf."

"Call me May, all my friends do."

We shake hands.

White beard combed, Captain Metcalf, sitting with his wife in the afternoon quiet of an English pub, looks remarkably like George Bernard Shaw. The tweed Norfolk jacket and matching plus-fours continue the theme, which becomes more pronounced when he produces his beloved briar pipe and leans back to enjoy the conversation.

Walking back from the bar, with a fresh tray of drinks, I eavesdrop half of Mrs. Metcalf's soliloquy.

". . . but I always knew he had two mistresses and now he's going to give one of them up! The *Isle of May* is, as we feared, for the breaker's yard. Now, all I have to do is get rid of my other rival, the sea, and he's all mine!" The Old Man laughs and puffs at his pipe.

"Now, May, I'm glad I've swallowed the anchor. I hate the bloody sea!"

"Don't you believe that old pirate for an instant!" she says. "The sea's in his blood. We met on a troopship, during the war, when I was a nurse. We were married by the captain of the old *Warwick Castle*, honeymooned at the seamen's mission in Liverpool, and have two sons, Nelson and Rodney. I'm telling you, there's saltwater in his veins. Even his Highland terrier is called Captain Flint!"

The captain knocks out his pipe and prepares for his defense by swilling down a large pink gin.

"Well, I tell you what I intend to do. I'm going to put an oar on my shoulder and walk away from the sea and when someone eventually asks why I'm carrying a long stick, that's where I'll settle down. As far away from the bloody sea as I can get in this tiny island!"

"Don't believe a word he says! We're moving to Rochester in Kent and he's already signed up for the River Medway Boating Club," Mrs. Metcalf taunts.

Mrs. Beaton leans over to the bo'sun.

"Now, Mr. Parry!" The bo'sun stands, slightly unsteadily, and blows his pipe again. This has the effect of summoning two white-coated waiters pushing a large cake on a trolley. On its crown is the candy likeness of a tramp steamer; delicately iced along her bows is her name. We all stand as Mr. Mackenzie pops the champagne. Glasses filled, he leads the toast.

"Lady and gentlemen, the ship . . . the *Isle of May!*"

"The ship!"

We down the salute. The bottle makes another pass over the waving glasses.

"Here's to Captain and Mrs. Metcalf."

"Cheers!"

The cake is assaulted and compliments go to Mrs. Beaton for its creation.

The afternoon glides into a golden haze, lit by a setting sun. Mrs. Metcalf, enlivened by half a bottle of port and several generous helpings of sherry trifle, is intimating an otherwise unknown story to the smilingly sozzled ship's cook.

"You see, the ship was called the *Ben Lucy* when she was bought by Arrowsmith's, and they wanted to change the name." May takes a large swig at her glass.

"Why did they want to do that, Mrs. Metcalf? *Ben Lucy* is a pretty name! I think it's a mountain in Scotland? Is that not right, Mr. Mackenzie?" The mate nods to the cook as the captain's wife continues.

"No, no, that's the point! It wasn't named after a mountain. Ben and Lucy were the previous owner's kids. So, they asked Rupert what he thought she should be called."

"Who's Rupert?" asks Geordie Whittle, as baffled as the rest of us.

"Rupert, him, your captain!"

The Old Man groans, putting his hands over his head pretending to hide, like a chimpanzee.

"Rupert," murmur some members of the crew, as if astonished that captains have first names.

"So, Rupert suggests *Isle of May,* just for me! What an old romantic, don't you think?"

Geordie stares blankly and shrugs his shoulders.

"I don't get it!"

Mrs. Beaton holds up a bottle of Mount Gay rum in bleary realization.

"Oh, I see, I love May, of course! Oh, Mrs. May, that's so lovely, that's the most beautiful thing I've ever heard, I think I'm going to—" The cook buries his tear-streaming face in Geordie's armpit.

"Don't take on so, bonny lad! There, there!" Geordie pats him on the back.

At the other end of the table, the mate is recounting the tale of Sawney Bean to the whiskey-infused Cowboy, who has lost the plot entirely.

"No, he wasn't a judge at all. He was a cannibal who was tried and sentenced to death, for eating people. I told you about him before!"

"Yeah, so you did. He held court in a saloon with a grizzly bear and Lillie Langtry, but I don't think he ever ate anybody."

"No, no, no, that was a different Bean. Sawney Bean was a cannibal, I tell you!"

"Yep, you're quite right, partner. He certainly was a real carnival!"

The mate smiles, thinking he's finally managed to get his message home.

Cowboy continues: "Judge Sawney Bean was a real live carnival and the only law west of the Pecos!"

Mate Mackenzie gives up and, with little prompting, ends the evening with a shaky rendering of "Auld Lang Syne." Mrs. Metcalf swings her glass to conduct the ragged choir, her cheeks as red as the fine Oporto wine sloshing around in her hand.

We spill out into the carpark, and the mate comes up alongside me.

"Did ye ever finish them history books I lent ye?"

"I have, Mr. Mackenzie, and I meant to bring them back to you today, but I was in such a hurry to get ready, I forgot. Are you staying anywhere near? I could pop the books over to you."

"Naw, forget it, ye can keep them. I ken all I need to know aboot my hameland. Anyway, are ye still going to Scotland? I'm shipping out the morn's morn. I'm running a supply vessel up to Hull. Maybe you'd like tae come along fer the ride?"

"No, I don't think I'll be going up north this year, I've got a cushy job working on the river, but thanks anyway."

"Well, if ye change yer mind, this is where we are." He scribbles on a piece of paper: "*Star Aldeberan*—Surrey Docks, Rotherhithe, sail tomorrow 0800."

Geordie Whittle sidles over, his yellow-rimmed eyes looking like piss holes in the snow.

"Ye'll have to wear the kilt up theere in Scotland. Divvy know why?"

"No."

"'Cause the sheep can hear a zipper a mile off!"

"Keep it clean, Mr. Whittle!" says the mate, bristling.

Geordie grins like an open wound gone septic.

"Don't take any notice of what a Geordie bloke says to you, Billy. They're nothing but a bunch of Scotsmen with their brains kicked oot!"

The night fills with farewells. Old friends and antagonists alike shake hands and disband, departing for God-knows-where.

Refusing a lift, I walk back along the moonlit river. The night is soft on the cheek.

As I approach the moorings I hear the rippling waters of the full tide gurgling and splashing under the rolling hulls of a half dozen tied-up vessels, and the smoke from the houseboats' chimneys hangs limply in the crisp fall air. The tide is very high, higher than I have ever seen it.

Riding at her anchorage the *Olive Oyl* seems to be moored uphill from the jetty, and being slightly unsteady on my feet, I wobble my way across the duck boards to find the security of my hammock aboard the old tugboat.

After I am tucked up for the night, my mind rambles over the day's doings. It has been a good day. I had parted on good terms with my old shipmates and said farewell to Captain Metcalf, a true old salt. This will be a cozy night. I have below decks to myself, just the peace and quiet of the river, unblemished by Martin snoring like a grampus.

"Ah yes, bliss in the arms of Morpheus," I whisper to no one.

The hammock swings gently in time with the rhythmic waters beneath the *Olive Oyl*'s keel. The full moon, distorted by the bulbous glass in the brass-rimmed porthole, projects its yellow amoebic image, slithering up and down the pinewood bulkhead between my toes. Good old moon!

I close my eyes. My thoughts become dreams and my dreams totter on the edge of oblivion. The solitary coracle of my mind drifts away on its nightly voyage of adventure, seeking fair winds and fortunate islands. But suddenly, something is amiss. A tempest seems to be gathering in my path, and the first poking fingers of savage squall force my frail craft toward jagged demons of surf-shattering rocks. Above the growing gale, a distant voice hails, calling, almost imperceptibly, from the banks of the wakened world. No form materializes, just a thin disembodied cry, its words unclear and the message hard to decipher.

"See . . . seek . . . sea cooks . . . remember?"

What could it mean? Sea cooks? I begin to toss and turn in my sleep. The still, small voice starts up again and slowly becomes clearer.

"Remember the seacocks . . . remember the seacocks!"

"Dear God Almighty!" I sit bolt upright. My hammock spins, dumping me onto the deck like a side of mutton.

"The seacocks on the *Comanche* are still open!" I yell out.

Scrambling out of the rear hatchway, I see the *Comanche* still tethered to the stone pier, but riding dangerously low in the high tide. Heart in mouth and wearing nothing but goose bumps and ragged underpants, I clamber across the gangplanks. Gaining the wheelhouse door of the stricken vessel, I snap on the interior lights. Below decks, the long vault of the central hold is awash, six fountains of tidewater erupting in the blinking light of a flickering forty-watt bulb swinging from the bulkhead. A snarling crackle discharges from the semi-submerged fuse box, sending puffs of white steam rising toward the main electrical bus bars above. Soon this unit will be underwater and the entire hold alive with four hundred and fifteen volts of lethal AC current.

"Oh dear Jesus, why didn't I ever learn to swim?" I whimper.

Wading into the icy pool, feet first, my toes slicing on the jagged iron ballast blocks beneath the swell, I attempt to close the first stopcock, but the upsurge of brackish tidewater from the open valve stem envelopes my head, choking and blinding me. I splutter back from the billowing font, coughing and cursing. At any moment I expect to feel the deathly surge of electricity fluxing through the filthy water. I'm left with no choice other than to dive beneath the slimy surface and locate the shut-offs. Convulsed with cold cramps, my fumbling fingers search for the elusive levers. Fear alone spurs my exertions. The first one turns and the inrush subsides—five to go. I make for the port side, slipping and getting snagged on the irregular iron moldings underfoot. Another groping search, another valve shut down. Nerve-piercing jolts of electrical current begin to wrack my muscles as the final intakes are stemmed.

In a frenzied nightmare of lung-bursting terror I erupt from the lethal soup, exploding onto the dry area above the galley platform, where I crouch shaking, safe from the fear of electrocution, but on the verge of hypothermia. I grab what dry clothes I can find. Wrapped in a bath towel, a floral apron, and a pair of duck-shaped oven gloves, I rub myself vigorously to warm up.

When the blood returns to my brain, it carries with it a dreadful reality. From where I'm sitting, I can see that the forward cabin has shipped water and Captain Johns's belongings float languidly in a pool of oily waste. Only the galley and the upper deck area have been spared, and here I squat like a nudist at a beach barbecue, shivering in a great puddle of bilge water and guilt.

"What should I do next?"

The waterlogged ship, sensing my thoughts, groans and slips her keel, leaning away from the pier and straining hard on her mooring ropes.

"Oh, dear God, she's going over!"

I clamber onto the foredeck, losing my pantomime costume in the process. Above in the monochrome moonlight, my worst fears are realized. Although I had stopped the inrush, the river is starting to ebb, leaving the water level inside the vessel higher than that outside. With the supporting buoyancy of the tide receding, the *Comanche* is listing badly to port and she's now in grave danger of parting her lines or ripping the mooring cleats out of the dockside. In desperation, I start the feeble bilge pump, which is like trying to empty a bathtub with a teaspoon.

Shivering in the cold moonlight, I watch the tidal race rushing toward the open sea. It's the fastest I've ever seen the Thames run. That damn moon's gravity is dragging the water away at a fleeting pace, just to spite me!

The vessel shifts her ground again, creaking her keel timbers toward the harbor wall, while her fore and aft mooring hawsers stretch like tortured bow strings. I go once more below to discover that the list has forced the water away from the electrical distribution boxes. Although this lessens the chance of electrocution, a residual voltage still tingles on the ship's timbers, giving small electric shocks every time I touch the bulkheads. Now, in a reversal of my previous labors, I dive to the sea-cocks again, this time to open them and let water out. Seized by chill spasms and tingling with voltage, I yank the handles upward and watch whirlpools of Thames water eddy above the drain cocks.

Shivering my way back to the *Olive Oyl* I light the gas cooker and warm up. For the next wee while, the tide must do its job and syphon the water out of the ship. Even now, dressed in dry clothes, I'm still shaking with the cold or maybe it's just raw fear. The *Comanche* is still in a bad way. If the critical angle of declination is exceeded, she will not be able to right herself and make a recovery. In desperation, I start the engine of the *Olive Oyl* and push my way through the moored houseboats to come alongside the listing vessel. By tying up on the outside of the ship and lashing onto the cat cleats on her deck, I hope to keep her from turning turtle at low tide.

Challenges and insults issue from the domestic vessels, now rocking and rolling in the whirlpool wake of the tug's backwash. Furious river residents emerge from their floating bungalows, fuming and cursing at me over the churning engine noise. Two neighbors from the nearest houseboat hail over to ask what's going on.

"It's the *Comanche*! She's filled up with water and going over!"

"Use the *Olive Oyl*'s fire pump to drain her hold!" calls one of the chaps.

"I didn't know she had one," I reply.

"She does—it's kept in the forward chain locker."

The man jumps aboard and ducks forward into the tugboat's prow. He returns, running out a spool of canvas hose.

"Feed this into the lower porthole of the *Comanche*'s engine room!" he shouts, throwing the syphon end over to his mate on the catwalk.

The newcomer fires up the donkey engine, and a spluttering plume of water leaves the brass nozzle on the foremast head spuming out into the silvern moonlight. The pumping continues until just before dawn, when the level in the hold lowers enough for the weight to equalize. With a rumbling jar the vessel rights herself and sits bolt upright on the remains of the tide. My helpers depart for their bunks, and I steer the *Olive Oyl* back to her usual station and close off the engine.

I remain awake until the *Comanche* settles high, dry, and empty on her tidal grid, with her seacocks firmly closed. In the early morning light she looks normal; her sleek exterior planking little betraying the ruin within. On the morrow, Captain Johns will return to his beloved ship to discover a world of sodden mattresses, oil-soaked clothing, and, worst of all, the oak chart box with the ship designer's irreplaceable blueprints a soggy mess of runny ink.

Sunday dawns, poking impudent icy fingers into the guilt-riven caverns of my waterlogged brain. In the sleep-starved delirium of day, I stumble about stuffing my few belongings into my duffel bag, while showering curses on the languid river. Tormented by my own fear of facing up to Captain Johns, I am a man bereft of spirit, my only thought being escape. As I wearily trudge up the gangplank to shore, a solitary duck paddling among the bulrushes bids me farewell with a derisive quack, and a lone steeple bell calls the hour.

Not wanting to let the cause of the disaster become a mystery, I search my pockets for a piece of paper on which to leave a message and find the note from Mr. Mackenzie. "*Star Aldeberan* . . . Rotherhithe . . . 0800 hours." That's it! I can just make it. Hurriedly scribbling on the other side of the paper, I pin an apology to the *Comanche*'s wheelhouse door:

> *Dear Captain Johns,*
> *I tried to empty your boat*
> *but ended up flooding it by accident.*
> *I am very sorry — Bill.*

The crumpled message wriggles like a mocking white moth pinned to a collector's board. I feel skewered, too. After putting many hours into that ship, I have almost managed to sink her in a single evening.

Turning my back on the *Comanche,* Captain Johns, and my idyllic river-rat life with Martin on the *Olive Oyl,* I sadly make my way to the railway station, certain that if there's any penance to be paid, it will surely come my way.

At Surrey Docks, the red-lead painted supply vessel *Star Aldeberan* rides the morning swell. Captain Mackenzie and his crew are already up and doing. This is his first command and he's eager to get under way. He spies me from the bridge wing and laughs.

"My God, laddie, what the hell happened to you? You're aw' covered in shite! You'd best get below and take a shower." He indicates the companionway.

"Thanks, Captain."

"What changed your mind about coming along?"

"Well, sir, I suddenly remembered the old adage, 'Time and tide wait for no man.'"

✦ Chapter 5 ✦

Here is that immense ocean from whence we see
All Europe supplied annually with an abundance of fish.

Bishop Jovius of Nocera
Discripto Scotiáe (Venice 1548)

Position: 53° 40′ N. 0° 03′ W.
Hull on the Humber

THE NOISE OF THE ANCHOR CHAIN RUNNING OUT WAKENS me from a deep sleep. I glance at the bulkhead clock. Dear God, I've been out for hours! I must have slept through the entire trip. The sound of a ship's hooter is my only answer as I hurriedly get dressed.

On the bridge, Captain Mackenzie is talking on the VHF radiotelephone.

"Aye, he wants tae hitch a ride up tae Aberdeen to see a friend o' his . . . aye, he's a good lad, we served together on the *Isle o' May*. Aye, Archie, aye, right enough, I'll send him o're tae see you . . . aye, cheerio." The captain hangs up the phone.

"Well, Rip Van *bloody* Winkle, you're in luck. Yonder trawler, the *Auld Allegiance,* is heading for Aberdeen and the skipper's an old pal o' mine. Get yersell across an' get aboard, she's aboot tae sail. Come on, man—jump tae it! They'll no wait for ye!" He ushers me out of the wheelhouse.

"My gear—I left it below."

"Grab his bag, someone! Go on now, scram! And hae a guid time

✦ 54 ✦

up in God's ain country!" I find myself standing on the dockside. The mate throws my duffel bag down from the deck above.

"Good luck, laddie—ye'll need it!" comes his cryptic parting shot.

Running down the quayside, jumping over hawsers and lobster creels, I close on the Scottish trawler. She is already under way, parting nose out from the jetty. I leap onto her stern as a great rush of screw wash spews oily green water up around her rudder. My voyage to Scotland is beginning at last.

"So, Mike Mackenzie tells me you're a keen laddie. Are ye willing to work yer passage?" the gruff skipper asks as he pours rum into his coffee mug.

"Of course, sir, I'll do anything to help. I'm a wireless operator, if that's any use to you." I smile with confidence. He seems singularly unimpressed.

"Aye, well, I need a wireless operator like I need an arsehole in the middle of my forehead. Can ye gut fish, laddie?" I shake my head.

"Well, then, ye'll just have to learn, won't ye?" This has me very puzzled; sure Scotland is just a few hours' sailing, a day or two at the most. Why would I need to learn to gut fish? The skipper slugs at his rum and waves to the children playing on the harbor mole. The trawler plows into the unsettled waters of the North Sea.

"Well, sir, how long will it take to get to Aberdeen, twenty-four hours or so?" Great belly laughs erupt from the bridge crew as the skipper turns to face me, a wicked smile spreading across his face.

"We'll be in Aberdeen the first week of October, God willing!"

"October? But it's only the beginning of September. That's a whole month away!"

"Och, well, we thought we might do a wee bit o' fishing on the way—just as long as that's okay with you, laddie?" Suddenly the penny drops, I've been had. Even worse, I've been shanghaied. The crew are having a field day at my expense. I am completely flummoxed by the situation and realize that Mackenzie has bested me again.

"A whole month?" I find myself saying.

"Aye, laddie, we usually have a twenty-eight-day turnaround. We go out with ice and we come back wi' fish. We also go out with wee laddies and bring them back men! Is that no right, lads?"

"Aye!" comes the chorus from the grisly-looking bastards he calls a crew.

Disconsolately, I stand in the wheelhouse watching the coastline of Yorkshire disappearing into the twilight. Jasus, I don't know the first thing about fishing, and twenty-eight days in this old tub? I should have taken the train, God damn it! I could have walked to Scotland in a week. As I'm taken below, I try to fix my mind on the scant solace to be found in my mother's oft-used maxim, "What can't be cured must be endured," but to the amusement of my guide, my mouth can only utter the words, "Fish? I hate fish, God damn it! I hate fish!"

On the slow trail northward, I learn a lot in a short time. First, the skipper isn't the old bastard he first seems; Mackenzie had put him up to it. Second, Elvis the mate is a complete rocket who'd once been jailed for hijacking a trawler and trying to sail it to Cuba. Third, all trawlermen are as mad as a bag of cats, and last, keeping dry on this floating funny farm is a skill that eludes me.

With all the hatches closed, ventilation is poor and the lack of circulating air causes rivers of greasy condensation to form across ceilings like little daisy chains, drip . . . drip . . . dripping down your neck, into your dinner, or onto your bedding, which becomes as comfortable as sleeping on a wet bath mat. I take this irritation in the spirit of my Catholic upbringing and consider it suitable punishment for flooding the sleeping accommodation on the *Comanche*.

The only peace and privacy to be had on this tiny craft is in the lavatory, but it comes as a nasty surprise to discover that damp toilet paper disintegrates while you're using it.

Above on the bridge, Elvis's long sideburns twitch in time as he croons a ragged version of "Blue Suede Shoes." His hair is heavily oiled and worn in the fifties style known as a DA, or "duck's arse." About his neck he wears a gold medallion in the shape of an LP record surmounted by a crown. He looks more like a fairground carnie than a trawlerman, except he is a man of few words. When he does speak at length, he invariably mentions "the King," and when I first met him, I thought he was a born-again Christian.

Seeing me enter the wheelhouse he sidles over with a knife in his hand.

"Gimme thruppence!" he growls.

I fish in my pocket and produce a three-penny bit. If this is a mugging it's a piss-poor affair, I'm thinking, but he pockets the thruppence, hands me the knife, and wanders back to his station. With total lack of enthusiasm I realize it's a fish-gutting blade.

Night and day we steam toward the rich cod-fishing grounds off the coast of Iceland; we arrive just as the weather hardens, to begin the gruesome task of harvesting the sea. After the most rudimentary on-the-job training, I'm kitted out in oversized boots and voluminous yellow oilskins and sent on deck seemingly for the amusement of the others.

A full trawl swings inboard, hovering briefly before a hand yanks open the cod end of the net, spilling a slippery avalanche of flapping fish, writhing and wriggling around our knees. The catch entraps my legs in a pressure hold, akin to being stood in a vat of water-filled inner tubes. The only way out of this torment is to haul up the nearest unfortunate fish and slit its throat, just under the gills, then slice open the belly to remove the entrails and liver. The liver is kept, but the guts are ejected with a flick of the wrist to the ever attentive swarm of seagulls, squawking their encouragements in the adjacent air. The experts clean ten big fish for each of my little ones, the horrid task being repeated ad nauseam until the last fish has disappeared down the slide to the ice room. The trawl is then prepared for another drop, after which I might get a cup of tea in the galley, if I can get near the teapot. Sometimes I just sit staring at the backs of the men huddled around the stove, waiting for the ghastly cycle to resume.

The wind can get above sixty miles per hour, and when it does it's nasty: cresting wavetops crash over the foredeck, pouring ice water down hatchways, into the steamy depths I am forced to call home. After the first round of dropping and retrieving trawls, I understand why people occasionally go nuts and shoot their coworkers. This is a job for maniacs. Never in the field of human endeavor has such a hideous enterprise been foisted on the unsuspecting neck of a hitherto optimistic Irishman.

I loved being a radio operator; it was the best job in the whole world. Even the term *radio officer* sounded grand. But now I'm a *snacker,* in fisherman's jargon: a semiuseless first-timer doing a job he knows nothing about.

I hate fish, with their gaping mouths and woeful eyes staring at me, as if to say, "Please don't kill me—please!" It gives me the bloody heebie-jeebies. I even see the hideous sods in my sleep. How the hell did I end up in this nightmare? No penance could be this severe. This is slavery; every shift I wake up expecting to find myself chained to an oar. Bloody Mackenzie! If ever I see him again, I'll skin him alive.

This fish-cleaning lark stinks in both senses of the word, and though I can't get the hang of it, I take my turn gutting the ugly buggers, mostly spoiling nice fillets by bad knife work. For the first few days out, the fishermen remain derisive and aloof. They make it plain that I'm not one of them. On deck, Elvis keeps an eye on me, and that makes me even more uncomfortable than the chiding of the crew. To show I'm willing, I try gutting one of the large female fish.

"Don't throw that away! That's the cod's roe, and it's worth more than you are, ya useless fuck!" Elvis roars over the howling wind. The old-timers laugh and fling guts at me. Mumbling curses into my jerkin, I lash out at the skuas and kittiwakes darting in to snatch at the fish entrails sliding down my yellow oilskins. In the frenzy, the knife flies out of my frozen fingers, almost cleaving the ear off the mate, before disappearing over the side into the sea. He curses me out, thinking I did it on purpose, then sends me into the hold to ice down the cleaned fish, a job normally reserved for imbeciles and the mentally deranged. I don't mind it, though; I'm daft enough to think this is some kind of promotion.

Hiding in the ice room out of the biting wind of the arctic squall above, I begin to feel more at ease, but my fool's paradise is about to reap the whirlwind. A sudden downturn in the weather has the old trawler pitching and buffeting, sending ice boxes and dead fish flying around at head height, like a manifestation of poltergeists.

Now I understand why the experienced hands tend to stay topside in bad weather. In the dark world below decks, evil spirits abound, laying traps for foolhardy twerps like myself. Anything not battened down is instantly possessed by mischievous demons intent on spreading havoc. Unseen hands hurl books from shelves, while ballpoint pens fly like medieval arrows seeking eyes and other soft targets. Legions of invisible lunatics bang and slap unlatched locker doors, striving to break the fingers of those attempting to fasten them. I soon realize that below deck in a storm is not the place to be either, and when the last codfish slides sluggishly down the chute, I clamber topside, only to find that, here too, the devil's work is at hand.

The solace of the galley teapot is a long way away. To gain its comfort, I dodge the green curls of white-spumed ocean crashing over the gunwales, traverse the lurching deck slippery with fish guts and diesel oil, scale the entanglements of line and tackle waiting to ensnare like barbed wire on a battlefield and avoid each foul fiend lurking in snarls of netting, rope, and steel cables, ever anxious to cause a fall, crush a few ribs, or inflict a broken limb.

Instead of excluding me as before, the men gathered around the galley stove move over to make a space for me. This is an unexpected honor. I wriggle in near the heat and pour a cup.

"Jock says ye threw yer knife at the mate. Is that right?" says a pugnacious-looking deckie with a punched-out nose.

"Naw, it was just an accident," I explain, sipping my tea.

"Accidents will happen," he says with a wink and I get the feeling Elvis isn't as popular as he thinks he is.

The mention of accidents gives voice to terrifying accounts of disasters lurid enough to scare the life out of greenhorns like me. They tell of injured men hundreds of miles from hospital care, having their legs sawn off by the mate, with no anesthetic, like in the days of Nelson. Old-timers speak of appendectomies being performed on the galley table, with instructions relayed by radio from doctors onshore, and of blokes being buried at sea, or their bodies boxed up in the ice room with the fish. Luckily, the almost impenetrable cadences of their northern Scottish tongue spare me some of the more gruesome details.

Winch operators, easily recognizable by the stubs of long-lost fingers, joke about their frozen digits being torn away by trawl cables without them even being aware of it. It seems that every trawling story has men swept overboard to perish in the arctic swell or limbs ripped off by winches, heads shattered by incoming otter boards, or necks snapped like carrots by swinging hoists. Not to be outdone by the winchmen, the deckhands impart to the inexperienced dire warnings about steel trawl lines snapping and the sudden recoil slicing men in two. Over steamy mugs of treacly, rum-laced tea, I am offered the prospect that the next time I'm waist deep in writhing codfish, there might well be a giant moray eel lurking at the bottom of the catch, waiting for an opportunity to sink its needlelike teeth into my boot, thus requiring crew members to cut off its head with a fire ax to release its viselike jaws.

When the crewmen sense that even the most horrifying tales of death and mutilation fail to turn me into a quivering jelly, they are more accepting. The fishermen also seem pleased that I am intrigued by their folklore and superstitions and do their best to instruct me.

"Ye see, whin yer setting foot on board a boat for the first time, ye must mak sure it's yer recht foot that touches the deck first off," says a crusty old cove.

"Aye," says his pal, "and dinnae get caught oot whistling, or ye'll have tae rin three times aroon the deck widdershins tae drive awa' the wind yer whistling up!"

I knew it was unlucky to whistle on a ship as it caused confusion back in the days of sail, when orders were piped to the crew by means of the bo'sun whistle.

"Why did Elvis charge me thruppence for a gutting knife when they're provided for free?" I ask. An old-timer looks up from rolling a cigarette and grins.

"Ah, well, laddie, ye cannae just give someone a knife for nothing. It's unlucky—cuts off friendship, ye see. The mate always sells the knives for a few pennies, and he needs all the luck he can get!" He licks the cigarette paper and presses it down before continuing.

"If ye want to stay safe, never mention a priest or a salmon in the engine room, or cut yer nails during a storm, that's real bad luck, and if ye ever want to sneeze, do it on the starboard side, not to port."

"That's an odd one. Why's that?"

"I don't know." The other lads shake their heads in agreement. The old boy warms to his lecture. He's somewhat of an authority on seafaring lore, and I'm beginning to enjoy myself.

"Children and hunchbacks are guid luck, but knives left crossed on yer dinner plate will invite the deil to dine and yer ship's doomed. A spilled pack of playing cards is a bad sign, too. An upright horseshoe nailed to the mast will hold in the good luck, but a cross-eyed seaman could lose that luck and be a 'Jonah,' especially if he happens to be Finnish, though I don't know why that should be." He puffs on his ciggie, relishing the blue scent of Old Holborn rolling tobacco. The others wait for his next pronouncements.

"I see ye wear an earring. Do ye ken why?"

"No, I don't, but I see some of you lads have them, too."

"That comes from the old belief that if yer drooned and washed ashore, though the sea has stripped every stitch of clothing from ye, there'd be enough gold in your lug tae gi ye a decent Christian burial." I finger the slim gold ring in my right ear, knowing that it wouldn't buy a bunch of flowers, let alone pay for a funeral. The ancient mariner laughs and ruffles the hair on the top of my head.

"I ken whut yer thinkin'!" he says, puffing on his smoke, then adding, "In the old days a man might have a p . . . i . . . g tattooed on his foot as a charm against death by drooning because it's a landlubber. Fisherfolk willnae mention the beast's name on sea or land, but ye can spell it oot. To meet a p . . . i . . . g on the way to the boats is very bad luck, and if ye want to wish ill fortune on a fisherman, 'Soo's tail to ye!' will dae the trick. I am telt that in Brittany they only kill a p . . . i . . . g when the tide is rising, but I'm no sure why that is." He draws hard on his roll-up, and I take the opportunity to comment.

"My dad always says that p . . . i . . . gs can see the wind."

"Aye, so they say, son, so they say. There be more superstitions o' the sea than hairs on a cat's tongue. In my day, the old-timers wouldnae utter the word *cat* either. They'd only cry it as 'the thing' or spell it oot, but cats are lucky to have on board and wifeys at hame will keep a black cat tae ensure the safe return of their men." He flicks his cigarette end into the galley stove.

"An' one mair thing: if ye chuck a knife at the mate and miss, that's the worst of bad luck!" He kicks the galley stove in his laughter, and the flat-bottomed kettle on the hob releases a belch of steam.

Later, lying in my damp bunk, I reflect upon this day's doings. I'm a bit nervous about Elvis thinking I'm a villain, but I am pleased that the men might. Aye, it's not a life for the faint of heart; a rare camaraderie exists among these tough lads, and if they are a bit clannish as a result, it's understandable. Fishermen think merchant seamen are a bunch of softies, and merchant seamen tend to think of fishermen as Neanderthals, but if danger is the common currency of the seafarer's profession, then these poor blighters are the loose change, worth little to the shipping owners and totally expendable to the uncaring elements.

The next day, determined to become more useful, I try to learn fish recognition from the large colorful chart hanging in the wheelhouse. Cod, ling, pollack, haddock, they are all an ugly bunch of bastards, especially the John Dory, which is all teeth and tail and would never be bought by the public if they saw it in its natural state. The gruesome-looking fish is sold in strips and given the posh-sounding name rock salmon.

I ask Elvis to sell me another knife.

"This time it costs ten shillings," he says with a smirk.

Off the port beam a couple of Spanish boats are engaged in pair trawling. Beyond them, Russian stern trawlers known as "Klondikers" ride the swell, speeding their catch back to distant factory ships. To starboard, gray-hulled fishing vessels, dappled with blood-red rust, continue the cycle of shooting and recovering nets. The skipper scans the horizon with his binoculars.

"Poland, Norway, East Germany, Bulgaria, Ireland, and what's that one?" He runs his finger down the international flag chart pinned to the wheelhouse wall.

"Oh, aye, Estonia. I tell ye, this fishing lark is bollixed. Years ago ye could steam aboot here for days and never see another livin' soul. Now every bugger is at it. It's like the fuckin' United Nations oot here." He hands me the glasses.

"Billy, keep an eye on these bastards to port, they're getting too fuckin' close."

I watch the Spaniards going about their work, trailing a huge net between them. A small black dot appears above the masthead of the farther vessel. Like a pair of porpoises, the twin ships abruptly change their heading, steering on a collision course straight toward us.

"Captain!" The skipper spins round.

"Hard astarboard! Hard astarboard—up trawl!" He pulls down on the steam whistle, sending long bellowing blasts into the hissing wind. The trawler answers the helm, describing a wide arc, running in front of the Spaniards.

"What the fuck do ye think yer doin'? Back off, ye dago bastards! Ye'll run us down!" The skipper is roaring into the VHF. The Spanish ships make no reply, but inch closer and closer.

"What in the name o' Christ are they thinking? Full speed ahead!" With the trawl out of the water, the boat spurts forward, leaving the Spanish trawlers cutting through our churning white wake. All eyes are turned on the rogue vessels. Elvis shakes his fist out of the wheelhouse window, and the skipper pours a stream of invective and torrents of abuse at the fleeing vessels. The bridge flashes into darkness, as an ear-splitting roar tears through the curse-ladened air.

"What the fuck was that?" says the startled skipper, as the view aft is obscured by the engine exhaust of an Icelandic coast guard plane. Just above mast height, the great gray span banks and sweeps back over us like a hungry albatross. The radio crackles out.

"Scottish schip . . . Scottish schip . . . *Alt Allegiance* . . . you are under arrest. You are fishing in Icelandic waters. Coast guard vessel *Thor* has been given your position. Cut your engines and wait for boarding party."

"You can kiss my arse!" says the skipper hanging up the radio-telephone.

"Hard aboot! Let's give them a run for their money. Just look at those smug Spanish bastards. They spotted that plane and got across the limit afore we even saw it. They might have warned us, dago bastards!" He sticks his finger up to the Spaniard ships, now in international waters, trawling away like nothing had happened.

"Right, Elvis, let's get the fuck out of here, before the *Thor* turns up, spitting fuckin' cannon shells and confiscating our fuckin' gear."

"Uh-huh!" says Elvis, spinning the wheel.

Safely outside the Icelandic fishing limit, the skipper becomes more relaxed, and unlike Elvis, he seems to enjoy chatting with people.

"Ye have to be careful where ye trawl hereaboots. No just because o' the Icelandic coast guard, but all the wrecked shipping lying on the bottom. See here?" He points to the chart covered in X's indicating a ship's graveyard.

"Seventy thousand mines were dropped in this area by the Germans in the last war, and hundreds of British and American convoy ships were sunk by them or the U-boat wolf packs attacking at night. With all the explosions and burning oil, the German submarine commanders called it 'the Rose Garden.' A good few Jerry U-boats were sunk here, too, either by their own mines or the depth charges of the convoy's destroyer escorts. Aye, it's a tangled mess doon there. Ye can easily snag yer nets."

I nod my head and stare out at the pitiless slate-gray ocean, rolling heedlessly onward, a silver-peaked shroud forever obscuring the barnacle-encrusted hulks and their long-dead crews below.

My third week at sea is drawing to a close, and I'm becoming reasonably proficient at divesting fish of their digestive organs. As I had previously found out, you have to be careful when gutting the fish, careful of what you throw away. The roe of the female cod are highly prized; they go into a separate box, as do the cod livers, which produce a vitamin-rich oil. The British government provides this free to schools, and gallons of the horrible-tasting stuff are ladled down the throats of unwilling kids every day.

The weather eases up and the sea is placid, but the work is still monotonous, and I'm glad when the order is given to make haste for Aberdeen harbor. At last, lights on a distant headland wink in the gathering dusk to the south.

"That's the town of Peterheid doon there. We'll soon be in Ayberdeen, an' yer wee holiday wi' us will be o'er. I trust ye enjoyed yersel?" says the skipper, smiling.

"Oh, yes, it was a great experience!" I say.

"Yer a bloody poor liar!" says Elvis with a Presleyesque curl of his lip.

We arrive at Aberdeen in the late evening and off-load the catch at the fish market.

"Here," says the skipper, handing me a bunch of fivers. "The lads had a whip-round for ye. Even Elvis chipped in."

Fifty-five pounds better off, I step for the first time on Scottish soil just as the trawler gives two short blasts on the steam whistle and moves astern to take up position alongside the fishing boats choking Aberdeen's inner harbor. It feels good to be here, and all in all it only took a month! I wave good-bye to the ship. Leaning on the taffrail, Elvis shouts something that the wind blows away and gives me the finger. By his side, one of the winchmen raises his remaining two fingers in a similar gesture, known to mariners as "the sailor's farewell." They weren't such a bad bunch. I might even miss them. I might even do another trip—yeah, fat chance!

With a heave, the vessel gets under way, its screw churning up stench and sediment from the anchorage seabed. As she turns out in the darkness her engines silence and the green starboard navigation light flickers off.

I swing my duffel bag up to my shoulder, and my Scottish adventure begins.

The staid granite buildings comprising Aberdeen's ancient city rise on all sides like a latter-day Camelot; each square block of stone is iridescent with quartz, mica, and feldspar, glinting and silvern in the spreading luster of the rising moon.

My task is to locate a redhaired Scotsman with a beard in a town of three hundred thousand—easy!

The skipper suggested that I try a pub called the Blue Lamp bar, much frequented by students and next door to the university union. It seems as good a place to start as any.

I walk up Market Street, swaying like a drunk. After all that time at sea, I'm having trouble finding my land legs, and solid ground seems to rise and fall in a most unpleasant manner. Being landsick would be odd, but luckily I've seldom been seasick, the only cure for which, I'm told, is to sit under a tree.

Just off George Street, the many spires of Marischal College poke up into the night, and across the road I find the Blue Lamp packed with students.

Smoky and warmed with dancers' sweat, the atmosphere of the crowded bar is infused with beer fumes and cheap perfume. Before too long, I realize that the other smell that I'm trying to identify is coming from me. It's the delicate piquancy known as codfish cologne, a heady mixture consisting of tar, diesel fuel, cod liver oil, and cheap red rum. After four weeks at sea, my clothing sparkles with a patina of fish scales, thousands of tiny encrusted sequins that look quite psychedelic in the pulsating lights of the disco. Well, I always was a snappy dresser, and, if this isn't enough to turn a girl's head, I haven't had a shower since leaving London. Still, I'm not on the pickup, I'm just looking for Angus.

After a pint of Guinness, I visit the first proper toilet I've seen in a month. It is pleasant to sit in a lavatory that isn't damp or revolving like a space capsule, and I make the most of it. A singularly curious spider lowers itself to eye level, staring at me with its neat little rows of eyes. I wonder what eight images of me grinning back at him must look like and why, given all the other places to build a web, it has chosen a toilet. Don't spiders have a sense of smell? My reverie is rudely interrupted by roaring and shouting, accompanied by a series of loud bangs on the lavatory door.

"Hold on, pal, I'm nearly finished!"

"Hmmm . . . yaaaa . . . urggh!" come the strangulated cries from the other side of the door. God, whoever this is, they're desperate! I hurriedly dress, and on snapping back the bolt, I'm buried under the weight of two writhing men, locked in a stranglehold. The larger of the two, propelled by his own momentum, smashes his face into the iron water tank and sinks to the ground. The other bloke struggles out of the cubicle and offers me his hand, to pull me free.

"Thanks, mate! That big bastard had me seeing stars, but I wouldn't let go. He'd have killed me!"

"Are you okay?"

"Yeah!" he says, looking at his bruised neck in the wall mirror. "The girls will think it's a hickey," he laughs, pulling his tie straight and cocking an ear to the long moan issuing from the toilet.

"What about him?" I point to the prostrate figure bleeding on the floor.

"Oh, yeah, I forgot about him," he says, giving the fallen geezer a crushing kick in the knackers. He offers his hand again; I think it prudent to take it.

"Terry's the name, Terry Sansome—Handsome Sansome they call me!" He looks at himself in the mirror and sniffs his armpits.

"Shaggin' hell, is that me? Something stinks of codfish?"

"No, I'm afraid it's me. I've just come off a trawler."

"Oh, really? I'm a trawlerman myself. Come on, I owe you a beer."

Back in the bar, I meet his two pals and he buys me a pint. He tells his mates that I was the hero of the moment and saved him from being throttled by a monster.

"What were you fighting about?" I ask.

"Oh, that bloke thought I'd shagged his missus last time I was in port."

"And had you—shagged her like?"

"Of course I did. They don't call me Handsome Sansome for nothing!"

"They don't call you Handsome Sansome at all, you lying fuck," laughs one of his mates.

"Yeah, never mind the bollocks. Everyone calls him Terrible Terry," says the other. Terry ignores them and instead pinches the arse of a passing young lady. To my surprise, she turns and smiles back at him.

"She could get lucky tonight, and I don't mean at the bingo!" He takes a long slurp at his pint, before turning back to me.

"So, what are you doing in Aberdeen, looking to do more fishing?"

"No, I'm a regular seaman, a wireless op. I was looking for a chap called Angus that I met in Morocco. Do you know him?"

"Oh God, yes! Angus MeTrousersUp, better known as Aberdeen Angus, the pot-smoking geologist. He was here about an hour ago, but I tell you where he'll be at midnight—outside the fish-and-chip shop, never fails. Well, if you ever need a place to stay, look me up! Oh, fuck, time to go!" The lavatory door is agape and a bleary-looking brute is scanning the crowd through blood-caked eyes. When I look back around, Terry and his pals are gone.

It is easy to spot Angus, standing beneath a cumulus cloud of bluish hash smoke, reading a "Furry Freak Brothers" comic by the aid of a street lamp. He seems neither surprised nor overly pleased to see me. He just offers me the joint, but on hearing my refusal, suddenly jerks himself upright and stares at me in astonishment.

"My God, it's yourself! Billy from Tangier! Jesus, guid tae see ye!" He hugs me into his parka, sour with the stench of old tobacco and stale pot smoke.

"Och, this is great—wait there and I'll get something special tae celebrate." He totters into the White Rose fish-and-chip shop, returns a few minutes later, and hands me a round greasy object from a brown paper bag.

"What's this?" I stare at the queer thing in my hand.

"That is a wee Scots pie . . . a wee Scots mutton pie . . . and it's the finest wee pie that ye'll ever taste—it's braw!" He shoves his pie into the hole in the middle of his beard, biting a half-moon into it. Without any apparent chewing, the delicacy is swallowed down, quickly followed by handfuls of brown-sauce-covered chips, fisted into the fathomless depths of gullet, secreted behind his wiry red whiskers.

"You know, Billy, when I get the munchies, I cannae get enough of these things. Go on—try it, man!"

I stare wanly at the uninviting flesh-colored pastry top, with its hard-crust rim and a single round hole like a cigarette burn in the center. It looks horrible and it smells worse, but I'd better eat the damned thing or Angus might take it as an insult. I try to put it in my mouth, but my head keeps shying away.

"If ye don't want the bloody thing, gie it tae me, ya wee poof, ya!" He grabs at the pie. I turn away in an arc to avoid his thrust and at the same instant bite into the hand-sized delicacy.

"Aaargh!" My senses are assaulted by an abomination of disagreeable stimuli, the epicenter of which is the scalding, slimy, gristle-ridden, malodorous mouthful that I have neither the nerve to spit out nor the courage to swallow. I stand goggle-eyed, cheeks bulging like a hamster's. A searing pain surges from my scalded forearm, as a rivulet of boiling fat runs down my hand, chilling into a ghastly white stalactite of pale lard hanging from my wrist.

"There you are! Is that not fabulous?" Angus fetches me a mighty slap on the back, which I use as an excuse to free my violated palate of this intrusive concoction.

"Oh dear God, if that's what you call fabulous, it's little wonder Sawney Bean turned cannibal!"

I surrender the rest of the pie to Angus and watch in abject horror as he swallows it in a series of chomping mouthfuls, while two flapping seagulls squabble over the steaming remains of my recent regurgitation. My astounded gaze drifts to a cheerful Tourist Board sign hanging in the chip shop window.

"Failte gu Alba!" it reads. "Welcome to Scotland!"

✧ Chapter 6 ✦

Nemo me impune lacessit
[No one attacks me with impunity].
The motto of Scotland

TWO MEN AND THE MOON STALK THE SILENT STREETS OF
Aberdeen. There are few venturing abroad as the town clock strikes one.
This is a town that goes to bed early. Apparently, it's a town that likes
to get up early, too, but not tomorrow. Tomorrow is Saturday.

"Well, Billy, what a turnup for the books, you arriving. I was just
thinking about ye the other day. What are ye doing here?"

" I . . . I don't know, it was all kind of an accident."

"I've not got yer money, mind. Ye'll have to wait till me next grant."

"That's okay, Angus, but could you put me up for a few days? I want
to have a good look at Scotland."

"Och, aye, God's ain country, stay as long as ye like. Come on, I live
down the road a wee piece."

We walk along cobblestone streets of brown brick terraced houses,
until after a couple of miles, he stops outside one and produces a key.

"Here we are. This street was the pride of the working class, but look
at it now. Just a decaying Victorian monument to the new golden age
that never came." He walks into the single room and collapses facedown
on the bed.

"Make yerself at home," he mumbles into his pillow.

Kipping down on the sofa, I spread a red tartan blanket over me for
warmth. Still feeling the roll of the ship, I sway into dreamland as if in
a hammock; my salt-spun dreams drift between the known and un-

known, rising and falling on the crests and troughs of Angus's snoring. Soon a brisk breeze off Cape Nao gives way to the balmy winds of the Balearic Islands blowing in from Formentera and causing me to smile and turn over in my sleep. Cruising along in my idyll, dressed in white shorts and shirt, I am lord of the ocean, admiral of the blue, pacing the bridge deck of my freighter with the warm wind tickling the backs of my bare knees. This agreeable sensation continues apace until becoming somewhat marred by the addition of tiny scratchy claws. I begin to fidget beneath the blanket. The tickling has developed into a full-fledged annoyance, dragging me from my pleasant fudge of unconsciousness into the stark realization that I'm in bed with a mouse!

After hurling a boot at the departing rodent, it takes a wee while to get back to sleep again. I mentally search for my Mediterranean cargo ship, but find myself instead coasting around on the deck of a fishing boat. Goddamn fish! I hate fish! I curse the gutting knife manifesting itself in my hand. No, no, not this ship, the other one, in the Med. My night demons take no heed of my pleas, and the rest of the trawler materializes around me, complete with sound effects. A lone railway engine, shunting in some distant stockyard, provides the clamor of clangs, whistles, and steam puffs associated with dropping the trawl, while under the blanket, my own breathing forms a hiss of ocean spray. Somewhere in the night, a chorus of squabbling cats' voices shape-shifts into the screeches and squeals made by the capstan winch dragging in catch after catch for cleaning. Eventually, chilled, unwilling hands pull the final net inboard and, with it, the icy dawn. A confusion of razor-gilled, skewer-toothed John Dory and moray eels avalanche from aloft, seething and snapping through the tangled triptych of my mind. I try to run, but, caught in the netting, a huge, blurry, red-spiked sphere hovers menacingly in front of my flinching face. I blink my eyes.

"Would ye like a wee cuppa coffee, Billy?" says the rusty metal orb, swaying indistinctly before me. I blink my eyes again, and the apparition slowly dissolves into a red-whiskered face.

"Jasus, Angus! I thought you were a German mine!"

The hour and minute hands of a traveling clock chase themselves around its Roman numeral face, while Angus gives ear to the saga of how I ended up in Scotland. His own story is a little more straightforward.

He took the ferry from Tangier to Algeciras, the train to the port of Santander, then a boat across the Bay of Biscay to England. What astounds me is that he had visited my parents in Birmingham and stayed several weeks.

"Yer dad's quite a character, isn't he? And yer mam, she's a riot, eh?" he says, grinning knowingly.

I can do no more than nod. I'm stunned that anyone would turn up on the doorstep of complete strangers with the line, "Hi there! I met your son in Morocco and borrowed money off him. Can I live here for a while?" I'd die of embarrassment, but Angus seems to think it no shame.

"Your dad and me often went boozing up the Dingle pub. I got to know all his mates!"

"Really," I say without enthusiasm.

"And I loved going shopping down the market with yer mam. It's great the way she has slanging matches with the stall owners, isn't it?" he enthuses, mad blue eyes seeking agreement.

"Oh, yes, she likes to give it out of her." I reflect. The truth is, I'm feeling a bit jealous. For one reason or another, I haven't seen my folks for nearly two years.

"Yer dad says ye're a silly bastard going to sea just when the industry's falling apart," he chides.

"Does he now?"

Oblivious to my cool reply, he tries again.

"And yer mam says ye are an ungrateful bugger who never writes home. And she telt yer dad that they should adopt me instead, and ya know what he said? He says to yer mam, he says—"

"Where's the toilet?" I cut him short.

"The what?" He looks confused.

"The lavatory, the loo, the wee hoose, or whatever you call it?"

"It's oot there. The one with the red door," he says, pointing out of the kitchen window to where a pair of brick-built privies grow tufts of green moss from their gray slate roofs. I shuffle sullenly past him into the brisk air.

The outhouse is a cold sanctuary to my thoughts and a patch of hoarfrost hiding in the shadows, safe from the sun. The door is a ragged collection of knotholed planks, haphazardly held in place by a pair of iron hinges and an equally rusted draw-bolt whose hasp was lost long ago. After expending Herculean effort to close this portal, I sit on the coarse wooden seat, between grimy, lime-washed walls, shivering with displeasure, my indignation illuminated by the dismal pale light filtering through the toffee-colored glass fanlight above the doorway.

"Cheeky sod!" I keep muttering. "What a nerve he had, moving in with my folks. I wouldn't do that to his parents, no way! And them saying I never write, what rubbish! I wrote a card only last . . . erm . . . when I was in Germany, last—good God, that was almost a year ago!" The realization has me dejected. In frustration, I pick at the ruby-red paint curling up from the surface of the door, like the fingernails of a Chinese emperor.

I think back to the night I told my folks I was leaving to go to sea. Mam cried, saying I'd be drowned to death and no one would know me, and my dad telling her, "Let the lad win his spurs," and saying, "Two years before the mast would make a man of him," and Mam telling me to stay away from dockside harlots and not to go into Protestant churches! Then imploring me not to leave. And me asking my mam whether she'd rather I continue working in the contraceptive factory, and her saying that was no job for a Christian either and I'd be better off feeding the poor sharks! Me walking out, slamming the door behind me and shouting, "I'm not a kid anymore!"

That was long ago and I'd seldom returned. Maybe Angus did the right thing after all, visiting my family and reminding them what it was like to have a young lad around. I don't know.

"I'm a bad son," I confide to the stubs of two long-dead candles nestling in a drift of dust on the small shelf in the corner.

"Write to your mother," they advise.

I stand up, emboldened by a new conviction. "I will!" I cry, yanking the toilet chain, which releases a turgid tide of liver-brown water into the rust-stained bowl beneath.

"Hitler Will Send No Warning!" a faded red wartime poster proclaims to the legation of spiders guarding the water tank. "Carry Your Gas Mask At All Times!"

Back in the room, Angus is now dressed like a World War I fighter pilot, in a long leather coat, helmet, and goggles. What I take for an explanation of his garb doesn't help either.

"There's no breakfast. I dinnae keep food in the house because of the mice."

"I don't understand."

"Well, grab yer coat and hat and come with me."

We stroll outside, where he indicates an exceedingly ancient A.J.S. motorcycle and sidecar parked at the curb.

"This is mine," he says with obvious pride.

"Is it safe?"

"Aye, sure it is. Jump in and we can get a big breakfast in the student refectory."

Having not had any food since it was at sea the day before, my stomach jumps into the sidecar, taking me with it. Before any further doubts as to the safety of the contraption can be cast, the motorbike roars off through the little suburb of Torry. This must have been a pretty little village once, with its working gas lamps and iron curbed alleyways. Now it seems like a lost world, dwarfed, as it is, by the shadows of the great circular storage tanks surrounding the marine fuel oil depot.

Food at the student union is wonderful, plentiful, and cheap, which is just as well since the money donated by the crew of the trawler will have to tide me over till better times.

"So, Billy, what are ye going to do? Hang around and get a job? Play the tourist? Go back on the boats? What?"

"I don't know . . . I'd kinda like to study something interesting."

"Ye could try social studies, history, or the like. Just go along to any of the lectures that you've a mind to."

"But I'm not a student."

"Who would know? And just look what this place has to offer. King's College Library has got to be one of the oldest collections of books in Britain. There's millions of old Celtic books in there, weird books, books on the occult said to be bound in the skin of condemned murderers— if you believe that sort of crap. Then there's always the student union, with its cheap restaurant and subsidized beer bar teeming with lots of nice wee lassies. Ye cannae go wrong!"

Angus scoffs down his food in silence, giving scant regard to digestion or table manners. He eats like a horse—mind you, he looks like one as well.

"Angus is dead right." I commence to thinking. "The scholastic life doesn't look half bad at all. If I hadn't left school at sixteen, this is probably where I'd be anyway, instead of bouncing around from one job to another. So, if I keep my head down, I could go to lectures every day, cram up on stuff, get one of those mail-order degrees, and who'd be any the wiser? My parents would be proud of me then! *"This is my son, the doctor!"* No, that doesn't sound right. How about, *"My son, the scientist!"* Hmm, better. Or maybe, *"My son, the teacher!"* Anything's better than, *"This is my son, the wanker!"* This is it—I have a plan, *"simple, but sustaining,"* as my dad referred to fried egg sandwiches.

Content with my career decision, I practice assuming the laid-back demeanor of the real students by putting my feet up on the velvet-covered seat opposite. A mother-of-pearl sheen reflecting from the cod scales on my trousers hastily reminds me who I am, and my legs disappear under the table again. That night in the little room in Torry, I scrub my clothes in the kitchen sink, rinsing them out in vinegar water to get rid of the fishy smell.

This weekend I resolve to catch up on a lot of sleep, and next week I shall attend the University of Aberdeen as a student—of sorts!

Monday morning duly arrives, and, dressed in clean togs, I accompany Angus to classes. Being shy of the procedures, I will stick with him to see how things work.

Angus's geology lecture turns out to be the most ponderous load of boredom imaginable. It's all mathematical calculations in regard to the point at which rock crystals metamorphose into stone or some such bollocks. The tutor's steady monotone, enlivened only by squeaks of blackboard chalk, is beginning to fossilize my very bones. Numb waves of petrifying apathy seep up from my ankles, disabling the knees and percolating upward to ossify my starving brain. I feel like Socrates' description of the onset of his death after he drank hemlock. Dear God, this is so boring—give me the hemlock!

Mercifully saved by the lunch bell, I saunter with Angus and the other students toward the café.

"Interesting stuff, wouldn't you say, Bill?" he asks.

"You're kidding. That droning old sod would put a glass eye to sleep!"

"Yes, you appeared to be doing a lot of squirming. I thought you were interested in geology?"

"I was, but it all seems to have evaporated. No, I don't want any more of that lecture—it's too technical for me."

The next day, sporting an old Aberdeen University sweater borrowed from Angus, I attend a philosophy lecture and one on forestry; sure enough, no one says a dickey-bird. Although I look the part and go unnoticed by students and teachers alike, I still have no idea what subject to pursue or which field to study.

Angus manages to get me a student union card so that I can use all the university facilities and, more important, a library card.

My first visit to the library is an extraordinary affair. I show the card to the security guard, who doesn't even look up from his copy of the *Press and Journal.* Making my way to the history section, I find myself alone in a shadowy maze of book-lined aisles stretching seemingly for miles. Like a lost soul seeking solace, I wander the puzzle, not knowing where to begin reading or where to start my research.

All around me ancient tomes groan under the sheer weight of the archaic wisdom trapped inside. Some sit tethered by stout chains to the wire cages that contain them. By their leatherlike appearance, I take these to be the ones bound in human skin. Although Angus doubts the veracity of the rumors, I mind my dad telling me of the "murder in the red barn." It happened in pre-Victorian times when a wealthy landowner called William Corder took a servant girl called Mariah Marten into his employ. As time passed he got a bit too friendly with the lassie, and when she became pregnant, he murdered her and hid her body beneath the floor of a red barn on his estate. No one seemed to care about Mariah's disappearance except her mother, who lived miles away. She dreamed every night about her daughter being killed and buried under a red barn floor. She eventually persuaded the police to dig in the barn and the body was discovered. In 1828, William Corder was hung for the murder, and a local doctor bought his body and skinned it for binding medical textbooks. Maybe one of these is Corder's last contribution to society. I don't stick around to find out, as I've heard that standing adjacent to these nefarious volumes can give you a headache.

I press on in an agony of indecision, moving farther into the labyrinth. Flitting from row to row, perusing each section, I touch the spines of these venerable volumes, reading the titles embossed into the deep rich leather: *Ayne Account of ye Aberdeen Witch Trials in ye year. 1596 . . . The Moft Illuftrious Perfons Who Died in the Year 1712.*

Now in the inner sanctum, I discover the mother lode, the crock of gold, the out-of-print books that can no longer be found in the modern world outside these hallowed walls: *Ptolemy: Geographia, 1789 . . . Sir Wm. Betham: Eturia Celtica . . . The Celtic Druids, 1829 . . . J. Frick: Commentatio de Druidis, 1744 . . . Phoenician Ireland, 1802 . . . Taliesin; or, The Bards and Druids of Britain, 1878 . . . Syntagama de Druidum moribus ac institutis, 1655 . . .*

Like an artist's apprentice standing for the first time in front of a virgin canvas, I'm terrified to make the first move. I realize that if I were just a bit smarter, I would have no trouble attaining that which is just beyond my intellectual grasp.

Hesitantly, I take out a volume of work by Francis Bacon and let the page fall open as it will. My eyes alight on a verse that instructs:

> *Read not to contradict and confute,*
> *Nor to believe and take for granted,*
> *But to weigh and consider . . .*
> *Histories make men wise.*

A revelation like no other I had ever experienced sweeps over me as I savor the text. That's it! I have found my calling and one well suited to my Celtic heritage. My Irish mother and Welsh father will be proud. I shall study hard and long; wisdom shall be my watchword, and in the hallowed halls of my ancestors, the cry shall resound: *"Behold! My son, the Druid!"*

⇥ Chapter 7 ⇤

We look to Scotland for all our ideas of civilization.

Voltaire

SHRIEKING RAW, THE CRUEL EASTERLY WIND SLASHES ITS WAY across Europe from the Russian steppes, but before it can scourge Aberdeen with its icy lash, a mild front blows up from the moist southeast, dumping a fleecy blanket of white on the sleeping city. The first winter snowfall has arrived.

Angus sits in front of the electric fire reading the evening newspaper. From behind the steadily growing barricade of history books stacked several deep on the kitchen table, I see only the top his wiry red Afro.

"Here's a job for ye, Billy: 'Druid wanted, no experience necessary, must have his own Stonehenge.' What d'ya think?"

"I think the joke is wearing a little thin, Angus. Surely, after five weeks you could come up with something a little different?"

"Well, ye asked for it, going around telling folk ye want to be a Druid. People think yer an idiot. Of all the things ye could be studying, why that? What's a Druid anyway? Some daft old tosspot sacrificing virgins to the rising sun?" He throws the paper onto the sofa and begins to roll his nightly reefer.

"I've told you before, a Druid is a Celtic wise man, a priest, and bugger all to do with Stonehenge or sacrificing virgins."

"Oh, tell me, great master, what is the secret of the universe?" he mocks, seating an album on the record player and lighting his joint.

"You're a wanker, Angus, 'cept that's a poor secret, 'cause everybody knows it."

He laughs. The room fills with blue fumes of pot smoke and a purple haze of Jimi Hendrix.

"A letter came for you today," he says, indicating the pile of unopened mail burying the sideboard.

"A letter!" I jump up and dig in the pile of bills. A small white envelope appears among the brown ones; it has a Birmingham postmark and the initials S.A.G. written in ink on the back.

"It's from my mam," I say, tearing at the seal.

Dear Willie,

Thanks for your letter which arrived on Monday. Your dad was surprised that you were in Scotland, he thought you were still in Germany and I said you was in Holland, but neither of us knew for sure as you never write. Your pal Angus stayed with us for a few weeks and him and your father had a good laugh. Angus seems to be a nice bloke, but he needs to get them buckteeth fixed. Your dad says, with teeth like that, you could eat an apple through a tennis racket—the misfortune.

Mrs. Fiddler's cat came home with an arrow sticking through him. Some dirty bleeder nearly killed the poor old moggy and him twenty-one years old. The vet was able to take the shaft out of him and he's walking about like nothing had happened. As for visiting us at Christmas, we're going home to Ireland to spend Xmas with your Nana, so we won't be in Birmingham at all. Did you hear that the contraceptive factory where you used to work, burned down? You dad thinks it was set deliberately, but I think it was an act of God. Anyway the whole town was stinking of rubber for three days and you couldn't see for smoke. Well that's it, I've no more for you, so I'll keep it short and sweet like a donkey's gallop.

Your ever loving Mam.

xxx

I stuff the letter back into its envelope.

"How's yer folks? Are they keeping well?" Angus asks, in that gasping way of speaking pot smokers have while inhaling.

"Aye, they're grand. My mam was asking after you."

"That's nice!" He coughs, wheezing the words out of his mouth in whiffs of stale smoke. "What does the S.A.G. mean on the back of the letter?"

"It stands for Saint Anthony Guide. He is the patron saint of lost things."

"Oh, aye, yer mother's right into all that mumbo-jumbo, is she no?"

"She's a good Catholic and stands by her faith."

"Superstition, that's all it is—Dark Age superstition!"

There's a loud click and all the lights go out. In the all-consuming darkness, Jimi's voice slides glissando into a baritone drawl as the record player slows to a dead stop.

"God damn it, the bloody shilling's gone in the meter!" Angus curses, feeling around for loose money in the inky room. "I've no change."

"I've none either, but I could pop down to the pub and get some."

"It's too late. It's past ten o' clock, the pub's shut," he says, turning the luminous dial of the traveling clock toward me, where it hangs in the coal-black air like a distant constellation.

"We'd best have an early night then."

"Aye!" he says, illuminating the gloom with a last draw on his spliff.

Angus could go to sleep on the point of a pin. He's gone in minutes. As for myself, a fatal last cup of tea has provided just enough caffeine to deprive me of slumber, causing me to lie wide-eyed in the dark, staring at nothing but my thoughts.

Angus was right, of course; what he had asked earlier was fitting. What *is* a Druid? I don't know much more than the dictionary definition, and the books I have deal more with what the Druids supposedly did than what they might be. Maybe this is all a waste of time. Perhaps I should stick to less obscure subjects, like hanging some meat on my skeletal knowledge of Scottish history and the invasions, dispossessions, betrayals, and usurpations that form its crooked backbone, or simply trying to perceive what makes the Scottish people unique, even among Celts—what makes them "tick." The Scots seem to carry their history around with them like dry tinder. You only have to mention the word *Bannockburn* and they'll flare up in patriotic passion. With this thought in mind, I puzzle over the psyche of my enigmatic friend Angus, who is proud of being Scots, but has trouble defining what being Scottish is.

"Well, not English—that's the main thing!" he had said, and when I asked him to explain why, he went on. "See, these English bastards, they depict themselves as polite, unassuming gentlemen, believing in fair play and cricket and all that. Then they make the Scots out to be penny-pinching, bad-tempered alcoholics, so mean they wouldn't piss on ye if ye were on fire! That's no very fuckin' fair-minded, is it? Sassenach bastards!"

This view of things is by no means peculiar to Angus. To the vast majority of Scots, there are two kinds of people in the world, those who are Scottish and those who aren't. It's a sentiment you may hear a lot.

If I had to write a thesis called "What Makes Scotland Different?" it would run something like this:

Scotland is like Ireland without rules. The population can be roughly separated into two groups; those who go to the Kirk and those who go to the pub. The Kirk usually means the Church of Scotland, which is a strangely democratic institution, with many spin-offs like the Episcopalians, the Presbyterians, and the po-faced Wee Free Kirk, who enjoy being miserable six days a week, except Sunday, when they're not even allowed to do that. What Catholics there might be are found mostly in the Highlands and some of the outer Hebridean Islands, still clinging devoutly to their faith despite dungeon, fire, and sword.

As for the pubs, they are plentiful and divided into three recognizable subgroups. First, the lounge bars, mostly found in hotels and the province of tourists and the more staid, well-to-do types. Second, the local pubs, vibrant and various, province of all walks of life and a joy to frequent. Finally come the blood tubs, dark, dangerous dives, territory of the vicious and to be avoided at all costs. All these establishments have one thing in common: fiercely draconian licensing laws, foisted on the country by the American prohibitionist Lady Astor. These accursed ordinances prohibit opening times outside of a few hours a day. Open from eleven in the morning until two in the afternoon, then from five in the evening to ten o'clock at night, the bars operate six days a week. All are closed on Sundays, except hotel lounges, which are often only available to hotel guests and residents.

Two peculiar Scottish traits emerge as a result of these restrictive regulations. The first is the ten o'clock rush, a quaint custom taking the form of a frenzied quaffing of several prebought beers and whisky chasers in the final ten minutes known as "drinking-up time." The second notable practice is the nightly habit known as "getting a carry-oot." This has to be done before last call and telltale brown paper bags, bursting with cans and bottles, are a good indication of who's going partying. Barmen clear the customers out with such phrases as, "Ain't you got no hames to go to?" and "Time, gentlemen, please. All your glasses, please." In response to these pleas, garrulous groups of men and women eventually drift into the exterior darkness, cradling their carry-oots like babies. The merry people of Scotland wander off to some nearby tenement for another spontaneous party, where a crowded kitchen formulates the hangovers of tomorrow and future generations of Scots are conceived under heaving piles of overcoats in the spare room.

There now! Histories make men wise and, thankfully, sleepy too. Good night!

The next morning is heralded by a flurry of hammer blows and guttural curses filling the frigid room. Angus is standing on a chair belting the bejasus out of the electricity paymeter above the door.

"What's wrong?"

"The blasted meter is full of coins—I can't get the shilling into it!" He continues walloping the coin box with a hammer.

"Be careful you don't break the security seal or you'll go to jail," I advise.

"If we can't get the electricity back on, we'll have no heating and freeze to death anyway! This is no use. It took me an hour yesterday to get the shilling in. I had to bang on the coin box to try and settle the coins down a little to make room."

"Did you call the landlord to empty it?"

"Of course I did, last week. He said he'd be straight round, but he's like that arse Bonnie Prince Charlie, a bloody long time coming! Gottcha, ya bastard!"

Reluctantly, the slot meter turns and the room is enlivened by a flood of light, the hum of a one-bar electric fire, and James Hendrix Esquire resurrecting from the dead.

The electricity meter is the primary bane of our lives. The only form of heating in the flat is the electric fire, which eats up units of electricity like a carthorse chomping oats. The more modern meters take the new fifty-pence coins, but we're stuck with an original shilling model that keeps getting full. The unlit outhouse is the next irritation, not merely because of the cold, but also because trying to read by the stub of a flickering candle is impossible. I rig wiring from the kitchen window and splice a couple of bulb holders on the ends. Stuck inside the bottoms of Tennent's lager cans, the twenty-five-watt bulbs are nailed to the back walls of the two neighboring outhouses. Mrs. Maclumphit, the old lady next door, is beside herself when she discovers that her toilet has a light and bakes us a big currant cake. Although the illumination shows the place to be more ghastly than previously witnessed, at least I can see to read.

The mild spate melts into a slushy thaw and as quickly again to a hard-crusted freeze, dusted by several inches of powdery snow. From the harbor to the east, to the old university to the west, the great city of Aberdeen, now cut off by snowdrifts, turns in on itself. In the old town, snuggling neatly between the rivers Don to the north and Dee to the south, spontaneous street parties erupt, as families take to skiing the streets and skating the frozen waterways, like the picturesque Russian paintings of ice carnivals in St. Petersburg long ago.

Aberdeen means "the mouth of the Dee," but the natives call themselves Aberdonians, signifying "the people of the mouth of the Don."

Of all the Scots, the Aberdonians have earned an unenviable reputation for being miserly, a charge that quite simply is not true. No doubt Angus would cry that this is "just another English slander," and he may well be right. The word *blackmail* came into our language from the Gaelic *Maol Dubh,* being the excessive taxes imposed by the English, the avoidance of which was called "getting off scot-free."

These folk are an abrasive, witty, independent-minded kindred as different from their English overlords as they were from the Roman invaders of the first century. They are citizens of their country, not subjects of the monarchy, like their counterparts in England. They may have lost their sovereignty to the wicked subterfuge of the greedy political eels in London, but they were never conquered, and that makes a big difference.

The Scots have scant regard for the laws of the English masters, and any rule they can break is considered fair game. Inventive and autonomous of spirit, they find unusual ways to ease life's everyday problems; poverty, being the worst of these, gives rise to some ingenious solutions.

Mrs. Maclumphit lives in the flat next door and has been a widow for a year longer than she was married. In the past twenty-five years, she had lost one son to polio and another to a Chinese land mine in Korea. She exists on the odd few shillings she gets from her lodger, Mr. Heggy, eked out with the tiny pension she gets from the state. Every morning, before the snows come, Mrs. Maclumphit walks along the beach pushing a baby carriage. Occasionally she halts, stooping over to pick something up, which she examines and then either discards or throws into the perambulator. The little old lady spends many hours in this pursuit, until, satisfied with the day's doings, she rolls her pram homeward at a leisurely pace. Anyone fool enough to attempt a peek at the infant in her charge would find themselves staring at hundreds of nuggets of shiny black sea coal. In the summer she sells her catch, but in winter she keeps back a portion for herself, always making enough money to afford a couple of bottles of Mackesson stout down in the local pub.

Sitting in the snug bar with Mrs. Maclumphit and Mr. Heggy is another old twosome, Albert and Maggie Murray. They are the life and soul of the place, always laughing and giggling like a couple of wee kids. I get a kick out of their youthful carryings-on and figure that they must put away a rake of drink in a night. I mention this to Bruce the barman.

"You must be joking. They're like that when they come in at five, pair o' nutters. They're milkies, you know, gassers."

"What? I don't understand."

He leans forward, so's not to be overheard.

"Milkies. Before they come down the pub, they get a pint o' milk and bubble coal gas through it with a rubber tube. Then they drink it!"

"Dear God! What does that do?"

"It gets them stoned, of course—right oot of their heids. They don't have to spend so much on drink then!"

"Is that legal?"

"Well, it's not illegal!"

"Jasus! I wonder if that's where the term *half-gassed* comes from?"

"It wouldn't surprise me if it did. You'd be amazed at what these senile delinquents get up to, wouldn't he, Andy?" The fellow on the stool next to me nods his head.

"Right enough. When I was working for the Electricity Board, we had a meter inspector reporting constantly that this one old wifey's coin meter never had any money in it. We tested the unit and it worked fine. The only thing noticeable was a damp patch on the wall below the meter, but that couldn't be conducting the amount of current the wifey was using. Then I got an idea: I opened her refrigerator, and in the freezer section was a rolled-out pancake of pastry, with ten fifty-pence-size cutouts in it, full of water. She was making fifty-pence pieces out of ice and using them to crank the meter."

"Did she go to jail?"

"Naw, there would be no point—she'd only make a key out of ice and escape!"

The barman takes up his own tale of crafty goings-on.

"Last autumn I was at a church rummage sale, an' I spied an old traveler man, eyeing up a fox fur coat. 'That'll keep you warm in the winter,' I said.

"'It will that,' says the old tinker. He gets it for fifty pence and disappears. Later on that day, as I'm taking a shortcut through the same churchyard, I spy the old boy sitting behind a gravestone, cutting the fur coat up into wee oval pieces, about three inches long. He puts matched pairs of these things into plastic bags and then adds some liquid from a small, brown, screw-top bottle to one of them. He sniffs at this stuff, pulling an awfully putrid face. Then he gi's a wee laugh an' wraps up the work carefully in his knapsack, except the one wee plastic bag with the smell, which he holds out in front of him, as though it might bite him. Fascinated, I follow him oot of the graveyard and up the road, and bugger me, if he doesn't march straight into the main hall of Lodge Walk police station. I follow him in, making like I'm looking at the public notice board, while the desk sergeant asks him what he wants.

"'Fox's ears—I've got a couple o' fox's ears fer ye,' he says handing over the bag to the policeman.

"'Pooh! They're a bit whiffy, we better put them in the incinerator, before they stink the place out.' He hands them to another constable, who hurries off downstairs wi' them.

"'Here ye go, Archie, here's yer reward, and don't wait till they're rotten before bringing them in next time,' the sergeant says, counting out some money into the old tinker's hand. The old boy shuffles off. Then I see the public announcement. Foxes had become so abundant they had been declared a pest, and the government had issued a bounty of a pound sterling for every pair of ears brought in. I figured the old fur coat might provide upwards of two hundred pair of 'fox ears,' netting the old rascal over two hundred pounds. Since the ears were stinking to high heaven no one was going to look too close! My God, I thought, I've just witnessed the perfect crime."

I rejoin the company with a story I'd read in the paper about two English get-rich-quick types who came up from London with the idea of setting up Scotland's first towing company and impound lot. They invested their money in a lock-up yard, an office trailer, and two new tow trucks, but after towing a few vehicles, the unlucky pair found themselves arrested by the police and charged with common assault. The Procurator Fiscal told the bewildered men that they weren't in England now and that Scots law is based on Roman law and that *car* is the Gaelic word for *chariot,* and a chariot is considered to be part of the person, which means forcible removal of the person is an assault upon that person.

Heavily fined, the two entrepreneurs return to their business only to discover a burnt-out office trailer and the smoking hulks of the two tow trucks. A victory to the wily Scots, albeit with the help of a two-thousand-year-old law.

We all have a good laugh and they raise a glass in toast:

> *Here's tae us.*
> *Wha's like us?*
> *Damn few—an' they're all deid!*

These are vigorous people that Himilco described—inventive, industrious, and above all, not giving a bugger what anyone thinks of them.

✦ Chapter 8 ✦

Fate rent Culloden's field,
Bloody and dreary;
Far from my native land,
Danger stood near me.
Traditional eighteenth-century ballad

NOT SINCE NAPOLEON FOUND HIMSELF CAMPED OUTSIDE THE
gates of Moscow did one person wish so hard for the onset of spring.
The winter sun never rises above twenty-three degrees in these northern climes, and midwinter nights are eighteen hours long. I yearn for some color other than the dreich shades of gray that constitute the brief daylight hours. Cold it is, too. The Siberian winds are storming the city, and being on the same latitude as Leningrad, we are besieged by similar weather. The outside toilet freezes solid, and even a pan of hot water fails to melt the drain.

Christmas week, Angus deserts to the luxury of his parents' villa in the posh suburbs of Edinburgh. I am left to spend Christmas in the company of fifty-million flu germs, which induce me to hallucinate right through the festivities and New Year celebrations as well.

What started with a dry throat and a slight headache now has me prostrate upon the bed, suffused in the orange glow of the single-bar electric fire. As delirium gathers apace, I perceive myself trapped like a bug in amber, unable to move or muster. Time loses all meaning; days and nights know no separation as skin-prickling torments of heat-driven chills wrack my quivering frame. The distant bugle of sleep calls my soul to the sweet repose of slumber, but here I am equally vulnerable to distress; fragments of World War I poetry flit through my fevered brain, haunting and macabre. One verse repeats, over and over:

> *At dawn, forlorn, on battlefield,*
> *As far away the sullen bell,*
> *Calls me now, my soul to yield,*
> *Either to heaven or to hell.*

Above the drone of the chanted stanza, I hear bells tolling, but they toll not for me. Their mournful song is for the fallen soldiers, rotting in the sepia photographs of my nightmare, khaki corpses heaped like ridges in a plowed field. Lying among the decaying daguerreotypes of death-clad youth is a fallen flyer who wears a long leather coat, flying helmet, and goggles. On the nape of his broken neck flicks of auburn hair grace his collar. He might well be Angus? I grab his shoulder and turn him over. He has no face. The verse changes as a disembodied voice declaims:

> *They shall not grow old,*
> *As we who are left grow old,*
> *But with the setting of the sun, and in the morning*
> *We shall remember them.*

Muffled drums beat their sad tattoo, rifle shots fire in chorus over the graves of the dead, and a lone bagpiper wails a sad lament that drifts like smoke over the field of battle:

> *The flowers of the forest*
> *That fought to the foremost,*
> *The flowers of the forest . . .*
> *Are all weed away.*

The sirocco embroiling my brain becomes soothed by the cool mistral of a broken fever. I'm dimly aware of lying in a room; my derangement seems to have passed. One by one, my senses return. First, I open my eyes and find the room full of daylight; I focus on the cobwebbed light fixture above my head. Then I hear a fog horn from the docks; that's a good sign that warm, moist weather is upon us. Touching my forehead, I confirm my impression that the fever is gone. Desert dry and acrid, my mouth tastes like the bottom of a parrot's cage. I sup at the fetid water kept in a beer bottle by the bed; it is flat and lifeless. The last of my reasoning to return is my sense of smell, and when it does, it conveys a deathlike stench pervading the tiny apartment. I struggle upright and gape around for the culprit. I don't have to look far. Two trash bags, festering in the kitchenette for the past fortnight, have become a pomander of mouse holes, vapors reeking from every one. Gagging at the stink, I open the window and eject them out into the sweet, crisp air.

"Oh, yer back from yer holidays!" cries Mrs. Maclumphit, pinning up washing in the backyard. "Ye better put some clothes on, young lad. Ye'll catch yer death o' cold! There's a flu aboot, ye ken?" She grins.

"Aye, Missus M. 'Verbum sat sapienti est!' A word to the wise is sufficient, as they say."

"Och, yer an affy tease, with yer wee Irish sayings, laddie!" she laughs.

Closing the grimy window, I fill the iron kettle from the single cold tap above the rust-stained porcelain sink. The brass faucet is green with verdigris and hard to turn. Realizing this is due to my own weakness, I look to the cracked mirror above the drain board for reassurance. The sallow and emaciated face that peers back is hardly my own. I am a wildman staring out with vacant gaze from under a matted nest of copper-wire hair. Though I'm barely twenty, my skin resembles the cadaverous book bindings in the old library at King's, colored only by the red stubble of scruffy beard. Lackluster eyes in sunken sockets appear as dead as those of iced codfish. A chill runs through me. The electricity supply has long since expired, so I shiver around the gas stove waiting for the kettle to boil.

A sponge bath, taken standing up at the sink, cleanses the patina of crystallized sweat from my body and with innards enlivened by the fiery glow of a cup of Bovril beef tea, I dress and take stock of my predicament.

On the downside, my money has all but run out, and I'm staying in a hovel with no bath, no inside toilet, and no hot water. Chronic unemployment and redundancy in the merchant fleet make shipping out impossible, unless I go back to trawling and, no, I ain't gonna do that!

The upside is scant, indeed, but I have a roof over my head, college courses to pirate, and Aberdeen is still one of the cheapest places in Britain to live. It's settled—I'm staying! Well, outside of this town, I still haven't seen Scotland.

Welcome news arrives in a letter from the Department of Health and Social Security. I have now been unemployed for thirteen weeks and am therefore eligible for eight pounds a week unemployment pay. Riches beyond the dreams of avarice.

The return of Angus is marked by a great flurry of cartography. One-inch-to-the-mile Ordnance Survey maps of northern Scotland cover the faded wallpaper, and the small room is transformed into operational headquarters for the great spring expedition.

Angus strides about studying the wall maps with a magnifying glass. In his German motorcycle jacket and goggles he looks like a latter-day Field Marshal Rommel. In this scenario I could well be General Montgomery, as I have no idea what he's up to, or where he will strike next.

"Here," he says, "this is where the goldfields are. See them wiggly blue lines? My dad and my uncle panned those mountain streams in the nineteen-forties. Mother's wedding ring is made from gold that dad panned there aboots."

"Kill . . . doe . . . nan?" I try.

"Naw, it's pronounced *Kildonan*."

"And there's gold there?"

"Aye, mair gold than ye can shake a stick at!"

"When do we get to go?"

"As soon as the weather improves, but we've much to do first. Preparation is half the battle. We need supplies, and you need a good-quality sleeping bag. I'll see if I can borrow one—they're expensive."

He goes back to his maps, drawing pencil lines in blue and circled X's marking possible overnight stops. It all seems a long way off, and I'm sure I'll succumb to cabin fever long before the seasons change.

But change they do, and spring begins with the welcoming sun climbing higher in the northern skies, pulling the first yellow and purple crocuses up through the green sward of the college lawn. I'm raring to go.

The Silver City, released from its winter hibernation, becomes a bustling metropolis, burgeoning with the special fraternity unique to isolated communities. Before 1494, it was just a small fishing community, but the founding of Aberdeen University in that year changed its fortune forever.

It's a fine March weekend morning, as Angus and I load up the motorcycle for our trip to the goldfields up north.

"One pound of sugar, one tin instant coffee, one packet of tea—Irish! Two-pound bag of brown rice, two pounds of dried vegetables, curry powder, soy sauce, petrol for the stove, matches. Guid! Guid! That will do for now. Load this lot up into the forward part of the sidecar and mind ye leave room for yer legs." Angus wrestles with his army tent, which seems far larger than its carrying sack.

"Be careful where ye put that ice ax—it's bloody sharp an' can do a lot o' damage if it's no stowed away safe. Oh, for the love o' God, Billy, watch what you're doing—ye've ripped ma sleeping bag, ya poxy wee skite ya!"

"Well, what in God's name do you want an ice ax for anyway? We're going gold panning, not hunting for Trotsky!"

"That was an ice pick that got Trotsky, ye ignoramus. This is an ice ax, a mountaineering ax. Do ye ken nothin' aboot climbing?"

"Only social climbing, Angus. Now, don't fret about yer sleeping bag. I'll stick some cloth tape over the hole—there, as good as new!"

I throw the sleeping bag into the motorcycle sidecar and for comfort sit down on it. With the sudden force of air pressure the cloth tape flies off and I'm engulfed in a swirl of downy feathers. Angus gives me one of those looks normally reserved for little boys and old men. He brings himself hard down on the motorcycle's kick start, and the old A.J.S. splutters into life.

"What does A.J.S. mean anyway?"

"All Junk and Scrap!" comes his reply. We swerve off in a whirlwind of optimism and goose feathers.

It gets a bit chilly in the sidecar and I wrap myself in the red tartan blanket, which I'm told is Stewart plaid. The wind in my face numbs my cheeks, but I'm exhilarated. This is what I've been waiting for all these long dark weeks. Scotland! To the majority of the British people, it's the least known part of their island.

Exotically named Scottish towns take substance. Keith, Fochabers, Elgin, and Nairn glide by, places I have only seen on a map. Each town, distinctively picturesque, is contrived of locally hewed stone, sustained in this wild landscape by guardian generations of civic pride. Ignoring the neat suburbs encircling the Moray Firth, the old motorbike chugs up the winding lane from the coast into the wilderness beyond, at last stopping by a large stone cairn situated on the desolate upland moor above Inverness, capital of the Scottish Highlands.

Tangy with pine smoke, the cool air drifts up from the coastal villages below into the afternoon sunlight, streaming in honeyed shafts through the lofty fir trees. Probing golden fingers of light cast angled shadows through the green-lined glade and circling squadrons of hooded crows squawk a raucous reveille.

"Lugh Lamh Fada," I say, stretching my arms above my head.

"What d'ya say?"

"Lugh Lamh Fada, Lugh of the Long Hand. He was the mighty Celtic sun god, and those sunbeams are his fingers reaching through the trees."

"Och, aye?" says Angus, rubbing life back into his benumbed knees.

"Yeah, he was the Celtic Apollo, till Christianity came along. Then he got demoted into being a wee shoemaker called Lugh chorpán, or Little-Bodied Lugh, which found its way into English as *leprechaun*."

"Bugger the leprechauns," says Angus, singularly unimpressed by the mythic and rubbing his numb arse to prove it.

I wander over to the great cairn in the clearing. I have read about these monuments and know that they are usually composed of loose boulders, placed there by ancient warriors prior to a battle. Those surviving the fray removed a stone, and the number left indicated the number of dead. The remaining heap was preserved as a monument to the fallen, and many such cairns stand as tributes to Scotland's turbulent past. This particular cairn is unusual, as it is both huge and cemented. Having the appearance of a round, rocky haystack, surrounded by an iron fence and crowned by a halo of yellow gorse bushes, the monument bears an inscription on its base:

THE BATTLE
OF CULLODEN
WAS FOUGHT ON THIS MOOR
16TH APRIL 1746.
THE GRAVES OF THE
GALLANT HIGHLANDERS
WHO FOUGHT FOR
SCOTLAND & PRINCE CHARLIE
ARE MARKED BY THE NAMES
OF THEIR CLANS.

"Oh my God! This is where the Jacobite army got butchered in 1746."

"Aye, I ken. I've been here before. I thought it would be a guid place to bide up for the night, nice and quiet."

"What? Bide up on a battlefield? Will we not get into trouble for camping out on National Trust property?"

"Naw, no bugger comes up here at night. They'd be feared of ghosts, and anyway there's no law of trespass in Scotland." He wheels the motorcycle down a short overgrown track, into a mossy clearing among the pine trees.

"Have you ever been camping before, Billy?"

"No, well, not in a tent at least. I've slept rough out in the wilds many times, but never under canvas. I could never afford a tent."

"Were you no in the Boy Scouts or the like?"

"No, there weren't any scout groups where I grew up. There was only the Boy's Brigade, but they wouldn't take me because I was a Catholic."

"Hmm, that's no way to treat a wee kid. Here's a good spot, nice and soft." Refusing any help from a tenderfoot like me, he quickly erects the green nylon tent. Soon he has the camp organized and the petrol stove hissing.

"You could go and get some water for the coffee. There's a well over there somewhere, near an old stone wall, if I remember right." He indicates the general direction, handing me the kettle. As the sun begins to set, I wander off into the shadowy brush in search of the water hole.

"I suppose this must be it?" I bend to scoop up a handful of spring water from a brackish-looking pool. It's a bit peaty, but it tastes all right. Kneeling on a flat stone, I gulp down a refreshing draft of the cool water. Then I fill the kettle. By my elbow a rotting wooden sign, green with age, lies facedown in the heathery scrub. I flip it over out of curiosity. A colony of wood lice scatters, revealing the fading legend painted beneath: Tobar mBas, the Well of the Dead. I shudder, either from the chilling air sweeping in around me, or more likely the thought of what I have just imbibed.

"Hurry up, the dinner's almost ready!" A distant voice drifts through the trees accompanied by the welcome smell of frying bacon. Taking a different route back through the dewy bracken, I stumble into a clearing where a row of green grassy humps grows out of the earth. Each mound has a lichen-spattered standing stone adjacent to it. The nearest one reads:

CLANS
MAC GILLIVARY.
MAC LEAN.
MAC LACHLAN.
ATHOL HIGHLANDERS.

Kettle splashing water every which way, I run back to the camp.

"What's wrong with you?" Angus hands me a bacon butty.

"Them hillocks back there, they're burial mounds, right?"

"They are, indeed. That's where the unfortunate buggers who died at the battle were thrown into the mass graves. Mackintosh, MacKinnon, Chattan, all heaped into the death pits, to lie as they'd fought, clan by clan."

"Poor sods, I see one of the markers just says, 'Mixed Clans.'"

"Aye, well, when you're blown to pieces by grapeshot, ye wouldn't be easily recognized." Angus places the kettle on the fuming gasoline stove and rolls a joint.

"What a shame, poor old Bonnie Prince Charlie."

"Charlie me arse!" He spits a hemp seed out of his mouth, before continuing.

"He was a fuckin' waster, a poofy, bourgeois bastard who led better men to their deaths and didn't give a tuppenny fuck aboot Scotland, either. When his troops captured Edinburgh in 1745, he could have declared a sovereign Scotland once again, but no, what did he do? He marched the Highland army on towards London, then at Derby, he turns them around and marches them all the way back up again, to die in this godforsaken place."

"But he'd run out of recruits and supplies at Derby—what else could he have done but retreat?"

"He could've gone back tae Edinburgh and declared an independent Scotland and the English would have been so relieved, they'd of let him have it. But he was only interested in the British throne and bollocks to Scotland!" He takes a long drag on his spliff.

"Do you want some of this?" He waves the reeking reefer in my face.

"No thanks. I told you before, it gives me toothache. So why did he come all the way up here for the final battle?" Angus breathes smoke out of his mouth and sucks it up his nose.

"I reckon Charlie wanted to throw the game, as they say in boxing. Look at his dilemma: his mission was to capture the British crown for his daddy and he had failed. He'd never lost a battle, but he was in full retreat. His Highland army was intact, with nowhere to go and liable to get mighty pissed off, if he tells them, 'Well, thanks a lot, lads, but my work's finished here, so I'm fuckin' off back to France, leaving you poor bastards to the tender mercy of the Brits.' His only way out was to let the English wipe out his army up here. Then he can bugger off down Loch Ness, to where the Frenchies had a ship waiting for the bastard, in the same loch where they'd dropped him off, a year before." Angus lies back into the tent, sucking at his joint.

"Well, I've never found that in any of the history books."

"No, and you won't, either. History books are there to give you clues, not facts. The first casualty of war is the truth, ya ken, and histories are written by the victors not the vanquished."

"So, you think Charlie did it on purpose?"

"Aye, of course he did. Just look at the evidence. With Lord George Murray as chief of his army, Charlie had never lost a battle. So why, on the night before Culloden, did he fire Murray and take command himself? Why did he switch the MacDonalds from their hereditary place of honor at the right of the line to the left flank, knowing that would piss them off? And why did Charlie never give the order to charge? Instead of keeping his men standing for a full hour, doing fuck all, while the English cannon blew the shite out of them? Bonnie Prince Charlie my arse—*Bloody* Prince Charlie, they ought to call him! The poxy bastard died of syphilis eventually—very fuckin' bonnie, that is." He takes his coffee mug and leans back, with a weird, inquiring look in his eyes.

"Are ye feared of ghosties, Billy?"

"Well, not really, but I don't like the idea of sleeping on the very blood-soaked ground where the poor Jacobites are still buried."

"Oooh, so ye *are* feared of ghosties!" Angus slurps down the last of his coffee and flicks the remains of his reefer out of the tent flap. In the gathering gloom, the discarded roach flickers briefly, before surrendering its vitality heavenward in a spiral zephyr of thin gray smoke. Angus too has succumbed to oblivion, quietly slipping into the inert, glassy-eyed state that he enjoys so much.

He's a strange lad, avowedly atheistic, skeptical of the ethereal, and suspicious of all forms of mysticism. If he has any religious thoughts, he keeps them to himself. He's always quick to denounce the idea of an afterlife, especially when it concerns my Celtic spiritual leanings. It's a mystery to me why a practitioner of such pragmatism spends so much time talking about reality and then smokes himself out of it.

In the warm womb of a borrowed sleeping bag, I begin to enter the long seduction of sleep. A blood-curdling scream wrenches me into bladder-loosening awakening.

"What the hell was that?" I struggle up, and Angus sits up, too.

"Shh! It's a cougar, a Scottish wildcat, and it's real close by!" he whispers.

"What, a bloody mountain lion? They don't live here, they live in America!"

"Naw, naw, they're native to Scotland, too. Vicious an' all, they are. You'd better not go for a pee, he might bite yer walloch off!" He lays his head back down and in seconds is snoring away. Lucky bastard, getting off to sleep that quickly. It's like throwing a switch with him.

Angus must have read my mind. The coffee has gone right through me, and I'm needing to go, bad. The more I try not to think about it, the worse it gets, until, unable to stand it anymore, I venture out.

A gibbous moon plays shadowgraphs in our sallowy bower, and the silvery stalks of the willows twitch as if touched by an unseen hand. A sharp crack issues from the bushes some distance behind me, followed by a scuffling noise and what, for all intents and purposes, sounds like a human sneeze.

"Hurry up . . . hurry up! Come on, or whatever it is will kill us both!" The silent plea to my nether regions is heard and I streak back to the tent, to peek timidly out from the flap. Angus snores like a chainsaw; several minutes pass by. Like a trick of the light, a strange shape waddles into view. It has the appearance of a small bear, with a black-and-white striped face. The creature spends some time sniffing the spot where I had peed and then adds some of his own. Still sniffing, the beast wanders calmly over to the tent, to stare myopically at me. Seemingly unimpressed, he turns with surprising agility and before departing, proceeds to eat all of the bacon fat out of the frying pan. It is a giant Scottish badger, the first I have ever seen.

I feel a bit of a coward lying here, scared of the creatures of the night, on a sacred field where the flower of Scottish chivalry fought so bravely. Angus dreams on, mumbling and cursing in the depths of his delirium. Eventually, sheer exhaustion overtakes me and I'm asleep at last.

The kilts-and-claymore nightmare I had expected fails to materialize and I awake in the gray mists of dawn, sweating profusely in the confines of a Swedish Army arctic-issue sleeping bag and again needing a pee. Damn coffee! Tea doesn't affect me like this. Wriggling out of my steamy nest, I wrap the red tartan blanket around my naked form and venture out into the clearing.

The sun is just on the nub of rising and a damp haze winds through the Scots pines like vaporous serpents. Walking some little way from the camp, I find the mossy ground beneath my bare feet cool and tingly, like stepping into a chill bath after a hot sauna. My long hair, still plastered to my head with perspiration, sticks like a skull cap, and ruffling it up to let the morning air through might look odd, but feels good.

I'm just finishing my pee when the patch of fog around me suddenly lifts, revealing a large brown dog carelessly cantering my way down the muddy track. Ten yards away, the mongrel screeches to a halt, staring at me uncertainly, as if awaiting my next move. I stand stock still, aware that, dressed only in a plaid blanket, I am in no state to tangle with a stray dog, and moreover, fearful that if I run, he'll chase me. In a show of bravado the mutt's hackles rise, rippling along his neck and down his back. A series of short, staccato barks jars from his throat, and when that doesn't move me, he shows a menacing line of jagged yellow teeth. Another flurry of thick white fog floats by, momentarily obscuring my tormentor. In the trees beyond the nebula, I hear a voice calling in a Yorkshire accent.

"Titus! Ti-tus! Where are you, boy? Come on Titus! Good boy!"

The fog-surrounded dog gives a single bark, and I hear the sounds of reunion.

"There you are. Have you done your business? You'll get lost in all this Scotch mist, you know." The dog begins to whine and sound agitated.

"What's wrong, lad? Did you think I was going to leave you? Tee-hee-hee."

I feel a sudden flood of warmth on my back, as a shaft of golden sunlight dissolves the veil in front of me into the scintillating swirl of color known as a Highland glorie.

A middle-aged, tweed-suited gentleman stands in my elongated shadow, attaching a lead to his dog's collar. He looks up and begins screaming. I try to reassure him by raising my arm to wish him a good morning, but my vocal cords, arid with a rabid fear of dog bites, manage only a parrotlike squawking noise. The ashen-faced man takes to his heels, followed by the equally terrified dog. A sudden fit of devilment seizes me.

"Come back and fight, ye Sassenach dogs!" I yell, in a Scots accent.

Man and dog are now fast-diminishing specks at the end of the overgrown trail. A slamming car door and a squeal of tires herald their retreat.

I fall to laughing so hard I could pee my pants, if indeed I had been wearing any. Back at the camp Angus is in the process of getting up. He stares at me.

"Crivens, you gave me a fright. Ye look like the ghost of Rob Roy in that fuckin' getup!"

✦ Chapter 9 ✦

All that glisters is not gold.
Old Scots proverb

THE SUISKILL BURN CRASHES AND SPLASHES OVER THE RAW rock strata of the pass of Kildonan. Peaty brown water swirls, foaming like fermenting beer in the rocky cauldrons of the tumbling Highland stream. I sit on a timeworn boulder in the midst of the torrent, staring hard into the multicolored granules of sediment scattering the bottom of a forest-green plastic gold pan.

"Aye, Billy boy, keep sifting. Any moment now we'll hit the mother lode, and all our troubles will be over. I tell ye, it's been years since these workings have been panned. There must be tons of gelt doon here. When news of our strike gets oot, there'll be a gold rush like in the Klondike. Aye, man, a great Scottish gold rush!"

The spring sun peeps briefly out from its hide of ragged clouds, causing a small misshapen golden lump to flash, twinkling up at me, through the wash water.

"Angus, is this a nugget of gold? Just here by that lozenge-shaped bit of quartz, see?" I pass him the pan for verification.

"Aye, man, aye, it is—it's gold! Gold! GOLD!" He flails about in the freezing stream, whooping and roaring, like a whirling dervish.

"Come on, Bill, join in! Gold! Gold!" Eyes blazing wild in a fury of auric fever, he continues his dance.

"But, what the name of sanity are you doing?"

"Ye have tae do a wee jig when ye first see color. It's traditional. Ye must throw yer hat in the air and holler Eureka!" To emphasize his point, he throws his bush hat in the air, loses his footing, and vanishes from view beneath the thrashing icy spate of the burn.

Like a reenactment of the last hours of Rasputin, Angus resurrects from under the freezing waters of the mountain stream, coughing and cursing all in creation. Then he shakes himself like a dog, sending silver beads of water spraying from his Ho Chi Minh beard, in a rainbow haze of sunlit droplets. He stands dripping, slowly performing the grimace that passes for his smile, displaying a clutch of ragged teeth that would put you in mind of a neglected prairie fence.

"Great man! Now we're real prospectors."

"What? Is that the first bloody gold you've ever had?"

"Aye, it is."

I'm somewhat taken aback by this revelation. I thought he'd been doing this for years.

"Where's me nugget?"

Angus stares into the pan.

"Aw, shaggin' hell, I've lost it!"

We trudge from the stream, up to the green wadi where we had pitched our tent. Before too long, the embers of the breakfast fire are fanned into life, and Angus begins the long process of drying himself out.

A steady plume of silver steam rises from his clothes, now hanging like becalmed sails from the willow branches surrounding our riverside campsite. I huddle close to the crackling pinewood bonfire in an attempt to dry out my soaked jeans. Angus throws the last of our bacon rashers into the smoke-blackened pan.

"I hope you cleaned out that frying pan before you used it. A bloody great badger had his kisser in it last night, licking out all the fat!" He ignores my warning and points at my jeans with a spatula.

"They'll dry quicker if you take them off," says the wild man.

"I ain't standing here in the nudey-noddy. What happens if someone comes along?" Strutting about naked, except for his climbing boots, Angus seems impervious to chilly air.

"There's naybody for miles aroond, laddie, except me and thee! Here, have a butty."

"Thanks."

"Oooh! That's better—oooh!" Eyes crossed in ecstasy, he uses the handle of the spatula to scratch hard into the ragged rug of red pubic hair around his bollocks. It's a ghastly sight and reminds me of the story of the tinker's old fur coat.

"Bugger off, you porridge gobbler, you're putting me off my supper!"

"Who rattled yer cage? Ye're no getting uppity with me, are ye?"

"Well, you did get me soaked, you mad bastard, leaping about like a lunatic. And then you dropped my nugget back in the river!"

Angus shrugs his shoulders and pulls out his canvas backpack.

"Now we've had our first gold strike, I can wear this," he says, producing a small bronze badge from the side pocket of his rucksack. It depicts a crossed pick and shovel with a tiny nugget of real gold soldered to the shovel blade.

"It was my father's. He got it in South Africa, when he was a prospector doon there. He said I could only wear it after I panned my first native gold. There we are, now!" He turns up the rim of his bush hat, pins it with the badge, and dons it, flat side to the front.

"I found that gold, not you, ya bloody cheat!"

"That's as may be, but ye didn't know what it was, did ye? I'm the geologist, remember? How d'ya think I look?" He strikes an odd heroic pose.

"You look like a congenital idiot from some hillbilly backwoods nudist colony, or maybe the cook who ran the chuck wagon in *Rawhide*."

"Who? Wishbone?"

"Yeah, Wishbone."

"Okay, smart arse, who played Wishbone in *Rawhide*?"

"It was . . . it was . . . ooh, don't tell me. It was—oh!"

"Right, that's got you puzzled for the rest of the night. No sleepums for you!" Angus takes his jeans down from the branches and checks the pockets.

"Oh no! Oh shit! My stash is soaking wet and my papers, too. I'll not be able to get my joint tonight!"

"Poor Angus, no sleepums for you, either."

"Don't you worry about me, laddie, I'll soon be resting in the arms of Morpheus."

"Ah yes, son of Somnus the old Greek god?"

"That's the boy!"

"Did you never believe in the Bible, Angus? God, and all that?"

"When I was a kid maybe, but not now. I'm a scientist. I only believe in that which can be measured, weighed, or counted. Peter Kropotkin was my man. He was a prince of the Russian court who gave it all up to study animal behavior. He wrote a book called *Mutual Aid*. That's my bible, the anarchist's bible!"

"What's it about?"

"It deals with the way individual animals help each other for the common good. It's like us. You helped me out in Morocco, and so I help you out now."

"Oh, tit for tat? Do unto others as you would be done—that kind of thing?"

"Aye, that's it," he says sleepily and then he says no more.

Warm in my sleeping bag, ears attuned to the noises of the night, I doze. Owls are abroad, calling from their stations; a soft wind rustles in the pine trees, crooning a descant duet with the distant, gushing cascade of the bubbling burn. Before the moon has a chance to rise, I surrender to oblivion, soothed by the soporific lullaby of the glen. My last awareness is the fragrant tang of pine smoke, rising from the dying embers, infusing like an incensed prayer into the purple night.

The tiptoes of my dreams take me on a jumbled journey through time, voyaging in hope to strange lands afar. On an exotic island in the Aegean, I tarry a while before descending into the dark cave of Somnus, the Greek god of sleep. The first-century Roman poet Ovid is there, looking rather sheepish. He takes me aside, whispering apologetically.

"I couldn't help it. I needed a god of dreams for my poem Metamorphoses, *but the Greeks didn't have one. I invented Morpheus so that he might become the god of dreaming. His name means shape-shifter."*

"I know. He also gave his name to the drug morphine."

"Yes, I heard. He's doing not bad for a false god. See, he takes his place among the panoply of despotic deities!"

The vault of the subterranean cavern becomes lined with elongated carved pedestals surmounted by waxen-faced marble figures. Some are obscure, some recognizable; all are hideous and enjoined in giving voice to a cacophony of lamentations. Baal, Beelzebub, Lucifer, Caesar, Oliver Cromwell, John Knox, Joseph Stalin, and Adolf Hitler sting the ear with a hellish chorus of dirge. Above it all, a still more discordant tongue is warbling a ghastly parody of an old hymn:

> *Morning has broken . . . cannot be mended . . .*
> *Blackbird has spoken . . . squawkety-squawk!*
> *Oatmeal for breakfast . . . oatmeal for dinner,*
> *Oatmeal for supper . . . forkety-fork!"*

Angus wanders around the campsite preparing breakfast.

"Hell's bell's, you're up with the lark. What time is it?" I say, trying to leave my dreams back where they belong.

"What's it matter out here what time it is? It's getting-up time, ya lazy sod. I've already been down to Kildonan village and phoned my dad. He says we're not in the right place. We need to be here." He sticks an Ordnance Survey map under my nose and points to a collection of wiggly lines.

"We have to find this place, where the stream and river meet, then move north about two miles, to where the streambed has a herringbone appearance. The rock strata here catch the alluvial gold in the apex of the wavy bits, so's we only need pan the last couple of inches of silt. It's like a natural form of gravity-trap, makes for less work, too."

"Sounds good to me," I say, trying to focus on the map.

"As I've said, all the local boys would pan gold for their wives' wedding rings. It was a tradition."

"I thought you didn't hold with tradition?"

"Shut up and eat yer porridge! Ye need to get your strength up. Ye never know what we might find—El Dorado? King Solomon's mines? Both?

"King Solomon me arse! Sure, weren't his mines in Africa?"

"Well, if they were, how do you account for all the Scottish gold found in the Valley of the Kings in Egypt?"

"I didn't know there was."

"Och, aye, the metallurgy proves that the gold came from here in the Highlands. Now do you see why the Romans were so interested in invading Caledonia? They simply followed the money."

"And that led them to Scotland?"

"Aye! And what's more, when I was living in Morocco, I saw standing stones with huge capstones on top, just like the cromlechs around here. The Berbers told me that they are called *bazinas* and were built by King Solomon, the father of all magicians, who also constructed the temple of Jerusalem by using the aid of supernatural beings known as djinnis."

"Oh, like the genie in Aladdin's lamp?"

"Aye! That's all bollocks, right enough. But, I think it's more than possible that the Phoenicians traded the gold from here tae the Middle East, and that's how Solomon got rich. Now give us some help tae pack up and we'll go find that gold."

A little while later we are on the road again or at least a stony rut-worn track.

We haven't traveled far when we come upon a very odd sight. In a small clearing by the side of the mountain road lies a collapsed tent covered with large stones and showing a central hump, on top of which two small boys sit, wailing unmercifully.

We discover that the hump from which mumbled curses and threats are issuing is none other than their drunken uncle. According to the wee lads, he had taken them camping and then tried to get them to join him in drinking a bottle of whisky. The more he drank, the friendlier he became. When they refused his amorous advances, he became abusive and a fight broke out. The struggle had caused the tent to collapse, and with great presence of mind, the wee lads clambered out and rolled rocks onto the canvas, trapping the old pervert inside. Being too scared to let him free in this lonely location, they've sat on top of him all night and are frozen through. Angus wraps the wee boys in our sleeping bags, while I stand guard over the miscreant.

"I'll run back down to Kildonan, Billy, and fetch the village policeman."

"Sure, I'll take care of Uncle Vanya here."

The hump rises up cursing and tries to struggle free, but a sharp blow from a hefty stick assures the occupant of my good intentions.

After some time, a white police Land Rover comes bouncing up the track and a giant, red-faced Highlander introduces himself as Sergeant

McLeod. The policeman is accompanied by a pretty wee district nurse, who wraps the lads in red blankets and sits with them in the back of the truck.

The sergeant thrusts a brawny arm into the tent, winkling the scowling pederast out like a hermit crab from its shell. The handcuffs go on and the wicked uncle sways, blinking in the morning sun. As he's led away, I notice his baldy head sports several egglike bumps.

The policeman's jeep departs down the way it came, tooting its horn.

Our quest begins anew, with much staring at maps and head scratching. Eventually, Angus decides that we are now in the right spot. There are some wavy rock formations on the riverbed, and we pan the sediment from these, bent over our washings like question marks.

After an hour of scraping, swirling, and sifting, Angus has found a few flakes of reddish-yellow gold, worth nothing, but he keeps at it, sure that the next pan will scoop up his golden fortune.

"To hell with this! I'm going cross-eyed, and my back's killing me. I'm off for a walk about." I throw my pan onto the grass and take myself for a stroll up the glen.

It's pleasant walking under an azure sky, brindled with the white cirrus plumes of mare's tails and the odd cloud scudding off to the east. The sun is climbing high, and for shade, I pass through a modern plantation of young spruce trees that abruptly ends near a row of tumbledown cottages. Here, a village of some ten households had once stood, under the watchful eye of an ancient chapel on the hill.

"Jesus, I've found Brigadoon," I say to the sky. The layout of the village is easy to define. Whitewashed ruined walls indicate the dwelling places, and the stark rough-hewn natural stones mark the byres, barns, and outbuildings.

I know the story. Here and in a thousand more heres all over the uplands of Scotland, the people are gone. Not of their own volition, but forced off the land by greedy landlords to make way for sheep, a vicious, calculating act perpetrated by the devotees of the Victorian one-eyed god called profit.

The people prayed, but the call of the new messiah was a louder voice in the callous hearts of the Tory landowners. The old Celtic church looked on as the crofters were shipped off like slaves to the Americas, but soon it collapsed from neglect or grief, leaving only its gable ends jutting skyward like a blackened bishop's miter.

The houses, too, have tumbled down. Where once wee kiddies played and cattle peeked over the kaleyard walls, only swaying clumps of early spring stinging nettles slowly move, filling the air with their bitter scent. Weed-shrouded chimneys, choked with birds' nests and dead creepers, totter above the gaping mouths of lifeless fireplaces, whose once-warm hearthstones lie cold and cracked within.

Like hands raised in divine supplication, the pale palms of many-fingered fungi grow from the decayed dust of silent kitchen windowsills. The wind lifts, and somewhere a rusty hinge swings in rhythmic cadence, a sad, lilting lament, floating across the barren glen like a lone piper's pibroch.

> *Once our valleys were ringing*
> *With sounds of our children singing*
> *But, now sheep bleat till the evening*
> *And the shielings lie empty and broken.*

"Brigadoon? More like Brigadoom," I mutter to the heather while making my way back from that sad place toward the river. After circumnavigating the wood, I find myself at the stream again. Angus is packing up his gear and loading the sidecar.

"This place is panned out. All the gold must be gone long ago."

"Well, Angus, to find gold you need to know the plants that have an affinity for it. That's how the Druids knew where it could be found."

"How's that?"

"There was a plant that only grew near goldfields. It had very long roots, and by following these down you got to the gold."

"Who told ye that load of tommyrot?"

"I think I read it in a book, or maybe my mother told me."

"Och, so yer mother told ye and what does she ken aboot where to find gold?"

"Well, I remember her telling me that the old Celtic way of collecting gold dust was to secure a sheepskin to the riverbed with the nap of the fleece against the flow. Then the women would go upstream and make a big stirring soup of alluvial mud and silt, which the current strained through the fleece, leaving the heavier gold dust behind."

"Are ye kidding me? Is that really what they did?"

"Aye, and I think that's what hatched the Greek legend of Jason and the Golden Fleece."

"Och, fer goodness sake, why didn't ye tell me this yesterday?"

"I didn't think about it, but what would you have done—killed a sheep and skinned it?"

"Aye, I might have done just that or even better still—skinned ye, ya bugger!"

I walk downstream to pick up my gold pan and spy something I hadn't noticed before. On a flat rock by the waterside lie three damp one-pound notes, held down with pebbles. On closer inspection, the face sides have faded somewhat, giving me the idea that they've been here some time. Since I can see no evidence of a votive well or an ancient shrine, I pocket the three quid to share with Angus later in the pub. It isn't much to show for all our time and effort, but it's destined to become the only money we ever make out of the great Scottish gold rush of 1970.

⇗ Chapter 10 ⇐

Of twenty thousand Cromwell's men,
Five hundred fled to Aberdeen,
The rest of them lie on the plain,
Aboon the Haughs of Cromdale.
Traditional seventeenth-century ballad

EASTER WEEKEND ARRIVES IN A GREAT BUBBLE OF FINE WEATHER. Angus spreads the map over the kitchen table and indicates a route that will take us to the rugged Atlantic coast of western Scotland. His pencil follows the red line of the A944 high road snaking up from the river Don into the Grampian Mountains.

"It's a bit of a switchback, but if the old bike can do it, it'll be a trip to remember."

I nod in agreement. The contour lines on the map show parts of our intended journey to be along cliff-top roads. Just north of the blue line marking the Don, there is a symbol depicting two crossed swords and the date 1645.

"What's this, a battle site?"

"Aye, that's where the Battle of Alford happened. Jamie Graham, the Marquis of Montrose, wi' only two thousand troops loyal to King Charles, routed a Covenanter army ten times their size."

"How did he manage that?"

"Montrose was a military genius, the finest tactical leader the Scots ever had since William Wallace. The problem was, he was a poor judge of character and put his faith in the Stuart cause, opposing the Covenanters."

"Weren't the Covenanters allied with Oliver Cromwell against the Royalists?"

"Aye, they were Cromwell's bastard spawn. A bunch of religious bigots led by Calvinist lunatics who nearly destroyed Scotland by dragging it into the English Civil War."

"What happened to the Covenanters? They kinda fade out of history?"

"Och, once they'd done Cromwell's dirty work and Montrose was captured, he called them all to meet him at Dunbar. The idiots lined up, thinking Cromwell was going to gi' them a medal, but instead his Roundheads annihilated the bloody lot o' them—just what you'd expect from the two-faced bastard English." He spits and continues to pore over the map.

"Hmm, nasty, but . . . what happened to Montrose?"

"He was taken to Edinburgh Castle and publicly hung, drawn, and quartered, just like Willie Wallace afore him."

"Ye gods!"

"Aye, and what's worse, it was his old pal Charles the Second that let him be executed, as part of a deal he cut with the Presbyterians for the restoration of the bloody monarchy!"

"Rotten sods!"

"Aye, right enough! So, is there anywhere you'd like to go, Billy—if we get the time, like?"

"Well, there's an old tree I was reading about called Pontius Pilate's Oak, growing near the ruins of the Roman fort at Callander. Legend has it that Pilate's father planted the tree on the day the baby was born, in honor of the child."

"What in the name o' Christ was Pontius Pilate's father doing in Scotland?"

"He was the garrison commander of the Roman fortress at Ancaster."

"Och, away wi' ye!"

The craggy peaks of the Cairngorm Mountains rise like sawteeth into the lark-filled sky. The old motorcycle puffs and wheezes its way up the mountain passes, sometimes slowing to walking pace. The trip down the other side, however, is a furious helter-skelter affair, engine disengaged and bike freewheeling in the petrol-saving style called "Aberdeen overdrive." Corners and sudden bumps in the road test the stamina of riders and machine alike; when my life flashes in front of me for the third time, I am able to remember Latin prayers that have eluded me for years.

Roadside signposts fly by, revealing romantic-sounding Scottish Gaelic place-names. Using my rusty Irish Gaelic, I decipher what I can from the name elements to extract their meanings. Some are easy. Cairngorm, "Greenish-blue pile of stones," is a true description of the smoky peaks jagging the clouds around us. Dalwhinne takes a little more detective work: *dal* signifies a field, but what's *whinne*? Maybe it derives from *cíoná*, meaning "champion." *Kin* is the old Gaelic *ceann*, the word for *head*, so Kingussie means "the head of the pine trees."

My backside is getting sore. I'm glad when we stop for a breather and a stretch on the banks of Loch Ness.

"So, do you think there's a monster in the loch, Angus?"

"Have a bit o' sense, man. How could a prehistoric dinosaur survive in Loch Ness? You believe in it though, eh, Billy?"

"Aye, I do. Didn't folk think the coelacanth was an extinct fish until they caught one in the Indian Ocean a few years ago?"

"That's different."

"How so?"

"Because that's the ocean and this is Loch Ness. But, believe what you like, it goes well with your ghosties an' pixies an' yer childish superstitions. This is the twentieth century, man. You're living in the Dark Ages." He opens up his map.

"Well, wouldn't life be boring if there were no mysteries left to solve?"

"I suppose it would. The place we're heading to is here, the curiously named Glenelg, otherwise known as 'the palindrome glen.'"

"Oh, aye, Glenelg, it *is* the same backwards—was it a cat I saw?"

"Where?"

"No, *wasitacatisaw*. It's a palindrome, too, like that thing about Napoleon sailing to Elba, remember?"

Angus shrugs his shoulders and kick-starts the bike. I scan the rough gray waters of the loch, wishing a big serpentine head would stick up and yell, *"Fuck you, Angus!"* As if he'd care?

It's getting dusk as we turn into Glenelg and begin searching for a likely campsite. It's handy having no law of trespass; we can put the tent up wherever we like. By a bend in the road is a grassy patch just off to the side where we can make camp in full view of the Isle of Skye, lying beyond the arm of the western ocean known as the Sound of Sleat. Angus fiddles with the tent poles, while I wander off to gather wood for a fire.

On the bank, by the bend in the road, lie several piles of cut firewood, stacked ready for kindling, but green with moss and splattered with lichen. I pull the top logs away to reveal the less rotten timber below.

"You wouldn't be thinking of burning that wood, surely?" comes a voice. Startled, I look up into the whiskery face of an old man, who had silently appeared and was now sitting on the stump of a felled tree, some ten feet away.

"I beg your pardon, I didn't see you there. Is the wood not for the taking?"

"It is not. Take what you may find around, but not that wood, it is cursed!"

"Cursed? I don't understand." The old chap takes a long puff at his pipe before continuing.

"For many years a tree grew from the stump I'm sitting on. Huge it was, the biggest tree for miles around. Its great branches spread out over the road and were home to many birds and pine martins. But— you're not English, are you?"

"No, I am not! I'm an Irishman."

"Good! Well, as I was saying, after the Battle of Culloden in 1746, the English redcoats used the tree to hang any Jacobites they found in the area, and later, in the Highland Clearances, many poor crofters, who refused to leave the land, met their maker in the same way. Over the years countless innocents were lynched here as well as the common sheep stealers, horse thieves, and various murderers. When the council chopped the tree down to widen the road, the wood was left in piles for the local folk to carry away. Those who did were sorry for it. The logs, when burnt, give off the stench of rotting flesh and the smoke screams out of the timber like the cries of the dead. You can see over there where some people even brought the charred wood and ashes back rather than have them near the house. No one hereabouts will touch that stuff. I advise you to do the same. It is said that if you ignore the curse, you will be dead within the year."

"There's no danger of me doing that, sir. As I said, I am an Irishman and take the signs and portents seriously."

"You are well to heed the signs. Oidhche mhath, Irishman, if you know what that means?"

"I do, sir. A very good night to you, too!"

In the gathering twilight, the stranger vanishes as quietly as he had come. I steer well clear of the Glenelg hanging tree and pick up sticks from along the hedgerows. Loaded down with firewood I make my way back to the tent.

"Where the hell have you been? I lit the fire without you."

"I met this old boy who told me not to take firewood from the tree back there. It's cursed." Angus shakes his head in disbelief and hands me a cup of java.

"Cursed, my arse. Some silly old bugger tells you a fairy tale and you take it in, hook, line, and sinker. You're pitiful! He's just pulling yer leg, man. They're famous for it in these parts—*famous!*"

"I don't think so. Old people have old knowledge and that should be respected."

"And you think this wisdom is handed down from father to son, sitting around the peat fire with a cow looking in the window."

"Aye, that's how I learned so many traditional folk songs, Angus. They were handed down by my folks. There's places in Ireland where people can recite epic poems that were ancient before the fall of Troy."

"So what? That doesnae mean anything. Don't you think they just make these things up for the tourists, like the tale of the Loch Ness monster?"

"No, they don't. It's folk memory, I tell you!"

"Prove it!"

"Okay, then, why do people say 'Oops!' when they have a little accident?"

"Because that's what folk say."

"Aye, Angus, but why 'Oops!' or 'Whoops!'?"

"Is there a point to all this or are ye just havering?"

"The point is that Ops was the ancient goddess of good fortune, as in opportunity. So when something bad happens, you correct it by invoking her name. This superstition has passed down the centuries from Roman times without losing its meaning."

"Aye, but folk don't know what they're saying when they say it. I'd never heard of Ops, till you mentioned it."

"It doesn't matter. The folk memory is still there, intact."

The night falls thick and black. Before too long, a chilly mist sweeps in from the sea and we seek the warmth of our bedrolls. In the confines of the small tent, Angus's bedtime joint smells acrid, but it overcomes the pungent whiff of his socks. I doze off, thinking about the old man of the tree and wondering whether or not he was real. Perhaps he was the guardian of the curse. I had heard of such things from my folks.

Angus is an early riser, and the coffee is made long before I even surface to consciousness. The campsite is flooded with early-morning sunlight, and the sea stretches calm and blue beyond Eilean nan Ceó, the Isle of Mist, better known as the Isle of Skye.

Breakfast always tastes better in the open air, and bacon, egg, and beans are a good way to kick off the proceedings. I take care of the washing-up at a nearby clear-running stream, accompanying myself by loudly singing a song I had learned at school:

> *Speed bonny boat, like a bird on the wing*
> *Onward! the sailors cry.*
> *Carry the lad, born to be king,*
> *Over the sea to Skye.*

Predictably, a ditty idolizing Bonnie Prince Charlie has Angus conjuring up a firestorm of invective hot enough to poach the pope. This pleases me no end, but wandering from the stream, I find him stoking a large log that he's introduced to the campfire, just to spite me.

"There, see? That's a piece of your spooky hanging tree, blazing away and I'm no deid yet." I empty some salt into my hand and quickly throw it into the blaze. Angus grins his toothy grin.

"Gowan, ya big jessie, if there is a curse d'ya think a wee bit o' salt will save ye?"

"Aye, I do!"

He takes down the tent and packs the sidecar with the camping gear. The log spits and hisses like a nest of vipers.

"You really should throw a pinch of salt into the fire, Angus—to break the spell."

"Away and shite with yer spells. I'm a geologist, no a fuckin' alchemist!"

Like it or not, the log is now producing a putrid stench that has even Angus crinkling his nose up. I kick it off the fire and empty the kettle over it. The charred limb lets out a hideous spine-chilling squeal of steam.

"Jesus, Angus! Even if you don't believe these things, have a wee bit of tolerance for thems that do!"

"Oh, aye! Like that Pontius Pilate's oak tree you wanted to visit at Callander. What a load of bollocks that is, and you still believe it!"

"How do you know the legend isn't true?"

"Well, the math doesn't add up, does it? Pilate was born long before the Roman invasion of Scotland. By the time Agricola got up here—in what, 74 A.D.?—Jesus had already been crucified."

"Then, maybe Pontius Pilate came here after Christ was executed and planted the tree himself and the story just got mixed up."

"Aye, and maybe Jesus came to Scotland and planted the bloody tree himself, just to give you something to haver on about."

"And well he might have. William Blake believed in the story that young Jesus came to Britain with his uncle, Joseph of Arimathea, like in the song 'Jerusalem':

'And did those feet, in ancient times,
Walk upon England's mountains green . . .'"

"William Blake was an idiot!"

"He was not, Angus. William Blake was a mystic and an Irishman, too, many believe."

"I rest my case," says Angus.

The road takes us down to where the sea cliffs expose sedimentary rock strata that Angus says is fifty million years old. I sing happy birthday to it, and he calls me an ignoramus. Angus crawls over the geological layer cake, poking this and staring at that and sometimes picking up things and hitting them with a hammer. He's in his oil-tot, but to me it's about as much fun as waiting for a bus in Manchester on a wet Wednesday morning.

Being in search of amusement I go for a wander into a part of the old Caledonian forest. The canopy is rich and leafy, and the tree trunks hang with beards of mossy green liverwort and earlobes of sprouting fungus. A savor of pine oil drifts through the dappled shade, and tiny drops of silver dew clinging to the spiderswebs break the light into spectra of scintillating coronas. Moths and butterflies flit in and out of the heather stalks, seeking nectar from the yellow gorse blooms, while a nearby woodpecker raps out a burst of hollow hammering that reverberates through the coppice like brisk machine gun fire. All nature is singing. Birds trill, bees hum, and the breakers from the rising tide spume and splatter on the distant crags beyond the woods.

In the moist bowl of a fern-filled clearing, a cupidic face stares down at me from the gnarled bark of an ancient oak tree. The apparition has the pleasant countenance of an ancient mariner, complete with a tuft of gray tree moss providing the visage with a luxuriant beard. Above this, a pair of wrinkled eyes smiles over a curly mouth, and for some reason I am put in mind of Captain Metcalf. The old sea dog watches me cross the open space and enter the tangle of creeper-festooned branches on the other side.

'Tis pleasant to walk in the wood. Once most of Scotland was covered with such forestation, until the great trees were destroyed, felled by English axes to make warships to fight Napoleon and the lesser ones burned to yield charcoal to make gunpowder. An unwelcome French thread in the weave of Scottish history.

I spy a flutter of black and white feathers, which, on landing, assumes the form of a magpie. Immediately, I scan the area for another of its ilk, as to see only one magpie is considered unlucky. The bird is alone, so I resort to an old magpie-tallying rhyme to counteract the bad luck:

> *One for sorrow, two for joy,*
> *Three for a girl and four for a boy,*
> *Five for silver, six for gold,*
> *Seven for a secret never to be told.*

In Ireland I have heard the bird referred to as *An Francagh*, "the Frenchman," but I'm yet to find out why this should be. Perhaps it's another Napoleonic connection.

The dingle of deciduous trees is curtained on the western side by a dry stone dyke. These mortarless walls carve the bare hills into irregular green patches on which dazzling white dots of sheep find scant grazing on the rugged uplands. I pull myself up to the top of the dyke and park my arse on a sun-warmed flat stone. Walls are great places to facilitate the mind. When I was a kid in Ireland, it was common to see farmers sitting on top of walls, thinking away furiously. Now all I need is a thought . . .

I sit for a while in the sweet bosom of nature, hoping that some revelation will overwhelm me with a rush of Druidic edification. All that happens is that the stone under my arse becomes cold.

The curse of youth isn't, as many older folk think, the absence of thought; my problem isn't lack of thinking, it's hacking my way through entangled ideas, trying to clear a path. I suppose, if ever an original thought came along, I could greet it with, "Doctor Livingstone, I presume?"

In this respect, I benefit greatly from my friendship with Angus. He is ever the sardonic skeptic, eager to keep my flights of fancy in check; a substantial rock on which my more whimsical notions come to grief, but most helpful of all, a gritty sharpening stone on which I may hone my wisdom as well as my wit. The pursuit of learning is the course that I have set and though the progress may be arduous, the goal is worthwhile. As the old Latin motto has it, "Per ardua ad astra, Through difficulties to the stars!"

The sun ducks behind a cloud and I vacate my perch. Returning along the way I had come, I soon find myself back in the clearing. The face is gone. The wispy beard still dresses the oak tree, but the avuncular smile above it has vanished. Try as I may, no further features can be discerned from the rough bark of the ancient tree. It gives me a chill that forces pace into my hurried retreat from the woodland. Once more in the open meadow of the glen, I feel to some extent that I have learned something. Powerful things abound that I have no control over, and I would be a fool indeed to mess with that which I do not understand. My father once told me, "Never open a door into the otherworld unless you know how to close it first!" Sound advice, but I had not opened the door, I had just been there when it was ajar, and I didn't feel threatened by what I saw, merely curious.

Away in the distance, a motorcycle engine roars into life, sending a flock of squawking hoodie crows, fluttering like black angels, back to the safety of the pine trees.

When I catch up with him, Angus is getting ready to leave.

"So, Billy, that was a day well spent. I found some dolomite—what did you do?"

"Well, I didn't find the mighty dollar, but I did get some sense!"

"Is that a joke?"

"Very nearly!"

"We'll take the Great Glen on the way back so that you can look for your pal Nessie. I figure tonight, we'll maybe camp somewhere by Invermoriston and tomorrow we can cut over the top of Loch Ness by Drumnadrochit and get back to Aberdeen on the Strathspey route."

"Drumnadrochit, eh? 'The ridge of the bridge.'"

"Is that what it means, Billy?"

"Aye."

We chug our way out of the palindrome glen, leaving the hanging tree and its cursed kindling behind. As we speed past the spot where the tree once stood, Angus doesn't give it a second glance, but I still have a bad feeling about it.

Rhododendron bushes line the roadside for miles in an endless dark-green tangle. Soon they will be burgeoning with their heavy clusters of white, pink, or purple flowers. Introduced into the Highlands by the Victorian English settlers, the plants, like their planters, have taken over vast tracts of the Western Highlands, where they flourish at the expense of native species. Where the rhododendron grows, nothing else will. The shrub is poisonous both to other plants and animals alike. Attempts to control the spread of the foreign invaders by hacking them down at every opportunity have usually failed, and even wholesale burning of infested areas has little effect; they keep coming back. The same is true for the plants.

On the road to Glenmoriston the bike starts to splutter and we stop to fix it at a place near Loch Oich called, in Gaelic, Tobar nan Ceann, or "the Well of the Heads."

By the side of the road, a large stone monument commemorates the events that took place here long ago. The four sides of the plinth are in-scribed in Gaelic, Latin, French, and English, the latter of which reads:

> As a memorial of the example and summary vengeance
> which, in the swift course of feudal justice, inflicted by the
> order of Lord McDonnell and Aross, overtook the perpe-
> trators of the foul murder of the Keppoch family, a branch
> of the powerful and illustrious clan of which his lordship
> was the chief. This monument is erected by Colonel
> McDonell of Glengarry, XVII Mac-Mhic-Alaister, his suc-
> cessor and representative, in the year of Our Lord 1812.

"Would you look at that now?" says I. "Right enough! I read about this in an old book called *Romantic Lochaber.* I can't remember why the Keppochs were killed, but the seven men who took part in their mur-der were decapitated and their heads washed in the well yonder, before being delivered to the feet of the clan chief in Glengarry Castle."

"Rough justice, indeed," says Angus, unscrewing an engine cover.

"Aye. In the last century, on the Isle o' Skye, a MacKinnon killed a tax collector and cut his head off. He washed that in a well, too. The an-cient Celts believed that washing your enemy's head in a spring cleanses the soul from the skull, so his spirit won't come back to haunt you."

"That's handy," says Angus, half-listening to my monologue.

"Most wells are old pagan sites, converted to Christian shrines by adding saints' names, like Tobermory on the Isle of Mull. That's from Tobar Moiré, 'The Well of the Virgin Mary.'"

"So, *tobar* means 'well'?" says my friend.

"Aye."

"So, if it *means well,* it will do you no harm?" Angus chuckles away to himself. Disregarding his dreadful pun, I continue rabbiting on about votive wells.

"In Ireland, you'll often see the trees and bushes around a well site festooned with the bandages of the sick. Folks believe that a cloth dipped in the water will create a cure. As the water slowly drips from the fabric, the disease leaves the body with each drop. Money would be left in offering at the wellhead, which only a fool would steal and be cursed by the spirits protecting it."

"Ah-ha!" says Angus, burning his fingers on the motorcycle engine. He takes little heed of what I say, but I'm used to that and say it anyway.

"I think the magneto points are gone," he declares, opening up a covered box and poking an oily finger inside. "Sure enough, one of the carbon brushes is broken. That means we're screwed. It's miles to the nearest town and it's Sunday anyway, so everything will be closed. We'd better find a place to camp for the night." He starts to walk down the road, scanning the surrounding glen for a flat piece of campground to bide up.

"Perhaps we can fix it?" I offer, but he's now turning the corner out of sight.

"Why don't you dip it in the sacred well and get some of your fairy friends to fix it?" he shouts back, disappearing from view.

I look at the problem part, which is lying on the grass, on top of the magneto cover. The broken brush is just a little round pole of carbon, about an inch long, with a coiled spring at the end. Taking one of the long-dead batteries out of my flashlight, I split it open with a penknife, revealing the almost identical carbon rod that acts as the cell's anode. With a wee bit of jigging about, I get the spring secured to the end of the rod and reassemble the magneto. The A.J.S. fires at the first kick and I stand revving the engine, aware from the motorcycle's mirror that a very puzzled Angus is running down the glen behind me.

"What's going on? How did you get her going?"

I just stand and smile, turning the throttle to tease him. Angus leaps on the bike, taking over the twist grip and gunning the engine, as if he fears it's about to die again. He cracks a gaping grin. Then he realizes his bum's soaked.

"Why's the seat all wet?" he shouts above the noise.

"I used some well water to bless the bike."

"Well, fuck me!" says Angus, obviously impressed.

"Agus an t-each air am marcaich thu!"

"What's that mean?"

"And the horse you rode in on!" says I.

With the setting sun dappling our backs, the three-wheeled wonder speeds up the tree-shrouded lane that runs along the north bank of Loch Ness. To the right, where the bushes allow, the vast expanse of the loch may be seen, blue and peaceful. No plesiosaur raises her mocking head and the water is still, except where a returning fishing boat carves a herringbone ripple toward the docks at Fort William.

✦ Chapter 11 ✦

There's a bed for me where'er I lie
And I've no want of care
As long as I've me belly full—
Me backside can go bare.

Traditional folk song

JUST BEFORE THE END OF THE SPRING TERM, ANGUS ANNOUNCES that he's going away to do some geology fieldwork in the mountains with a group of his fellow students.

"So, do ye want to come? I'm sure there'll be room on the bus."

"I don't know, Angus. Do you think the others would mind?"

"No, and I ken there's a spare seat, 'cause Andy Ritchie is taking his own transport. He's just bought a wee scooter and he wants tae try it oot."

"Okay—if nobody minds."

The next day, gray and early, I meet the snooty bunch of herberts that constitute the "rock smacker's club." These sons of the rich and famous appear very aloof in their brand-new designer gear and matching accessories. They stand around in the chill morning air, like mannequins in a catalog, each wearing equipment costing more than I've managed to earn in my entire life. If the morn is frigid, the company is even more so.

"What are *you* tagging along for? You're not a geologist. Are you hoping to discover some new element or something?" the leader, "Lord Snooty," sniggers in the haughty, pinch-arse accent of the British upper class.

"Well, while you and yer muckers are running around the hills, splitting stones in half with yer wee hammers, I thought I might go seeking the Holy Grail."

He stares at me like I'm shit on his shoe.

"Well, okay, but don't get in the way, there's a good chap."

It's as well the buggers have fine long noses, it gives them something to look down when dealing with peasants like me. And look down they do. I sense them mocking me and my old clothes. Bollocks to them! as my mother would say. I'll be all right in my new army boots, plus the addition of a red, lightweight nylon jerkin, called a kagool, that cost me ten shillings in the military surplus store. Apart from my sleeping bag, my only other encumbrance is an old gas-mask satchel, containing some packets of brown rice, powdered soup mix, and a small six-pack of herbs and spices.

The minibus meanders the country roads west of Aberdeen into the area known as the Mearns, some of the finest farmland in Scotland. From this rich soil was sprung the ploo-boy laddies, who tilled the fields with horse and plow, and the Orramen, who did the myriad other jobs to be found on the farm. These tough lads worked hard and played harder, living in communal hillside shacks called bothies and making their own entertainment. Some were talented songsters, and many bothy ballads survive to tell of their lives before the Great War:

> *When I was a ditcher and drainer*
> *And up tae me oxters in snaw*
> *The Deil grabbed a houd o' me bollocks*
> *And I thocht that he'd rugged them awa'.*

Those who didn't volunteer for the war of 1914–1918 were conscripted into the British army by the thousands. A disproportionately large number came from Scotland, and of those, few survived. By 1920, there was hardly a man left alive in the Mearns who knew how to yoke up a plowing horse. The merry ploo-boys had gone, decimated on the barbed wire of Passchendaele or gassed in the mud-filled trenches of the Somme. The small towns and villages—Banchory, Aboyne, and Braemar—remain, huddled around their war memorials like mourners at a tombstone. No hamlet is without one. Even the smallest row of farmers' cottages has a commemorative plaque with half a dozen names recording the carnage of World War I. Sometimes the village, too, is gone. Long abandoned and plowed over, leaving only a Celtic cross in a field to mark the passing of a lost generation.

The wave of melancholy that has pervaded my soul since leaving Aberdeen is suddenly evaporated by a crocus-yellow sun bursting through the gray vapors above.

A belt of blissfully warm weather creeps in, and the road through the Grampians becomes a trip across the roof of the world. Far away, the imposing, ragged pinnacle of Schiehallion proclaims its right to be "the Fairy Hill of the Caledonians," guardian to the vast expanse of Loch Rannoch, the aptly named "Lake of the Ferns."

One hundred and twenty miles from Aberdeen, the eight-seater minivan climbs up to the plateau known as Rannoch Moor and stops at a point where the main road is bisected by one of General Wade's old military roads, built by the English redcoats to subdue the Highlands just before the 1715 rising. At the crossroads stands a few gray stone buildings, a garage, a tiny shop, and the Bridge of Orchy Hotel.

"Break time!" calls the driver, pulling into the pub carpark.

"Where's the campsite?" I ask.

"It's an old grass-filled quarry, about four miles down the military road on the banks of Loch Orchy," says the driver.

After we have a couple of beers, the bus conveys our party over a humpbacked bridge and along a single-track road, coming to rest in the midst of the pine trees skirting the loch. Pitching our tent among the others in this sheltered bower takes little time. The ground is soft with peat moss, and the springy grass makes for good bedding.

From the open door of the tent, the view across the loch to the snowy pinnacles is breathtaking. The placid waters of the deep, blue lake cradle in the green arms of gently rising foothills, reflecting the snow-capped peaks above. It's just how I imagine Switzerland.

"God's ain country, eh?" says Angus, with pride.

"It's beautiful—aye, beautiful."

Lord Snooty lights a fire, and one of his minions places a large cooking pot full of water on top of the sticks. In five minutes their fire is out. They try again, with similar results. I tell Angus of my lack of confidence in these would-be fire raisers.

"Och, to hell wi' them," he says. "I've got my wee petrol stove here, though by the whiff of it, I fear it must have been leaking on the road up."

Angus is right. His rucksack reeks of gasoline, and we have to leave it outside the tent.

His lordship is cursing at the fire, as if that's going to help. I get up to give them a hand. Taking three waterlogged sticks from the loch shore, I fashion a tripod over the fire and hang the cooking cauldron from its peak. The fire flares up, and soon the water in the pot begins to boil.

It's obvious these chaps have never lived rough in their lives, a conviction of mine that's compounded when the laddie elected to cook for the group opens a tin of Spam and throws it whole into the pot, along with a packet of dried beans and a loaf of sliced bread.

The resultant goo is served up and eaten with the greatest reluctance by the campers. The beans are as hard as bullets, but a few bottles of beer soon raise their spirits and hopefully aid their digestion. When darkness descends, the lads take to their sleeping bags and indulge in muted conversation until a lone heron calls for peace to fall upon the glen.

The heat of the morning sun on the nylon overhead has the camp rising early. Lord Snooty wants everybody to go prospecting near the village of Strontian on Loch Sunart, where he says the element strontium was first discovered in 1790. Angus is in his anarchist mode and tells him to fuck off and stop giving orders. He's not in the mood for prospecting; instead, he's going to climb Stob Ghabhar, the pretty, Swiss-looking mountain across the loch.

After a disastrous breakfast of burnt toast, spoiled eggs, and incinerated bacon, Lord Snooty's group departs in the minibus, leaving Angus and me sitting at the campfire.

"Whoever these kids are, they must have butlers to look after them when they're at home."

"And chefs too, nae doubt!" Angus waves an Ordnance Survey map under my nose.

"There it is. This is the best way up, along this ridge to the central corrie. Then up the waterfall tae the lower peak, then over the saddle back tae the summit."

"Why are you telling *me* this?"

"You're coming too, aren't you?"

"No."

"Ye have tae. What happens if I fall and kill myself?" He folds up the map and packs it away in his fume-filled backpack.

"What good would I be, if you fall and break your neck? What's so special about this hill anyway?"

"It's not a hill, it's a Munro, and one I've not climbed yet."

"What in hell's name is a Munro?"

"A Munro, dear boy, is one of the Scottish peaks over three thousand feet, named after a certain Hugh Thomas Munro, who was the first to climb all two hundred and seventy-seven of them. I'm a Munro bagger and I've done about fifteen. Stob Ghabhar at three thousand five hundred and sixty-five feet is one I've no climbed yet. So, are ye going to chum me along?"

"No chance. It's me that would break me bloody neck. You've done this before."

"Ah, Billy, don't be a shite. Come on, it'll be fun!"

"Aye, all right. Call me stupid, I'll go a bit of the road with anybody, like Doran's donkey."

"Rub this into yer boots. It'll keep the water oot!" He hands me a tin of Mars Oil, a slimy concoction that smells of almonds and soaks quickly into my fingers, as well as my boot leather.

We strike out in a westerly direction, making our way around the loch, to the foothills of Stob Ghabhar, "the Peak of the Goats."

Beginning the ascent is quite enjoyable, but before long the disagreeable sensation of being chilled by the mountain air, while sweating like a pig in my nylon kagool, sets me wondering why people do this for fun. I wouldn't do it for money.

Angus tells me that the great central bowl of the mountain was scooped out millions of years ago by a glacier. What he doesn't tell me is that a herd of wild deer lives here now, which, on seeing us approach, begins stampeding from one side to the other. Apparently trapped, the beasts shy away to a far corner where they watch us cautiously as we trudge through the squelching morass that constitutes the bottom of the hollow. With a trumpeting roar, a hefty great stag, carrying what looks like a cluster of radio antennas on his head, appears from nowhere. Head down and bellowing, he charges through the rocks, spurring us to splash up the central stream toward the safety of the fifty-foot waterfall pitching in long tails from the cliff above. At the rock face, Angus climbs like an ape. Terrified, I follow, trying to put as much distance as possible between me and the jagged horns of the furious stag below. Thirty feet off the ground, the realization comes upon me that I'm stuck.

"Angus!"

Clinging to the spray-soaked vertical rock adjacent to the waterfall, I find myself standing on a two-inch-wide, slime-covered lip of stone, with one hand holding on to a loose boulder and the other searching for a finger grip.

"ANGUS . . . ANGUSSS!"

A head appears over the top of the cliff above me, followed by a camera.

"That's great, Billy—hold it there. No, actually, can ye make it look a wee bit more dangerous?"

"IT *IS* DANGEROUS, ANGUS, YOU MAD BASTARD! GET ME OUT OF THIS!"

He pulls a nylon rope from his rucksack and throws a looped end down.

"Put this under your arms and I'll pull you up."

Struggling to keep my balance on the slippery precipice, I lasso myself with the rope, but before it can be secured under my armpits, my foot slips and the rope catches around my neck. Twenty feet above, Angus feels the dead weight and pulls. I lose all contact with the rock and dangle like a condemned man from the gallows. In desperation, I try to cry out, but the pressure of the noose is too much. On the verge of strangulation, I grab the rope to take the strain off my neck. The momentum swings me out into the icy cascade of the waterfall, then back again. Angus, oblivious to my predicament, retreats from the cliff edge and wedges himself between two boulders to get a better purchase. Grunts and curses fill the air above me as he heaves on the rope. Like a dead pig being hoisted in a butcher's shop window, I'm unceremoniously dragged upward, through the slime-oozing strata of crumbling rocks.

Lying on a saturated moss bed, with cold water seeping through to my underwear, is not how I imagined the life of a mountaineer.

"Ye were supposed tae put the rope under yer oxters, no roond yer neck. Ye could have gotten hurt!"

"I know . . . I tried . . . but . . ."

Talking is much too sore. I give up and sit, rubbing my rope-burned throat.

Angus smiles and shakes his head, like people do in the presence of idiots. He opens his rucksack to stow away the rope and decides to dig out some supplies.

"Okay, we'll stop here for a whiley and have a wee bit o' lunch," he says, unperturbed by my moanings. "How do ye like mountaineering so far?" he asks, as if a stupid question will cheer me up.

I croak out my feelings as best I can—speaking straight from the heart.

"My, my, Billy, ye surely know a lot of sweary words! Ye got a mite wet, too. Never mind, the next bit's easy."

Angus has lied. The easy part consists of climbing a forty-five-degree slope; my wet boots, almost coming up under my nose, give off a smell of almond oil that soon has me hiccuping. These are no ordinary hiccups. The hunks of dried beef we ate for lunch had sat for several days in Angus's rucksack, marinating in the petrol fumes from the leaky stove. This introduces a rare, not to say, explosive element when it comes to a simple bodily function like belching.

The air is getting chillier by the minute. We are now above the snow line, and my wet boots and trousers have frozen solid. I realize why Angus wears those queer-looking orange gaiters around his legs and ankles. He's perfectly dry and shows off by leaping ahead to the lower of the two peaks, where he poses on the summit, waving his ice ax in the air. Eventually I catch up with him and stand gasping in the raw mountain atmosphere.

Angus fishes out the rope and ties it around my waist. He thrusts the ice ax into my trembling hand.

"I want ye to go first. Probe the snow either side of the ridge to make sure there's a foothold before treading down, okay? If ye slip, I'll hold ye, right?"

"No, I don't want to do this! I want to go back down—I'm c . . . c . . . cold!"

"What? Past that fuckin' great stag? This is the only way back doon! Ye'll have to keep going, understand?"

I nod; speaking is still too much effort. A gaseous burp and I move off, slowly threading my way across the saddle-shaped ridge. Keeping one foot on either side of the snow crest for balance, I negotiate the traverse, probing the snow, but not knowing what to feel for. The sheer drop to the left ends in the stone-scattered corrie where the pacing red stag still blares his challenge. The right-hand side of the ridge is a steeper escarpment, descending like jaggy shark's teeth two hundred feet to an ice-covered mountain loch. Whether through frost or fear, my teeth begin an involuntary chattering dance, sending audible clicks echoing around the polar caverns of my skull.

"This is, by far, the d . . . dumbest thing . . . I have ever d . . . d . . . done in my life," I say to the wind.

"Don't look down!" shouts Angus, seeing me wobble. I make an effort to comply, but my movements are becoming as slow and erratic as my thoughts. I look down again. Clouds are filling the valley below, obscuring the safe green world in a shroud-white mist that adds to my sense of disorientation. The tickly terror, welling deep in the pit of my stomach, is barely restrained by the pretense that I'm the first person ever to scale the Alps, or the Himalayas. Yes, I could be on Mount Everest—dear God, what am I thinking? People die on Everest—regularly!

Icy drafts and petrol vapors alternate through my lungs as I trudge the last few yards to the snow-covered summit. Here, on the topmost pinnacle, I stop. A small wellspring of triumph bubbles up briefly through the cracks of my frozen soul, but the elation doesn't last long. From my vantage point I can see the other side of the ridge, where twin rows of footprints dent the snowfields leading to the top. Far from being the first to scale the unsullied peak of my fantasies, others have beaten me to it and recently, too. Even worse, they have left their mark, depriving me of what little comfort my fancy could avail. To my great chagrin, "the Peak of the Goats" is crowned by a cairn of orange peels and an untidy mess of blue chocolate bar wrappers.

"Bastards!" I curse those who have violated my virgin mountain.

"They're all a bunch of bastards!" I belch in disappointment, giving the orange peels a kick. The pieces spin off into the void, tumbling into the mist below. As they disappear, I realize that the top of the mountain is only the halfway point on this miserable trek and it's a bloody long way back down. I think of Sir Edmund Hillary, who, when asked why he wanted to climb Everest, replied, "Because it's there!" What sort of a bloody stupid reason is that? Mountains my arse! This is the first one I've ever climbed and, as God is my judge, it will be the last!

Angus arrives at my side and slaps me on the back. He wants to shake hands. I decline, figuring I'm shaking enough. He pulls out his map and tells me that he wants to carry on and climb the Munro behind Stob Ghabhar, which is linked in turn by another snow ridge. I wish him well to wear it and give him the end of his rope and his ice ax. He seems shocked.

"Ye can't go back doon now, not on yer own. Ye've no experience and it's dangerous! Ye'll break yer fuckin' neck!"

"I d . . . d . . . d . . . don't care. This was a d . . . d . . . dumb idea. I'm g . . . g . . . getting hypothermia I'm off, before I f . . . f . . . freeze to death!"

"Well, fuck off, then! You're no fun, no fun at all!" He stands his ground.

We stare at each other for a while, neither giving an inch. Then I turn my back and trudge through the crispy snow, burping my way down the other arm of the mountain. I had half expected Angus to follow, but when I look around, I see that I'm descending on my own.

"Stubborn bastard," I confide to the thick mist, wrapping me in its cold, moist blanket.

Once I'm across the snow line, the ground underfoot becomes a scree slope of tiny irregular stones. I quickly discover that stumbling downhill is just as hard as scrambling up. Soon my own momentum has me skidding out of control. I gambol and slide, rolling in ever larger loops, until a massive flat boulder halts my flight, knocking the wind clear out of me. I lie for several minutes in the armpit of the moss-topped stone, terrified to move, in case some part of my battered body announces the unwelcome news that it is broken. A loud belch swells my lungs enough so's I know my ribs aren't cracked.

The route down now takes me through the sticky suction of a dribbling, gorse-scattered peat bog. Only a small circle of visibility can be maintained in the fog. I move on through this miserable nebula, as if trapped inside the filmy glass of a goldfish bowl. For all its pestilence, at least the clammy veil may well obscure me from any wild stags that might be roving the vicinity.

"I am delivered!" I announce, sloshing out of the tormenting mists, into the lush sunlit glen beyond.

I rest upon a sun-warmed slab of granite to take stock of my situation. Although I seem to be in one piece, my neck aches and appears to be considerably longer than previously. I have no fingernails left, and my hands are covered in small cuts and bruises. My mud-soaked jeans are ripped out at the arse and knees, and my fisherman's jersey is a mass of holes surrounded by homeless wool ends. As for my new kagool, it has become a shredded guise of strips and streamers, giving me the appearance of an angry cockerel.

"Fun? If this is Angus's definition of fun, he's working out of the wrong dictionary!" I mumble, but at least the waterproofing on my hiking boots has done a wonderful job: they're both full of muddy water and not a drop has leaked out.

It's about two miles back to the campsite from this arm of the foothills. I steam like a dung heap in the warm afternoon sunshine.

Nearing the camp, I hear a strange sound coming from around a bend in the road; a hollow noise, akin to the thwacking of a ball on a cricket bat, echoes through the woods, soon to be followed by another a little while later. Walking stealthily, I advance on the source of the odd sound. In the middle of the track stands a large curly-horned, black-faced ram, facing off with a massive gray boulder, which he no doubt thinks is his rival. *Crack!* The half-witted creature butts the solid mass so hard that his back legs shoot skyward with the impact and he nearly stands on his head. Staggering back for yet another run at it, the bone-headed beast paws the earth and snorts snot and steam from its flaring nostrils. *Crack!* The ram reels backward and collapses sideways in the ditch. I sit on the unshakable boulder and wonder if stubbornness isn't a part of being Aries the Ram. I reckon it must be; sure I'm one myself and so, come to think of it, is Angus.

The heat of the resurrected campfire feels good as it drives the chill out of my bones, and a mug of milk does something to settle my confused digestive system. At the lochside, I scrub the big cooking pot with sand and shingle to get rid of the congealed stucco of last night's supper. Soon the great iron cauldron is bubbling above a blaze, sending the zesty fragrance of leek and onion soup into the cloudless afternoon sky. The addition of some dried vegetables and a big tin of chopped tomatoes gives color and substance to the brew, which begins to simmer nicely. To enhance the flavor, I add a couple of tablespoons of curry powder, a sprinkling of garam masala, and a few shots of soy sauce. Further, I discover that boil-in-the-bag rice cooks well if hung above the steaming cauldron like clothes on a washline. I have raided the expedition food store and cooked a half-decent meal for the lads. All that remains now is to sit and wait to see if they appreciate my efforts. I help myself to one of their beers and leave the rest to cool in the nearby stream. Then I have a lie-down.

Awakening from my slumbers, I find the students wandering around the camp as stunned as villagers at a UFO crash site.

"Who cooked this?" says Lord Snooty, tasting the curry. "Ay say, it's jolly good, too!"

"A Burmese woman taught me how to cook when I was a kid," I offer, emerging from the tent. "There's boiled rice to go with it, and there's beers cooling in the stream—help yourselves!"

Half an hour later Angus strides up and I hand him a beer. He accepts it with exaggerated grace, which gives me the impression that he's irked about me leaving him on the mountain.

"I made a curry," I say, trying to get on his good side.

"Aye, I ken," says Angus. "I could smell it from aboot two miles away."

"Aye, well, get stuck in before it's all gone." He does, but he eats alone in the tent. Lord Snooty comes over with an empty plate.

"You wouldn't mind cooking again tomorrow, would you, er . . . em—"

"Bill, my name's Bill," I remind him. "No, I don't mind, but it would be handy if I could get some supplies from the village—fresh vegetables, milk, and the like."

"What a champion idea! You could borrow Andrew's motor scooter, if you wish. Couldn't he, Andy?" Andrew seemingly has no say in the matter, so I agree.

"Thanks, I will. Now, if you all have a whip-round for money to buy the goodies, I'll run off tomorrow morning and stock up."

The night draws on and Angus continues to sulk in the tent. I try to win him over with some cheery banter, but he's having none of it.

"Hey, Angus, what d'ya think? I'm the official expedition camp cook."

"Are ye, indeed? Well, ye'd better get tae sleep. Ye'll have tae be up early the morn's morn, tae make breakfast!"

Miserable git! I think. Just 'cause I didn't want to die up on his precious mountain.

Fed and watered, the geologists depart for another day of staring at strata. This time Angus goes with them. I have fun riding Andy's Lambretta down to the village, but half a mile from the gas station, it runs out of petrol. I don't mind; mostly it's downhill and the quiet allows me to appreciate my surroundings all the more.

The Bridge of Orchy Hotel nestles by an old stone bridge, out of the way of winter winds and summer heat waves. Along its back reaches, the peaty water of the river Orchy gushes and spumes over a boulder-peppered bed, making sweet gurgled music in the stillness of the glen. Pushing the scooter the last few yards to the crescent of the hump-backed bridge takes a little effort, but riding down the slope side takes me right up to the solitary petrol pump. The sign in the garage hut window says Open. I beep the horn and wait; nobody comes.

The road is deserted for miles in both directions, and raggedy sheep wander freely up the middle of the A82, seeking out grazing at the roadside. Way off, on some distant plantation, a chain saw begins whining its descant, soon to be joined by the steam whistle of the logging train from Fort William, chuffing its way south across the curved arches of a far-off stone viaduct. I honk the nasal-noted horn again, and a man explodes from a nearby henhouse in a great flurry of chickens.

"Help yoor ploody self, leaf da munny hinside!" says the stranger, disappearing back inside the coop.

"But I need a gallon of petrol."

The old man reappears carrying a basket of speckled brown eggs.

"Hoe my Cod, can hue not work da pump?" he says, striding up to the forecourt.

"No, sir, I've never had cause to."

"Hwan gallon, his hit?" he says, waving the nozzle under my nose.

"Yes, just the one." I recoil from the gas vapors.

"Do hue not like the schmell hov peterol?" The old boy laughs.

"I used to, but not anymore! Is the bar open yet?"

"His hit a dram hue want?" he smiles, filling the scooter's gas tank.

"No, I want to buy supplies. We're camping up the glen. I need some groceries."

"Crowserees, his hit? Do hue want fresh-laid hegs?"

"I do, certainly."

"Come hinside!"

The garage man sells me a dozen eggs still warm from the roost and I pay for the gasoline.

"When will the bar be open?"

"For a wee dram, his hit?" he says, with a twinkle.

"No, for the other groceries."

"Hoe, habout fife minits, hi think. Cheerio!" The old chap picks up an ax and vanishes around the corner. I hear the sound of firewood being split.

The five minutes becomes fifteen and then thirty. A black-and-white border collie emerges from the bank of the river, followed by an ancient gentleman carrying a ram's horn crook.

"Could morning!" he says, making his way to the pub door. "Han ice day—byootifool, hisn't tit?"

"Yes, it's beautiful." I'm about to add that the hotel bar isn't open when the dog gives a single bark and the bolt inside is immediately drawn back.

At the bar, the retired shepherd, who goes by the name of Lachlan, asks me where I come from. His accent is very Highland and Gaelic words enrich his speech, like currants in a cake.

"Har hue han Hamerican, har hue?" he quests through crinkly white eyebrows.

"No sir, I'm an Irishman."

"Glé mhath, Éirennach. Cimar a tha thu?" Irishman, Are you well?

"Tha mi an eatorras." My friend, I'm doing not bad.

"Hue have ha letheolas of the Gaelic?" The old boy is pleased.

"I do, yes, just a wee smattering."

The barman arrives.

"What will it be, poys?"

I look up. It's the same man who collects eggs, pumps gas, and chops wood.

"A pint of heavy for me and whatever this gentleman wants."

"Hue har very kind. Hiel haff a dram, hif you don't mind?"

"And a whisky, please." The barman nods.

"Haff hue peen to Hamerica?" asks Lachlan. "My prother was there, hand he tolt me hit was a country hov marvels." He chuckles into his whisky before continuing in his Highland brogue.

"He tolt me the shepherds haff a device called a lasso for rounding up the beasts. Hits a kind hov mechanical sheepdog and his to be seen hon the telafission apparatus as well. Haff you heard hov the like?" The old boy is very amused by the idea. For myself, I had to admit that I'd never heard of a mechanical sheepdog called a lasso, but I have the growing feeling that the old crofter has the description of a cowboy's lasso mixed up with the TV series *Lassie,* and it seems less than courteous to put him right on the matter.

By high noon the barman arrives back to tell me that the grocery shop is now open. Not before time either, as I'm feeling decidedly tipsy after a breakfast of MacEwan's ale. It's no surprise to find the same old chap behind the counter as the store clerk. I hand him my list and he fusses among the shelves, muttering the names of the items to himself as he finds them.

"Whel, dare hue are now, dat's da lot. Hexsept hive no horanges." He hands me a cardboard box.

"That's okay, sir."

"Och, don't be calling me *sir*. Me name's Hamish. Now, his der any-think else?"

"Do you have a newspaper?"

"Yes, do hue whant today's or yesterday's?"

"I'd like today's."

"Whell, yool haff to come back tomorrow. Whee get them a day late."

Riding back up the glen, with a box of groceries, a carton of eggs, and yesterday's newspaper, is a precarious affair, but the wind is mild and sustains the scent of pine trees on its breath. Soon the air around the campsite conveys the fragrance of onions and fried mutton. An Irish stew is in the making, and the nice thing about Irish stew is that you put it in the pot and it makes itself.

The evening shadows call the hunters home from the hill, and the geologists return to lounge around the campfire, like Roman senators, eating, drinking, and talking bollocks.

"First class!"

"Jolly good show!"

"Awfully tasty!"

It's as much as they ever say to me. I'm pleased that they enjoy my cooking, even if they don't enjoy my company. Once the food is eaten they completely ignore me, which I don't really mind, but it would be nice if someone offered to help with the washing up. Yes, they're a strange lot. Lord Snooty and his acolytes sit as much apart from Angus as they do from me. It's amazing to think that the class system could be alive and well out here in the middle of nowhere, with His Lordship at the top, Angus in the middle, and myself at the bottom. Bollocks to them! As Scotland's great bard, Robbie Burns, said:

> *Is there for honest poverty*
> *That hings his head, an' a' that*
> *The coward slave, we pass him by—*
> *We dare be poor for a' that!*
> *For a' that, an' a' that,*
> *Our toils obscure, an a' that,*
> *The rank is but the guinea stamp*
> *The man's the gold for a' that!*

The haughtiness of the rock smackers grinds on, and Angus remains aloof as well. Maybe it's catching? I notice that he doesn't smoke dope in front of these sons of the empire, but sneaks off at bedtime down to the lochside, where he does whatever he does while coughing away on his joint.

"It's for herself the cat purrs," the old Irish saying goes, and tomorrow after breakfast I'll ride back to the village and have a good yarn with some of the everyday people down at the hotel.

"Another fine morning!" I call to Hamish, who's busying himself in the kitchen.

"Yesh! Help yoorself—hiel pee out presently!"

I pour a beer and sit alone in the bar, reading yesterday's paper. Like a soft wind brushing my cheek I feel the presence of someone standing beside me. With neither sound nor salutation, an old woman has entered the room and now stands next to me, pointing to a section of the paper that contains a full-page advertisement for the Egg Marketing Board.

"Big Egg," she says, tapping a scrawny fingertip on the image.

"It is, mam, yes," I agree, somewhat taken aback by her stealthy arrival.

"Eggs put lead in yer pencil!" She giggles, nudging me in the ribs.

"I guess that's fine, if you've got someone to write to." I smile back at the diminutive white-haired woman.

"Do ye whant yer fortune told?" she asks, her pale blue eyes looking earnest.

"No, no thanks," I say, but she grabs my hand anyway, sending a cold shiver down my spine.

"Muir bhaithte!" mutters the old lady, in strange old Gaelic.

"Doesn't that mean 'the sea of drowning'? I don't understand?"

She puts her finger to my lips to silence me.

"Ye will understand when the time is right!" she says in English. "Streap air muin nan ard mullach na saigheadean," she adds in Gaelic, cocking her head sideways like a parrot, to see if I take her meaning.

"Climb . . . erm . . . on top of . . . the high hill of the . . . *saigheadean*? Is that 'arrows'?"

The old woman nods her head.

"An turuis . . . chun nan eileann-naomh, na tha, na bha, agus na bhitheas," she continues.

I make a stab at the complicated translation.

"A journey . . . to the holy island, which is, is not, and is again. Correct?"

"Just so!" She smiles, then abruptly turns and walks toward the kitchens.

I am left alone to puzzle over her odd pronouncements, until eventually, the barman appears out of the passageway carrying a crate of Glenmorangie.

"Hey, Hamish, who's the little old lady that talks in Gaelic riddles?"

"I don't know—giff me a clue?"

"No, it's not a game. I was just talking to this old woman, and she said some weird things to me. You must have seen her—she walked straight back into the kitchen!"

He shakes his head.

"Come on, are you trying to wind me up?"

"Maybe hue met the Cailleach, the Old Woman Hov the Roads. She's peen seen here pefore, sometimes as a byootifool young maiden and others as an old crone. Take heed of what she sez to hue. Hit has peen known to come true!"

"Naw, she was real all right, she even nudged me in the ribs!"

"Has hue will!"

Later, I tell Angus about the strange conversation with the disappearing woman. He coolly tells me that I'm an idiot and can't tell when people are taking me for a ride, like the old man at the Glenelg hanging tree. I feel odd about that, too.

The day comes when the stone molesters crack their last rock and pack away their hammers. Tomorrow we return to the Granite City.

The lady called the Cailleach does not reappear, though on occasions there are other women to be seen in and around the village. But I do see someone dressed like her as we are leaving. Just as the minivan crosses over the old river bridge, I think I see her down by the water's edge, staring off into the distance with her back toward me. I may be mistaken, but I find her words still haunt my mind, though the significance of their meaning eludes me. Maybe Angus was right, and the old lady was just having me on. Aye, maybe.

The fine weather follows the expedition back to Aberdeen and arrives about the same time, but does nothing to warm the chill atmosphere surrounding Angus. Since he still seems to be brooding over the events on Stob Ghabhar, I leave him to it.

Summer is the time when a young man's fancy turns to affairs of the heart. Today I am such a beast, strolling down Union Street and looking at the girls. A particularly lovely young lass in a green-and-white miniskirt breezes past me.

My head turns with her. "Oh, my, she has legs like a gazelle," I mutter.

Suddenly, the world goes black. When my vision returns, it's accompanied by a throbbing headache and an awful pain in my face. From the passersby aiding me in my discomfort, I learn that I walked headlong into a stop sign.

"That'll teach ye tae go keeking at middens!" says an old lady who had witnessed the whole thing.

Back at the flat, Angus smiles when I tell of my disaster. He's been so moody of late, it's good to see him happy, but it is hard to know whether he's laughing with me or at me. He has cleaned the place up, for once, but I notice that my gear is all stowed away in my duffel bag—which is sitting near the door. I take this as a veiled hint and decide to go looking for Terrible Terry, who had offered me a place to stay when I first arrived in Aberdeen.

The next day, still sporting a black eye and a sticking plaster across my nose, I make a round of some of Terry's haunts, one of which is the Kirkgate bar.

A nasty wee bloke, all tattoos and rotten teeth, wanders in and plonks himself down on an adjacent bar stool. He's already much the worse from drink, so when the barman refuses to serve him, this does nothing to improve his humor. The drunk decides to snarl at me and, muttering gibberish, makes a grab at my bandage. I try to brush him away in a lighthearted fashion so as not to cause offense, but like a wasp at a picnic he keeps coming back for more. The barman keeps glancing over, no doubt looking for an excuse to throw him out, but my attention is focused on a silver half-crown piece that I've just spotted lying among the discarded cigarette packets and other trash on the floor.

A swift duck forward and the coin is in my hand. Unfortunately, in the same instant, the drunkard decides to give me a "Glasgow kiss." His badly aimed head-butt smashes his nose into my forehead, producing the opposite effect to which he intends. Bleary-eyed, he rockets from his stool, cracking his head on the beer-soaked piano in the corner. From there, holding his nose, he dreeps down the side of the instrument, leaving a red trail. Dazed and uncertain, I look around. The burly barman leaps over the bar. I think he's going to hit me, but he shakes my hand.

"Well done, laddie! I was waiting for someone to pagger that bastard. He's an effin' nuisance!" He picks up the fallen hero like a limp rag doll and uses his face to smash open the heavy oak doors. With a heave, he throws him into the back alley, where a scattering of beer bottles announces his arrival.

I look at the date on the half-crown. That's a piece of luck—it was minted in 1950, the year I was born.

Terry doesn't show at the pub, but I do meet up with him later on my way to the White Rose fish-and-chip shop.

"Ahoy there, Billy! What have you been up to? I heard you got into a punch-up at the Kirkgate?" says Terry, sidling up, all teeth and testicles.

"Naw, naw, nothing like that. I was bending forward when some drunk geezer put the head on me. He got the worst of it, mind you."

"Good lad yerself!" He grins. "But he gave you a black eye, like?"

"Naw, it was sex rearing its ugly head that gave me the battle scars, not brawling in a pub."

"Pray tell," says Terry, putting an arm around my shoulder with renewed interest.

My companion is amused by the tale of how I lusted after a pretty girl and ended up kissing a stop sign. When I go on to express my concerns about Angus, Terry seems to know more than I do.

"So, I hear Angus is about to give you the old heave-ho, isn't he? I'm not surprised. He's doing a turn with that tart, Senga, you know."

"Who, backward Agnes? You must be joking! She's a junkie—*and* a dockside whore."

"That's right. I heard she's wanting to move in with him. If that's true, he'd better hang a red light on his front door. Is he poncing off her, I wonder, or just getting a free ride?"

"Beats me! All I know is, he's been acting really weird of late, sort of moody and grumpy. And he took the sidecar off his old A.J.S. He seems to be making a racing bike out of it. It's strange, it's like he's become a different bloke."

"Yeah, but as they say, 'If you lie down with dogs, you'll get up with fleas.'"

"What d'you mean?"

"People who hang out with junkies usually become junkies themselves."

"Naw. I don't think it's that. Not Angus, he's just a pothead."

"Maybe so, Billy. If you want to stay at my place, here's the address."

"Thanks."

We stop at the end of the road, where the brightly lit chip shop belches steam into the night air. I read the menu board while waiting for the queue to move in off the pavement.

"What exactly do they put into a haggis, Terry?"

"In my experience, it's best not to ask," he says.

"It's a sheep's stomach, filled with offal, unmentionables, and seasoned oatmeal," offers a bloke behind me in the line.

"And what about all those different colored puddings?"

"Well, the black pudding is pig's blood and oatmeal, the white is pig's fat and oatmeal, and the red's a cross between the two. Maybe you'd like a Scotch pie?"

"Not on your nellie! I had one of those grease-filled land mines when I first arrived in Aberdeen. It was ghastly."

The stranger laughs.

"How about a fried garlic sausage? They're good."

"Aye! That's what I'll do, I'll have that with chips," says Terry. "God knows I won't be kissing anyone tonight."

"I'm sticking to cod and chips," says I. "At least I know what's all in it and I might have caught the bugger myself."

"I thought you hated fish," says Terry, laughing.

"I don't mind them cooked. It's when they've still got their clothes on I don't like them."

On the bus back to the small flat in Torry, I continue to puzzle over Angus's odd behaviour. Although I have only known him a few months, we have been good pals. Now he seems to have become a stranger. Terry reckons this is because he's on heroin. I don't know. I'm almost totally ignorant about the effects of hard drugs, but I pray that Terry's mistaken. I prefer to believe that maybe Angus is in love.

Outside the little apartment, illuminated by the spluttering gas street lamp, the old aluminium sidecar lies abandoned in the gutter. No more jaunts into the country for you, it spells. In the flat, there is a note from Angus saying that he won't be back until the weekend and asking me to move out by then, as he has a girlfriend wanting to stay. The P.S. at the bottom adds that he's more than paid back any debt he owed me from Morocco and bids me "Good luck."

Feeling more sad than aggrieved, I snuggle under the old red Stewart tartan blanket, reading my book until the shilling runs out in the electricity meter. Closing in around me, the night is acrid with the stench of stale pot smoke, mingled with the sickly scent of body odor and Senga's cheap perfume.

✦ Chapter 12 ✦

Have ye pain? So likewise pain have we
For in one boat we all imbarked shall be.

Thomas Hudson (1584)

THERE'S A CERTAIN CONTENTMENT IN HAVING ALL MY WORLDLY
goods stuffed in a duffel bag on my shoulder and being footloose and
fancy free. I'm no Gene Kelly, but I dance up the street all the same,
jigging among the puddles spilling and welling on the cobblestones beneath my feet. Come rain or shine, I feel alive, and even if Angus has
gone bad ways, I leave my worries behind me.

"Ah! Blessed mother Gulf Stream that nurtures your children in
these northern climes, with your warm salty milk, without you, this
would be another Siberia!" I croon to the scudding clouds.

My joy is endless, but I don't know why. Perhaps I'm just glad to be
free of the tiny room in Torry, though I'll miss old Mrs. Maclumphit,
with her girlish laugh and bags of sea coal. My elation lifts in a song
my dad used to sing:

> *I am just a country boy,*
> *Money have I none.*
> *But I've got silver in the stars,*
> *And gold in the morning sun.*

Singing like a linty, in the sparkling rain shower, I draw ever nearer to
the address where Terry shares a house with a bunch of students near the
university buildings in the center of Aberdeen. I have heard tell of wild
parties happening at this place, and I make my way toward it, feeling as

if my real adventure is about to begin, but despite his nickname, Terrible Terry acts more like a gentleman about town than a roughneck deckhand on the *Margaret Rose.*

Number 42 Powis Place, this is it! I confide to myself, ringing the doorbell. I wait, nothing happens. I snap the shutter on the brass letter box a few times, nothing happens.

"Just a minute!" calls a voice from within.

The doorknob turns and then falls off at my feet. A flurry of curses and the spindle end of the handle probes its iron finger out of the hole, opening the door with a squeak.

"Welcome aboard," Terry smiles, revealing the gap in his front teeth that he reckons drives women wild.

"Thanks. Is there a place where can I put my bag?"

He motions to the hall cupboard.

"You can stow your gear in here and kip down on the couch whenever you like. We're a bit short of beds. Do you want a cup of char?"

"Sure!"

Terry places an ancient iron kettle on the fat-encrusted blue enamel gas cooker. I chuck my bag on top of the heap of rucksacks and sleeping bags cluttering the hall cupboard.

"Who else lives here?"

"You'll meet them soon enough! I think there's six of us in all or maybe seven—we never seem to be all in at the same time."

"And they won't mind me moving in?"

"Naw, don't worry. They couldn't care less," Terry says.

The gas hob fumes and splutters, sending searing jets of steam and boiling water ejaculating from the kettle spout. Terry absentmindedly picks it up by its roasting handle. "Agh! Ya bastard!" He drops it quick, splashing scalding water over the cooker and the front of his jeans.

"Agh! Ya bastard! Ow! Ow!"

He does a tarantella-type dance and throws handfuls of greasy gray washing-up water over himself from the coagulated pool in the sink. The poor old kettle is crucified with a stream of seagoing abuse, and to save himself any more pain, Terry wraps the dusty kitchen curtain around the hot handle and marches defiantly to the table in the center of the room. This causes the curtain rod to pop off its mountings and land on the open flames of the range below. The threadbare fabric erupts in a crimson fireball, and the plastic rod bows and buckles on the stove top like a writhing serpent. Terry leaps back to the cooker, emptying the spitting kettle onto the pyre of the gold brocade drapes. As the last drops of hot water put out the conflagration, he turns around and grins apologetically.

"Fancy a pint instead?" he says, blowing on his injured hand.

"I think that might be a safer bet!"

"I'm a bit accident prone, you know—things happen to me."

"I know. I remember the night we met."

"Come on, let's go get a beer."

We swing the half mile up the road and into the Marshall bar.

"Yeah, I'm the original square peg in the round hole! It's a bit embarrassing, too. The skipper of the *Margaret Rose* says, if I was stripped bollock-naked and put in the hold with nothing but two ball bearings, in half an hour, I would have lost one and broken the other. He's probably right too. Lots of things go wrong for me. You've no idea."

After witnessing how Terry makes tea, I can well believe it. He seems to move quickly, even jerkily, akin to someone always in a hurry. This gives the impression that he doesn't let the grass grow under his feet and likewise emits a certain jaunty vitality.

His long brown hair, hanging straight to his shoulders, is suited to his rakish image, and he would do well to be the lead singer of a really ugly rock band. Terry might be a Jonah and a bit of a clown, like when he reacts to anything unexpected by assuming the puzzled look of a startled gorilla, but he's a good lad and as honest as a new penny.

A cool pint of beer soothing his burned hand, Terry reflects on his twenty-one years on this earth. He tells me he's been trawling for about three years. As his story unfolds, his green eyes alternate between the soulful and the astute, sometimes appearing only as thin slits in wrinkles of merriment.

"I wasn't always a fisherman, you know. I used to be a tire fitter in Birmingham, but I hated the industrial belt, the stink and the smoke. So I came up here for a dirty weekend with some Scottish lassie I'd met at the Glastonbury pop festival and I never went back."

"I was at Glastonbury, too, Terry. And here's another coincidence. I also worked in the rubber industry in Birmingham, in a factory that made contraceptives—worst three weeks of my life." We laugh. Terry takes up where he left off.

"You're an Irishman, right? You ever heard of the Bretons?"

"Of course, my grandmother's family were from Brittany."

"Well, my people were Breton somewhere down the line. I don't know much about them, but one of my ancestors was Sanson the executioner, the bloke who operated the guillotine in the French Revolution. It's from him we inherit the curse."

"What curse?"

"Oh, never mind, I was just rambling on. It's funny, that incident with the kettle," he says, finishing his pint.

I sense Terry is trying to change the subject, but I let it go.

"What's funny?"

"It's funny how hot water can put out a fire!"

The barman gives him one of those looks and picks up our empty glasses.

We return to the flat later that afternoon and I meet the irreverent crew who are to be my roommates. Terry introduces each of them in turn.

"This is Bloggs, the tallest man in the world with curly hair and glasses, who plays the violin in bed with his boots on!"

I shake hands with a friendly giant of a man, who, if he'd been born green, could have made a fortune selling frozen peas.

Terry continues. "Here we have Nuff the Scruff, the ragged-arsed bastard from Coupar Angus, fastest banjo player this side of the Cuttle Burn!"

A black-haired chap, resembling Cornelius out of *Planet of the Apes,* smiles over the rim of his five-string banjo and plays a lightning-fast "shave and a haircut—two bits."

"There's a guy called Johnny, who sometimes lives in that tent behind the sofa with a girl from Shetland. And through here we have Davy, the clown and jongleur, who travels all over Europe doing clownish tricks!"

In the back room, the two iron bedsteads are empty, but a large wardrobe lies on its back in the corner. With an ominous creak, the door lifts open and a voice says, "Hello there, neighbor!"

I peer in and a round-faced naked man beams up at me. The equally nude girl by his side extends her hand, so I might kiss it.

"Bonjour," she says, smiling.

"Enchanté, mademoiselle."

Living in this zoo takes some getting used to, and a full night's sleep becomes a distant memory. A constant stream of odd people comes and goes at all hours. How they maintain their grades at college, I don't know. They never seem to do any course work, and I seldom see them, except when I'm reading in the King's Library and they're lying on the grass out front.

Billeted in the living room, I live like a cat, sleeping whenever I get the chance and prowling around the rest of the time. By midsummer, the flat is too hot even for the flies, and I spend most of my days in the city, finding solace in the cool corners of libraries and public houses. But when the day's heat evaporates, we return from the shadows to have music sessions and play, unencumbered, often till dawn.

I have long known how to play the mandolin, but the boys teach me the intricacies of American bluegrass: "Dixie Darling," "The Arkansas Traveler," and Earl Scruggs and Lester Flatt's "Foggy Mountain Breakdown," played ever faster; with Nuff's banjo and Bloggs's fiddle dueling for advantage, the competition is fierce, but in the end, the banjo always wins. I add a few Celtic jigs and reels to the mix and, when fingers get sore, a couple of wild Irish songs. Luckily, the neighbors above are stone deaf, and the little old lady across the hall lives in the back of her apartment.

Three of us sleep in this room and sometimes four, whenever Johnny's girlfriend is around. Terry has a bunk bed in the corner by the window and I sleep on the settee between the tent and the fire. What little privacy Johnny's tent may offer visually, it fails to provide aurally, and, with no radio or TV, Johnny's nocturnal romps with his Viking girlfriend make for poor entertainment.

The walls of the room are bare, except for a picture of Adolf Hitler that hangs above the fireplace; the lank hair, the postage stamp mustache, and the piercing coal-black eyes are the first thing I see on awakening. I don't like it at all.

"Bloggs, what's a picture of Hitler doing up there, anyway?"

"It's hiding a nail! Why?"

"Don't you think it's odd having Der Führer gazing down on us, night, noon, and morning? It's creepy."

"Och, ye'll get used to it. Think of the torture he's going through, having to look at you lot, and there's madder bastards than him come around here."

As if summoned by Bloggs's statement, the door is pounded by a timber-splintering series of knocks.

Enter Nigel, "the mad axman of Nairn." This chap calls himself Wartooth and goes about stripped to the waist, wearing a kilt. He believes himself to be a reincarnation of a Viking berserker, that fearsome warrior elite, who, inflamed by concoctions of hallucinogens and alcohol, sprang from their long ships to run berserk and deadly among my terrified ancestors in Dark Age Britain long ago.

A rat's nest of long, matted yellow hair and chest-length forked beard enhances the ferocious appearance in which he revels. Large leather sandals continue the theme, and his crowning glory is the huge twin-headed war ax that accompanies him everywhere.

"All hail to the blood eagle!" he shouts and sits down, long bony fingers clutching the haft of his ax.

"All hail!" answers the company, and he breaks into an open-mouthed version of a laugh that makes a *"huh-huh-huh"* noise in the back of his throat.

Wartooth's few remaining teeth have indeed seen many's the long campaign and are a scant rearguard waiting to be overwhelmed by the forces of decay. These motley veterans click like knitting needles when he talks and jut out of his gums at crazy angles, akin to gravestones in an old cemetery. His pockmarked nose, not unlike the crooked handle of an old whitewash brush, thrusts southward from the frenzied eyebrows that bisect his wrinkled forehead. Deep in their sockets, eyes like red-rimmed cauldrons into which blue-yolked eggs have been carelessly cracked gaze detached and distant as if beholding the events of another time and place. Although he fronts a startling apparition and is often painted purple, he seems kind and gentle and I like him.

The warrior in Wartooth talks a lot about battles, but the man in him likes to expound odd theories on the human condition, and the world in general, to anyone who will listen.

He tells me that he never wears a shirt because shirts begin to stink on their own after a few days, and this smell contaminates the body, making it necessary to change to a nonsmelling shirt, which continues the odorous cycle. He also maintains that only ships and open-backed buses are safe to travel on, bolstering his belief that these vehicles are stationary time machines, designed to fit the criteria necessary to make the world move around them, while you remain seated. The open-deck stipulation ensures the passenger a generous supply of oxygen while traveling through the vortex. He instructs me in the mysteries of the digestive system, which, he contends, is external to the human body. Food entering through the mouth passes down a hollow tube to its eventual reemergence, without ever actually being inside "the body proper." Therefore, the function of the alimentary tract is as external to the human form as is the hole in a doughnut.

Wartooth's thoughts are as unconventional as his appearance, and, for all I know, he may well be right.

He tears a piece of paper into a strip about a foot long.

"Does this piece of paper have one side, or two?"

"Two."

He forms the paper into a loop, with a single twist on one side.

"So how many sides has it now?"

"Two!"

"No, it only has one! If this pen never leaves the surface of paper and yet writes on both sides, then there must only be one side, correct?"

"Correct!"

He pulls the loop through finger and thumb. The pen makes an inky trace on the white surface. Before long, the point at which he started joins neatly line to line. He opens up the loop and the pen mark is on both sides of the paper.

"See! The two-sided paper has only one side!"

I had heard about the Möbius strip but had never seen one constructed. Johnny lets out a gasp of incredulity and dives into his tent, saying that his mind has melted. Terry doesn't understand the entire thing and uses the strip of paper to light a cigarette from the fire embers, while Wartooth, flushed with success, gapes and makes the *"huh-huh"* sound again.

We sit until the wee hours, talking about the space-time continuum. I ask him if he understands the theory of relativity.

"Oh, aye, that's easy. The space-time phenomenon is best illustrated by relativity, the premise being: the more you dislike a relative, the longer they want to stay with you."

He talks on, until a pale dawn streaks the eastern sky. Then, as the early morning buses begin running, or standing still, as Wartooth would have it, he departs.

"I must go to my hame moot, to wear the bear's shirt!"

"I thought you didn't wear shirts?"

"The bear's shirt is worn inside the body. That's what a berserker is— one who wears the bear's shirt, in here," he says, tapping his head.

He leaves me with the growing feeling that one of us is as mad as a bag of cats.

At least Nigel has a home somewhere, unlike Fingers Fergie, who materializes one night from some parallel universe and becomes another permanent resident of the madhouse. He gets his nickname from his chosen profession as a sneak thief, and good he is at it, too, when he can be bothered. As my mother would say, "He'd steal the eye out of a blind man's head and shite in the hole!" Not that the gaunt Fergie poses much of a threat to us (we have nothing worth stealing), but it's handy having a shoplifter around to supplement the weekly groceries.

Alas, Fergie has a darker side.

Like so many young Scots, he is exceedingly fond of his drugs and takes any pills he can find, both for imaginary illnesses and to see what they might do. His main hobby is being a hypochondriac, although he denies it. To prove his innocence, he plows through the *Reader's Digest Home Doctor,* announcing that he's had every ailment in the book *except* hypochondria.

Fergie is nocturnal, to the point that he sleeps all day and lies awake in his bed all night, except when the moon is full and he's out thieving. Terry likes to tease him.

"Geerupp, ya lazy fucker, and go steal something!"

"I can't, Terry, I've got a bad back," Fergie whines.

"Aye, Fergie, let's take a look at it?" Terry rolls the skeletal felon over and probes his knobby spine.

"Just as I thought, you have a ghastly condition called osteocoital-atrophy."

"Oh my God, what does *that* mean?"

"It means you're bone-fucking-idle. Now get up and do something, or my boot will go up your arse—three lace holes deep!"

After exhausting the bathroom cabinet's supply of aspirin, laxatives, and out-of-date birth control pills, Fergie takes to injecting himself with Doctor Colis Brown's patent cough mixture, which has a morphine-opiate base. Not surprisingly, before too long, he develops hepatitis and starts dying all over the place, which Terry thinks is "dashed inconsiderate."

Come autumn, Fergie is too ill to join us for the long-weekend campout at the Kinross folk festival, and when we return he is a sorry sight. Sallow and emaciated, Fergie lies in the middle of the kitchen floor on a moldy mattress, like a pile of dirty washing. His jaundiced face is the color of a wilted daffodil and the stench of impending death pervades the room. Arrayed about him, like candles around a corpse, are a dozen or so milk bottles full of highly infectious, murky yellow piss.

"Yellow Jack!" whispers Terry, in my ear.

I know what that means. It's the yellow *Q* for quarantine flag, flown by plague-ridden ships. Fergie stares up at us through tawny tomcat eyes.

"Listen, Fingers, you need the hospital, pronto! We'll walk up and call for the ambulance. You just stay there and we'll get you sorted out."

It's half a mile to the pay phone at the end of the road. Terry makes the call, and as we toddle back down the long cobbled street the ambulance speeds past us, blue lights flashing. Something is wrong! In the distance we can see the ambulance men leave the house and drive away without Fergie. Nonplussed, we run in to find Fergie up and dressed, pretending to read the newspaper.

"What in the name of Jasus is going on?"

"Have they gone?" he answers in a weak voice.

"Yes! And you should have gone with them!" Terry growls.

"I told them I was all right and they went away. I don't like hospitals, they make me feel sick."

"You are sick, ya bloody idiot, and whatever you've got, we don't want it, savvy? Don't like hospitals my arse! What sort of a fuckin' hypochondriac are you?" Terry's hopping mad and shaking Fergie like a rat. He drops him back onto the stinky mattress and pulls me into the other room.

"I've had enough of this bollocks! Go back up to the phone and call the ambulance again. I'll keep a weather eye on Lazarus here!"

"Okay!" I disappear out the back door, make the phone call, and run back to be there before the ambulance arrives.

Fergie lies motionless on his filthy bed, looking like a lifeless skeleton carved out of rancid beeswax.

Ten minutes later, there's a knock at the door.

"Ambulance here!"

Fergie is up like a shot, trying to look normal, patting down his matted hair.

"Come in!" shouts Terry.

Fergie makes a dive for the back door. Terry's ready for him with a right cross to the jaw that fells him like a tree. Fergie lies motionless on the mattress.

"This way, gentlemen, the patient is in here."

The two medics tie the lifeless figure to a gurney and wheel him past us. We snap to attention.

"Mighty are the fallen," says Terry, saluting.

Now the real work begins. Gagging at the stench, we clean up as best we can. Having nowhere else to put it, we stuff the frowsty mattress into an old air-raid shelter at the end of the weed-infested yard. Carefully, as if they contain nitroglycerine, the piss-filled bottles are removed at arm's length, by means of the fire tongs. One by one, each lethal fermentation is emptied into the outside toilet and the bottles dropped into the backyard burning barrel containing Fergie's soiled sheets.

"Fire purifies," says Terry with grim satisfaction, as the late incumbent's shite-filled underpants are consumed by great licks of orange flame.

With the doors and windows open to clear out the smell, the room is chill from the first arctic winds now blowing from the north. Terry hunts for firewood and finds a large plank, nailed years ago to the crumbling brick wall that overlooks the railway line. Legs spread for balance, he gives the spar a mighty pull. With a crack like a pistol shot, the board snaps, smacking him in the knackers. Cross-eyed and sucking air, he falls sideways into the weeds behind the air-raid shelter.

Terry nurses his bruised bollocks by the fireside, anointing them with witch hazel as the flames from the scavenged timber take the sting out of the air.

From his place above the mantelpiece, odious Adolf glares down on the sordid scene.

A delicious quiet descends and sleep comes, falling upon me like nectar from the honeydew, as sweet as an angel's kiss . . .

"Get up, ye lazy bastards! Open the door! I've a message fer ye!"

Wartooth is hammering on the door with the end of his ax.

"What time is it? For the love of Jesus, Nigel, it's the middle of the night! Come back tomorrow."

"Open the door, ye skraelings, or I'll chop it down!"

"Open it, Terry, I think he means it."

"You open it, I'm scared of him!"

Wartooth follows me into the living room and sprawls across the sofa, thus depriving me of my bed. He looks around.

"Where's Johnny?"

"He's staying at the Viking wench's."

"Where's Fergie?"

"He's in hospital."

"Oh."

"Well, what is it, Nigel? What's so important, to be waking us up for?"

"Oh, yes, I was taking a walk down at the fish pier to get some raw cod liver to eat and I met the skipper of that last boat you were on, Billy.

He wants you to sign on for a wee stint up in the Arctic, and the mate of the *Margaret Rose* is looking for you, too, Terry."

"I know he is. I owe him a fiver."

"Naw, it's about shipping out. He needs crew. I volunteered my services, but he declined!"

"Aye, that mate can be a funny bugger. You'd think he'd jump at the chance to sail with a purple Viking. Whatever's the matter with him?"

Nigel shrugs his shoulders and looks to me.

"No, Nigel, I don't want to go trawling again. Never! I hate fishing and I hate fish, especially codfish. By the way, Nigel, what's a skraeling?"

"A skraeling? It means a savage—it's an old Norse word."

"You're a mine of useless information, Wartooth. Do you want a cuppa tea?" I ask.

"No! I never drink anything until I receive the heat that is in the light of the sun."

"Oh, no! He's at it again. Please, not tonight. I'm too knackered to deal with it, and me bollocks hurt." Terry pulls a pillow over his head and slumps in his cot in the far corner of the room.

"What do you mean, Nigel?"

"Billy, don't ask him. No, no, please. Oh, me poor bollocks!"

Wartooth, impervious to Terry's pleas, launches into an early-morning raga on the subject of sunshine.

"You see, the light from the sun is light only. There is no heat element anywhere at all in it."

"How d'you make that out?"

"Billy boy, I'm glad you asked me that."

"Well, I'm fuckin' not," comes a muffled voice from the corner.

"The sunlight reaches the ground, where it agitates the molecules of the earth and all upon it, thus rubbing them together. This produces friction, which in turn, produces heat."

"What a load of old shite!" says the muffled voice.

"But your theory doesn't take the polar regions into account."

"Ah, but it does! The reason that the poles are cold is because the intense magnetic fields surrounding the polar regions stop the molecules moving, and so no heat can be produced. That's why there's plenty of sunlight at the poles, but no heat."

I nod a halfhearted assent to the mad Viking and the room falls silent, except for Terry groaning in the corner.

I awake to find the purple marauder gone. Terry is up, sitting on the edge of his bed, engrossed in squeezing pus from the rows of red pimples on his thighs.

"What in the sweet name of Jesus are you doing, Terry? That's disgusting!"

"I'm having a Dutch bath. Got to look my best—I've got a hot date tonight with one of my tarts, and I suppose I better find out if me bollocks still work."

"Ye gods, if only she could see you now! So which one of your ever-expanding harem is going to be the lucky girl this evening?"

"Er . . . what day is it?"

"Wednesday, why?"

"Well, I've got so many bints in tow, I have to keep them rationed to one day each, you see. So, I have a wee rhyme, made up to help me remember who's who:

Sunday—Mandy
Monday—Judy
Tuesday—Wendy
Wednesday—Kirsty
Thursday—Heidi
Friday—Sandy
Saturday—Cindy

"Och away, Terry, you're full of shite!" I mock, mimicking the Scottish accents of his various girlfriends, but I had to admit that he did have a way with the ladies, a way that eluded me entirely.

"Yeah, Terry, there's an old maxim that reminds me of my past girlfriends."

"Oh, really? How's it go?"

"It goes: 'April may, but June won't!'"

He laughs, then takes to examining the backs of his thighs for pimples, swaying in front of the mirror like a lassie checking to see if her stocking seams are straight. What a showman—he could put Rudolph Valentino to shame. How does he do it? He's not much to look at, God knows, and his chat-up lines are abysmal, but his inexhaustible supply of excruciating chat seems to work wonders with the fair maids of Aberdeen. They hang on his every word.

"There now!" says Terry, splashing aftershave on his recently preened legs.

"Aw! Ow, ya bastard!" he cries, doing a little dance, while pulling on his blue permanent-pressed pants.

"So, are you going to ship out on the *Maggie Rose*?"

"I'll have to, Billy, I'm nearly skint. How about yourself, are you going to rejoin the *Auld Allegiance*?"

"No, no, no, not shaggin' likely. I've had it with trawling, I hate fish! And I'm still getting the dole."

"Oh, that reminds me. A letter came for you today from the unemployment office. Maybe they've found you a job?" He hands me a small manila envelope. I tear at it.

Dear Mr. Watkins,

    Your unemployment benefit has expired.
    You may be eligible for Social Security payments,
    depending on your work record.

                                       DHSS

"Oh no, they've cut off my dole money! What will I do?"

Terry raises his hand in mock blessing, making the sign of the cross.

"Put your faith in Cod, to the glory of Cod and the Piece of Cod that passeth all understanding. See you at the docks, Billy boy!"

He departs to find his shipmates. As he walks up the road, I can hear him singing.

"There's a plaice for us, somewhere a lemon sole for us . . ." The thin voice fades into the distance.

"There's no way I'm going back fishing . . . no way . . . no bloody way! I'd rather starve!" I confide to Hitler.

"*Arbeit Macht Frei!*" The cruel eyes scowl back.

Work makes you free!

✦ Chapter 13 ✦

Whether morning, whether evening,
By land or by sea, I shall die,
Alas, I know not when.

Ninth-century Irish text

Position: 68° 17′ N. 9° 04′ W.
Steam Trawler *Auld Allegiance*
Jan Meyen Ridge
Arctic Ocean

THE NORTHERN LIGHTS FLICKER, DANCING IN GHOSTLY curtains of electric filigree high in the arctic night. Crisp icy air, fresh and tangy, is drawn in with each breath of the starboard watch. Our bow splits each swell effortlessly, casting hissing white spume onto a funeral-black sea, flowing and spilling in undulating humps, like the curves of a Titian nude.

Two points off the starboard beam, the lights of a Russian factory ship blaze golden in the night, and the red and green navigation lamps of her attendant stern trawlers wink in and out of the crystalline ice floes. Another hour's steaming and we are alone in the vastness of the inky ocean, our only company the floating cathedrals of icebergs, cruel and beautiful.

As we rise on a wave, the air lights up. Fuzzy, viperous tongues of static electricity coil and spit from the masthead, flickering and darting along the twitching twin wire antennas. I can feel my hair standing on end, and, as I raise my hand aloft, strange filmy auras of luminescence stream from my fingertips. This is my first experience of the phenomenon known to seafarers as St. Elmo's fire. In the olden days sailors thought this corona discharge was a sure sign of the good saint's protection from storms and bad weather. I know it to be a natural occurrence, but it gives me the willies just the same.

The foremast signal lights flicker on, red above red, a Whole Gale warning. My walkie-talkie crackles.

"Billy, give it one last deek aboot and get in here, the old man wants ya!" comes the voice of the mate, who's very pleasant to me now that there's a new snacker on board and I'm not the lowest of the low.

"Roger, Elvis, on my way!" I scan the ocean. There's a vessel dead ahead, crossing at a right angle to our course, but not posing any immediate hazard.

"Elvis, there's a ship crossing the T with us. She seems to be under way. I'll give her a call on the VHF, all the same, just so she knows we're here."

"Aye, good idea. Mak it so!"

I switch the walkie-talkie to channel 16 and call the black-and-white freighter now looming large in our path.

"Vessel dead ahead, this is trawler *Auld Allegiance*. What's your status, old man? Over."

I hold the hissing radio speaker up to my ear to better hear the reply.

"Trawler abeam to us, this is the Icelandic Steamship *Fjellfoss*. All is good with us, old man. How you? Over."

"All fine here, we will be passing astern of you, shortly. Where are you bound? Over."

"We are heading back to Reykjavik with a cargo of timber from Leningrad. Over."

"Okay, *Fjellfoss*, you're nearly home. Good luck! Over."

"Yes, good luck too, fishing men. *Fjellfoss* out!"

The gigantic stern of the cargo ship towers above us like a cinema balcony. A young man posting watch from the freighter's fantail flicks a red-ended cigarette butt into the night and waves farewell. The churning screw wake fades into the gloom, and now we are alone.

The sea is rising, sending ice-floe calves buffeting along the rows of steel rivets that hold the hull plates in place. In the half-light, the distant bergs are a circle of menacing shapes. At all points of the compass, they lie like tenacious timber wolves, waiting to strike down their prey and devour it. I shiver, not so much from the cold, but from a growing feeling of foreboding that has haunted me for the past few minutes.

The night descends, morbid and malignant on the Arctic Ocean, quenching the friendly flicker of the aurora borealis. To the southwest, frozen stars vanish as treacle-thick storm clouds eat into the fanciful configurations of fabled constellations. Lone sentinel of the northern wastes, our tiny vessel is a Christmas tree of colored lights in an otherwise lightless crypt of cresting swell.

I give the sea one last scan, to make sure we aren't standing into any unforeseen danger, before heading for the warmth of the wheelhouse. All I see is our own navigation lights reflecting back from the glassy mountains, like the ethereal running lights of long-gone ghost ships.

I shiver again.

"Looks like we're in for a bit of a blow. The arse has fallen out of the glass in the last hour," says the skipper, tapping the bridge barometer. Above his head, the ship's declinometer records an ominous roll.

Sleet and hailstones begin to pepper the wheelhouse windows, and the coxswain turns on the turbovisor to clear the glass. Deckhands are sent fore and aft, to make fast rigging, lash down otter boards, and stow nets where the wind won't carry them off. Now with hatches secured, decks cleared, and life rafts made ready, the old trawler, veteran of a thousand storms, steels herself to the biting wind.

The men return to sit around the galley stove while they can, blowing frozen curses into their cupped hands.

There is a keel-shuddering thump. The crew shoot nervous glances at each other as an ice floe scrapes the full length of the 163-foot ship.

"Sorry aboot that, lads!" says the helmsman. "I cannae see fhug all, it's as black as the devil's toenails oot there!"

"Aye, so it is! Reduce speed and take the heading into the wind. Billy, you ken how to operate the wireless, don't ye? Find oot what's going on. I tried using the VHF, but it's bugger all but crackles!"

"Aye, Skip! You'll get nothing on the 'fish fone' in these conditions.

We need to use the medium wave transmitter." I clamber into the wire-less cabin immediately aft the bridge, which is usually a dumping ground for everybody's junk. This is more like it, back to the old job. I flick the main on/off switch, and the radio warms up with a pleasing glow of thermonic tubes; presently, the receiver comes to life.

"All ships, all ships . . . Wick Radio, Wick Radio. Severe storm warning for sea areas Viking, Forties, Cromarty, Rockall, Malin Head, north and southeast Iceland. Violent storm imminent! All ships listen . . . 2182 kilocycles." Through the static-laden ether, shore stations all over the north of Scotland and in Scandinavia are sending urgent warnings: "Get to the nearest port—there's a hurricane on the way."

I relay the news to the captain. "Fat chance of that," he says, staring at the chart. "Tell them we'll bide on our own."

I contact the Stonehaven maritime radio station on a frequency of five hundred kilocycles per second using Morse code, the old reliable method of wireless communication. They ask me to wait until traffic for an Atlantic container ship is dealt with. I listen to messages flying back and forth between Scotland and the homeward-bound vessel. It's routine stuff; greetings being sent by crew members on board to loved ones ashore, mostly signed off with the P.S., "If kisses were snowflakes, I'd send you a blizzard," or the other old maritime cliché, "Every turn of the screw brings me nearer to you."

Screws and snowflakes finished with, Stonehaven calls me back. I reply. The small blue spark dances between the silver contacts of the brass Morse key, sending a thousand watts of power radiating from the twin-wire antennas above. The dots and dashes of the staccato signal cut through the hissing static, as I give our position and status. A thousand miles away in Scotland, Sandy Aitchesson, the shore operator, knows we can't make port. He sends goodnight and wishes us the best of luck.

The 461-ton vessel begins to roll like an unctuous pig on a grease-covered waterbed. Mountainous waves break over the bow, sending nervous fingers in search of secure handholds. Like characters on the lid of a sardine tin, the crew swathe themselves in yellow oilskins and sou'westers, to stand legs braced, as the trawler pitches and rolls in the fury of the gale.

The helmsman curses, peering through the wheelhouse window,

straining to see anything in swirling curtains of sleet-filled rain. I'd been in storms before, but this one is different. It looks and sounds different, and with the sea air laced with corona-discharged ozone, it even smells different.

Jagged forks of lethal blue lightning tear open the gathering darkness, the accompanying thunder lost in the screams of shrieking wind. Caught in the flashing xenon strobe light of the flickering elements outside, the bridge crew appear like jerky disco dancers intermittently lit in sapphire-bright silhouettes.

Without warning, a cross-wave lifts the trawler's stern clean out of the water. The over-revving 950-horsepower engine begins screaming as the propeller spins free. Then the ship jars as the screw crashes back into the ocean foam, sending a shock wave whiplashing from stem to stern that awakens fear in every man on board. I see Elvis make the sign of the cross. This worries me even more because I know he's not a Catholic.

Vertical and horizontal become locked in a three-dimensional death dance to see which will prevail in the struggle for the ship's equilibrium. Seawater, weighing sixty pounds per cubic foot, crashes over the rails in gigantic swamping waves. Sea spray and rain freeze to the rails and superstructure, like icing on a cake, building up an inch per hour and adding tons of top weight to the rolling trawler.

We have no survival suits. In a gale like this, the bright orange Mae West is your best friend. It probably won't prevent you from drowning, but its thick padding is great protection against cracked ribs and broken collarbones. I can't swim anyway, I don't think any of the crew can either, but that's common among cold-water seamen. If you go over the side in these latitudes, you wouldn't want to be able to swim. Hypothermia gets you in seconds, and heart failure speeds you off to Fiddler's Green shortly afterward.

My worry starts to become fear. I distract myself by testing the transmitter. Just as well, too, because something is wrong. The indicator needle on the output meter tells me there's a fault. It doesn't take me long to realize that ice is forming on the aerial insulators, shorting the signal out to ground. This means having to go up top to clear the buildup. I go to the skipper to report the situation and get my life jacket.

With the ship now rolling at forty-five degrees, all routine work has stopped. The survival of the vessel is now our only concern.

From below decks, with a stream of invective as foul as his cooking, Peter the Poisoner emerges from the galley, covered in flour and broken eggs. He looks like a ghost.

"The fookin' starboard, fookin' food lockers, are awf their fookin' moontings an' the fookin' flooower and the fookin' eggs is all over me fookin' heid!"

"Any chance of a wee cup o' tea, Peter?" says the captain.

"Aye, there's a chance—*nay* fookin' chance! I'm noo going back dooon there! Wi' all the shite in the wurrelled fleeing aboot me fookin' heid! Is it mad you think I am?"

"Well, get oot on deck and chip away some ice then, afore we're top heavy. ALL HANDS TO THE ICE!" the skipper roars into the intercom.

Peter looks at the snaking flurries of wind-crazed snow streaking past the glass.

"I'll go below and try an tidy the fookin' place up, afore we're fookin' bottom heavy! I'll mak some fookin' tae when you find some fookin' calm water!"

"Well, fook awf then! ALL HANDS TO THE DE-ICING!"

Men don crash helmets and life lines, preparing each other for the foray, like squires attending medieval knights. Armed with fire axes, we take it in turns, venturing out onto the rolling deck. Chipping ice from the rigging is almost suicidal. Crewmen slip and slide along the deck like curling stones, until pulled back to safety by their mates. Some climb the rigging, only to be plucked off by the blast, to dangle on their safety wires like flailing spiders. Willie the winch man and myself are next out. He blasts away the icy buildup on the superstructure with a steam hose, as I prepare to climb the mast.

"Why does anybody do this?" I shriek, as a freezing wave flattens me against the forward cowling and boils around my knees.

"For the glamour, what else?" shouts Willie.

"This is the dumbest thing I ever done in my life!" I screech to the wind.

"I've heard that before!" the gale howls in my ear. "Up on the top of Stob Ghabhar, wasn't it?"

"Bollocks!"

I begin my climb, ice ax dangling from my wrist. The wind hates me and pulls at my back with octopus suckers. I don't yield, but climb, slowly, like a slender loris; each movement deliberate, precise, exaggerated. I remember the old sailor's maxim "One hand for yourself, one for the ship!"

When I look up the mast, the spar seems to stand still, while the world swirls sickeningly about it. Maybe Wartooth was right after all! At last I'm in position, arm hooked around the mast. Several cracks of the ax send a curtain of pallid icicles breaking free from the antenna wires, daggering to their deaths on the careering deck below.

"All clear for now, topside!" I shout into the walkie-talkie, as I begin my stealthy descent down the mast rungs.

The old-timers stand at the open wheelhouse door, beckoning. I crouch in the spray, trying to gauge myself between rolls and pitches, to make my dash inside. At the opportune moment, I jump for the door and am pulled through. The ship lurches to port, giving sudden momentum to the steel portal closing behind me. The heavy slamming door scatters us like ninepins, bouncing me off the far wall, where I slip in a pool of fresh vomit, crack my head on the binnacle, and slide on my back under the legs of the captain's chair. He gazes down at me, shaking his head in mock despondency.

"As a seaman, you're as much good as a hat full of arseholes. Get below and let the Poisoner take a look at ye—you've cut yer heid open."

A trail of blood smears along the companionway walls marks my descent to the galley, where Peter wraps a turban of crepe bandage around the blood-encrusted gap in my scalp.

"There you go, now you look a right fookin' idiot. Like Gunga Din, up the fookin' Khyber Pass," says the cook.

"That's shaggin' rich, coming from someone who looks like the lead zombie in *The Curse of the Undead!*"

"FOOK AWF wi' ye, Sparky. I've nay mair fookin' yoose for ye!"

Using hand and footholds like a mountain climber traversing a glacier, I inch my way back through the tumbling ship to the radio shack. Regaining my seat, I strap myself in for safety, but my head thumps with the exertion of it all. Once immobile, I start feeling seasick and have to get up again.

What was fear an hour ago is slowly building into terror. I have faith in the ship. She's been around since 1936 and seen plenty of bad weather. I've faith in the crew, too; they may be roughnecks, but they're not cowards.

It's me I'm worried about. If we do start going down, I don't know how I'll react. Will I take death calmly or start screaming? I just don't know. Is this what real fear is? What does it feel like, trying to breathe with your lungs full of icy seawater? Is it agony or is it sweet? Is God waiting beyond the pain, with warm outstretched arms, or just cold oblivion. I don't know—and I don't want to find out!

"Oh God, oh dear God!"

I'm kneeling on the radio shack floor, wedged between the bulkhead door and the operator's table. I'd like to be praying, but I'm too busy heaving my breakfast into the wastepaper bin.

"Oh dear Jesus, help us all!" I spit the acid-hot residue into the trash can. The bloody bandage begins uncoiling like a dying cobra into the slopping waste. My wire-rimmed spectacles hang momentarily from one ear, before slipping off into the goo. Trying to clean them, on the drier end of the bandage, smears blood with the vomit on the glass. This makes me sick all the more. My stomach aches from retching, but now, thank God, it's completely empty. Hopefully, I can resume my seat, without fear of spewing all over the radio equipment.

The cyclone-driven breakers pound from windward, trying to shatter the ship. When this proves ineffective, the wicked wind smashes a rogue wave into the hull from leeward side, in an attempt to burst us like a walnut in the jaws of a nutcracker. The trawler doesn't give in. Her plates groan as she takes the foul punch, then she shudders like a shaggy dog shaking off bathwater. First I'm pitched forward and steady myself by hanging onto the antenna insulators. Then I'm thrown back onto the radio table, where my bottom depresses the telegraph key, sending a thousand watts of radio frequency power up my arse and out my fingertips. Shocked and singed, I fall to the steel floor, to lie steaming in the vomit spilling from the ricocheting trash bin.

My misery is compounded by screaming coming from the companionway outside. I drag myself up and look out into the passage. The young snacker has his index finger caught in the steel bulkhead door. I shout through to the bridge crew on the intercom and the door is released from the other side. The young lad's finger looks like a melted candle dripping ruby red wax onto the deck plates. The white skin is split from the fingertip to the palm, where it hangs like a burst condom from the base of the raw, red stump.

"You look after him," says Elvis. "We're too busy!" He slams the steel door.

I prop the kid up between the watertight door and a wall-mounted fire extinguisher. He's in shock and his eyes keep rolling. Calling down to the galley for help eventually brings Peter the Poisoner clambering up with the first aid kit. The cook pulls the flap of skin back into position and sews it up with a few crude stitches before applying a dressing. I hold the young fella as steady as I can, but he keeps wriggling around and whining.

"I want me mam . . . I want me mam . . . I want me mam."

"For fook's sake, sonny! Were you vaccinated with a fookin' gramophone needle?" Peter growls, trying to hold the squirming kid still.

I nervously start to giggle. Peter takes one look at me and cracks up, too. The pair of us sit helpless with laughter, either side of the terrified deckboy. Eventually, Peter gains a little of his composure.

"Ye want yer mammy, do ye? Stick yer arm oot, sonny, I'm yer mammy now."

Peter holds up a big syringe of morphine. The poor wee snacker takes one look at it and faints.

"Well, that saves me the fookin' trouble!" Peter grins and disappears below.

I drag the limp body into the wireless cabin and strap him into a Mae West. He comes to and throws up, adding to the rolling sea of puke coursing across the floor. And there he stays, alternately vomiting and crying for his mammy, while cradling his bandaged hand, like a nurse holding a baby.

Well, he's not much company, but if we're going to die, at least I won't be dying alone, I console myself, putting on the headphones so's I don't have to listen to his blubbering.

What had been terror mixed with hysterical elation a while past has now progressed into a detached state of sadness, a strange numb feeling, like when someone drinks himself sober. All around us, the hurricane gorges on victims. The herring drifter *Oaken Ark* is swamped and the crew take to the boats; they've no chance. The airwaves are crammed with a dirge of Mayday distress signals from distant vessels; the *Landreger Hovingham* is going down, so is the *Kimya,* but I know they're all too far away for us to go to their aid, so I try not to think about it. It's like it's not really happening.

The wireless operator on the Atlantic container ship, previously heard swapping pleasant banter with the shore station, sends his final position and his last message.

"We've lost the plant . . . sinking . . . tell my wife I love her." He screws down his Morse key to give a continuous tone.

When the note finally fades in my headphones, I know she's gone down, all hands with her. My reflection stares back from the glass dial of the Marconi Atlantic radio receiver, blood and puke streaking my face. "If kisses were snowflakes, I'd send you a blizzard," they had joked a few hours ago. The poor buggers got their blizzard all right, but the kisses were the kiss of death. What feels like an enormous bubble wells up in my throat. I don't know if I am about to burp or throw up, but when I let it go, I find that I've burst into tears. My numbness ferments into anger.

"What sort of a loving God allows this to happen?" I shout at the radios.

"I want me mammy," moans the snacker.

"Bollocks to yer mammy!"

Hour after hour, the roll call of doom recites like a mantra in my Brown's D-type headphones. I jot down the names of the vessels, time and position of sinking in the radio logbook. One by one, the distress signals cease and an eerie silence pervades the airwaves. Through the crackling static, I hear a weak signal from far away. The *Fjellfoss* has made port safely in Reykjavik.

Fear, sadness, and anger give way to the agony of fatigue. I want to sleep, sleep long and unencumbered by dreams and nightmares. Sleep calls to us all. The snacker huddles in the corner half-awake, great golden harp strings of yellow phlegm connecting his nose, chin, and shoulder. Still buffeted by monstrous seas, the ship keeps her prow to the wind and bites hard into the head waves. The worst is over. I help the sniveling snacker to an empty bunk and lash him in.

"ALL HANDS TO THE DE-ICING!" squawks the Tannoy. I climb up to the bridge to report for duty.

To the east, a pale, ragged-edged gash ruptures the tormented sky, announcing the breaking dawn. As the pallid daylight becomes full, we see the depth of our deliverance. Tossed continuously from one sixty-foot wave to the other, the sturdy trawler has taken everything the elements could sling at her. Still she fights back, alternately deep in the trough, a green wall of water curving above her, casting its dark shadow down on the frozen deck, the next instant, riding high like an iron-clad surfer on the peak of the wave crest, towering aloft, jeering at the retreating tempest. Death has passed over. We have survived. *Auld Ali* has done us proud. Now, as the storm winds abate we must attend to her needs.

Out on deck, a jumble of broken rigging and smashed equipment juts out of the ice pack. An oxyacetylene cylinder zigzags around the fore deck, like a confused torpedo, sending flurries of ice shavings into the air. One of the old-timers gets a lasso onto the valve end and we drag it to where it can be lashed safely to a cat cleat. The deck abaft looks sparse; the trawl gear and gutting tables are missing, two of the life rafts have gone over the side and the aft winch spar dangles like a broken arm from its mast.

In a fury of revenge, we attack the ice, hacking like berserkers in a frenzy of flashing ax blows. Six men abreast, driving back the dazzling army trying to engulf our craft. Breastplates of hard arctic snow are stove in; legions of icicles lose limbs and fingers to the severing strokes, and helmets of frozen brine shatter where they had grown on capstan and stanchion alike. Behind us come the steam hoses blasting away anything we miss and taking no prisoners. Half an hour later, we are relieved by fresh reinforcements and swarm below decks to find warm mugs of cocoa waiting.

"All well, but wet! There's a foot of water in the engine room, we'll need to use the pumps," reports the engineer, the pounding of the great reciprocating steam engine all but drowning out his words.

The galley looks like Rome after the attack of the Visigoths. But in the midst of the chaos, Peter the Poisoner has managed to make the captain his pot of tea.

"Better keep in with the old man." He winks, climbing up to the bridge with a tray.

By late afternoon and early evening, the worst of the storm has passed and what's left is blowing itself out. Now the hurricane is well to the north of us. In that direction, the black sky is still torn with ragged lightning.

"Put yer faith in God and an Admiralty chart! Hmm, what should we do?" sighs the skipper, tapping the map with a pair of dividers. We all await his decision.

"Let's mak for Lerwick, so's we can get the wee snacker to hospital and mak some repairs. Put her aboot, we'll no broach now!" he orders, twiddling the dividers southward across the chart, to where the elongated archipelago of the Shetland Islands looks like a big bug splattered on a windshield.

The crew members file out of the wheelhouse to get some rest while they may, nodding to me as they pass, each stubbly visage a haggard crust fractured by the worry lines of a hundred past storms. Their frost-cracked lips say nothing, but I get the message: you're okay, say the raw-rimmed eyes of the old-timers.

I grin back through the dried blood and puke caking my own face and feel proud to have stood the test with them and endured, but I feel their sadness, too. I know the aftermath to come; it's always the same. News of missing men and lost vessels will trickle in over the next few days. Wives and sweethearts will jump to every ring of the telephone, their hopes rewarded or turned to sorrow by a few short words. Kinfolk will stand on pier and headland, scanning the distant horizon for the sight of a familiar silhouette, but all too often, their prayers go unheeded by the cruel elements. Aye, it's a hard life at the fishing.

"Muir bhaithte," the old Cailleach of the Bridge of Orchy had seen in my hand. "The sea of drowning" she had foretold. Now I understand.

Exhausted, I return to the radio shack and put my feet up on the table. Saying a silent prayer for those who died that night, I drift slowly off to sleep.

Alone on the bridge, his face lit by the pallid sky and the flickering glow of the radar screen, the solitary figure of the helmsman peers through the spinning turbovisor at the unforgiving sea. Feeling each rudder response through the brass-rimmed walnut wheel, he quietly intones the seaman's hymn:

> *Hear us, Lord, we cry to thee,*
> *For those in peril on the sea.*

→ Chapter 14 ←

Sometimes all you can do is,
go to the bar and drink the storm dry.

Tom Carrera, Alaska tuna fisherman

Position: 60° 20′ N. 02° 00′ W.
Lerwick
Shetland Islands

A MOTHER STANDS WITH A BABY SWADDLED IN THE LINES OF her cloak. Her hair does not ruffle in the wind nor does her heart flutter in her breast, for she is carved from solid gray stone. The Madonna and Child stand sentinel on the windswept cliffs above the town, staring out over the bleak ocean with sad, cold eyes. Just as many women did in the great storm years long ago, when the hurricanes quenched the lives of so many fishermen in these northern islands.

I watch, too, since landing and making fast. I have tried to find out if there was any news of Terry and his ship. No one knows anything.

Like the bedraggled wagon train of a vanquished army, vessels of every size and nationality limp across the harbor bar, mooring their battered hulks in the rock-hewn safe haven of Lerwick, the principal town and port of the Shetland Islands. I make my way down the stone pier, visiting each in turn, as they tie up: the *Polo Norte, Freedom, Skandia, Dauntless II, Jan Ove,* and *Hellesfisk.* I have the same question for each.

"Has anyone heard anything of the *Margaret Rose*?"

Heads shake, shoulders shrug, and negative replies come in half a dozen different languages. I continue down the line, but draw a blank.

A convoy, escorted by the fisheries protection vessel *Scarba*, enters the harbor with a blast of steam whistles. Fishing boats in line astern straggle like ducklings behind their mother: the *Venture, Grimsby Pride, Swiftwing, Samfrost* all make it in, followed by the *Nordstjern, Tobarchin, Norseman's Bride,* and *Shady Lady.*

As before, I go from ship to ship, asking the same question.

"No, sorry, mate," says the skipper of the *Grimsby Pride.*

"Nae chance, pal," growls an old boy in yellow oilskins.

"Not a sign, no," the deckhand tying up the *Venture* replies.

I move on to where the *Norseman's Bride* is coming alongside and hail her.

"The *Maggie Rose*? Aye, min, I saw her east of the forty-mile bank, dead in the water, just before the gale hit. She was having a wee bit of engine trouble," shouts a dark-haired young laddie on the foredeck.

"Oh dear God! Did she lose the plant? Did she broach?" I call back, fearing the *Maggie* had lost power and been swamped by the rising seas.

"Naw, the *Margaret Rose* is okay, min. I spoke to the skipper on the VHF myself. We stood by till they got her engines started, then she made off toward Norway."

"Thanks, pal, you've made my day." I smile, much relieved.

The fishing boat comes alongside the dock, and I catch her thrown bow line.

"Have ye got family on board?" asks the stranger, jumping ashore.

"No, it's just my friend Terry Sansome, and he's kind of accident prone. If something's going to happen, it's bound to happen to him."

"Just yer friend, ye say? Sometimes that's the best thing. Ye can choose yer friends, but you're stuck with yer family! Anyway, the East Norwegian Basin didn't lose any shipping to my knowledge, so I guess yer pal will be all right." He ties off the lines and walks up to me. "My name's Fred Corsie, from the Orkney Islands," he says, holding out his hand.

"Fancy a pint, Fred?"

"Aye, min, I do."

We walk through the fading daylight to where the Thule bar is a golden glow amid the blue shadows.

Opening the door releases a belch of cigarette smoke and Patsy Cline lyrics into the gathering night. Inside the pub, the air hangs low with fumes. It's as hot as a boiler room and every bit as noisy. Several different fights and arguments seem to be happening at the same time. Some people appear to be taking part in more than one of these.

Sitting at a table on his own, paying no heed to the ruckus about him, is a huge, longhaired Shetlander with a Viking beard. He could well be Wartooth's twin brother. Fred introduces me to this gentleman. He is Big Magnus from Whiteness.

"Were you caught in the storm, too?" I ask him.

"Aye, min, I was. We were sailing west when it hit," he says, grinning.

"How did you get on?"

"We used an old Viking trick and hid behind St. Kilda!"

"What, that tiny island way out in the Atlantic?"

"Aye," says Magnus. "The Norse knew that ships were safe in the lee of the island. That's why they called it *Skilda*—'the Shield.'"

"So how did the name get changed to St. Kilda."

"God knows! Some drunken monk who cannae spell, maybe."

We are joined by John Robertson, the skipper of a Grimsby boat that lies beaten and bent at the harbor mole.

"How did you fare, John?" asks Magnus.

"Oh God, Magnus, I lost two full sets of gear, nets and all. One of them's tied around my starboard screw, between the propeller and the bloody P bracket. I'm going to have to get a couple of divers to cut her free."

"Dear God, min! That'll cost a pretty penny," says Fred.

"Yeah, it will, about two thousand pounds a piece for the nets and the wintertime diving expenses on top of that. Still, we made it through and there's many worse off than ourselves."

"Aye, that's true. Shite always floats!" says Fred, raising his glass in the old seafarers' toast to absent friends.

"Men destined to be hung need never fear drowning," adds Magnus.

The talk turns to past disasters. The winter storm of 1832, in which thirty-one boats were lost, along with one hundred and five men. Black Sunday, August 19, 1848, when eighteen boats went down in a sudden squall, drowning an unknown number of boys and men. And the great storm of 1881, where ten boats foundered and fifty-one men lost their lives.

I learn a lot at this table. The lads tell me that a death onboard a fishing vessel is usually followed by a "dead man's auction," in which personal effects are sold off to the crew and the money sent to the widow or other family members. If there is no family, the money is spent on a wake in the next port of call, which seems only right. It's bad luck to owe money to a dead shipmate, so it can also be put into a weighted bottle and dropped in the sea for the departed soul to receive down in Fiddler's Green.

"I've heard a lot about superstitions at sea, but what about curses? Are they a big thing?" I inquire, looking to the old seadog Magnus.

"Oh, aye, did ye ever hear of 'the Curse of Captain Kendall'?" he says.

"No, can't say as I have."

"Well, do ye remember Dr. Crippin the murderer?"

"Aye, of course, he killed his wife and went on the run with his mistress."

"Was he no the first person to be arrested through the use of a wireless message?" asks Fred.

"The very same!" says Magnus. "In 1910, Crippin took passage from Antwerp to Canada on the liner *Montrose* along with his lover, who was disguised as a man. Captain Kendall of the *Montrose* had seen enough lassies in his time and wasn't fooled a bit. He sent a wireless message to Scotland Yard, and a detective was dispatched on the much faster White Star liner *Laurentic*, who caught up with them off the coast of Newfoundland. When Crippen and his lover were taken into custody, the murderer put a curse on Captain Kendall, and four years later, when Kendall was the master of the *Empress of Ireland*, she collided with the Norwegian coalship *Storstad* and went down with terrible loss of life at the very location where Captain Kendall turned Crippin over to the police—on the very spot where he had been cursed! What do you think of *that*?" Magnus slaps the table in front of me.

"Aye, that's an odd one, right enough. I've been told that the curse of a murderer is very potent."

Fred nods his head in concurrence. Magnus calls for more beers, and I recount the story of Dr. Corder and the murder of Mariah Marten in the red barn.

Magnus goes on to say that the *Laurentic*, sister to the *Titanic*, lies virtually intact where she was sunk by German bombers, just off the coast of Shetland in shallow water, but no one ever dreams of raising her.

Fred says that the first bomb the Nazis dropped on the British Isles landed in the north of Shetland and killed a rabbit. Which seemed ironic, since the first British bomb to land in Germany hit the Berlin zoo and killed an elephant.

Murderous doctors, wrecked ships, and unfortunate animals fill our stories and laughter fills the tavern, until the events of the last few days are quite forgotten, for the time being. This is how it must have been centuries ago when the wild Vikings whiled away the long arctic nights telling their interminable sagas. "The winter is the less for it!" the old Norse storyteller would say at the end of a tale, and now it is the end of this session, too. After pitching around the Arctic Ocean, the mixture of strong ale and being on dry land has me distinctly wobbly. I say my good-byes and weave my way up the stone-slabbed streets to my bunk on the *Auld Allegiance*. It's a November night, but you wouldn't know it by the temperature. Soft Mexican winds, blowing from the southwest, drift down the dark streets, carrying a thick wet fog. The warm Gulf Stream waters that had pushed the crazed hurricane northward now bathe the islands in a tepid steam bath.

Cradled in my bunk on the trawler, I listen to the wavelets rippling and gurgling beneath the hull. It reminds me of the sound of the Thames, when I lay in my hammock on the *Olive Oyl*, a whole other lifetime ago. From out in the misty night, the long, low moan of the harbor foghorn lulls me to sleep. I have no dreams.

Just before the start of the next short day, I take a walk around the narrow stone-laid streets of the picturesque town. Lerwick looks like it grew from the living rock of the harbor inlet. The streets are so narrow that the fingertips of outstretched arms can touch the shop fronts on both sides. It's a bit like wandering the rabbit warren alleyways of Tangier, but Morocco never knew this climate or such tall blond people. For all its isolation, Lerwick not only sees itself as the center of the Atlantic fishing grounds but looks to the world at large. The Pacific and Orient Steam Packet Line was founded here by a local lad and P&O steamers are still going strong, providing island-linking ferry services as well as luxury cruise liners.

The weather has stayed warm. Not that this affects the locals; they seem as impervious to heat as they are to cold and wander around in below-zero temperatures wearing less clothing than I would wear on a summer's day. "Scratch a Shetlander and you find a Viking; scratch a Viking and you'll find yourself in hospital," as the old saying goes.

Having walked around the wee town, I take my rest on the harbor wall. Hissing mats of exhaust bubbles surface from aft of John Robertson's boat. Like a blowing whale in a red rubber suit, a corpulent figure erupts from the greasy depths. He flips up his mask and waves a greeny-black lobster at me.

"Hey, pal, put this in that bucket over there, will you?" He throws the leggy crustacean over and I chuck it in the pail where several others are crawling about.

"There's hundreds of the buggers down here!" His heels go up and he vanishes back down to the work at hand.

He surfaces a while later and another diver appears with him. We take to chatting while they change their air tanks.

"Aren't you cold in those wet suits?"

"No, not really, the air is usually colder than the sea, and the Gulf Stream heats things up at this time of year. If we want a really warm glow, we just think of the money we're making!"

Out in the silvery mouth of the bay a small rowing boat is dropping a necklace of wicker lobster creels baited with dead fish. Leaving the orange marker buoy floating behind, the fishermen heave back toward the shore.

"The plot thins!" says the first diver, with the merry twinkle of a ruse gleaming in his eye. He whispers to his buddy, and they both slip quietly into the water; a trail of bubbles marks their progress toward the distant creels. When they return, I ask them what they've been up to.

"Come back at the turn of the tide and see."

Later as the tide ebbs, I wander back to the pierhead to find the divers now dressed in their regular clothes and enjoying a beer on the harbor wall. The reappearance of the unsuspecting lobstermen has them in rib-nudging fits of schoolboy giggles. They let me in on their secret. Swimming around on the sea bottom, the divers had snatched up every lobster and crayfish they could find and stuffed them cheek by jowl into one lobster pot, just for fun. Now they watch and wait.

The fishermen pull up the first pot; it contains nothing. The second and third pot contain the same. The fourth comes over the transom of the dinghy empty as well. The two fishermen curse their luck as they strain for the remainder, their words clearly audible as they drift across the darkening bay.

"She must be stuck on something! Heave away, Jamie!" "Pull harder man, I can see her coming up. She's—Holy Christ, will you look at this! Pull, man, PULL!" The laden pot comes sluggishly over the stern, the writhing claws of dozens of demented lobsters protruding and snapping through the hoops of the wooden creel.

"Whatever sort of bait did ye put in that pot, Wullie?"

"I've nay idea! So help me, God, I've nay idea!"

Holding their breath, as only divers can, the two pranksters stagger off up the road before releasing their stifled laughter. To this day, the mystery of the miracle bait remains an enigma among the lobster fishermen of Lerwick.

The *Auld Allegiance* sails next day with a bright new orange inflatable dinghy taking the place of the lost life rafts. I stand in the wheelhouse as we pull out from the gray stone haven, past the swaying mast of a Viking long ship moored in midchannel.

"That's the *Dim Riv* at anchor there. She's a full-scale replica of a Viking war galley, clinker built and as sound as a pound," says the skipper.

"What's *Dim Riv* mean?"

"It's the old Norse for 'morning light.'"

I stare at the fearsome dragon's head nodding with the rippling tide.

A cold chill runs through me, as ancient memories of the Viking raids on Ireland well up in the deep pools of my subconscious:

Since tonight the wind is high
The sea's white mane a fury
I need not fear the hoards of hell
Coursing the Irish Channel.

"What's that you're saying?"

"Oh, it's just an old Irish verse called 'The Viking Terror,' from the ninth century."

Steaming into the Sound of Mousa, we slip through the straits, under the stern gaze of a great circular stone fortification standing on the cliffs. It resembles the concrete cooling towers seen at power stations.

"What's that thing, Skipper?"

"That's the Broch of Mousa, built by the Pictish folk who lived here-aboots. They built dozens of they things all over the place, way the hell back, when Jesus was in short trewsers, eh, Elvis?"

"Uh-huh!" says the mate, with a Presleyesque curl of his lip.

I study the ancient guardian fortress through the binoculars. It has only one door and no windows on the outside wall, a perfect refuge for the mysterious Picts.

"Aye, strange folk, the Picts. They vanished completely. Naebody kens what happened to them," muses the skipper.

"I know the Romans called them Caledonians. I think they inter-married with the Scots who came over from Ireland and the Viking settlers, and sort of got lost in the mix. There's nobody can understand their language now, but it's carved on standing stones all over Scotland."

"That's maybe right enough," says the skipper.

"I've often wondered if they spoke a Celtic language? My mam speaks Irish and my dad speaks Welsh. I still remember a wee bit of both. I should try having a shot at cracking it."

"Aye, you'd be better off doing that than the fishing, son. This game's shagged. I cannae see the industry lasting oot the seventies. We'll soon be as vanished as the Picts. They bloody klondikers and purse seiners tak even the wee baby fish — the breeding stock, for Godsake! This is the first time I ever returned with more boxes of ice than codfish. Mark my words, laddie, this is a taste of things to come. Tak my advice son, sign off in Aberdeen and go an' dae something useful wi' yer life."

"I tell you, Skipper, I think I'm jinxed. I seem to have the uncanny knack of getting a job just as the arse falls out of the industry!"

"It's the luck of the Irish, son. What d'ya say, Elvis, is that no right?"

"Uh-huh!"

I watch the silent, empty fortress sink behind the horizon. I feel its redundancy and that in turn makes me feel lonely. A shiver sends me below for a cup of hot tea and a chance to get the chill out of my bones before the start of the next watch.

The old-timers say that fishing is a hell you can overcome. That's as may be, but I can never get used to the damp. I sit in thought by the galley stove, watching the flat-bottomed kettle spit sizzling drops of water onto the glowing stovetop.

Sartre said, "Hell is other people." But no two hells are the same. Jews and Arabs have the burning hell, so do the Christians, whereas Viking myth speaks of the icy Elijudnir, presided over by the evil goddess Hel, daughter of Loki the wizard of lies.

Trawlermen live their hell at the whim of the raw elements, never knowing when disaster may strike. Storms aren't the worst of it, however. Damp and boredom are the real enemy in this netherworld of sluggish saturation and brain-numbing monotony populated by devils' hordes of slimy, stinky fish.

Back on watch, the thin drizzle does nothing to raise my spirits. Salty spray lifts from the bow wave, seeking every crevice in my cracked lips, stinging like iodine. The sea is flaccid and dismal; each wave top hardly bothers to turn a fleck of foam. Above, dazzling white seagulls wheel and dart against a gloomy gray sky as bleak as my thoughts. I am depressed. Ever since the night of the hurricane, I have nursed another strange feeling that I can't explain. I struggle to recognize the problem, but just as is seems about to manifest in my mind's eye, it evaporates. My brain rounds up the usual suspects: no money, no girlfriend, no real place to stay. No, it can't be them. That was the situation beforehand, when I didn't feel like this. I puzzle on, knowing that if I was just a wee bit smarter, I would have no trouble grasping the concept that eludes me. I content myself with the discovery that I've reached some sort of intellectual plateau. For the first time in my life, I have realized that I'm just smart enough to perceive how dumb I am.

At last the genie is out of the bottle. Slowly the reason behind my elusive uneasy feeling becomes manifest. Although I'm daydreaming now, I haven't dreamt since the night of the storm. The terror of those events casts a longer shadow than I expected. I've always had vivid dreams and sometimes complex nightmares, but the helpless anguish and impotent rage I felt that night was an ordeal I wasn't prepared for. The last messages of dying men on sinking ships make for a poor lullaby, and I fear reliving their horrors so much that I only take to my bunk when stupefied with rum. After that, what passes for sleep is merely unconsciousness. "Drink has drowned more men than Neptune," the saying goes, and it's true: in the fishing fraternity, alcoholism is just another ever present danger to be contended with.

A mile or two off on the port beam, a fishing vessel is dead in the water and showing a queer signal. I give her a call on the walkie-talkie to ask her status, but receive no reply. Through the binoculars, I can see a knot of men struggling with some dark object caught in the nets, aft of the boat. I fear it may be a dolphin. They spot us and wave. From the wheelhouse an Aldis signal lamp flashes:

dot-dash-dash-dot / dot-dash / dash-dot P / A / N. PAN.

"Skipper, the vessel on the port side is in distress. She's sending an urgency signal. I've called them on channel sixteen—no response."

"Okay, Billy boy, hold on to yer hat!" The trawler makes a great arcing turn to the left, dipping her gunwales deep into the wave tops. Soon we are alongside the herring drifter *Bon Adventure.*

"What's the problem, Duncan? Is your radio out?"

"Och, no, Airchie, I wouldn't be bothered aboot a deid radio. No, it's that little memento of World War Two we've picked up aft."

All eyes follow to the stern of the fishing boat, where the curious object can be seen, rising and falling in the moderate swell. The drifter is indeed distressed. A large barnacle-encrusted antishipping mine, tangled like a spiky steel oil drum in the herring drifter's nets, is threatening to clip the stern and blow the boat to pieces.

"Shouldn't we call in the navy, Skipper?"

"Naw, Billy, that's why he didn't want to use the radio. If ye get the navy involved, it's a right song and dance, wi' sheets of paperwork and being stuck here for hours while they pussyfoot around, making an exercise oot of it. Naw, we'll sort this bugger oot ourselves. LAUNCH THE ZODIAC!"

I help the deck crew make ready the inflatable raft, and before I know it, I'm over the side with them. We secure the raft as a buffer between the spiked detonators and the stern of the fishing boat. The drifter launches a tiny rubber boat of her own, and together, we unravel the nylon gill netting from the dome-topped canister. A sudden cross-wave lifts the drifter's jollyboat skyward, on top of the mine.

"Nobody move!" shouts the skipper from the rail above. "Wait for the next cresting wave!"

Seconds tick by. The small raft slides around on the bobbing mine, squeaking like a soapy sponge on a window pane. Then the swell lifts her clear off and dumps her ten yards away. Our dinghy is still trapped between the mine and the drifter's transom, which gives us some stability. With much cursing and delicate hand maneuvers, the netting is picked clear of each detonator spike and the hideous weapon finally freed from the gear.

The mine floats away toward the jolly boat. The *Bon Adventure*'s mate ties a long length of nylon rope to the ring on top of it, then fastens a small bag of luminous green sea stain and an orange plastic warning buoy to the line, marking it as a dangerous object.

"Airchie, could you call and report this tae the Coast Guard on yer big wireless? I've only got the wee VHF," the skipper of the drifter shouts over.

"Aye, nae bother, Duncan. Fair fishin' tae ye noo. An' don't go picking up any more tin fish!" The two skippers wave and depart as we climb aboard.

"Did you hear that, Billy?"

"Aye, Skip," I say, making for the radio shack.

"Then mak it so, but don't give oor name oot!"

Feeling at last that I'm doing something useful, I fire up the big transmitter.

"Wick Radio . . . Wick Radio . . . Wick Radio, do you receive? Over."

"Wick Radio here . . . what vessel, please?"

"Wick Radio, this is the yacht . . . er . . . *Cormorant*. We have spotted an unexploded mine at position fifty-nine degrees, seven minutes North, two degrees, eleven minutes West. Over."

"Yacht *Cormorant* . . ." The voice repeats the information and coordinates. "Is this correct? Over."

"That's correct. Someone has marked it with an orange buoy and green sea stain. We are heading away from the location now. Over."

"Well, aren't some people very obliging. I'll bet it was marked by the fishing boat who caught it in their nets. Thank you for the information, *Cormorant*. Happy fishing! Wick Radio out."

The skipper stands at the radio room door and winks.

I feel better.

✦ Chapter 15 ✦

Do you mean there's more than one foreign language?
Jon Bjornson, Icelandic Steam Packet Company

SURVIVAL SHOULD BE A SCOTTISH WORD, BECAUSE IT'S certainly a Scottish trait. You hear it all the time: "How's it going?" "Och, nae bad—I'm surviving, just!" A newspaper headline reads, "Will the Fishing Industry Survive North Sea Oil?" BBC Radio Scotland asks, "Can a prehistoric monster really survive two million years in the peaty waters of Loch Ness?"

Survivre, old French, from Latin: *super-* above or beyond + *vivere* to live. The dictionary definition is more prosaic: "*Survive:* To live or continue beyond the death of another, an event, etc.; remain alive or in existence."

We had survived wind, waves, and the flotsam of World War II, but with little to show for it. At the pier in Aberdeen I watch the catch being off-loaded. It doesn't take long—there isn't much of it. Without a catch bonus, a fisherman's wages are small, subsistence, in fact. I've now done two trips up to the Arctic Circle and have hardly made a penny.

Subsistence, my inner voice echoes as I watch the three ten-pound notes counted into my hand. Coined from the Latin, *sub-* under + *sistere* to cause to stand, I tell myself.

The skipper looks at me apologetically. There's no pink slip. His eyes say it all.

My dad was right when I told him I was studying Latin. "Oh, that will come in bloody handy one day—you never know when you'll meet a passing centurion!"

✦ 182 ✦

"Thirty quid for freezing me ass off and nearly getting killed. Still, 'Nil desperandum!'" I mutter, drifting into the Bon Accord bar for a couple of beers with some of the crew. The talk is dour among the trawlermen. They buzz like a swarm of bees. The drone of conversation flings fragments into my falling-asleep mind.

"Fuckin' lousy catch!"

"Piss-poor wages!"

"We got oor gear snagged on one of thay new oil pipelines—ripped the erse oot o' the trawl!"

"Misfortunate bastards! They reckon they must have caught one of thay nuclear submarines in their nets. Pulled them doon faster than they could put out a Mayday—poor bastards."

I leave my beer and the depressing chatter behind and take off to the flat in Powis Place to flop down, fully clothed, on the settee. Now all I want is to sleep. Sleep long and have dreams, sweet, sweet dreams. Before nodding off, I notice my roommates have done a fine cleanup job in the wake of Fergie's squalor. The flat is indeed neat and tidy. The air smells fresh, with just a hint of jasmine. There are even new curtains, and the picture of Uncle Adolf has lost its privileged position to a colorful *Jesus Christ Superstar* poster. I begin to doze off. The bedroom door opens and a scantily dressed lassie enters, pulling on a dressing gown.

"Hello! You must be Bill. I've got something here for you."

"Oh, I'm dreaming and all my Christmases have come at once," I mumble.

"I don't know about that! Your friends are gone. They got thrown out by the landlord, but they left this letter for you." She takes an envelope from behind the clock on the mantelpiece.

I sit upright and sadly open the note.

"You mean you're not a dream?"

"Erm . . . no, I'm Allison," she says, her dark eyes darting nervously and one hand demurely closing the open neck of her dressing gown.

She looks rather sweet, so I smile.

She coughs politely and moves from one foot to the other, tucking a lock of brown hair behind her ear.

I turn my attention to the roughly scrawled note:

Fergie, the dimwit, gave this address at the hospital and so the drug-squad raided the house. The landlord flipped out, so we have set up a new menagerie at 9 Granton Place. We have all your gear—see ya! Bloggs.

"Granton Place? Where the hell is that?"

"It's way up the other end of Union Street, and please don't swear!"

"Can't I just stay the night?" I plead.

"No, we girls have to be up early for lectures tomorrow—and anyway, it wouldn't be proper."

"What's a pretty girl like you studying?" I ask, trying to win her over with an easy smile.

"I'm a third-year divinity student," she says frostily, opening the front door.

"Oh my God!"

"Don't swear—and I'll take this, *you* won't be needing it," she says, picking up my door key from the table.

It's a long walk on tired feet to the top of Union Street and then on to Granton Place. Here I discover, to my chagrin, that the new apartment is on the top floor of an old four-story tenement.

The boys seem in good spirits and tell me that Terry had arrived back yesterday and had immediately gone to see one of his girlfriends, so I can use the spare bed in the kitchen. Bloggs's great hairy face begins telling me of the police raid and subsequent eviction, but stretched out on the bed, I nod off before he can finish.

Dreams close in, many-layered, luscious fantasies, scented and sensual. Allison the divinity student is divine indeed and indulging in her own prayer of passion.

"Oh God . . . oh God," she gasps.

"Don't you be swearing now!" I nuzzle into her jasmine-fragranced ear. *"Can I have my key back* now?" I whisper through the kisses.

"Oh yes!" She surrenders. *"Yes . . . yes . . . yes!"*

In the delicious depths of the dream, a door creaks open. I hear Terry's voice saying, *"Jesus, I'm knackered!"*

"Oh, no, Terry, please don't interrupt now, not now. Can't you see I have company?" my dream shape pleads to the darkness.

Terry, in the wakened world, does not hear my cries or heed my presence. My erotic reverie is terminated by one hundred and sixty pounds of trawlerman crashing down on top of me, splintering bed boards and rib cage alike. Torn from the arms of my phantom lover, I let out a scream. Terry struggles back up, mouthing a string of curses, and flicks on the light.

"Billy, ya bastard! I thought you were dead!" he says, hugging the life out of me.

"I can't breathe," I wheeze.

"Oh, sorry, old mate, I'm just so glad to see you—I was worried when we heard nothing of the *Allegiance*."

He takes off his overcoat and I think I'm hallucinating again.

"Terry, why are you wearing a dress?" I ask, rubbing my eyes.

"It's a long story, you wouldn't believe it," he says, sitting down on the bed.

"Well, if I'm going to share a mattress with you, you'd better tell me!"

"Okay, so we were doing repairs off the coast of Norway when the storm hits and the skipper says, 'To hell with this, set a course for Bergen.' So, after docking, I went to that Christian Salvasen whaling club you told me about, and you're right, it is the cheapest drinking hole in Scandinavia. Anyway, I get pissed up on akvavit and get back on board just as she's sailing. Like an idiot, I'm leaning over the sternrail, jacket draped over my shoulders, when the ship crosses the harbor bar and out past the breakwater. The breeze yaws, tearing the coat from my back. Passport, seaman's card, and nearly a week's wages plunge to their doom in the wake of the boat!"

"So, what happened when you got back to Aberdeen and found out the lads had moved?"

"Well, I saw them in the pub, then, fancying a bit of 'how's yer father,' I went down to the flat of that hippie girl Inky, you know? The one that always smells of incense and patchouli oil. Well, being a gentleman like, I feel obliged to pay for my night's lodging by giving Inky a fierce old shagging. Anyway, we're having a great bunk-up with her old brass bedstead wobbling and creaking, but me trousers fall from the bed rail and land on top of the single-bar electric fire. *Whoosh!* The fuckers go, causing a serious coitus interruptus. When I look, me polyester trousers have evaporated. Well, of course, Inky, being a bleeding earth mother, doesn't wear jeans or the like and I've lost both my jacket and trousers in the past twenty-four hours, so I have to be getting the early morning bus dressed in a flowery frock and a girl's overcoat."

"Jesus, Terry, what next?"

"No, it gets worse. I was doing well at the start. I keep my head down, so's no one notices me, but then bloody Nigel, the mad axman, gets on! 'Hello Terry,' he says, plonking himself down next to me all purple and whatnot. 'Why are ye dressed up like a tart? Are ye turning into a wee poofta, are ye?' I nearly died of shame. Every eye on the bus is gawping at us till Nigel notices them. 'What are youse bastards looking at? Have ye never seen a transvestite before?' He goes into one of his tirades about lily-livered peons of bank clerks, pox doctors, and arse lickers making their way to their pointless jobs to fulfill their meaningless lives and how he is going to die like a Viking with his two lungs sticking out of the ax wounds in his back. 'A blood eagle! That's the way to go—straight to Valhalla! All hail to the blood eagle!'

"He's waving his ax about, and the conductor is feared to go near him. I'm glad when the bus stops at the lights, I jump off and run like fuck! I didn't draw breath till I got home! So here I am, no money, no papers, and nothing but women's clothes. I tell you, if it wasn't for bad luck, I'd have no luck at all!"

"You could always go on the game, Terry! Here's a blanket, and if you start dreaming about one of your girlfriends, keep yer hands to yerself."

"No danger of that—I'm shagged out."

"Lucky bastard!"

A cold morn finds us huddled around the feeble flames of a damp kitchen fire. We had taken to gleaning sea coal from the beach, but getting the damn stuff to light was nigh on impossible. I knew that Mrs. Maclumphit had regular sea coal customers who wouldn't spend good money on the crap we're finding. So what were we doing wrong?

The following morning, Terry and I see the old lady pushing her pram along the sand and venture to ask her opinion on the fire-lighting problem. Furthermore, I notice that she never takes coal from the little cove where we had filled up our bags yesterday.

"Good morning, Mrs. Mac."

"Och, hello there, Billy, it's yersell. Fit like, loon?"

"Grand, Mrs. Mac—and yourself?"

"Och, survivin', so I mustn't grumble. Are ye haukin' mere o' that steam coal?"

"Aye, we have nae fuel for the fire except what we can chorrie," I offer, using as much of the local Aberdeen dialect as I can muster.

"Ged, dear loons, ye'll ne'er burn thon coal in the fire. Das fer ships' boilers, das no sea coal. Das steam coal, aw washed up from thon wreck oot yonder. Deek where the auld ship's boiler is blawing off like a muckle great whale?"

She points to a spot out in the surf line, where the North Sea waves crash over a large rusty cylinder, occasionally sending a jet of white sea spray into the sky, from some old vent or other.

"Oh no! We spent hours collecting that shite and humping it up eight flights of stairs."

"I bet aw that humping had ye fair warm, gettin'? An' that'll be the onlee heat ye'll get oot o' it tae. Ye widnae get thon clinkers to licht if ye wiz the deil hissell blawing roastit fireballs oot yer erse! Ye'd be thare from noo till doomsday!" The old lady pushes her pram off into the distance to attend to her solitary business, her laughter mingling with the calls of the seagulls.

"What did she say?"

"She says that steam coal doesn't burn, Terry."

"Blimey, is *that* what she said?"

Back at the madhouse, we recount the sad tale of the unburnable coal to our pals, who find it extremely amusing. We do discover that starting the fire with regular coal and then introducing crushed pieces of steam coal seems to work after a while if you blow at the coals through a copper tube. We show our alchemistic process to Nuff, who has been away all week and missed the debacle of the flameproof fuel.

"If ye want to warm a kitchen, this is what ye do!" He lights a ring on the gas cooker and inverts an iron pot over the flame. Within minutes the room is warm and cozy.

"What's with you guys? Did ye never grow up in poverty?"

Both Terry and myself, who *had* grown up in poverty, gaze amazed.

Winter draws on, folding thick carpets of wet snow around the sidewalks and eaves of the Silver City. Washing and personal bathing take place in the kitchen sink, but since water can only be heated by the kettleful, the curious spectacle of the dust bath is performed weekly by the inhabitants.

Naked as babes, two grown men are standing on a folded-out newspaper, sprinkling talcum powder onto their heads from a tin marked Spring Lilac. The resultant cone of white powder is rubbed briskly through the hair, until it falls onto the shoulders. Then it's worked into the armpits, whence it falls toward the private parts, subsequently burnishing the genitalia before drifting to the feet, where, after dusting the toes, it is carefully collected and put back in the tin for next time. As the winter progresses, the talc turns through many shades of gray and begins to resemble lumpy oatmeal.

None of the families who live in the tenement have indoor bathrooms. Going to the outside toilets in the dead of winter is like a trip to the Russian front, and leaving the comparative warmth of your bed at night makes for a miserable trek to a frozen unlit toilet.

All of our neighbors use chamber pots, and the morning ritual called "the parade of the pots" takes place on the stairs, between seven and nine o'clock each day. Eight flights of stairs have to be negotiated to empty the piss pots into the freezing shanties in the backyard, but the women make the most of it and it is not unusual to see two wifeys chatting away on the staircase, seemingly holding giant teacups covered with white linen handkerchiefs.

Ordinary folk call the pot a "guzzunder" because it goes under the bed. The ones who like to think themselves a cut above the rest refer to it as a "Napoleon." This curiosity dates from the late eighteenth century, when chamber pots made in the factories of Stoke on Trent had likenesses of England's archenemy, Napoleon Bonaparte, staring up in anguish from the bottom. Guzzunder or Napoleon, we have neither.

The same winter snowstorms that did for Emperor Nap are dumping many feet of snow on Aberdeen. All traffic stops, and a delicious hush descends on the city.

Outside, things are not so rosy. The backyard toilets, already half-obscured by the blizzard, are now completely buried by an avalanche from the tenement rooftops.

Generations of Scots had long used the kitchen sink for peeing in, but to overcome the present crisis requires a greater degree of subtlety.

The kitchen's bay window stretches tall above an archaic porcelain sink. To its strong wooden plinth the boys bolt a long springy plank that can be bent in an arc and trapped under the empty bed frame. To the free end is fixed a white enamel washbowl. Defecation is effected into this utensil, and on completion of the job at hand, the bed is jerked back. With the top of the kitchen window previously opened, the entire apparatus, similar to a medieval siege engine, catapults the bowl's contents forward at enormous velocity, neatly clearing the casement and propelling the offending objects into the wasteland beyond.

This latter-day masterpiece of sound Scottish engineering practice is called "the turd hurtler" by its designers and is their pride and joy. With great aplomb the boys invite visiting dignitaries to view it and, if they so desire, to give it a whirl.

The infernal concraption, as Terry refers to it, remains in nightly service until the neighbors complain of the shuddering noise the thing produces and threaten to call the police. Luckily, the warm Gulf Stream returns to the rescue and the snowdrifts depart, allowing us access to the outside toilets again.

On December 24, Wartooth arrives and wishes us a Happy Bastille Day. Nuff, who has worked translating French, takes pains to put him right.

"Bastille Day, Nigel, is on the fourteenth of July. It's a French national holiday."

"True, that was the case when it started, but the French revolutionary calendar, introduced in 1793, had twelve months of thirty ten-day weeks in a year, so that left five days over each year, and, since the first revolutionary year began on the twenty-second of September 1792, the date has slowly incremented forward by 890 days in 178 years. Thus, after removing the leap year days from the Gregorian calendar, which was eleven days out anyway, I calculate that this year, the anniversary of the Storming of the Bastille falls on the twenty-fourth of December." Wartooth looks around expectantly.

No one rises to his bait. In the silence, I ask what I think is an innocuous question.

"What do you do, Nigel?"

"I'm a berserker," he says, grinning back at me, glad of the conversation.

"Yes, I know that, but what do you do for work, like a proper job?"

Wartooth smiles his victory smile.

I realize that I have fallen for one of his loony lectures, like it or not. Nuff plugs his ears with his fingers and goes off to his bed, singing *la-la-la* noises. Terry glares at me.

"I work 4.66 days a year, which is all that is allowable under the current legislation."

"Four and a half days a year. Nigel, what are you talking about— what legislation?"

I know asking him is a mistake and will only lead to a mental concussion, but like a lemming running toward a cliff top, I can't help myself.

Nigel takes a piece of paper and a pencil.

"There are 365 days in a year, okay?" he says, writing down the number 365. "You spend a third of your life asleep, correct?"

"We might if you didn't keep coming around, keeping us awake with yer bloody nonsense," says Terry.

Wartooth studiously ignores him.

"Okay, so, 365 divided by 3 equals 121.66. Now there are 52 weeks in the year, each containing a Saturday and a Sunday on which we don't normally work."

"You don't do anything *normally*, ya mad bastard."

"Shush, Terry, this is interesting."

"You're getting as daft as he is," Terry mutters.

"So that's 104 weekend days we don't work. So, 121.66 minus 104 equals 17.66 working days left. Now, there are 13 days of national and bank holidays in the year, okay? 17.66 take away 13 leaves only 4.66 days per year on which you may work."

Wartooth sits in the corner of the kitchen clucking to himself in triumph, his long bony fingers plucking twangy discords from Nuff's banjo.

Terry shakes his head in resignation, and his own curiosity takes hold.

"Why the sudden interest in the French? I thought you were a Viking to the core?"

"The French *were* Vikings," says Wartooth. "Well, *some* of them anywise."

"What new shite is this?" Terry groans, flopping down on the bed.

"The Norsemen under their leader, Rollo, were invited down from Scandinavia by the French king Charles the Simple, to settle in northern France to help subdue the wild Bretons."

"He must have been fuckin' simple if he thought a few Vikings would scare the Bretons, eh, Billy?" says Terry, sitting up and expressing some pride in his own Celtic bloodline for the first time.

"Aye, well, the Norsemen began to speak French and became the Normans, who eventually invaded England with William the Conqueror in 1066, so, vive la France!"

This revelation is probably the most reasonable story I've ever heard Wartooth utter. Even Terry seems impressed, and inquisitive, too.

"Okay, Nigel, my great-great-great-great-grandfather was a Breton. Sanson was his name. He operated the guillotine in the French Revolution, chopping the heads off aristocrats. What do you know about that?"

"Well, it's a common misconception that only the rich and noble went to the blade. The truth is that of the forty thousand beheaded, less than fifteen percent were aristocracy, the rest were peasants."

"But why should that be? Surely the revolution was caused by the peasants?"

"No, Terry, the French Revolution was caused by pigeons."

"*Pigeons?* I knew I should've kept my mouth shut! Pigeons, my arse!"

"Yeah, *Columbidea vulgaris,* the common pigeon."

"Okay, Nigel, I'll buy it one more time, but this is the last time."

Sitting back with his hands folded behind his scraggy head, Wartooth spins the tale of the pigeons that brought down the monarchy of France.

"There were fat cats in those days, real fat cats. They lived in chateaux, and like any other cats, they liked to eat pigeons. These chateaux were like walled townships where only the nobleman and his servants lived, and in each was a dovecote."

"What's that?"

"It's a building for keeping pigeons, Terry, usually a tall tower with hundreds of roosting nooks set into the sides. Anyway, the breasts of these birds were a delicacy to the bourgeois rural French, who liked them baked in red wine. The problem was, no one in the chateau fed these birds, so they flew out each day to forage for seeds in the poor people's fields. Every time some impoverished peasant sowed his spring corn or winter barley, hundreds of plump pigeons descended on the furrows and stripped them clean. That's why the peasants were starving and the fat cats were fat!"

"Okay," says Terry, "so why didn't the peasants kill the pigeons and eat them?"

"Because it was against the law."

"Well, why didn't they break the law, so's they could survive?"

"They did eventually. It was called the French Revolution."

Terry groans again and pulls a blanket over himself.

From far away in the chilly night, a city clock tolls the midnight hour.

"Happy Christmas," says Wartooth.

"I thought you said it was Bastille Day?" I offer.

Before Nigel can answer, Terry makes a series of staged coughing sounds. Then looking over at me, draws his finger across his throat as if to say, Pursue this and I'll slit yer gizzard.

✦ Chapter 16 ✦

Lament him a' ye rantin core . . .
Nay mair he'll join the merry roar,
In social key;
For now he's taen anither shore,
And owre the sea!

Robert Burns

IT'S CHRISTMAS DAY AND A WONDERFUL SMELL OF ROASTING
turkey pervades the normally frowsty air of the small kitchen. The festive afternoon dinner is laid out with a colorful array of sprouts, carrots,
and potatoes, both roasted and boiled, all waiting for the anointing of
rich brown gravy. Terry raises a glass in poetic toast:

"It was Christmas Day in the workhouse,
The one day of the year
When the paupers' plates were full of grub
And their bellies full of beer.
Up spake the workhouse master, a nasty little sod:
'If you don't do your task today . . . you'll get no Christmas pud.'
Thus spake a brave old pauper, his face as bold as brass:
'You can keep your Christmas pudding and stick it up your . . .
Ar . . . tidings of comfort and joy, comfort and joy,
Oh, tidings of comfort and joy.'
It was Christmas Day in the harem,
The eunuchs lined the walls,
He said, *'What do you want for Christmas, boys?'*
And the eunuchs shouted, *'Ba . . . Tidings of comfort and joy,*
Comfort and joy, Oh, tidings of comfort and joy.'"

Hands clap, hands slap backs, hands grab knives and forks, and are stilled in reverent expectancy, as Bloggs sharpens the carving knife with a series of great sweeping flourishes.

The gentle giant carves the bird, laying the thick cuts of white breast in a semicircle on the serving plate. I look from face to face and am put in mind of Pavlov's dogs. The last offcut reveals an unwelcome intruder in our midst. A small, shiny, plastic bag, full of steaming innards, begins bursting out of the side of the turkey carcass. Bloggs blinks at the swelling protrusion as if it's an alien from another galaxy.

"What the hell's that?" he cries, poking it with the carving knife.

"Holy Jasus, Bloggs! Didn't you think to take the bag of giblets out?"

"I didn't know you had to," says Bloggs. "It says 'oven-ready' on the label!"

We had never eaten a proper cooked meal together in the little attic flat. The boys had done us proud. With the exception of the plastic haggis, the meal is devoured with no ill effect, other than that curious dopey feeling that sets in after eating turkey. One by one, the lads drift off to their beds, leaving me and Terry lounging around like Victorian gentlemen, supping glasses of port.

"What are you going to do tonight, Billy?"

"Oh, I thought I might go see Angus. I hear he's fallen down some mountain or other and he's in the Royal Infirmary with a broken leg. D'you want to chum me along?"

"No thanks. Anyway, I've got a date, and *she's* got a sister! Maybe you fancy chumming *me* along?"

"No, I better go see Angus. He's bound to be lonely, it being Christmas an' all."

"Go on, ya big softy! I bet if *you* was in hospital with a busted leg, he wouldn't bother his arse going to see you."

"That's as may be, but two wrongs don't make a right."

"Aye, Billy, and ye can't make a silk purse out of a sow's ear."

Inside the old hospital, the smell of iodine, ether, and pine disinfectant soon drives all recollections of Christmas dinner from my nasal memory. Angus is in a room by himself. For a laugh, I ask him if he's in quarantine. He tells me his parents have paid for a private room. He seems distracted as I tell him about Bloggs's Christmas dinner and even more uninterested when I mention the other gossip and goings-on in the city. He asks me to close the door to the hallway and put the bolt on. Thinking he wants to use the bedpan, I'm happy to oblige. Instead, he takes a spectacles case from his bedside drawer and fills a hypodermic syringe with fluid from an ampoule, then sticks the needle into a vein near his crotch.

"What are you doing that for? Don't the doctors do that for you?"

"Don't be so fuckin' naive, Billy. The doctors don't know fuck all about this and don't ye be tellin' them either. No man, this is morphine. You should try it . . . moooorphiiine!" He lies back dazed, mouth open, like one of those stupid-looking codfish that used to haunt my dreams.

I turn the bottle over. The label reads, "For Use by the Royal National Lifeboat Institution Only."

"Where did you get this?"

"From . . . eh . . . that guy down at the uni . . . Rennie his name is . . . aye . . . you can get it from Rennie."

A red blaze of anger engulfs me.

"You're fucked, Angus—you and your false god Morpheus!"

I smash his syringe into the trash can and stomp out of the room.

It doesn't take long for Terry and me to track down the guy who has the stolen ampoules: he is openly selling them in the university union. A bit of detective work reveals that his name is Macintosh and he's known as Rennie to his friends. Two days after Christmas, we hear reports that he will be in the beer bar that night. In preparation for our meeting, I comb my hair back with Brylcreem and borrow Nuff's leather motorcycle jacket. Terry has his hair tied back in a ponytail and is wearing a cutoff Levis jacket and a pair of Polaroid sunglasses. We stand in front of the mirror trying to look like drug dealers. I look like a poor man's James Dean, whereas Terry would pass for Willie the Pimp.

The union bar is half-full when we enter. Our informant is by the door.

"Which one?" Terry asks, scanning the crowd.

"The bloke with salt-an'-pepper hair in the corner booth."

"Good lad!"

Terry and I watch for a while before wandering over to the table.

"We hear you have the makings of a happy holiday season?" Terry says, in a transatlantic drawl.

"I might have. Who told you?"

"A mate of ours recommended you. Angus is his name."

"Oh, yes, of course. Sit down, gentlemen. Angus is one of my best customers."

Terry sits. I remain standing. I notice with glee that this makes the weasel-faced student very nervous.

"Is it good stuff? We don't deal in crap," Terry whispers in his ear.

"Oh yes," he intimates. "It's government issue. I stole it myself from the medical supplies at the RNLI Lifeboat Station."

"Good for you!" says Terry. "By the way, what is it you're studying? Chemistry? Medicine?"

"Law," he smirks. "I'm a third-year law student."

This was one revelation that didn't surprise me at all.

"Well, Rennie, we're willing to buy your whole stash and pay good money for it, too. Meet us at midnight outside the rubbish dump and be careful—there are cops about!"

"Can't we do the deal here?"

"Hell, no! It's too risky. We have an investment in this stuff . . . not to be messed with. Get my drift?" Terry says cryptically.

I suddenly realize that Terry is playing out the role of "Connection," the drug pusher Phil Spector played in the film *Easy Rider.* I have a hard time keeping my face straight.

Terry picks up on my apparent inner turmoil and says, "Make yer mind up, Rennie. My buddy Knuckles here is getting agitated!"

At this point, the effort of controlling my stifled laughter has me making fierce facial grimaces. I stride out into the corridor for the relief that only a fit of giggling can bring. Terry strolls out past me.

"He fell for it," he says.

The papers the next evening carry a story about a law student found tied to the gates of the local rubbish dump. Terry reads it out loud as we walk along by the docks:

It was freezing last night when the police, acting on a tip-off, discovered twenty-two-year-old Iain Macintosh lashed to the iron gates of the refuse collection center with his trousers around his ankles and wearing just a T-shirt. A placard strung about his neck stated "I Sell Morphine Stolen From Lifeboats." A large quantity of stolen morphine was recovered on his person, along with a signed confession detailing his part in breaking into the Lifeboat Station. He was unable to give any details of his assailants and is being presently held under police supervision at the Royal Infirmary, where he's being treated for hypothermia. Criminal charges are pending.

"I hope the wee bastard now has some idea of what the pain of frost-bite feels like," says Terry, counting yet again the contents of Rennie's wallet, "Two hundred and forty-five quid! Blimey, makes you wonder if selling drugs isn't worthwhile?"

I dart a nervous glance at him, but his half-arsed grin tells me that he's only pulling my leg. One by one, Terry folds the banknotes up and stuffs them into the slot on top of the lifeboat-shaped charity box outside the Seaman's Mission. He flaps the leather wallet to show it's empty, then throws it in a great curving arc into the greasy waters of the harbor.

"Good riddance to bad rubbish," he says, smiling.

The midwinter solstice passes. Now the short, bone-chilling days are getting slightly longer, giving greater respite from the endless hours of dank, dark winter nights. I've heard that there's a curious form of depression associated with living in these northern latitudes that's brought on by sunlight deprivation. If that's true, it will suit Angus, who's now released from hospital and hanging around with a sullen crowd of death-hungry wankers who'd smother their mothers for the price of a shot of heroin. Not that he speaks to me anymore. He doesn't even seem to recognize my existence. At first I found this hurtful, then I was angered by it, and now I couldn't care less. The happy-go-lucky guy I knew is gone. Only the husk of Angus is left.

Time to move on. Life is waiting, and so is the morning post.

"There's a letter here for you, Terry, from the government."

"God, what now?" He opens the envelope as if it might explode. "Oh, it's okay. It's just my replacement British passport."

He shows me the black cover with its gold-incised royal coat of arms.

> *The lion and the unicorn*
> *Were fighting for the crown.*
> *The lion beat the unicorn*
> *And chased him 'round the town.*

"What's that mean?"

"You see the armorial beasts either side of the shield?"

"Yeah."

"Well, the lion represents England and wears the British crown on his head. The unicorn stands for Scotland, and if you look closely, you'll see the Scottish crown is used as a restraining collar around the unicorn's neck and there's a chain running from it, anchoring the defeated beast to the British soil at the bottom of the shield."

"My God, so there is," says Terry.

An ugly rumor drifts like a bad smell through the back alleys and dockside drinking haunts of Aberdeen. It stings all who it comes near, and leaves each with the same stupefaction of shock.

Nuff hurries in. We know this means trouble: Nuff doesn't hurry anywhere.

"It's true, lads, I heard it from a cop I know downtown. Nigel is dead."

"How?" says Bloggs, blinking like an owl.

"I'm not sure. He'd been arrested for chopping down some wooden addition to a house that he thought was an eyesore or something, and when he heard he might get the jail for it, they reckon that he somehow committed suicide!"

"Jesus, poor old Wartooth."

"Sorry, lads, I couldn't find out anything more. It's all a bit shrouded in mystery."

"Shit—and I was always such a mean bastard to him," sighs Terry.

"No, you weren't. He never took a blind bit of notice what you said anyway. It was all water off a duck's arse to him."

"Yeah, I guess."

Terry opens his last bottle of duty-free Trawler rum and pours it into four glasses. We toast our fallen comrade.

"To Nigel!"

"To Wartooth!"

"To Valhalla!"

"All hail to the blood eagle!"

Salute finished, we smash the last four glasses into the fireplace. Nigel would have liked that.

"Where do you think he is now?" asks Nuff.

"He's surely riding with the Valkyries to be received and feasted by Odin and his name added to the wall in the great hall of Valhalla," I muse, hopefully.

"And laughing his balls off!" Terry adds, poking the sea coal hissing in the fire grate.

Bloggs says nothing, but his fiddle weeps out a slow Celtic air. Terry listens a while, then shakes his head. He puts a hand on Bloggs's shoulder.

"Come on, Bloggsy man, Wartooth wouldn't want us to mourn. Give us something a wee bit lively."

"Aye, right enough."

The huge-handed fiddler bursts into a good old Scandinavian-sounding tune called "Villasfjord." I grin and clap my hands; so do the others, but we know it's a hollow gesture, all the same.

Until now, death had been a remote occurrence either through distance or time and hadn't happened to anyone close to me since I was a kid. I find it very difficult to believe that I'll never see Wartooth again. Hear his clicking, knitting needle laugh and try to stay awake through his all-night lectures on heaven knows what.

Wartooth was the first of my friends to die, and I hardly knew him. I didn't even know his real name, or how old he was. It all seemed so final. Not that Nigel himself believed in death as we know it, or life either. That would be too simple. He espoused, instead, the "palindrome theory" that you live your days in two separate time lines that operate in opposite directions. If one way is good, then the other is bad. *Evil* is *live* backward, and, likewise, *devil* is the inverse of *lived,* so like the yin-yang symbol, the two forces balance out, trapping you in the middle. The only way to break free from this "Vale of Tears" was to die an honorable death, thus ensuring your passage to the higher plains of existence that lie beyond. I just wished I had known him more and known more of what I'm sure he knew. Damn it!

"Up like a rocket and down like the stick," they say in Ireland.

That was Nigel, all right—a sky rocket, launched on a blazing flight that could never touch ground until the bitter end. Even then, to prevent the dishonor of being locked up like a common criminal, he "fell on his sword" like the true Viking he was. I'll miss him.

The wake for Nigel Wartooth takes place at a small gathering in the university union beer bar. The majority of students are away for the holidays, and even I attend, more out of duty than enthusiasm.

Playing at being a student has lost much of its early appeal, especially when I realize that most of these kids are more in fear of being disinherited by their rich parents for flunking than they are interested in achieving a good education.

Nigel's death, along with watching my old friend Angus becoming a junkie, only adds to my sense of disenchantment. Aberdeen has soured for me. I have learned a lot from studying books, but unless the secret of the Druids lay in gutting fish, any practical experience I may have gained is much wanting.

The voice of the head porter calls over the public address system: "Telephone call for Uther Pendragon . . . telephone call for Uther Pendragon, box three, please!" Passing through the lobby, on the way to the toilets, I notice no one goes to the phone. The call is repeated: "Uther Pendragon, please! There's a phone call for you at box three."

Who could be paging King Arthur's father? Finally, curiosity gets the better of me and I pick up the receiver.

"Hello?"

"Hello! Is that you, Billy? Billy Watkins?"

"Aye, it is, who's this?"

"It's Gordon Jones."

"What! Gordie Jones, the folk singer from Liverpool?"

"Yeah!"

"Bloody hell! How did you know I was up here?"

"I heard you were hanging around at Aberdeen University, and I figured the beer bar would be a safe bet. Anyway, I've got a flat in Edinburgh, if you fancy popping down for New Year. We're having a Hogmanay party, and it would be good to see you again!"

"Sure, Gordie, that sounds great. Is there room for me to bring my pal Terry?"

"No bother, bring him down. My mate, Chris Dale, is coming up from Birkenhead. Meet us in the Café Royal bar—it's right by the bus station—and we'll have a good laugh."

"Okay, I could do with a good laugh. By the way, why did you page Uther Pendragon?"

"Because I knew if you were there, the Arthurian name would make you prick your ears up and you wouldn't be able to resist answering the call."

Terry and I set off the next morning. A day of hitchhiking through the wild glens of Perthshire is a pleasant respite from the angular granite walls of Aberdeen. Lifts are slow, so it is nighttime when we're dropped off at the beginning of the mile-long suspension bridge spanning the savage tidal course of the Firth of Forth estuary. From here on, we walk.

To our left the lozenge-shaped trusses of the mighty Forth railway bridge have stood since 1888, corroding away in the salty wind, just as fast as the workmen can dab red-lead paint over the rust. To the right, the lights of Rosyth Naval Dockyard ripple across the black waters below, writhing like multicolored eels on the surface of the coal black.

"Have you ever done a Scottish Hogmanay, Terry?"

"Aye, and you?"

"No. I was here last year, but I had the flu. I hear it's bigger than Christmas."

"Oh aye, it's the big event all right—usually takes up the whole week. People renew friendships, bury the hatchet with old enemies—hopefully not in their heads, sing 'Auld Lang Syne,' and all get steaming drunk. It's great!"

"What's this 'first-footing' thing about?"

"Well, after the bells at midnight, thousands of folk go off to 'first foot' good luck into their neighbors' houses. Everybody's door's wide open to everyone, but a tall, dark, man who brings you a piece of coal is considered the best luck of all. He gets a free whisky."

"What if it's steam coal?"

"He gets a free kick in the arse!"

We laugh our way up the steadily rising curve of the bridge pathway. A stream of cars speeds by, honking and hooting in honor of the festivities to come. Across the center line of the old rail bridge, a mile away, a commuter train clanks toward Edinburgh. Dwarfed by the gigantic bridge span, its lit windows look like a string of tiny fairy lights twinkling in and out of the iron latticework of the Victorian marvel. Everybody seems to be in a festive mood and heading to the capital city. The excitement is infectious and infuses me with the buoyant feeling that my real adventure is about to begin.

"You know, Terry, it's amazing how a pagan festival like Hogmanay has survived all the squabbling over the calendar and the religious wars and—"

I suddenly realize I'm talking to myself. Halfway across the bridge, Terry has stopped some distance behind me. He stands motionless, staring at a wreck marker buoy, blinking out in the watery darkness. I walk back to him.

"What's up?"

"It's so lonely. My God, it's so lonely," he repeats, as the buoy clangs out its doleful warning bell.

"What is?"

"The buoy out there, on its own. It's so . . . isolated . . . so lonely."

I've never seen Terry like this. He holds on tight to the iron railing like a condemned man in a death row prison cell. The wind whips tears from his face.

"So, so lonely!"

I start to move him along, but he resists my efforts. I put an arm around him.

"Terry, come on, mate. We're nearly in Edinburgh. We've got to meet up with Gordie before the pubs shut. Come on, man. I'm so thirsty, I've got cactuses on my tongue!" I laugh, trying to make light of what I can't understand.

I steer him away from the spot. He comes reluctantly. Without another word, we descend the gently sloping pathway leaving the bridge that leads down to the bus stop on the Lothian side of the Forth.

Whatever had come over Terry on that toll bridge, he feels very relieved to be off it. He sits hunched up in the bus shelter, a cigarette trembling in his fingers.

"I'm sorry about that, back there. I don't know what came over me."

"Was it the height? It's one hell of a way up off the water."

"No, it's not that."

"What then?"

The arrival of the bus spares Terry the discomfort of answering. We climb aboard and he makes to go to sleep. I let him be, but I'm left with the certain feeling that if I hadn't been with him on the parapet, he would have jumped to his death and I don't know why.

"Failte gu Dun Eideann—Welcome to the City of Edinburgh" reads the roadside sign and beyond it, bejeweled with sparkling lights, the dark contours of the ancient capital slumber on the Plains of Lothian like a sleeping giant. Not that he'll get much sleep tonight: this giant is about to awakened by a million New Year's revelers.

Even though it's packed to the gunwales, it's easy to spot Gordon Jones in the Café Royal bar, as he's six foot two. He stands at the top of the steps dressed in a World War II tan sheepskin flying jacket, which, along with his long nose and lank brown shoulder-length hair, lends him the appearance of an Afghan hound looking for mischief. At five foot eight, his partner in crime, Chris Dale, is a less imposing figure, but I take an immediate liking to this bespectacled young jokester from Cheshire, who, like the cat in *Alice in Wonderland,* often disappears but leaves his smile behind.

With a whisky in his hand, Terry has cheered up considerably. He and Gordie are deeply engrossed in discussing the sex life of the arctic tern, a subject that they both seem to have prodigious knowledge of.

"This doesn't seem to belong to anyone," says Chris, taking a huge slug out of the creamy top of a pint of Guinness that had sat on the bar unattended for half an hour.

"Oh my God—I hope it's not his!" I say, staring over Chris's shoulder to where a tartan-clad monster is slowly filling the enormous doorway that leads to the toilets.

The gigantic hairy creature stares incredulously at the empty spot on the bar where his pint had sat. Only a wet ring remains as a clue to it having existed.

"Oh sweet Jesus, it's Sawney Bean," I hear myself whimper.

"WHAUR'S MY GUINNESS?!" A fist resembling a leg of mutton covered in red ivy crashes down on the solid oak bar, sending glasses flying skyward like badly launched bottle rockets.

"WHAUR'S MY GUINNESS?!" the monster screams again, thrusting a flaming red beard into each of a dozen faces along the bar. He grabs the one he thinks is a likely suspect.

"I didn't touch it! I don't drink Guinness—it's disgusting!" The huge hand loosens its throttling grasp on the innocent man.

"DISGUSTING, IS IT? NO AS DISGUSTING AS YOU, YA WEE NAFF!"

The "wee naff" is discarded to the side like a used tissue, and the brutish glare descends toward us. Only Chris, Gordie, and I are left. Terry has already fled.

"WHAUR'S MY GUINNESS?!" The great mass of kilted death is making his inexorable way in our direction.

"Oh shit—RUN!" Chris shouts, plowing through the crowd like an icebreaker. I need no encouragement, I'm gone, leaving Gordie behind. Out on the dark cobbled street, Terry is in the lead, Chris is well ahead of me, running like the wind. At least I'm not the last one, I'm thinking, when Gordon's long spindly legs sprint past me and suddenly I am.

"COME BACK AND FIGHT, YE BASTARDS!" the giant roars into the night, his voice lost in a peel of bells. From all corners of the city an enormous cheer goes up, joined by a great ethereal sound filling the night sky above Leith docks. Like the *vox humana* of an immense celestial organ, the horns, hooters, and steam whistles of a hundred moored ships blend together in one enormous chord to welcome in the New Year.

✦ Chapter 17 ✦

Burke and Hare cam doon the stair
Wi' a lady in a box . . .
Tae tak her to doctor Knox.
Nineteenth-century street kids' rhyme

EDINBURGH, MYSTIC MISTRESS AND NEWFOUND FRIEND, RISES
gently from the salt-soaked cobbles of Leith docks like Aphrodite from
the sea. The medieval Old Town uncoils in concentric castellations, descending the high castle rock until it meets the New Town, a cascade of
Georgian crescents, unfolding across the Lothian plain in classical symmetry, stretching far distant to the verdant folds of the Pentland Hills.

In summer, this promontory city sits snug and content like a dozing
dog on a long afternoon. When winter blows, she bides brisk and
defiant, cradling her offspring in warm nooks and hollows, whilst bar-
ing her black basalt teeth to the gnawing north wind. No matter what
the season, the ancient capital breathes an air suffused with the health-
giving aromas of fragrant malt and tangy yeasts, emanating from bak-
ery and brewery alike.

Legend has the city founded in the mist-shrouded Celtic past by two
Irish giants named Gog and Magog. Castle turrets, steeples, minarets,
and monuments crown every hilltop.

New Year's Day has passed and gone, but the frenzy of the January
sales has still not abated, as we four friends wend our way through the
crowds to take in the sights. We won't be buying anything, but it's fun
to wander among the throng. Here are the "vigorous people, proud in

spirit, skillful at their work," who have the "inborn genius for commerce" that Himilco the Carthaginian had reported.

Princes Street, bustling as a beehive, was once the shop front of the British imperial world and still teems with chocolate-box Dickensian emporiums, pungent with the scent of lavender and beeswax.

Top-hatted doormen and blue-uniformed commissionaries ply the brass handles of massive oaken doors, ushering the spending hoards into the great open vistas of Victorian department stores, whose proud boasts are engraved on their windows: "By Royal Appointment to Her Majesty the Queen, purveyors of . . . Whisky, Woolens, Tartan, Bagpipes, Aberdeen Angus Beef, Wild Mountain Venison, Salmon, Spring Trout, Pheasant and Bonnie Prince Charlie's Petticoat-tailed real butter Shortbread."

"There you go," says Gordie, acting the tour guide. "There it is, the once great Highland Celtic culture, condensed, canned, and sanitized for consumption by Sassenach fops and the delicately stomached British upper classes."

"Ah, but despite the tartanalia, the Georgian New Town is beautiful, Gordie."

"True!"

We walk up the Mound. A man-made street, built over what Gordon tells us was the city's medieval garbage dump, snakes across the now drained Nor loch, below the castle, joining the old city with the new.

"This is the Royal Mile and that's Deacon Brodie's Tavern, once owned by William Brodie, who was a pillar of society by day and a house burglar at night. He eventually got caught burgling the Excise House, and that brass plaque in the road shows where he had the pleasure of being hung on the very gallows that he had designed himself."

"Wasn't he the bloke who inspired Robert Louis Stevenson to write *Jekyll and Hyde?*" asks Chris Dale.

"Aye, and Stevenson also wrote a wee song much sung by street kids:

> *Oh Deacon Brodie,*
> *Somebody should have told ye*
> *Or were ye just perverse,*
> *Louping fences after dark,*

Ye'll whiles get snaggit by yer sock
And land upon yer arse."

We walk on. Halfway down the cobbled flagstones of Edinburgh's Royal Mile Gordie stops. He points to an ornamental heart shape picked out in colored stones set into the ground outside St. Giles Cathedral.

"That's the Heart of Midlothian. It's the only place in Scotland where you can legally spit. Folks do it all the time for good luck!"

We sit for a while watching the passersby to see if it's true. Within the space of five minutes, three men, two women, and a child have all gobbed onto the splattered stone heart. A group of American tourists are appalled by the spectacle, especially when they see a young policewoman dribbling a plume of saliva onto the pavement before wishing them a nice day.

Wandering down the High Street, Gordon reminds us that we're actually walking on the roof of a hidden street beneath.

"It's hollow under here, all the way down from the castle to Holyrood Palace."

"Why's that?" asks Terry.

"In the seventeenth century, the present street was built over the ancient alleyways below because the wealthy townspeople thought the poor folk in the rat-infested lower levels carried the plague."

"What happened to them?"

"Well, entombed by their fellow citizens, they died in their hundreds. I've been down there—it's amazing. Mary King's Close looks fairly modern. It has houses and a butcher's shop with the original meat hooks and what they think was a whorehouse because it has an iron-clad front door with a little spy hole in it."

"Are there any bones lying about?"

"No, just piles of dry dust in the corners of the kitchens and bedrooms—that's all that's left of the people. The bones were removed for burial in the last century. Lots of ghosts, though."

"When did they do this?"

"The last time was around 1645, that's when they sealed off two hundred families, condemned them to certain death by starvation. But fear of bubonic plague led to hysteria in those days, and wicked measures were taken against it."

"That's true. I read that in Aberdeen they closed the city gates and shot a cannon at anyone coming within a mile of the town walls," says I.

"I bet that was effective!"

"You ain't kiddin'!"

"Did you ever hear of Burke and Hare?" Gordie asks.

"Yeah, they were a pair of itinerant Irishmen who made a living digging up freshly buried corpses and selling them to the medical school, weren't they?"

"Just so, Billy. They sold cadavers for Dr. Knox and his students to dissect. He must have known it was illegal, but if he did, he kept quiet and just paid for more."

"So what happened?"

"Burke and Hare realized that if Knox couldn't give a monkey's where the bodies came from, why should they? They considered themselves legitimate businessmen and called themselves resurrectionists, but digging up corpses was hard work and they might get the jail for grave robbing, too. Murder was an easier option and if they just killed beggars and other lowlifes, no one would miss them. They were arrested in 1828 after killing a pretty young prostitute named Mary, well known and loved by the City Fathers. Hare turned King's evidence and implicated Burke. Burke went to the gallows and Hare disappeared."

Gordie is not only taller than us, he's a couple of years older, too. This he revels in. He plays the part of the older brother, with a grace and eloquence that belies the fact that he's only twenty-three.

"When you're as old as me, son, you'll understand!" he jibes in a rich baritone. His nickname is Gordie, the Knower of All Things, the Old Tome, the man who was advanced in years when the world was still a slime!

At the Netherbow, brass plates in the roadway mark the site of the Old Town's watchtowers and its eastern gate. A house on the corner bears a plaque proclaiming that it was once owned by a certain John Knox.

"Is this the same guy who bought the dead bodies?" Terry asks Gordon.

"No, this was the Protestant preacher in the 1560s who wrote the pamphlet *The First Blast of the Trumpet against the Monstrous Regiment of Women*. 'Women are weak, frail, impatient, feeble and foolish creatures,' he said, 'and any rule by them is contrary to God and repugnant to nature!'"

"What a charmer. It makes you wonder if he even had a mother at all."

"Aye, Billy. A statue of the old fraud stood here until recently. He was removed to prevent people from pissing on him and pelting him with the dregs of their fish-and-chip suppers after the pubs close on Friday nights."

"Fish-and-chips sounds good, Gordie."

"Gordon, I'm getting peckish, too—history makes me hungry."

I can smell the fish-and-chip shop long before we get there. An eddying breeze carries the tang of malt vinegar and hot cooking oil. Inside, we join the queue as the cook slides a pizza into the hot fat fryer to heat it up.

"Dear God, they deep-fry pizzas!" Chris whispers.

"Pizzas? They'll deep-fry Mars Bars too, if you ask them!"

"That's disgusting," mutters Chris.

"Talking of which, a bloke once told me that a haggis is made out of a sheep's stomach, full of oatmeal and chopped-up unmentionables. What do you reckon they are, Gordon?"

"I told you before, it's not safe to ask!" says Terry.

"They're a sheep's sexual organs," says the Knower of All Things.

"Are you happy now you know?" smirks Terry.

"No."

Consuming a carryout supper while wandering down the cobblestone streets of Edinburgh is a cultural icon. People of all social classes can be seen promenading the Georgian crescents eating out of newspapers. The only difference being, snobs prefer their fish suppers wrapped in the *Glasgow Herald* or the *Scotsman* and wouldn't be seen dead with the more proletarian *Edinburgh Evening News*.

"Gie us a chip, mister?" a scruffy wee street kid barks as we pass by.

"Thanks, mister, you're a barry gadgie!" he smiles, grabbing a handful.

The Scots aren't stingy with their fish: you get at least two good-sized fillets, with a sprinkling of salt and soaked in malt vinegar or thick brown sauce.

"The meal that defeated Hitler!" says Chris, tucking into his fish-and-chips.

"How d'ya mean?" asks Terry, with a puzzled look.

"See, back in the Second World War, fish and potatoes were amongst the few things that weren't rationed. Farmers could grow spuds almost anywhere and the lads in the fishing industry kept the cod rolling in, so for a few pennies, people could buy a hot meal to keep them going—nutritious, too."

"Blimey!"

"Yeah. If old Adolf had bombed the tattie fields and sunk more trawlers, Britain would have been starved into submission in no time."

Before discarding his empty wrapper, Chris reads aloud the head-line on the front page: "'Move to Knock Down Cemetery Wall Angers Residents.' That'll be an interesting town meeting, make no bones about it!"

Chris Dale is a character. He looks like John Lennon but sounds like Ringo Starr. He works in the Lever Brothers factory in Liverpool, where he claims to be one of the people who polish the little blue speck-les in the soap powder. If Gordie, Terry, and myself are the Three Musketeers, Chris is our D'Artagnan, a little younger than us, still liv-ing at home with his parents and keeping down the steady job that he must return to now the holidays are over.

"I don't want to go back to Liverpool," he mopes, packing his shoul-der bag back at the flat.

"I don't want to go back to Aberdeen," says Terry.

"Me neither," I add.

"Then don't!" says Gordon. "You can all stay here. I don't mind."

What a temptation. Gordon's attic apartment in Stockbridge is bright, airy, and smells of pigment, turpentine, and rich linseed oil. There is no phone, no TV, and no bath, but—a thing to marvel at—he has an inside toilet! I almost faint with the sheer luxury of it all. Last term Gordon attended the art school. Now he is an ex-art student, dis-illusioned with academia, as the spare room full of half-completed oil paintings can attest. Gordie has a vast selection of books, many of which deal with wizardry, the paranormal, and the occult. His interest in sorcery and the cryptic is benign. He does not approve of the black arts or their practitioners. Instead, he is in love with the antiquity and allure of Edinburgh. He calls it "the City of Enchantment," and it is charged with a special magic that crackles like static electricity in the crisp air.

On the morn, Chris reluctantly departs for his work down south. Terry and I have no work to return to; redundancy in the fishing industry has hit an all-time high.

"Don't you need to go back to Aberdeen to get your gear?"

"We're wearing all the gear we have!"

"Hell's bells!" says Gordie, who has more clothes than Liberace.

Gordon Jones treats life with all the eruptive flamboyance of the wizard Merlin in a medieval pageant; nothing is too insignificant for his artist's eye and inquisitive mind. Since leaving college, Gordon has been unemployed, but he's not worried. Friends of his own a string of basement and street-level shops, in nearby St. Stephen's Street, that will shortly be renovated. This will hopefully provide jobs for us all.

To get Terry and me acquainted with our new habitat, Gordie whisks us from one end of Edinburgh to the other, explaining each aspect of the metropolis in a whirlwind of history, anecdote, and folk tale. The capital city holds few secrets from him. He is well versed in its glorious antiquity, doughty courage, and timeless refinement. These qualities Gordon exposes as a rich vein of golden legend, rippling through the darker enigmas of the city's tormented past.

High above on the Castle Rock, Edinburgh's mighty fortress towers abruptly on a wedge of black volcanic basalt. Several hundred feet above the town it glowers, threatening or guarding, depending on your perspective. It's still a garrison for the English army, and the Union Jack flutters from its parapets as a reminder to Scottish people that the Celts are no longer in control.

"That's where we're heading next," says Gordon, looking at his watch. "I want you to see something. Forward!" he cries, leading us in a march up the High Street, across the esplanade, and up to the gates of Edinburgh Castle.

The British army sentries at the portcullis pay us no heed. Neither do the stone statues of the great Scottish patriots, William Wallace and Robert the Bruce, either side of the drawbridge, who, in days of yore, would have cleaved the heads off these Brits and drunk wine out of their skulls.

On the parapets, Gordie shows us Mons Meg, a huge-mouthed cannon that took seventy pounds of black powder to prime it and could shoot a cannonball the weight of a cow over a mile. He tells us it was used at the siege of Roxburgh Castle and points out a fractured piece at the top of the barrel, where a lump of iron flew off and killed King James II of Scotland in 1460.

"Serves him right for standing too close to it," mumbles Terry. "Hey, will you look at that now!" he smiles, as a posse of young American girls begins taking happy snaps of each other sitting astride the ancient black cannons of the battery.

On the north side of the castle defenses, overlooking Princes Street Gardens, a corporal of the guard marches with clockwork precision to a modern twenty-five-pound field cannon pointing directly over the battlements toward the Georgian New Town. He carries a long brass cylinder that he snaps into the breech of the artillery piece. Next he produces a pocketwatch and stands to attention studying the dial. The soldier remains motionless until, with a cry and a lightning-fast movement of his white-gloved hand, the cannon discharges with an ear-numbing roar. The echo of the shot rolls across the city and away to the hills beyond.

"Holy Christ! What the fuck was that?" splutters Terry, who was still gawping at the American girls and had seen none of the preparations.

"It's the one o'clock gun," says Gordie. "They fire it every day."

"When?" Terry says, fingering his ears.

"At one o'clock, ya numpty, when d'ya think?"

"Blimey! I thought he was shelling the city—I nearly shit my pants."

An hour later we are across town, standing outside the Scottish Museum of Antiquities in Queen Street.

"If the one o'clock gun had fired a live shell, this is where it would have landed," Gordon reports, with that confident knowledge that seldom requires questioning. The museum's collection of Pictish and Celtic artifacts is mind-boggling. Entire rooms are crammed with gold torques once worn around the necks of warriors, intricate brooches that maybe pinned together the cloaks of maidens, and golden armlets that once adorned the princes of the ancient tribes of Alba.

"All this has been turned up by the plow or discovered by workmen digging drains and the like. This must only be a fraction of what's lying undiscovered under the ground. Just think," dreams Gordon.

I do think. I ponder that perhaps the idea of King Solomon's mines being in Scotland might not be so far-fetched; taking into consideration the tons of gold exported, plus the treasures looted by the Romans and the Vikings, the amount of gold Scotland once produced would have been staggering. It's little wonder Angus and I found bugger all up in Kildonan.

The central hall of the museum houses a display of Pictish standing stones. All are etched with strange indecipherable symbols that tell a tale that none so far has been able to unravel.

"Do you know what these are?" Gordon points to the lines and notches incised into the stones.

"Yes, it's the writing known as Ogham. Named after Ogma, the Celtic god of eloquence and literature," I say with certainty, having seen the Book of Ballymote, in which ancient Irish monks had recorded the myriad meaning of these strokes.

"Yes, the Ogham can be deciphered. It's personal names mostly and 'here lies the body of,' et cetera, but these are the real puzzle." He indicates a group of flat-faced stones bearing similar sets of carved symbols. Although from many different parts of Scotland and the northern isles, the stones display a constant theme. Often the main symbol is a crescent moon with a V-shaped arrow superimposed upon it. Others have emblems resembling a pair of spectacles with a zigzag arrow producing a Z sign through the bridge. Some stones have both symbols, and others have variations on the motifs with the arrows cutting through other objects, such as snakes and things that look like pairs of trousers. I have never seen anything like them. I'm intrigued.

Gordie tells me of an American lassie called Marianna Lines, who has a wonderful knowledge of the Pictish stones and has developed a unique way of taking rubbings from them, using white cotton cloth and the natural dyes found in native mosses and plant fibers. This process gives a true image of the inscribed details without causing any harm to the integrity of the stone.

I feel a strange power emanating from these obscure monuments. They transmit a homing signal like an emergency radio positioning beacon.

Can anyone hear us? they whisper. *Is there anybody out there?*

Yes, I'm here, I think to myself, but I don't understand what you're trying to tell me.

Seek your destiny, the voice says, in a cadence that sounds familiar to me. *It is up to your generation to take up the struggle for the resurgence of our people.*

Yes, I recognize the call now. These are the words my father uttered, when I left on my strange odyssey long ago.

The stones fall silent.

"Where's Terry?"

"Oh, God, Gordie! You made me jump!"

"Yeah, you were in a world of your own for a while there. Anyway, we better find Terry, he's wandered off somewhere."

"Yeah, he's been doing a lot of that recently. Do you think he seems preoccupied?"

"I dunno, Bill, I never knew him when he was just occupied."

We discover Terry in an annex of the main building. He stands transfixed before a great oaken black guillotine whose rusty blade had removed the heads of a great many religious dissenters in the sixteenth century.

"The Iron Maiden" says the sign. "Fore-runner of the French Guillotine."

"Get me out of here," he whispers.

❖ Chapter 18 ❖

Speleology is the art of climbing a mountain from the inside.
The Knower of All Things

SPRING BEGINS WITH THE DECIMALIZATION OF THE BRITISH currency. The old coins we have known so well are replaced with tiny new pence mintings that don't even look like real money. It's a shame. I'll miss the old pennies, even though they had the likes of King William of Orange, or the usurping Hanovarian bastards, Georges I–IV, on their worn faces. Two issues came out in the reign of Queen Victoria. The first, showing the young queen with her hair tied back, was called "the bun penny." The second, showing her in mourning, not for the millions of famine deaths in Ireland, but for the passing of her consort, Prince Albert, was known as "the Widow of Windsor." After them came the various fornicating lineage of Victoria, Edward VII, George V, the Nazi-loving Edward VIII, George VI, and finally Queen Elizabeth II, whom the Scots won't even recognize under that title:

> *Scotland hasnae got a king*
> *And she hasnae got a queen*
> *How can there be Elizabeth the twa*
> *When the first yin's never been?*

Aye, the Scots have a long memory and mind well that when Elizabeth I ruled over England, Scotland's monarch was the ill-fated Mary, Queen of Scots.

I continue to muse over the new coinage. It will take some time to learn that now there are 100 pence in a pound and not 240 as there has been since Roman times. The silver sixpence, known as the tanner, is gone. With it the copper ha'penny, the brass thruppeny bit, the shilling or bob, the florin or two-shilling piece, and the half-crown, also called the half-dollar. LSD we called our money: Lire, Silarius, Denarius—pounds, shillings, and pence. Now LSD was taking on a new meaning, and it wasn't Latin either.

Binning is a popular, though illegal, pastime and a social necessity. Gordon, Terry, and myself make several nocturnal circuits of the neighborhood dustbins on bucket night, and what we find helps furnish the spartan attic flat.

This night our haul is spectacular and includes a World War I gas mask, a pair of handcuffs, a cast-iron kettle, a hobbyhorse on the end of a wheeled shaft, and a huge stuffed tiger with its tail missing. For a laugh, I put on the mask, and the red breathing cylinder dangles from its ribbed rubber hose like an elephant's trunk. Gordon, handcuffed to a kettle, rides his hobbyhorse up the midnight pavements of Anne Street. Behind him, Terry carries the dilapidated tiger over his shoulders in the style known as "the fireman's lift." A young man in the corner garden is attempting to light a cigarette from a street lamp when he catches sight of us. He slides down the pole and stares at us, crazy-faced and fidgety.

"You're one of me, aren't you?" he says, obviously hallucinating.

"We're all in your mind," says Gordon, waving the handcuffed kettle at him.

The young chap throws his arms in the air and screams off.

"Ferocious aggravations! Ferocious aggravations!" he howls into the night.

Then, in a fit of derring-do, the acidhead scales the iron fence at the end of the road and batters his way into the shrubbery, where a loud splash announces his arrival in the river called the Water of Leith.

"Bloody idiot," says Terry. "Fancy trying to light a fag from an electric lamp."

"Freaky, man!" I mumble inside the gas mask.

"That's not freaky. Tomorrow we'll do something really freaky. Come on, we better get an early night."

The following morning, Gordon leaves early and returns sometime later in a borrowed car with a pile of odd-looking equipment.

"Right, lads, come on, let's go caving."

Soon we are crossing the Forth bridge into Fife. I notice that Terry doesn't reference the midway point where he'd stood the night of his panic attack. He just looks straight ahead. Maybe he's forgotten, or perhaps it was the darkness that time that scared him.

Once in Fife, the motorcar switches through a twist of lanes until stopping in an overgrown wayside.

"Are you claustrophobic, Bill?" Gordie asks.

"No, I don't think so. I grew up in a sixteen-foot caravan. There wasn't enough room for claustrophobia." Gordie smiles and turns to my pal.

"How about you, Terry, any problems in that department?"

"Erm . . . no . . . I don't think so either. I don't know, I've never been underground before."

Dressed in hard hats and overalls, we sort through a pile of miners' lamps and batteries, until we are kitted out with a full set of each. Gordie takes a rope out of the trunk of the car and signals for us to follow him across the road and down a steeply inclined track.

"This is the old railway line into the mine. They had a big steam engine set up here that pulled the full tubs of limestone up to the surface."

We walk through the weed-infested tangles of rusty red iron. Before us, the great black orifice of Ninelums Limestone Mine craters the side of an overgrown hill.

As we descend into the dark, the dank smell of soil and earthy decay gives way to the chill piquancy of dry, dusty chalk. On this level, the main chamber is huge. Radiating from its central hub are numbered roads, wide enough for big trucks to drive. Old signposts betray their wartime secrets: "15 inch HEX" reads one.

"What's that mean? I don't like the sound of it, Gordie."

"Don't worry. It's nothing to do with witchcraft. It's where they stored artillery shells during the Second World War, fifteen-inch-high explosives, probably for the coastal batteries protecting the Forth bridge."

"Yeah, this one must be for the Bofors antiaircraft gun." Terry's helmet lamp illuminates "Bofors Cannon Ack-Ack."

We spiral downward into the narrow sections, where for the first time, in the hush of this immense dark cathedral, the sound of steadily dripping water becomes distinct.

"Stop here! We need to rope up for the next descent—it's a bit tricky."

The thin nylon cord is attached to the carabiners on our safety belts, giving about fifteen feet between us. With Gordon in the lead, Terry in the middle, and me bringing up the rear, we look like a string of Christmas tree lights twinkling in the darkness of the cavern.

Scrambling our way across a sloping bank of rough, boulder-strewn scree, we reach the ominously named Dead Section. Here, the steep angle of the shelf inclines toward an immense still ocean of silent gray water. I try to ascertain the size of the flooded cavity, but the beam from my headlight is lost in the black nothingness above the lake. It gives me the chills.

The odd thing about caving is that you can only see where your head is pointing, and using the helmet lamp takes a lot of getting used to. Terry stumbles along like a drunk, his oversized helmet slipping over his eyes, or falling off his head altogether.

"Hang on, Gordie. I can't get . . . Gordie, hold on a minute . . . oh bollocks!" He bumbles along in front of me, like a rag doll on a puppet string. Twice I stop to help him up, twice we get pulled over by Gordon, who's lurching ahead like a dog on a scent.

"Come on, lads, stop fooling about. There's lots to see and not much time!" Our fearless leader marches on, over rocky banks, down crevasses, and finally into a narrow limestone shaft, from which the regular ping of water droplets echoes like pistol shots along the glassy calcite walls. Here we get a breather.

"This is beer can alley—and there's the can." Gordon points to the source of the noise. Standing under a steady drip falling thirty feet from the passage roof, a once red MacEwan's Export beer can now petrifies under a creamy-white shroud of calcium carbonate.

"That's too weird. Can anything get calcited, Gordie?"

"Well, Bill, it depends on what it's made of. If it's hard enough not to get dissolved by the water, I suppose you could calcify most anything. I'll show you what I mean. It's about half a mile along this passage."

Farther down the marbled tunnel, the roar of falling water becomes deafening. A gushing stream of freezing water cascades down an old wooden ladder, which is stuck into the open top of a large oak barrel. The wood is no longer visible, but it's still there, solidified in the calcite, which gives the two objects the appearance of being carved out of tallow candle wax. At the end of the long passage comes another surprise.

"Halt! This is the tricky bit I told you about."

Gordie stands at the top of the rim of a vast yawning chasm of incalculable depth, a gaping ulcer in the limestone duodenum of Ninelums Mine. I drop a stone into the abyss and hear nothing. Terry stares at me, wild-eyed.

"I can't do this!" he says, shaking his head at Gordie.

"It's not as bad as it looks. We just traverse that ledge around the lip of the hole—there's plenty of handholds. Follow me!"

Roped together, we don't have much choice. Gordie drops down onto a six-inch-wide shelf edging the chasm and begins circumnavigating the crater. Terry is still staring at me in terror. I can't see the whites of his eyes anymore.

"I can't do this—I'm scared!"

As if in answer, the rope around his waist yanks him over the edge and he screams, grabbing at my boot. I hold him steady on the rope, until he gets a grip.

"Come on, Terry, it's easy."

Gordie pulls at the rope, Terry follows, clinging like a spider to the crevice-filled rock face. Then it's my turn. Inching along at the end of the rope, I'm not only scared of falling myself, I'm frightened of pulling my mates down with me. I'm sure this hole reaches clear down to hell.

"This is the dumbest thing I've done in my life!" I mumble to the nothingness.

In the cold of the underground world, I'm sweating so profusely that steam is rising off me. At the end of the traverse, I see I'm not the only one, but in Terry's case, the steam is rising from the crotch of his trousers.

"I peed me pants," he says, with an apologetic smile.

"Okay, lads, we'll take a break here so Terry can sort himself out, and then I'll take you on to the pretty bit."

Gordon opens his rucksack and produces sandwiches, pop, and a bar of chocolate. We take our repast sitting in a white crystal cave where long, dripping icicles of living rock probe downward, seeking their kinsmen below.

"Stalagmites and stalactites—which are which, Gordie?"

"That's easy to remember, Bill: mites go up, tites come down!"

We finish our meal in silence, listening to the echoing *plink-plonk* of a hundred water droplets hitting the rocks and pools below.

"Sounds like a Japanese orchestra," says Terry, trying to put a brave face on things.

Gordie looks at a hand-drawn map, following the outline of passages and galleries with his finger.

"We are at the midway point now—about two miles in and a mile down. The next section is a climb up toward the organ gallery . . . here . . . but first I want to show you this."

We follow Gordon to the mouth of a long, low tunnel, bricked off halfway across its opening. Behind the brick wall is what looks like a canal extending off into the immeasurable darkness.

"Touch the surface of the water, Terry."

Terry stretches out his hand and finds himself immediately up to the elbow in cold water.

"That's amazing! The surface isn't where you think it is!"

"No, it's an optical illusion. A friend and I discovered it last time we were here."

"Bloody hell, that water's freezing." Terry has a wet sleeve to contend with, along with his wet pants.

"Onwards and upwards! We've a good way to go yet." Gordie is staring at the ceiling of a mighty domed cavern. "Do you see that crack in the roof, up by the edge of that ledge? Well, that's where we're headed."

Terry is getting nervous again.

"I can't climb up there—I'd bloody well kill myself!"

"Yeah, Gordie, Terry's right. It's no climb for beginners like us. Isn't there another way up?"

"Yeah, if you like. You can follow this passage around in a spiral till it comes out in a vault above where we are. I'll meet you up there." He casts off his belaying rope and begins free climbing up the glistening rock.

"Gordon, I want to go back. I've had enough fun for one day . . . pissed me pants an' all." Poor Terry is starting to shiver, whether from fear or cold, it's hard to tell.

Gordie gazes down at us from his perch on the top of the ledge.

"We can't go back—there's not enough power in the batteries to make it. The only way out is up." He wriggles into a crevice near the top of the dome. Soon only one foot is visible, and then he's gone altogether.

Terry looks frightened and busies himself in coiling the rope.

"I don't like this, I don't like all this dark. We could die down here and no one would be any the wiser."

"We are not going to die, but we better get a move on—I notice my lamp's beginning to yellow."

"What's that mean?"

"It means the battery's getting low."

I take the lead, with Terry cursing along behind me. The path isn't too bad and the gradient rises gently. Ten minutes later, we have circled around and are in the organ gallery, above where we started. There is no sign of Gordon.

"Gordie! Gordie! Where are you?" Terry's voice reverberates off the barren walls.

We stand in silence listening for a reply; we hear nothing but the echoes of steadily dripping stalactites.

"Gordie! Gordie, can you hear me?"

"Of course I can bloody hear you. Give me a hand—I'm stuck!"

The muffled voice issues from a cervical cleft in the face of the rock some five feet off the ground. We stumble to the hole and peer in. Gordon had been maneuvering with one arm stretched out, pushing his hat and lamp in front of him, but now he is wedged in tight.

"It's my battery pack. I need to unclip the cell and hand it on to you. Can you reach the helmet? If you can, give it a tug and the battery should pull free."

"Can you not crawl back?"

"No, that's worse. I'll have to come out this way—I've done it before."

Alarmingly, Gordie's lamp is also beginning to go yellow. Catching hold of the helmet, I haul on the thin cable and the battery pack pops out from under Gordon's waist.

"Gordie, hang on to the wire and we can pull you out."

"I don't think it will be strong enough—it might break. Use the rope!"

"Terry, give me the rope and I'll try to chuck the end to Gordon!"

"The rope? Erm . . . I don't know what I did with it. I think I left it on a rock back where we were."

"Okay, I'll go get it! Now don't you go anywhere. Stay put, okay?"

Terry sits beneath the hole like a troll guarding a cave. I shuffle back down the circular walkway. The rope is lying where he left it. I snatch it up and hurry back, not before time either. Terry isn't holding up well in the crisis; he sits morosely smoking a cigarette and muttering something about his curse.

"Come on, Terry, look sharp! Make a bowline loop on the end of the line and chuck it to Gordie."

Terry makes the knot and pitches a coil of rope into the hole. The cast reaches Gordon, but in doing so, knocks the end off Terry's cigarette, which disappears down the open collar of his overalls. Terry's yowls and accompanying dance take him over to the pool side, where he ladles handfuls of water down his neck. Now he's more wet than dry. He looks at me balefully, expecting a witty comment. I say nothing.

"Hey, you guys, what's happening?" comes the voice from the crevice.

"It's okay, Gordie. Now get the loop around your wrist and breath out!"

"Okay, Terry, PULL! Gordie, PUSH! Okay, once more, PUSH!"

Like veterinarians birthing a troublesome calf, we delve into the orifice, tugging hard on the rope. Groans and curses echo in the yellow womb of the tunnel. With a final contraction, the rock delivers forth. First a head, followed by heaving shoulders, two long spindly legs, and a pair of mud-encrusted boots.

"Congratulations, Terry, it's a boy!" I joke, but he's not in the mood for humor.

Gordie struggles to his feet, rubbing the circulation back into his legs. He limps off into the darkness, putting on his helmet and lamp.

"This is what I wanted to show you," he says, turning his headlight onto an immense ensemble of silver, blue, and orange columns of calcified rock, rising from the shallow lagoon beneath like the manifold pipes of a great cathedral organ. We stand in awe, three tiny black dots silhouetted by the light reflecting from the magnificent edifice.

"It's beautiful," says Terry.

"This is another place we found—look at the bottom of the pool!" He indicates the rock surface just beneath the water, where millions of drips have formed irregular rings of pearly-white calcium deposits, making the whole area seem to be floating on top of a giant lace doily. It is beautiful.

"We better think about getting out of here, Gordie. I'm already switched to backup power and my lamp's beginning to yellow."

"I know! Let's call it a day or a night—it's impossible to tell which down here. I think it's this way."

He takes off up a previously unnoticed passage. Ten minutes later, we're back in the organ gallery.

"Bugger, I could have sworn that was the right way."

He stares uneasily at the map. Terry is looking even more agitated and has gone ominously silent.

"We have to find a passage which forks left and right and there's a cairn of five stones marking the left way, which is the right way. Okay, Terry, switch off your lamp and we'll conserve that battery for any emergency."

"Oh, so being lost in a fuckin' great mine with no extra batteries isn't an emergency?"

Terry is trembling again. He grabs Gordon's arm.

"Look, Gordie, I lied when I said I wasn't claustrophobic. I fuckin' hate it down here—I think we're all going to die!"

"No, we're not. Anyway, I've got two candles, if we run out of power. Now, come on, I think it's this way." He gestures and marches off into the gloom.

"Terry, do as he says. He's the only one who can get us out of here. Switch your lamp off—I'll stick close behind you."

We follow the flashes from Gordie's headlamp into a dank catacomb that narrows as it climbs into a dusty, dry vault.

"I can smell earth, soil, we must be near the surface!"

Gordon scans the three tunnels radiating away from the central vault. He strikes a match in the entrance of the first tunnel. The flame burns steadily upright. He moves to the next, but it's the same story. At the mouth of the farthest passage, the flame flickers, bending away from the draft.

"This is it!"

Gordie's lamp picks out the five-stone marker cairn and we scramble into the tunnel. Soon we are on all fours. The passageway becomes a low crawl about eighteen inches in width, then it narrows to an earthen burrow that pays out in a tiny circular igloo of roots and damp dirt. Gordie tears at the rough, domed roof, cascading clods of grass and boulders down into the shaft. Cramped behind him in the hole, I am engulfed by the falling detritus.

Terry is almost entirely buried in the stale confines of the tunnel cavity, but with a last effort, the sweet sea air rushes in from the Firth of Forth and a sparkle of silver stars appears in a circle of early evening twilight in the indigo sky above.

Gordon wriggles up out of the ground. His boots vanish from above my head and as quickly, two long arms come reaching down, pulling me up into the middle of a lush meadow of long rough grass.

In the fiery afterglow of the setting sun, the figure of a red deer stands silhouetted with a luminous target painted on its side. Behind us, squinting into the golden haze, a bewildered archer with a half-drawn bow and arrow stands, legs akimbo and mouth agape. He can't believe his eyes. In the shadows between hunter and mark, two humanoid figures, with lights flashing from their foreheads, have suddenly materialized from nowhere, soon to be joined by a third on all fours.

"Where are we?" I rasp in a dust-choked cough.

For a moment the dumbstruck sportsman is lost for a reply, then his tremulous answer comes.

"Earth!" he says.

⤳ Chapter 19 ⤶

"These buildings are beautiful, Mr. Yates. Are they Georgian?"
"I dunno, mam, I've never been to Georgia."
Rowdy Yates, *Rawhide*

EDINBURGH'S NEOCLASSICAL FACADES AND GOTHIC SPIRES
still hide beneath a pall of grime-black fallout from the soot and smoke
that gave the town its nickname "Auld Reekie." The Fresh Air Act,
which outlaws the burning of soft sulfurous coal, has improved the air
quality, but only the suds of the restorers' spray guns will change the appearance of the city, revealing the yellow and brown sandstone buildings buried under three hundred years of dirt.

People who owned apartments in Edinburgh are just waking up to
the fact that they're living in places designed by Robert Adam, many of
which have original Adam fireplaces hidden under many coats of old
lead paint. When cleaned, these fire surrounds are exquisite and fetch
good money in the antique trade. This I learn from Dougie Ford, an
old mate of Angus's, whom I had first met in Aberdeen. He offers me
a job with his renovation squad, stripping pine doors and woodwork
from old houses.

"Bare wood is *in,* Billy," he tells me, "and fashion has decreed that
walls should be painted flat-white and all previously covered surfaces
scraped and sanded to reveal the unspoiled wood underneath."

My ill-fated career as an interior decorator begins with great enthusiasm in the Georgian house of an elderly woman named Mrs. Gilmour
and ends soon afterward.

The old biddy is circumspect from the start, when we three scruffy fellows knock on her door and tell her we are the painting contractors her husband has hired.

"I don't believe you!" declares the sickle-sharp nose jabbing like a bayonet over the brass links of the door's safety chain.

"We talked to Mr. Gilmour on the phone this morning."

"Go away!" says the nose, and the door slams shut.

Dougie spends the next five minutes on his knees, pleading with her through the letter box.

Eventually, after a phone call to her husband, she lets us in and we begin work. Before too long, it becomes increasingly clear that some-one is denuding the house of valuables faster than Hermann Göring could strip a French art gallery. Worried that it might be one of us, Dougie calls me and Archie Ogg into the hallway.

"Where's all that silver stuff that was on the sideboard, a bit ago . . . aw, they spoons and things?"

"It's the old girl, Dougie, she keeps walking in and taking things away on the sly. I've seen her do it—putting wee statues and things into her pocket and shuffling out with them. I think she's a wee bit odd."

I nod my assent just as a scraggy neck thrusts around the kitchen door supporting a face as cold as an unplugged soldering iron.

"What are you lot whispering about? Are you here to work or have you just come to rob me?"

The haughty old besom retreats to the kitchen, which by this time is full of everything portable in the house. From the doorway her beady brown eyes continue to keep us under surveillance.

"Madame, we are artisans, not thieves, and we come with the high-est references. I told your husband on the phone that we are legitimate contractors."

"My husband is a fool! He only hired you because you were cheap— and cheap people are all thieves and drug addicts!" She slams the door, and we filter back into the front drawing room.

"Jasus, who rattled her cage?"

"Now, now, Billy, even if she does deserve a free tumbrel ride to the guillotine, remember, she's the client."

"Sorry, Dougie."

"Archie, go ask the old gal for some hot water. We need to sugar soap these walls before we give them a lick of paint—er . . . no, come to think of it, Billy better go, his hair isn't as long as yours."

Archie shrugs his shoulders and looks relieved, I get a sickly sinking feeling, like when an elevator descends too fast.

Outside the kitchen door, I stand fist raised like Chairman Mao, but lacking the willpower to knock and waken the beast within. This is stupid, I think to myself. Here I am, a grown lad, feared of a silly old woman. As I venture to knock, the door flies open and Mrs. Gilmour is there waving a hideously long carving knife under my nose.

"I heard you coming, so don't try anything with me—I was in the army, you know. What is it you want?"

"Jasus, missus! All I'm after is a bucket of hot water to wash down the walls before we paint them."

"Don't you dare take the name of thy Lord God in vain and don't try to say my walls are dirty either, if you know what's good for you! Now be off with you—go on, SHOO!"

She slams the door and I hear the sounds of something heavy being dragged across the floor to prop against it. Empty-handed, I return to the lads.

"Where's the water?"

"She wouldn't give me any! She told me to bugger off—well, not in so many words. She told me to 'shoo.'"

Archie finds this highly amusing. He would, of course—he was spared the humiliation.

"Did you try the bathroom?"

"Aye, she has that locked up, too!"

"Well, this is no good. I'll have to have a word with the husband. He said she was a little strange when I talked to him."

"Strange? She's as nutty as a fruitcake, waving a bleedin' great knife around like Jack the Ripper. And she's barricaded the door with something heavy, most likely the body of her husband."

"Billy, don't exaggerate. She was probably just peeling potatoes."

"What, with a thing like a bloody great sword?"

"Well, it's her house. She can do what she wants. So, why don't you and Archie start with dabbing paint stripper on the mantelpiece. And look out for that stuff, it's fiercely corrosive and use gloves, too, or it will burn the hands off you."

Being a novice at this game, I watch Archie dab and smear the gelatinous paste into the finely chiseled wooden filigree decorating the Adam fireplace.

"The trick is to keep it moist and let the stripper do a' the work. Then, when the paint lifts, we carefully cream it off, exposing the raw wood."

"How do you get into all of the fancy nooks and crannies of the carving?"

"Ye use a cocktail stick or a toothpick. Something with a fine point."

"I could ask that old doll for her carving knife."

"No, ye don't want to use metal. It can scratch the wood."

We work on in silence, until Archie gets bored and starts chatting.

"D'ya know the main difference between the working class and the middle class?"

"What?"

"When ye go into a working-class home, the first thing the woman will say is, 'Do ye want a cup of tea, lads?' and 'Make yerself at home, I'm just popping doon the shops fer some biscuits.' When ye go into a wealthy middle-class house, they tell you to wipe your feet and they never let ye use their toilet."

"Well, this paranoid old so-and-so would rather kebab me than give me a bucket of water. If I asked to use her loo, I think she'd kill me outright!"

We both laugh, more to break the frosty atmosphere than anything else. Dougie prises the top off of several paint tins and peeks in at the contents.

"Well, we've plenty of white eggshell. I'm away to the store to get some methylated spirit and some steel wool."

"Steel wool, Dougie? What are ye going to do, knit a suit of armor?"

"Aye, very funny, Archie. I'll be back in an hour—try not to upset the old girl."

Dougie vanishes and with him goes any semblance of seriousness. Archie Ogg and myself sit on the floor in front of the fireplace, sniggering away like infants at the slightest whimsical word. Somehow, knowing that "Mrs. Madwoman" is barricaded in her own kitchen, wielding a thing the size of William Wallace's claymore, has us in peals of merriment. In trying to suppress a further fit of giggles, I wipe a tear from my right eyelashes. A searing pain like the splash of boiling fat blinds my eye.

"Jesus, Archie! I've got some of that crap in me eye!" I jump up, scattering the paint tins.

"What crap?" He grabs me as I slip in the slick of spilled emulsion.

"The stripper!" I scream, struggling back up.

"AW, NO, AW, JESUS, NO! We need to get ye to the sink quick afore ye're blinded."

He shuffles me out of the room and up the hall to the kitchen door.

"Mrs. Gilmour, quick, open the door! We need some water!"

"I've told you, my walls are clean!"

"No, missus, you don't understand! I've got an injured man here! We need to get to the sink! Mrs. Gilmour, quick, open up—PLEASE!"

"I'm not falling for any of your tricks. If he's really injured, take him to the hospital."

"Mrs. Gilmour, fer Christ sake, there's no time! He'll be blinded for good in a few minutes."

"Do not take the name of thy Lord God in vain!"

"Open the fuckin' door, ya mad old cow!"

"How dare you—I'm calling the police!"

"Fuck this!"

Archie, with a mighty heave, shoulders the door open with a splintering crack. The barricade of kitchen furniture slides across the wooden floor. In agony, I stumble in behind him.

"Archie, this shit's alkaline, right?"

"Aye, it is—get some water on it, quick!"

"NO! Vinegar, vinegar would be better."

"Where's your vinegar, missus, quick!"

"I'll never tell you—not even if you torture me!"

"Someone ought to torture you, ya daft old bat!"

Archie tears open cupboard after cupboard in a mad scramble as I cry out in agony.

"Here—here it is!"

Lying face up on the kitchen table, I shake the spurting vinegar bottle over my eye. Sweet, soothing acid quenches the gnawing fiery pain but just as quickly stings of its own accord, and I start screaming again. Archie grabs me and holds my face under the cold tap in the kitchen sink, which sends freezing water up my nose and into my lungs. Coughing and spluttering, I struggle free and bury my face in the kitchen curtains.

As my vision returns I see Mrs. Gilmour sitting slumped on a chair in the corner, her knife pointing at the tangle of fresh white footprints crisscrossing the dark oak floorboards.

"You are all mad! Quite mad!" she gasps, goggle-eyed.

Dougie has no alternative other than to give me the golden elbow. Like I could care. In the five years since I'd left school, I'd been laid off and fired more times than the one o'clock gun.

My next attempt at finding a job is prompted by an advert in the *Edinburgh Evening News*:

> YOUNG MAN REQUIRED TO WORK ON SHIP
> Sea-going experience preferred, but not essential.
> Must be able to work unsupervised. Mon.–Fri.
> Wages negotiable.
> Apply, 9am–5pm. MV *Gardy Loo,* Leith Docks.

"What d'you make of this?" I hand Terry the newspaper.

"Monday to Friday? Must be a coaster or a ferry. Are you going to try for it?"

"Yeah, why not? I'll take the bus down now. It can't be worse than fishing."

"You'd better borrow some clean clothes then," says Gordon, "You're still covered in paint from that last job."

I look in the mirror. It's true. The paint-stripper-in-the-eye fiasco left my only shirt and jeans in a right mess. Gordie lends me the only shirt he has that fits. It's turquoise denim with white piping around the collar and pockets. It looks like it belonged to a country-and-western star. Next he finds me a pair of his old blue jeans, which are gone at the knees.

"Five foot eight from six foot two equals . . . erm . . . there!" Gordon hacks six inches off the trouser legs with a pair of scissors.

"There you go," he says, handing me the jeans.

I try them on. They fit fine around the backside and the legs are just the right length, but the ragged worn-out knee areas are dangling in front of my shins, giving me the appearance of a tall man with his legs cut off.

"I can't wear these—they look daft."

"If you wear a pair of my boots and tuck them in, no one will ever know."

"Good idea, Gordie. My own boots are all covered in paint."

He fishes in the wardrobe and extracts two pair of boots.

"You've a choice. There's these"—he holds up a pair of floppy, green suede Robin Hood–type knee boots—"but if I were you, I'd go with these ones," he says, flourishing a pair of yellow-and-black snakeskin cowboy boots.

"Oh dear God, what a choice! Haven't you got any ordinary boots, Gordie?"

"No, all my boots are extraordinary, especially these ones—and they go nice with the shirt."

I have to stuff newspaper into the toes to keep the stupid things from sliding off, and the sheer weight of them has me walking like a moon man. Gordon reaches for a brown Stetson hanging on the back of the door.

"Don't even think about it, Gordon!" I say, pulling on my fisherman's jersey and peaked cap.

The man at the dock office hardly gives me a second glance. He's probably used to people looking like sailors from the waist up and cowboys from the belt down.

"Ye need to talk to Mr. Matheson from the Sanitation Department," he says, "but he's no here at the moment."

"No, no—I was looking for a job at sea on a ship called the *Gardy Loo*."

"Aye, ye need to see Mr. Matheson. He's no here, but I can give ye the paperwork."

The *Gardy Loo,* the dock official explains, is a sludge vessel. Twice a week, she sails from Leith with hundreds of tons of Edinburgh's sewage, which is dumped several miles out in the North Sea to feed the fishes. The job in question calls for a laddie with a strong stomach and a pointed stick to burst the gas-filled condoms of fermenting sperm that tend to clog the filter grid on the ship.

"People shouldn't tie knots in them when they flush them down the loo. It's disgusting what some folk do with condoms, isn't it?" He smiles, handing me the job application forms.

"I wouldn't know—I'm a Catholic," I say, leaving the papers behind on the desk.

Clomping back up the stairs to the attic flat, I can hear the lads talking in the room.

"Here he comes now," says Terry.

"Well, what did you find out?" asks Gordon, hopefully.

"Gentlemen, though it pains me to say it, I have finally discovered that there are worse jobs than gutting fish!"

→ Chapter 20 ←

Mony a mickle, maks a muckle. (Things add up.)
Old Scottish adage

WITH NOTHING IN MY POCKETS BUT MY HANDS, I WANDER down the long winding hill that runs past the iron railings of Queen Street Gardens and onward to the bohemian suburb of Stockbridge, where Terry and Gordon have started work on the shop restoration projects in St. Stephen's Street. I didn't get asked to be part of the job. Perhaps the news of my antics at Mrs. Gilmour's house preceded me, or maybe fortune has another fate in store for me.

Passing the Laughing Duck tavern, I spy three new copper pennies glinting up at me from the bottom of an ornamental pond on the portico. Deciding that thruppence is better than nothing at all, I hop the wrought iron paling and glean my prize.

So far, so good! It is eleven in the morning, and I'm already showing a profit.

At the bottom of the hill, outside St. Vincent's bar, an enormous bonfire rises up in tattered terraces from the cracked black cobbles, like the giant nest of some fabled bird. A pair of street urchins, their dirty faces knit together with snot and pimples, are dragging more bric-a-brac from a nearby demolition site. With surprising agility, these little herberts clamber up the ragged mound of branches and old furniture to add fuel to the eclectic pyre.

"What's the bonfire in aid of?"

My innocent question is met with a work stoppage and two blank stares.

"Is it for a special occasion like May Day?"

"Naw . . . it's . . . naw . . . it's fer . . . erm . . . Victory Day," a scruffy wee laddie guesses from the apex of the heap.

"Do you mean Queen Victoria Day?" I smile up at him.

"I dinnae ken . . . somethin' like that," he says, returning to his arrangements.

From a side street, another waif appears carrying a walnut-framed print. Holding the picture high above his head, he makes to smash the glass out on a nearby log.

"Hey, sonny, wait on! Let me see what you have there!"

The kid spins on his heel and looks uncertainly at me.

"It's just junk. I found it in the bins, mister, I dinnae steal it. I found it, so it's mines—it is so, aye!" He shuffles from one foot to the other, clutching the piece to his threadbare Fair Isle pullover. He looks up nervously at his mates.

"I ken it's yours—I just want to take a wee deek at it, that's all, pal." I speak softly in a Scots accent, so as not to scare him into dropping it.

The bigger of his chums flutters down to his side and bares a row of khaki-colored dental disasters at me, in what only an optimist would be tempted to construe as a smile.

"D'ya wanna buy it, mister?" His pal grimaces and turns the print face about in hope.

I look at the thing, fingering the three coins in my pocket. It is an Edwardian litho depicting the pyramids of Egypt and some angular-looking camels.

"Aye, I'll chance it. I'll ge' ye a penny fer it!"

"Piss awf—I'd rather burn it!" spits the elder, obviously disgusted at my display of guid Scottish parsimony.

"Youse can get four sweeties fer a penny, ya ken? Listen, I'll gi' ye tuppence—that's a penny each. There's a deal?"

"But there's three of us—me, Jake, and Wullie—and it's Wullie's picture, he chorried it. So a penny each, or no dice!" My God, if this kid ever becomes chancellor he'll wipe out the national debt.

"Okay! Ye drive a hard bargain—thruppence it is and guid luck tae youse."

The big fella nudges his grimy, grinning mate with a satisfied elbow, as I count out the change. They scamper up the sides of the bonfire, where they stand defiant to the world, outlined against the gray sky like standing stones on a tumulus. Smiling, I turn down the cobbled street past the Luftwaffe-scarred tower of the old church.

"Hey, mister!"

I'm being hailed by young Sir Greenteeth, now safely ensconced with his henchmen atop the ramparts of his wooden Camelot.

"What?" I shout over my shoulder.

"Yer a fuckin' balmpot, paying thruppence for that piece o' old shite!" the boy informs me.

Cheeky little monkey, he needs a kick in the arse. But I suppose life has already seen to that in the case of these ragamuffins. Oft-quoted lines of my father's spring to mind:

> He was a vulgar little boy
> I knew without a doubt,
> For he put his thumb up to his nose
> And spread his fingers out.

Edinburgh is full of these ragged-arsed wee kiddies; sometimes you're wading knee-deep in them. They seem to appear from nowhere. The only clue as to where they might live comes at feeding time. On the back drying-greens behind grimy rows of six-story tenements, the off-spring's cries for food rise skyward amidst the grid of washing lines, their voices shrill above the city's din: "Mammy, can I no git a jeely piece? Mammy, gi' us a jeely piece!"

Each parent knows the call of its own, and sooner or later, a dingy upper-floor window flies up and a strawberry jam sandwich, done up in an old bread wrapper, glides down like a Frisbee to be unerringly caught by the hungry hands.

I think about young Mahmood, my onetime guide in Morocco, and wonder how he's getting on. I bet he's never seen a jam sandwich, but I'm also sure he could order one in seventeen different languages, if he so desired.

"The poor are always with us," Jesus said, but he didn't say why.

I meander down St. Stephen's Street to a particular antique shop gracing the far end. Gordon introduced me to the owners of this hallowed emporium, and I have become greatly enamored of their venerable company and sense of fun.

"Heaven's Alive Antiques, Curios and Primitive Objets d'Art" the hand-painted sign above the shop announces to the world. I stride up the yellow sandstone steps and through the bell-tinkling door.

From the musty depths of the cluttered interior walks the tall welcoming figure of Tom Reid, aesthetic, mystic, and part-owner.

"What have you for me, my friend?" he says enticingly, electric blue eyes arcing in the shadow of enormous bushy eyebrows.

"It's a lithographic print of an Egyptian scene . . . er . . . maybe Edwardian or late Victorian?"

"Good, my friend, very good. It is, as you guessed, Edwardian, mass produced, but quite charming in its way. It's worth about three pounds— I'll give you half of that." His ivory-white teeth gleam under a huge black Stalinesque mustache as he counts three new fifty-pence pieces into my hand. I'm beginning to like this. The antique business is a sight more lucrative than fishing and a thousand times less dangerous. Ye gods! That's eleven and a half pints of beer or six fish suppers.

"Come through into the back room. My friend Bob is just about to start on one of his stories."

In the inner sanctum, Bob, artist, wizard, and high priest of the esoteric, is holding court to a quaint collection of worthies gathered around a great roaring fire of old oak furniture. Square-framed, stocky, and ebullient, he is the antithesis of Tom's serene, sinewy aestheticism and sports a *Laughing Cavalier* upswept mustache and pointed beard.

To experience Bob telling a yarn is a delight. Even the most innocuous parts of the narrative are illustrated with grand gestures, stubby, air-stabbing fingers, and intricate body language that translates universally. Great crow's-feet laugh lines spread from the corners of his iodine-colored eyes, marking the past pathways of a million monologues, while the rich velvet of his native Scottish tongue ensnares the listener in a fatal web of absurd intrigue:

> *"So Donald, you see, comes in the shop with this saucer-shaped*
> *piece of old tarnished bronze metal that he'd picked up on*
> *Calton Hill. 'What is it?' he says. 'It must be very ancient,'*

*he says. So I have a wee look at it, and it's what I thought—
nothing but a piece of old bronze furnace slag that had
splashed up, forming a crude bowl shape. Curiously enough,
by accident, a solidified drip on the bottom resembles an erect
phallus and testes.*

*"So I says, 'By Jove, that is old!' and he gets all excited and
hops up and down. I start to act amazed and exuberant, to
wind him up. For devilment, I tell him, 'Donald, you have
something there I thought I'd never live to see, a piece of un-
surpassable quality and antiquity, an artifact so old, so ancient, that it was not made by* Homo sapiens *at all. It is
Cro-Magnon and priceless! What you have there in your
hand, Donald, is a . . . is a prehuman bowl!'*

*"His eyes nearly pop out of his head as he stares at the
thing. He leans forward. 'What exactly does that mean?'
he says, all conspiratorial.*

*"'It means, Donald, that you are the proud owner of one
of the oldest and finest archaeological finds ever made on this
planet. You'll make a million out of it, if not more!' Well, this
got him going again, hopping from one foot to the other.*

*"'What was its purpose? What was it used for, this pre-
human bowl?'*

*"So I tell him it is a ceremonial salver used to cradle the
testicles and catch the blood in Cro-Magnon circumcision
rites. You will notice the male genitalia depicted on the base.
This is the giveaway. To my knowledge only the Smithsonian
Institution in America has one similar, so you can name your
price!'*

*"Poor Donald thought all his birthdays had come at once.
He sends it, with a covering letter, under massively heavy
insurance, to the curator of the British Museum in London.
Well, the weeks go by and nothing is heard, which gets him
into a terrible state of agitation. So eventually he telephones
the museum and is put through to the woman in charge at
the Anthropology Department.*

"'Have you had a chance to look at the piece that I sent you?'

"'Yes, sir. What is it?'

"'What do you mean, what is it? You know fine! It's a prehuman ball bowl!'

"'I'm sorry, sir, I've no idea what you're talking about.'

"'Can you not tell from the shape of the thing?'

"'No!'

"'Have you looked at the object on the base?'

"'Yes, I am looking at it right now.'

"'Does it not suggest anything to you?'

"'No!'

"'Madame, I hardly dare ask, are you a married woman?'

"'She hung up, Bob! She just hung up! I can't understand it! She hung up the bloody telephone on me. What's the world coming to?'

"Poor Donald, I didn't have the heart to tell him it was all a leg-pull, but I guess he's found out by now."

The butt of Bob's joke is a great bearded bear of a man who resembles King Edward VII and has the grandiloquence to match. He has an antique shop up the road with a stuffed, four-legged bird in the window. I like Donald. He is an optimist who always thinks he's on the verge of discovering some long-lost masterpiece in a junk sale or, alternately, marrying himself off to a rich widow, neither of which he's managed to do so far.

In the infamous back room of Heaven's Alive, I find my real alma mater: a rich university of arcane knowledge, a spiritual temple, and, above all, a retreat from the mundane business of survival.

Bob studies Druidism and is glad to have an apprentice to serve as a willing acolyte to his sage. From him, I learn more than any book can furnish.

Tom, on the other hand, is eclectic in his spirituality, and his mixture of Celtic, Hindu, Shinto, and Buddhist beliefs always exudes a guiltless love of humanity that is as godlike as any mere mortal can attain.

Tom had served in the British navy during World War II and had visited Hiroshima just after the atomic bomb was dropped. What he witnessed there changed his life. Sometimes he plays Puccini's *Madame Butterfly* on the shop's ancient windup gramophone and sobs uncontrollably. I find his love of humankind poignant and when he urges me to "Caress a tree, my friend," I know that he is in earnest and means just that. Lesser people may make snide remarks about tree huggers, but Tom is right:

> *What is more noble than a lofty elm*
> *More solid as the oak,*
> *More sacred than the ash?*

From his Eastern leanings he has earned the revered nickname of Rama Reid.

The inner circle of friends to which I have recently been admitted is an eccentric lot indeed. Stuart, a former African bush pilot, and Carney the Car are both used-vehicle dealers. Robert, a handsome, devil-may-care type who loves gambling, operates as a diamond mining engineer in Zaire. Jerry the Pole deals in voodoo fetishes and Art Deco. Then there's Ralph, who carries both a bronze leaf-shaped sword and the belief that he is the reincarnation of King Arthur, who, with admirable fortitude and patience, is still waiting for the present incumbent of the throne of Great Britain to vacate it in his favor.

Each weekday evening, Bob and Tom hold court at the St. Vincent bar at the end of the street. Donald, of the prehuman bowl, and Stuart, of the equally elderly cars, are regulars at the domino table. We play for a shilling a corner and two shillings for a granny, which occurs when a player wins three games in a row.

"Threes and twos never lose!" "The Duke of Buccleuch!" "Never bar a double!" "There's no honor in winning your own down!" "I'm champing!" "He's downed a blowser!" "Gentlemen, it's down to a count!" "Dead man's hand!" "The whore of Leith!"

This is the language of the esoteric world of dominoes echoing amid the shuffling of domino pieces and clinking of beer glasses.

It's cozy in this malt-scented, oak-paneled room, listening to the endless leg-pulling jibes and the steady click and clack of the dominoes. I daresay, more antique dealing goes on here than in all shops put together. The trader's motto is a simple one: "One man's junk is another man's treasure."

Above the bar, a walnut-framed beveled glass mirror, emblazoned with the brave legend "Campbell, Hope and King's . . . Purveyors of Fine Ales and Stouts," provides a distorted reflection of the early-evening clientele gathered beneath. In the dingy light, the eyes play tricks, and perhaps it's the mirror that's true and the customers that are warped. Either way, I have made more friends here than anywhere else in my life.

Ralph, or Ra-Alpha, the Egyptian Sun God, as he likes to be known when he's not being King Arthur, sits in the corner nursing an orange juice. I sit down next to him.

Like Nigel Wartooth before him, Ralph doesn't drink. He doesn't have to—he's intoxicated with his vision of the Celtic past and the glory days to come after the restoration of the Gael, which he assures me is coming soon. Normally, his dark eyes smolder with the intensity of certitude, but tonight his heavy brows are knit in puzzlement.

"Where could it be?" frets the once and future king.

"Where could what be?"

"The Lia Fáil, better known as 'the Stone of Destiny,'" he replies, fixing me with his gaze. The old fire is back.

"The Stone of Destiny is in Westminster Abbey, isn't it? Stolen from Scone by that old bollix of a king, Edward the First, because whoever sits on the sacred stone is king of Scotland," I offer.

"No, that's not it, Bill. The stone that sits under the coronation chair is just a hunk of red sandstone with a cross incised on it and a metal ring embedded. The ancient stone on which the Celtic kings were crowned was a pillar of white marble inscribed with all manner of cabalistic symbols and ancient texts. It was the pillow that Jacob slept on when he dreamed of the ladder going up to heaven."

"So how did it get to Scotland?"

"It was brought from Egypt to Ireland by Goidel, whose mother, Scota, was the daughter of the pharaoh and wife of Niul. When the Scota tribe migrated to Pictish Caledonia, the stone went with them, and when the Picts and Scots united under Kenneth MacAlpin in 848, the stone was located at Scone, which had become the capital of the new nation of Scotland."

"So, the stone that Longshanks stole and took to London was a forgery—and every English monarch since has been crowned on a piece of worthless rock!"

"Correct."

"All well and good, but where's the proof?"

"Okay, so Edward the First grabs the stone and thinks that he's scuppered Scotland's royal line for good. When Robert the Bruce beats the English at Bannockburn in 1314, Edward the Second sues for peace and renounces his father's territorial claims on Scotland. To sweeten the deal, he offers to return the Lia Fáil to Bruce, who politely refuses it because he had already been crowned at Scone in 1304, whilst seated on the real stone. Do you see?"

"Yes, but—"

"Hold hard, I haven't finished. So on his deathbed, legend has it that Robert the Bruce, King of Scotland, asks his friend, Angus Og, Lord of the Isles, to take the Stone of Destiny into safekeeping and to hide it somewhere out in the Hebrides, well away from the English. There is no way he would have done that, unless he had the real stone, is there?"

"I guess not. So where is it now?"

"I don't know, your guess is as good as mine. If I knew, I would be the king, wouldn't I? It's passing strange that the two things that we must quest for are so similar."

"What things?"

"The Lia Fáil and the Holy Grail. Both are biblical in their origins, both have mystical qualities, and both are a missing part of the puzzle."

"Fáil and Grail—they even sound similar. And there's a connection there if I was only smart enough to see it! It's like when you have someone's name on the tip of your tongue, but it just eludes you."

"Maybe you're the rebirth of Sir Percival, the virgin knight. He could almost see the Grail, but he couldn't, as his name suggests, *pierce the veil*," says Ralph, in all seriousness.

Ralph gathers his things and begins walking toward the door, leaving me in bemused silence.

"Well, that's bloody typical, that is," I mumble to myself. "If I'm to be one of the Knights of the Holy Grail, why do I have to be the one who doesn't get laid?"

"I shall go now. Good night, loyal subjects all," says the king, with a regal wave of his hand.

"Aye, good night, Ralph, or Ra-Alpha, or King Arthur, or whoever the hell you happen to be this evening."

Ralph's place at the table is taken by two brothers that I have recently gotten to know. The first to sit down is thin, bespectacled Theo Tammes, a quiet-mannered art connoisseur who works part-time in Bob and Tom's shop. Accompanying him is his older brother, who outwardly couldn't be more different. André is robust of stature and sports both a Henry VIII beard and a hail-fellow-well-met persona that puts one in mind of a merry medieval baron. Theo is the first to speak.

"Bill, there was a phone call for you at the shop yesterday. They said they'd call every noon until they get you. I think it's urgent."

"Thanks, Theo, I'll pop in tomorrow. You don't know who it is, do you?"

"No, sorry, mate, but it's someone with a Scottish accent."

"Maybe it's an offer of a job?" I wonder.

"What sort of work are you looking for?" André asks.

"I was a radio operator at sea, but those jobs are hard to come by."

"Can you do electrical work, wiring and suchlike?"

"Sure, I always repaired my own electronic equipment, and I've wired boats, too."

"Good, well, I'm trying to set up a theater lighting business for myself. If it works out, we could maybe use your electrical skills, and there'd be a job in it for you."

This is good news indeed. André reckons to be up and running before the Edinburgh festival in August. I go home happy. It has been quite a day.

The following morning, I join Theo in the dusty enclave of the old shop. True to expectation, the telephone rings at exactly noon.

"Bill, is that you? This is Bloggs in Aberdeen. Can you hear me? I can barely hear you—it's a shitty line!"

"Aye, Bloggs, I can hear you fine. What's happening?"

"It's Angus. He's dead . . . killed in a motorcycle accident. I thought you should know."

"When?" I feel the world stop for a second. All I can see is Angus grinning at me through the cursed smoke of the Glenelg firewood.

"Hello, can you hear me?"

"Yes. When did it happen?"

"Two nights ago, on the bypass. He was killed outright, broke his neck. He was speeding and he lost it on the curve."

"Do you mean he was going too fast or—"

"Who knows? Both probably. Sorry, Bill, I know he was a friend of yours."

"He was, yes."

❧ Chapter 21 ❧

Byrr eu hoedyl hir hoet ar eu carant.
[Short were their lives, long the grief of their kin.]
Aneirin

THEO STANDS BEFORE ME, BLINKING LIKE AN OWL.

"Bad news?"

"Aye, my pal in Aberdeen got killed in a motorbike accident."

"Oh my dear chap, that's ghastly. I tell you what, I'll close up for lunch and we'll pop off for a beer. What do you say?"

"No thanks, Theo, I think I'll just go for a walk."

I leave Theo pottering about in the dusty shop and trudge off toward the city center in a muddle of jumbled thoughts and memories. I make my way through the cobbled streets to the war memorial on Calton Hill. I climb to where the folly stands on the crest of the round-topped hill, a glorious duplicate of the Parthenon, built in honor of the dead at the Battle of Waterloo. The seven-pillared frontage is all that was ever completed. The euphoria of defeating Napoleon melted away as quickly as the construction funds, leaving a ruin less complete than the original in Greece. Angus used to say, "If Edinburgh is the Athens of the north, does that make Athens the Edinburgh of the south?" Poor Angus. I never got to walk around his hometown with him, but I feel as if he is here in spirit, even though I know he didn't believe in such things.

I buy an apple pie and a bottle of milk from the mobile shop in the carpark and take my lunch sitting on the steps of the Parthenon.

A four-engined maritime reconnaissance aircraft growls across the blue spring sky above the Firth of Forth. It's an Avro Shackleton, "ten thousand loose rivets flying in close formation," as they're known. Higher still, a crocus-yellow sun plays catch-as-catch-can with tufted clouds. The throb of the Rolls-Royce Griffin engines reverberates in the warm air as the old plane makes a slow turn and heads out to sea on patrol. Trawlermen called them "the Gray Ladies." They know that these aircraft can often find sinking vessels, even in the worst conditions and, like angels of light, drop rescue gear and rubber dinghies to the men below.

The hum of the contrarotating propellers fades and the twin-tailed giant disappears into the pall of smoke climbing from the chimney of Morton Hall crematorium. For all I know, that might be Angus now, rising into the clear air like a puff of pot smoke. Perhaps that distant vapor is composed of his wild hair, crooked grin, and gangly frame, now reduced to an essence, drifting and dissipating among the herringbone exhaust trails of the Shackleton. I don't know.

My troubled thoughts turn to wondering. Should I have told the hospital about Angus's drug habit? Would they have put him into treatment or called the police? Maybe the doctors did know and didn't want to get him busted either. I guess I'll never find out now. All the same, I wish I'd just left him playing the piano in Morocco, safe from Senga and her junkie pals and far away from bad mixers like amphetamines and fast motorcycles.

"What a waste of a young life," I confide to my pie. "I'd better write and tell my folks, they're bound to be upset." An attentive pigeon watches me finish the pie and darts in for the crumbs. I remember dear departed Nigel the Viking and his theory that pigeons caused the French Revolution.

"Vive la France!" I say. The bird puffs out his chest, as if in pride, and scans me with a golden eye.

To the east, the smoke from the crematorium has ceased and with it the sense that Angus is accompanying me on my tour.

"Good-bye, old friend. I'm sorry we fell out on the mountain," I say to the wind.

Shuffling down the stony track, I arrive in the tree-lined Georgian crescent that leads to the top of Leith Walk. On a soot-shrouded building, a bronze plaque announces that Sir Arthur Conan Doyle was born there in 1859. I smile, imagining myself like the ever-astounded Dr. Watson, inviting the great detective, Sherlock Holmes, to speculate on the questions that still confound me.

"So, Holmes, what happens to your soul if you don't believe in God?"

"H'mm, interesting question. Ask me another."

"Do atheists get a chance to recant or do they go straight to hell?"

"Ah, a greater conundrum. Anything else?"

"Yes, would a God of mercy not give lost souls a last chance?"

"Perhaps you may find what you are looking for over there."

A hundred yards away, tucked behind the Sherlock Holmes pub, stands the almost hidden edifice of St. Patrick's Catholic Cathedral.

"Thank you, Mr. Holmes."

"Elementary, my dear Watkins!"

A great iron-studded oaken door opens to a silent refuge from the bustle outside. I swither at the portal in two minds whether to enter or not. This is pathetic. Last week I was all set to become a hardheaded pagan, but now, seduced by the familiar waft of incense, my old faith seems so serene and comforting. What is it they say? "Once a Catholic . . ."

I kneel in the chilly church, leaving the proto-Druid of my aspirations outside. It feels strange praying for the repose of the soul of a young man to a God he didn't believe existed. I have misgivings, too. If God is perfect and we are created in his image, why do men have nipples? I try hard not to get distracted by such vexing questions and concentrate on the crucifix above the altar. Something about the pallid face of Christ on this cross baffles me. It doesn't bear the look of forlorn anguish that I'm used to seeing. Here, the visage has a more contented aspect, happy even; it's the face of a man whose job had been completed. Christians believe that Jesus had to die to conquer death, and, for once, the sculptor seems to have captured that moment, bestowing on Jesus an air of job satisfaction. As an Irish Catholic, I must have seen thousands of images of Christ on the cross, but for the first time, I see him not as the son of God but as a man, a young man of just thirty-two. Angus was just twenty-two.

A door opens somewhere behind me and a black-robed figure paces the distance from the sacristy to the confession box in dignified, measured steps. I glance about. I'm alone in the vastness of the quiet space.

Even in the cool confines of damp pews, the certainties of my childhood faith continue lighting fires in my soul that my adult ego tries hard to extinguish. I slide along the wooden bench and kneel in momentary genuflection in the aisle. It is only a few yards to the oak door and the waiting world outside, and yet I find my steps drawn to the dark, carved portal of the confessional.

This is the dumbest thing you've ever done in your life, my internal, evil twin chides me as I enter the tiny room.

I kneel on the plush red hassock in front of the walnut-framed window that connects priest with penitent. The cover of the oraculum slides back silently, silky smooth from years of usage. Behind the black gauze the dim outline of the priest invites me to begin my confession. He has a pronounced Irish accent.

"Bless me, Father, for I have sinned. It is ... erm ... three years since my last confession."

"Three years, my son, that's a long old time. Have you been away from the church?"

"I was, Father, but I was away at sea a great deal of the time."

"I understand. Make your confession."

"I don't really know what to say, Father. I suppose I swear a lot and get into arguments, but apart from that, I don't remember doing anything really bad."

"Well that's good, if it's true. You say you swear—do you mean taking the Lord's name in vain?"

"Yes, Father."

"Well, don't do that. You wouldn't like your name being used as a profanity, now would you?"

"No, Father."

"Anything else? You've missed a lot of mass, haven't you?"

"I have, Father, yes."

"Is there something else? Sins of the flesh perhaps?"

"No, Father. I'm just about celibate."

"Celibate? Out of choice?"

"Not really, Father, more out of sheer bad luck."

"Well, let's not go into that. What other things may you have done that would displease Almighty God?"

"I don't know, Father. Is it a sin to be superstitious?"

"If you mean things like it being unlucky to walk under a ladder, surely that's just common sense—something might fall on your head. But as for black cats crossing your path or Friday the thirteenth being an unlucky day, I don't think that is sinful as long as no one is hurt by it. Why do you ask?"

"I . . . er . . .erm . . . Father, what happens if you die and you don't believe in God?"

"How do you mean?"

"A friend of mine was just killed in a motorcycle accident. He was an atheist."

"Perhaps he made his peace with the Lord in his final seconds of life. Ours is a God of infinite mercy, remember."

"Yes, that's what I thought, Father. I had another friend who died recently. He committed suicide. What about him?"

"Oh dear, suicide is a very grievous sin. Was he troubled in his spirit?"

"I don't know, but he wasn't right in the head. He thought he was a Viking warrior and he wanted to go to Valhalla."

"Then he surely wasn't culpable, poor chap. May he rest in peace."

"Thank you, Father. I feel greatly relieved for my friends."

"Don't thank me, thank our Father in heaven. Is there anything else you wish to confess?"

"Is it a sin to look lustfully at young ladies, Father?"

"Of course it is, ya fool. If it wasn't, we'd all be doing it!"

My friend Angus is gone, but now with the benefit of absolution I feel my prayers may get a better hearing, so I put in a good word for him, wherever he's bound. Ah, the old-time religion, there's nothing like it. Ten Hail Marys and five Our Fathers and I have a clean slate again. The Protestants don't know what they're missing.

I walk to the Queen Street museum and buy a postcard depicting a Celtic cross. Sitting in the airy hall, surrounded by ancient standing stones, I write a short account of what I know of Angus's death. A trip to the post office next door and a three-penny stamp sends the sad news speeding off to my parents in Birmingham.

Angus had often told me of his favorite haunts in Edinburgh and of how he liked to rummage through the junk shops in the Grassmarket or climb Calton Hill to get a panoramic view of the city he loved. In his honor, I make a tour of some of the places he'd described to see if they bore any resemblance to what I had imagined.

Edinburgh seems to take great pains to honor its dead; reminders of the fragility of life rise up on all sides. Statues of fallen soldiers stand defiant over the names of faraway places where they died: Afghanistan, the Somme, Sud el Bahr, Spion Kop. Monuments to writers, poets, sailors, and clergymen nestle in lilac groves or by the side of the ornamental walkways lining Princes Street. Equestrian statues, Celtic crosses, and dedicated park benches all bear the names and dates of departed citizens.

At one end of King's Stables Road, a round watchtower in the common graveyard once housed the town guard, whose job it was to thwart the skulduggery of Burke and Hare. Adjacent is the spot where "Half-hangit Mary" was hung for witchcraft. A plaque tells that this particular lady amazed her executioner and onlookers alike by coming back to life shortly after being cut down from the gibbet. She leapt from the body cart with the cry of, "See, I telt ye I was innocent!"

The Grassmarket was often used for public executions and houses memorials to both Protestant martyrs that were burned to death and Catholic Jesuits who were beheaded for the way they prayed to the same God.

Sawney Bean and fifty-eight members of his family met their grisly demise here too. There's no monument to them, but I remember the scene vividly described in one of the history books that Mate Mackenzie gave me: "The men did their hauns and leggiss cut off and left tae bleed taa daith. The weemen and barins, hiving watched this, were burnt in three saiveral fires, a' cursin' tae their laust gasp."

Up from the Grassmarket, at the top of Candelmaker's Row, I meet the bronze figure of Greyfriar's Bobby. This faithful little dog lay for years on his master's grave, cared for by passersby, until he was granted the Freedom of the City and a life pension for the loyalty he showed to his dead owner. The grave is just inside the railings of Greyfriar's Church-yard, where carved skulls and crossbones adorn the mossy blackened headstones and hourglasses and Grim Reaper scythes remind the living that time is running out and death waits in the wings.

A motto carved in crumbling limestone is barely legible: "Tempus fugit—tempus edax rerum": Time flies—time devours all things.

My steps return northward and back downhill toward Stockbridge.

"Hey, Billy!"

A voice hails from the direction of the bus station. I look around, shading my eyes from the glare of the afternoon sun.

"Billy—over here!"

Across the busy corner of the square, the wiry figure of Chris Dale is waving his arms like the flight deck officer on an aircraft carrier.

"Hey, how ya doing?" I shout over, as he dodges the traffic to cross the road.

We shake hands.

"I'm back!"

"How long for?"

"For good!"

I walk with Chris down to Gordie's flat in Stockbridge. Halfway up the stairs, the landlord juts his head out from the door of his first-floor apartment.

"You'd better just be visiting!" he says and slams the door.

"What's wrong with him?" Chris whispers.

"He's getting pissed off that me and Terry are staying here and not paying rent."

"Pity for him. I'll dump my stuff and we'll go get a pint, eh? It was a bloody long bus ride from Liverpool."

"What happened to your job at the soap factory?"

"The bubble burst."

On the way through Stockbridge to the St. Vincent bar, I tell Chris about Angus. He'd never met him, but he had heard me talk about him.

"I hate junkies. They're a pain in the arse," he says.

In a nicotine-stained alcove, next to a spluttering gas heater, sits the diminutive figure of Madame Doubtfire, dangling her Minnie Mouse legs from an overlarge moth-eaten fur coat.

"Come over here and sit with me, William," the sedate old dowager says, raising her bottle of Guinness and patting the wooden bench next to her.

"Hello, Madame D. How are you?" I say, sitting down while Chris gets the beers.

"I'm fine, but how are you? I heard your friend was killed the other day."

I smile at the kindly old girl. Despite her advanced years, not much gets past her. She's as bright as a button and as sharp as a bag of needles.

"Yes, he was."

"Do you know what I was doing on the night of the fourteenth of April, 1912?"

"No, Madame, I don't, but I know the Irish consider it an unlucky date."

"Well, it certainly was for me. On that date, I was traveling to New York on the White Star liner RMS *Titanic*. Have you heard of her?"

"Of course, Madame, everyone has heard of the *Titanic,* but I didn't know you were one of the survivors! You couldn't have been more than a child."

"Ha! Enough of your flattery! I was born in 1892. I was twenty years old and on my way to America to marry Mr. Doubtfire of the famous circus family. When the great ship went down that night, I learned a lot about death, and do you know what the biggest thing to come out of it was? I learned to live each day as if it was a complete lifetime."

"Yes, ma'am, I'm just beginning to learn that. All in all, it's been an odd experience, losing friends."

"Oh yes, I know only too well. All of my old friends are gone . . . Lady Astor, Nancy Cunard, Max Beerbohm, all dead and gone, but I remember them, I remember them all. But you know what they say: 'You can't prevent the birds of sorrow from flying over your head, but you can prevent them from building their nests in your hair.' That's an old Chinese proverb, you know."

"Very appropriate, Madame," says Chris. "Did you pick that up on your travels when you were young?"

"No, my friend, I got it out of a fortune cookie at the Ping-On restaurant last week!" She cracks a wicked laugh, which settles into a beatifying smile that would free anyone's soul from gravity.

I shake my head. At the venerable age of seventy-nine, she has a ready wit that can still outgun the best of us.

Chris and I chum the frail Madame Doubtfire up the hill to the little secondhand clothing emporium that she keeps in a basement. Arm in arm with her two gallants, she giggles out stories of the old days. In her dingy shop, smelling of lavender and camphorated oil, we sit a while listening to her accounts of the raucous era of Al Capone, suffragettes, and the Charleston. As she speaks, her pale blue eyes twinkle like stars on a frosty night. Tucking up a wisp of snow-white hair, the faded diva shows us an album of photographs taken during her roaring twenties. Time frozen in sepia, there she is, radiantly beautiful in her flapper's dress and bobbed haircut, Clara Bow, Myrna Loy, and Mary Pickford all rolled into one; a veritable temptress of her time and gladly, a true vamp of ours.

"I'm not much to look at now, boys, but in my youth, I was well kissed . . . aye, well kissed," she sighs, closing the book.

Before we go, we give our lady friend a couple of pecks on the cheek. She chases us out of the shop.

"Be off with you, you bad boys. A girl's not safe around you. My reputation will be in ruins!" she giggles.

⚜ Chapter 22 ⚜

But as every man sayeth, every dog has its day.

John Heywood (1562)

I RECEIVE A MESSAGE THAT IAN THE OPTICIAN IS LOOKING for me. This could be lucrative, as Ian is a wheeler-dealer type and has his fingers in many pies. When I reach his modest premises on Lothian Road, he is standing in the front of his shop, arguing with a little old lady.

"I tell ye, Mrs. Murray, there is nothing wrong with your glasses. I've checked your prescription twice over and it's correct."

"Well, I'm for telling you that I cannae see right wi' these things."

"What can't you see right, Mrs. Murray?"

"I cannae see things that are far away."

"Right!"

He grabs her by the hand and ushers her out onto the street.

"Can you see that big yellow thing up there?"

"Aye."

"What is it?"

"It's the sun, of course."

"Aye, well, that's ninety-three million miles away. How bloody far do you want to see?"

He motions me in, slams the door on the bewildered woman, and puts up the Closed sign.

"Come through to the back, Bill. I've something for you to sell, and I'll make it worth your while."

I follow him into the kitchen part, where a dozen gray-green crabs snap and splash in their attempt to climb out of an old stone sink.

"I got these beauties in payment for a pair of spectacles. I want a pound a piece for them, and anything else you can make over that is yours. There's a bucket with a lid over there—a drop of water and you're in business."

"Why me? I don't know anything about selling crabs."

"Because you're a fisherman, and I'm a respectable optician. I can't go round the pubs hawking crustaceans, I've an image to keep up. Anyway, you look the part with your wee sailor's cap and your woolly jersey. Now come on, this is a golden opportunity. What d'ya say?"

"I say you're a cheeky bastard! Okay, gimme the bucket. I'll try selling three at a pound twenty-five each."

Sloshing down the hill with a pail of water containing a trio of disconsolate-looking crabs is not how I had planned to spend the day. After a few refusals, Jean-Pierre, chef de la maison at the Purple Onion, is kind enough to purchase the two medium-sized crabs, but he won't buy the big one.

"I not like eem. Ee asn't got all eez legs."

I hadn't noticed that the poor bugger had a couple of legs missing—probably lost them in a fight.

"You can have him for a pound, and that's me making no profit out of it."

"No, no, I not like eem—take eem away."

He pushes me and my bucket out of the kitchen door. I attempt to bargain.

"Aw, come on, Jean-Pierre. He's my last one and I can't wander around with just one crab in my bucket. I'll look like some prat who's just come from the seaside."

"You are breaking my eart . . . boo-oo. There now, you make me cry—now peese off!"

That was that. No more to be gained there, but I had made fifty pence and a pint of beer was only thirteen. Me and my crab retire to the St. Vincent bar.

"What have you got in the bucket, Bill?" asks Angie Rue, looking up from her evening paper.

"It's a crab, Angie. I'm selling them."

"What, as pets?"

"Naw, for eating. They're edible crabs. You boil them and they change color—they go that sort of red, you know?"

"Oh, aye. My Dave loves crabs, but they're so expensive."

"You can have this one for a pound, just so I don't have to cart him about all night."

"Okay, I'll bring back the bucket tomorrow. Same time?"

"Aye, that will do fine. Boil him good, mind. I don't want you both getting food poisoning."

"Sure enough. See you happy-hour tomorrow." Angie waves as she and her dinner toddle off into the long shadows of the sunset.

Terry wanders in to the bar. He looks disheveled, which is not surprising since he didn't come home last night.

"Hi, Terry. Where've you been, you old tomcat?"

"Don't mention tomcats to me."

"Why not?"

"Well, you know that lassie I went home with last night, Pauline? She turns out to be a crazy vegetarian who feeds her cat on nothing but brown rice."

"What's wrong with that?"

"Cats have to eat meat. If you feed them on brown rice, all their bleedin' hair falls out!"

"Their fur falls off! No kiddin'."

"Too bloody right! Have you ever tried getting your oats with a bald tomcat watching you? I couldn't do it, it was just too weird."

"Why didn't you turn the light off?"

"'Cause they can see in the fuckin' dark, can't they? No, she's too odd for me. Brown rice, my arse—far too odd."

"I think all your girlfriends are odd—they'd need to be."

"At least I've got girlfriends—not like you, ya fairy! When was the last time you got yer leg over?"

I laugh it off, but he is right. I haven't been out with a girl for nearly a year. As my lustful comrade harangues my involuntary celibacy, questions my sexuality, and berates my bachelorhood, I muse over my pint and decide that I need to take "the pursuit of the legover" a little more seriously. Ah, to hell with worrying about it! As my dad would say, "You never know your luck in a big town."

The following afternoon, as I make my way up the tenement stairs after buying a newspaper, I am met by a middle-aged woman dressed in a tweed skirt and jacket. She has recently moved in from the country, and I figure her to be one of the horse-and-hounds set known as the "Jolly Hockeysticks" type. Normally her conversations consist of a rather priggish "Hello thair!" but this time she firmly blocks my way and begins speaking to me in an upper-class drawl that sends disagreeable shivers down my back.

"Yoo thair! Am I right in thinking you're unemployed?" comes the haughty voice of the faded beauty.

"Er . . . yes, ma'am . . . I am at present."

I thought she was going to give me one of those "In my day people like you were put in the army, or the workhouse, or stuffed up a lum like a chimney boy!" speeches, but no. Instead, she looks me straight in the eye and announces, "I'll give you three pounds a week to exercise my rufus!"

I stand there blinking in incomprehension. What does she mean? I'd heard about older women seducing young lads for a price. Was *that* it?

"Come in here, if you're interested," she says, opening her apartment door and marching inside.

As if drawn by a magnet, I follow. Through the open door I catch a glimpse of a large brass bedstead. Then she opens another door and an enormous dog of the red setter variety leaps upon me, knocking me on my arse in the hallway. I am engulfed by his acrid breath and slobber-tongued kisses.

"This is Rufus. He's a thoroughbred and he's very highly strung!"

He bloody well ought to be, I think—from the nearest lamppost.

Seeing only my flailing arms, the old debutante adds: "I've just brought him up from the country, where he is used to a good long run each day. About ten miles should do it. Here's his lead and the first week's money. Now awf with you and don't bring him back until he's tired!"

As if in a trance, I find my doggy-ravished face dripping with saliva out on the stone staircase with a disagreeable shaggy mutt in one hand and three quid in the other.

It's little wonder these folk needed an empire to boss about. She never even discussed the deal with me, but the money will be handy.

"Come on, Sunshine, let's see what sort of a dog ye are."

Sensing adventure, the slobber hound pulls me down the stairs, into the street, and almost under a bus. I need to take the upper hand.

"Sit!"

He sits.

"Stand!"

He still sits.

"Walkies!"

He takes off down the road, dragging me like a kite behind him.

Around the corner by the garages, I belay the dog lead around a lamppost and give him a face-to-face growl, which he readily translates as, Me big dog, you little dog. You behave or you die!

Suddenly Rufus realizes the scheme of things. Now we are on better terms and his behavior improves—slightly.

Apparently these dogs are bred to sniff people's crotches, which Rufus does with embarrassing regularity. When not engaged in sniffing, his main pursuit is to get as muddy as possible, then leap up on some unsuspecting soul, leaving clarty paw prints on coats and dresses. The dozy bastard is a royal pain in the arse. Ten miles a day—no bloody way!

Still not sure of what to do, I wander down the back streets, away from the traffic that this silly bugger keeps trying to jump into. At the large iron-railed rectangle of Broughton schoolyard, I stop for breath. Lying in the gutter is an old tennis ball; I pick it up, and suddenly I have the dog's full attention. He sits, earnestly eyeing my every move for an invitation to play. I throw the ball down the steep playground steps and the setter is after it like a red flash. He bounds back up the thirty or so steps and nuzzles the ball back into my hand. I chuck it down again and he repeats the same retrieval. After an hour of this Rufus is completely knackered.

I walk him into the Broughton bar, where he curls up by the fire, licking his pads, while I imbibe a couple of pints of good Scotch ale on the doggy money. After another hour, I lead the panting dog back to "Mrs. Jolly Hockeysticks," or whatever her name is, and she is delighted.

"Good work, my boy! He looks all fagged out. Oh, see there, he's gawn straight to his basket. Jolly good show! Same time tomorrow, then? Pip-pip!" Without waiting for a reply, she shuts the door in my face.

Well, I'm a happy boy! This beats the hell out of fishing, I think, as I wander down the street to the St. Vincent. Something is nagging me, though. What have I forgotten?

On entering the subterranean hostelry, I spy a white plastic bucket with my name scrawled on it. Oh, shit, the crabs! I grab the pail, turn tail, and make the trek up to the optician's shop.

"Where the bloody hell have you been?" Ian is not best pleased.

"Sorry, Ian, I was kidnapped by aliens. How's the crabs?"

"It's a fuckin' pity the aliens brought you back. The crabs are dead!"

"How did that happen? They looked all right yesterday."

"So they might, but that was before they pulled a bottle of bleach into the sink with them. Anyway, you owe me three quid, so pay up!" I hand over what's left of my dog money and I'm broke again. Easy come, easy go. Pity there's always more goings than comings.

On the way back along George Street, I spy some young folk dodging traffic to stand in the middle of the road adjacent to the statue of His Royal Highness, George IV. In fits of giggles, the students point and take photographs of the old Hanovarian usurper. Intrigued by their behavior, I ask one what's up.

"Come here," he says, taking me to a certain spot in the middle of the street, three-quarters onto the royal plinth. "Look!"

He points at the statue, whose regal poise is now somewhat marred by the appearance of a sad-looking penis dangling out of the codpiece in the front of George's Knight of the Garter regalia.

"That's brilliant! Did you just notice it?"

"No, the whole story was in our student magazine. Apparently, the statue was commissioned by the English and they hired a local sculptor named James Stewart, who, unbeknownst to them, was a Jacobite."

"I'm not surprised, with a name like that!"

"Aye. Well, he fashioned the likeness so's that when you viewed it from the side, the end of the royal scepter sticks out like the king's old tadger! And see what he put on the back of the plinth."

I walk to the rear where "Erected 1822" is carved into the limestone block.

"The Brits were furious when they found out about the prank and ordered the arrest of James Stewart, who by that time had fucked off to Canada with the commission money."

"Good!"

Leaving the rude king displaying his wares to the students and burghers of Edinburgh alike, I stroll down the hill toward the sea, singing a children's song about the maid-loving monarch whose dynasty was almost toppled by the Jacobite Scots army:

> *Georgy Porgy puddin' and pie,*
> *Kissed the girls and made them cry,*
> *When the boys came out to play,*
> *Georgy Porgy ran away.*

By the time I get back along to the St. Vincent, Angie's Dave is sitting in the back, drinking a pint of cider. I'll have a friendly chat with him and maybe he'll buy me a beer as thanks for the nice fresh crab I put his way.

"Hi, Davy! How was your crab dinner?"

"Don't fuckin' ask me aboot it!"

"Did you not like it then? Was it not good eating?"

"I dunno, I never ate it."

"Why not? Angie said you loved crab."

"I did, until I came hame last night. There was a barry smell of boiled seafood as I came into the hoose. Angie says, 'I've got your favorite . . . it's boiled crab for supper. It's in that big pot with the lump of concrete on top.'

"I says, 'What the hell is a lump o' concrete doing on top of a pot?'"

"So she says, 'Billy told me to boil the crab, so I put him in a pot of cold water and lit the gas. Well, he was awful strong and he kept knocking the pan lid off and trying to climb out, so I had to put a heavy weight on to it, to keep him in.'

"Dear God, Bill, she boiled the poor fucker alive! After that, I didn't have the heart to eat it."

I'm beginning to enjoy walking the dog, and the ritual of his workout becomes refined over the next few weeks. A tartan blanket makes the schoolyard steps more comfortable, and sandwiches and a newspaper or a book add to the pleasure of invigilating the beast's exercise. Quietly reading on the top of the stairs, I only have to flick my foot every couple of minutes to tip the ball down the steps and play the game. The bone-headed dog never tires of this monotony and is pleased to play the same game, over and over, until his legs give out. He has become a dependable source of income, however, and is certainly easy to entertain.

It's a beautiful day as myself and Rufus, after a session of playing ball, close on the St. Vincent for an afternoon noggin. Chris is there and takes the mutt for an extra walkies around the block. He's no interest in the dog; he does it to chat up the women out walking their dogs. He lets Rufus have a sniff at a bitch, then he says, "Can my dog have your dog's phone number?"

This has to be the worst pickup line in the world—and what's worse, it works!

I try this caper one day in the park, but Rufus takes off between the girl's legs, and before I can let go of his leash, my hand is in a personal place and the lassie's hand is smacking the head off me.

One Monday afternoon, I go to pick him up as usual, and his owner opens the door. She stares at me for some time, until a flash of realization lights up her face.

"Oh, you've come for the dog. I regret to say he's dead . . . killed yesterday up on Fetties Row . . . hit by a car, poor darling. I had just let him off the leash behind the tennis courts, when a stray ball whistled over the bloody fence, into the main road. Well, he took off after it like a charging rhino and was run over by a cement truck. Died instantly, poor love. He always was a bit giddy. I suppose you'll miss him. Here's a pound for your trouble—cheerio!" The door slams in my face again. I'm stunned.

The discreet charm of the bourgeoisie, I think, as I make my rueful way down to the pub. I raise a glass to the passing of man's best friend. Damn it all! I will miss the silly sod, and I'm going to miss the money even more.

→ Chapter 23 ←

Esus of the barbarous altars . . .
Lucan the Roman

IN THE WEEK SINCE THE DOG'S DEATH, THE WORLD HAS
turned upside down. André has indeed opened his lighting company,
but as luck would have it, the first job he has available is for a van driver. Chris Dale has a driving license, so he gets it. I've never learned to
drive; there wasn't much room to practice on a ship.

Bad luck comes in threes, they say, and sure enough, the landlord
has ejected us from the attic flat and told Gordie to get out, too. We
move our belongings into one of the old damp basements that Terry
and Gordon are renovating. Here we unroll our sleeping bags on flat-
tened cardboard boxes, which do little to make the concrete floor more
bearable.

An unexpected cold spell blusters in from northern Russia, stopping
spring in mid-blossom. Lethargy falls upon me, too. It's like wearing a
backpack full of bricks that I can't put down. No money, no hope of a
job, and even less chance of romance now that I've nowhere to live.
Compounding these evils, I also sense a loss of direction. What am I
doing here? Where am I going? I feel adrift, a ship not under command.

The capricious winds of fortune blow me to the top of the schoolyard steps where I used to play with Rufus. In a somber cloud of soli-
tude, they dump me on my backside, where I indulge in something I
have rarely done in my life, feeling sorry for myself.

Kids' voices float across the glass-speckled schoolyard like the cries
of wild geese. In each corner of the playground, groups of children

gather in knots, playing games that were old in my grandfather's time. The wind whirls their songs around in eddies of dust and shredded paper, and snatches of rhyme reach me atop my stone staircase.

The wee lassies skipping jump rope sing:

> *Jean McPherson was a person, wi' long yellow hair,*
> *She took the boat along the water, last Glasgow Fair,*
> *The rain came pouring down in torrents,*
> *Her hair she couldn'y keep dry,*
> *And all the day the streaks of gray were runnin' through the dye.*

The wee laddies playing at the ball sing:

> *Old Jocky wears the kilt, he's always in the fashion,*
> *An every time the wind gets up, he canny help but flashin.*

One of the boys comes over to the bottom of the steps and shouts up: "Huy, mister, where's yer dug?"

"I'm afraid he's dead . . . he got hit by a car."

The small kid calls over his shoulder to his mates: "I telt ye! The big dug's brown-breid . . . got a slap o' a motor!"

His pals start drifting over to me on hearing the news. They form a sullen semicircle at the foot of the steps. I find it quite moving the way these scruffy boys share my grief. I feel a lump forming in my throat.

"I had a dug once and he's deid, too."

"Oh, that's a shame . . . I'm sorry to hear it. What happened to him?" I ask, almost on the edge of tears.

"Well, I was teaching him not to eat and he just got the hang of it . . . and he deid!"

They piss themselves laughing, and more boys, sensing blood, gather around.

"Do you go to this school then?" I say, trying to shift the conversation away from my embarrassment.

"Aye, I do, mister, but I've got a brother at the university."

"Oh, really. What's he doing there?"

"Nothing much. They keep him in a bottle . . . he was born with two heids!"

The rabble flee to hoot and holler from a safe distance.

"Got ye, neh-neh!" the vulgar skite needles me, waving the V sign at me.

"Aye, you got me all right, you raggedy-arsed little urchin . . . you living monument to faulty contraception! You got me fine! Now bugger off!"

> *The raggit childer o' the Gael*
> *Wi' hides as tough as auld chin-mail,*
> *Fleet tae smile an' swift tae curse,*
> *Touch no' the cat, ye'll cam' off worse.*

The wee wag and his pals retire to the opposite side of the playground. By the backslaps and grins, I can tell that he's king for the day.

Like poor kids the world over, they have their dignity and show it through their quick wits and kindred sense. They also seem to know the songs of their forebears; the rhymes, sung whilst bouncing rubber balls off the gable end wall of the school, are quaint to say the least:

> *One—two—three O'Leary*
> *I saw Wallace Beery*
> *Sitting on his bumbaleery*
> *Eating chocolate soldiers.*

These street songs are handed down, child to child. I'm sure none of these kids has any idea who Wallace Beery was.

> *Our school's the best school,*
> *It's made with bricks an' plaster*
> *The only thing that's wrang wi' it,*
> *Is the baldy-headed master.*
> *He goes to the pub on Sat'day night,*
> *An' goes to church on Sunday,*
> *Tae pray tae the Lord to gi' him strength,*
> *Tae murder us all on Monday.*

Aye, there's fierce power in song, I'm thinking. All humankind has found release in the lilted word. From the primeval keen to the unknown lines that became the first hymn to the love-fired lyrics that happy hearts sing universally, life's labors are salved by the passing of song. Nations rally to anthems; the grief-stricken cry lamentations. The lullaby crooned at the cradle of beginning inevitably becomes the dirge of death at journey's end. My mental musing ends abruptly in revelation.

That's what's wrong with me—I'm a singer who's not singing the songs!

The gloom of the morning evaporates in the yeast-laden air. The time has come to get up off my arse, both literally and figuratively. I am restored.

A brisk breeze pushes gently on my back as I head down to the old antique shop in Stockbridge.

The doorbell tinkles, but no one appears from within. Making my way into the inner sanctum, I hear the sounds of furious labor.

Like a hermit in his cell, Bob, with a ferocity born of frustration, carves, chips, and chisels at the knotted gnarl of oaken wood on the bench before him. A necromantic ambience surrounds his earnest efforts.

"I know he's in here somewhere."

"Who's in there, Bob?"

"You'll see soon enough!"

A frenzy of mallet slaps produces a flurry of shavings that spiral to the floor like hewn helixes of DNA. Picking up a fine rasp, the old wizard, with infinitesimal care, chamfers the yielding wood. Through the calendar of concentric tree rings, the keen-edged chisel cleaves, until incrementally a small, almost human hand appears in delicate relief, brought forth from the sinewy veins of the stubborn oak grain.

"There you are, my lad. Now, only one more thing to do before revealing the rest of your wee body."

The scraping of the fine file and the crackling fire are the only sounds that greet the birth of the unseen creature. I venture to speak, but instinct holds my tongue in reverence during this moment of intense incarnation. Deftly, Bob carves a manacle around the wrist of the unsculpted figure. This is soon joined by a neatly chiseled chain shackled to a wooden pin. He smiles in triumph.

"Now I have you, my boy, now I have you!"

For the first time in these proceedings, Bob seems to relax and take full notice of my presence. He falls back into a frenzy of chipping, but no longer preoccupied by his prenatal task, addresses me with devilish glee.

"Tree spirits are elusive creatures—even when you sense them in a piece of wood, they may still escape you in the carving stage. The trick is to find a hand or a foot and put a shackle on it quickly. Then they are trapped and can be hewn into a recognizable form without escaping altogether. The shackle also binds them to your will and not their own, so they may be of use to you in divination or the like!"

"How did you know he was in there?"

"Well, I know what to look for. A while ago, whilst walking in the woods, I noticed an oak tree with branches that had rubbed together to form an X shape. This I perceived to be the dwelling place of a tree spirit, so I cut out the section that you see here. When you hack away the surrounding wood, the form that is left is a child of Esus, the father of tree spirits. That's him up there!"

He points to the wall, where an intricately carved plank of driftwood, resembling the god Pan, stares at me puckishly through lewd, goatish eyes.

"Well, who was this Esus then?"

"There's no *was* about it! He *is* an ancient Celtic deity worshiped in the cult of the trees. Often shown as a wood cutter, Esus is the spirit of the life force and sacred wisdom of the trees, the *Dru Vid* or oaken knowledge from which is derived the term *Druid.* He is in the yule log that you bring into your house at Christmas, the father that nurtures the sacred mistletoe, which you also bring into your home at Christmas. The connection here is more apparent than it first seems. In the dim distant past, when Christianity came to these islands with Joseph of Arimathea, the Druids are presented with a new religion which states that Jesus, which they would have pronounced *He-sus,* was crucified and died on a tree and thus became the new messiah. To tree-worshiping devotees of Esus, this would seem to be just a new twist on their established religion, so no conflict of interest. This is how Celtic Christianity flourished when all of the rest of Europe was a dark, vandalized morass. All the Druids did was change the religious emphasis of the deity from being a male Thunder God, to being the female entity they were more comfortable with. Hence, Jesus takes the backseat, and his mother, Mary, is promoted as the divine supplicant, the one you pray to. *Now* what do you think?"

He holds up the finished figure, which, modulated by the firelight, seems to pulsate with vital force. The motherless child of Esus is altogether queer looking. Wizened and twisted, the lank-limbed urchin stares with piercing intensity through the slits of his gimlet eyes. I shudder. Bob laughs.

"He has a power, does he not?"

"He sure does, Bob, he gives me the willies."

"Well, you'll never be a Druid if a wee tree spirit can put the fear into you. Stand up to him, show him who's boss." Bob passes me the fetish, which I hold as if it may bite me.

"Study his form, for there is a clue as to his nature combined within."

I stare at the oak orphan and look for recognizable signs.

The reclining spirit forms the rough X shape indicative of his humble origins; one hand rises in a form of a salutation, and the other is firmly shackled to its pin. Two spindly legs splay out, suggesting the appearance of an upside-down sky diver, while the expression on his face is one of shrewd cupidity, tempered with a hostile smirk that gives an all-round air of mischievousness. But what could be the clue to the spirit's nature? There is something familiar about the form of the augury, but I cannot put my finger on it. Yes! That's it! Fingers. Just like his creator, the figure is endowed with pudgy little hands and stubby wee fingers— ah-ha!

"Is it the hands, Bob?"

"It is! Well done, my boy. I'll make a Druid of you yet! You see, a spirit's hand carved in the likeness of one's own will never turn against you, and that's of primary importance if you are dealing with the gentlemen from the otherworld!"

Bob bends over the bench attending to his infant imp, like a figure from a Christmas crib setting. A cold breath of wind chills the hairs on my neck as I sense some silent presence manifesting behind me.

"Caress a tree, my friend."

"Jesus! Tom, you scared the wits out of me!"

"It is cold out today, is it not? Caress a tree before they die and become ugly furniture." Without fear of consequence, he throws pieces of an Edwardian dresser onto the crackling fire, which burnishes the room with a coppery glow.

"It's incredible that you two make a living—you burn more antiques than you sell."

"There are things that must be done, that are not yet begun, my friend." Tom's bushy eyebrows lift in the direction of the workbench. He nods over at the wooden figure.

"Who is our new arrival?"

"That's Bob's tree spirit, that is. A newborn child of Esus!"

"And what are you going to do with him, Bob?"

"I'm going to put him up here." Bob clears a place for the fetish on the encrusted marble mantelpiece.

My friends and I sit in a semicircle around the most expensively fired hearth in the known world, as Esus and his offspring gaze down on our unholy trinity.

I am blessed to be among such learning and good humor and do my best to adopt a little of the ample wisdom and charisma that abound in this gentle company. These men give generously of both and never demand recognition or reward for their efforts. An open labyrinth lies ahead, and my mentors guide me through the maze of the mind to where the cauldron of the Celtic soul steams and bubbles with incorruptible enlightenment. Bob, an effervescent evangelist, entreats my immature imagination to soar above the confines of convention, whereas Tom, steadfast anchor to Bob's dirigible capering, is solid and sure, as trustworthy as the trees he loves.

Tom puts the kettle on for a cup of tea as Bob takes up the tale.

"There's a carving of Esus in Paris that was discovered under the choir of Notre Dame Cathedral in 1711. The Christians often build their churches on pagan sites. It is a way to show the natives that the old culture has been conquered. Did you know that, Bill?"

"Yes, I've seen it in Wales. The church at Cascob is built on an old tumulus, and so is another about five miles away. I remember my trips to Radnorshire when I was wee and my dad telling me that many churches are on ley lines because they are built on the sighting mounds for the leys." Tom sips his tea and begins.

"The same is true in Mexico. The conquistadors destroyed the temples of the Aztecs and erected their chapels on the ruins. That is the hallmark of invasive cultures. Look at London. The White Hill was the burial place of the head of Bran the Blessed, the great mythic Celtic warrior, whose head could travel along ley lines. The tradition was that while Bran faced across the sea to the Continent, no attack would come from that direction. It is said that prior to Caesar's invasion of ancient Britain, the head was secretly dug up and removed by Roman spies, paving the way for the later occupation. This story, in altered form, lives on in English tradition. The Normans built the Tower of London on top of the White Hill and it became not only the prison for the king's enemies but home to a small flock of ravens. The English believe that if the ravens leave the tower, then Britain will fall to a foreign invader. This is a curious echo of the much older superstition, don't you think? But I doubt the modern-day English realize this, or that the Celtic word for raven is *bran*!"

Bob nods his agreement and Tom sorts through a dusty pile of books on the back windowsill.

"I sense that you are experiencing some inner turmoil," he says, over his shoulder.

"Yes, I'm sort of looking for answers at the moment."

"Do you know the questions, my friend?"

"No."

"*Y Gododdin*," he says, handing me a slim volume of Welsh poetry, "written by Aneirin, great bard of the Celtic British tribes, when he dwelled in the primitive fortress where Edinburgh Castle now stands. It tells of the coming of the Saxons and how the flower of Edinburgh's warriors mustered and marched to their deaths at the Battle of Catterick in 605 A.D. The Saxons won, but we know little of them, because they had no bards, whereas Aneirin has made sure that the bravery of the Welsh-speaking British warriors will be remembered forever. You're a bard . . . use your talents to free yourself first, then look to the fortunes of your people!"

I open the book and, glancing at the first line, I read:

An gelwir mor a chynnwr ym plymnwyt
Yn tryvrwyt peleidyr peleidyr gogymwyt . . .

We were called! The sea and the borders are in conflict.
Spears are mutually darting, spears equally destructive . . .

"Isn't Welsh a beautiful language? You can convey so much in so few words," I say.

"That's the true sign of a poetic tongue," Bob answers.

"What do you think I should do, Tom?"

"If I were you, my friend, I would make a pilgrimage to the top of Arthur's Seat and take on a renewal of spirit. A great man once said, 'Strange insights are vouchsafed to those who seek the high places.' He was an Irishman, too, by the name of Flann O'Brien. Much might be gained from such an enterprise."

"Tom's right, Bill, Arthur's Seat is a powerful place. On the first of May, the feast of Beltaine, multitudes of Edinburgh folk will climb the slopes before sunrise to collect the first fall of dew. They will anoint their eyes with it and try to see visions. As the sun rises they will light bonfires in honor of Bilé, the Celtic god of death and rebirth. Go and be reborn, carry your Beltaine fire in your heart."

"When should I go?"

"Now, before it gets dark," says Bob.

It's late afternoon when I reach Arthur's Seat. My mind echoes with the noble stanzas of Aneirin's fourteen-hundred-year old poem, spurring me up the rugged track leading to the summit. The twisted neck of volcanic strata rises tall and sinewy from the epicenter of the city, an ancient place surrounded on all sides by modern urban sprawl.

Dappled with tough grass and whin-bush, the twin peaks of the sacred hill resemble a sphinx. The craggy head, to which I climb, is the high point connected by a sloping saddle called the Hunter's Bog to a rounded haunch known as the Lion's Rump. Here on the green slopes, the mighty Arthur, prince of the Votadini, called his countrymen to arms and dealt a fierce blow to the marauding Saxon war bands at the

Battle of Guinnion or the White Tower, fought close to the village of Stow in the Borders. He left three hundred dead on the lush plain, beneath the white moss-covered remains of a huge Pictish Broch. Next, he defeated them in the Ettrick forest and once more at Solway. His mounted troops harried the Saxons over Hadrian's Wall and down into Somerset, where it is believed he was fatally wounded at Camluan and carried to the Isle of Avalon to die in the sacred Celtic sanctuary of Ynys Whytyn, or the Island of Glass, said to have been founded by Joseph of Arimathea and better known as Glastonbury.

The hut circles of these proud people still form grassy horseshoes on the level parts of the mountain, and parallel rows of cultivation terraces striate the south face of the ancient hill. Within this natural citadel rise the man-made earthworks of Dunsappie hill fort, thrusting square and impregnable above its adjacent lough. On the obverse side of the mount, great skeletal stacks of russet rock form the cage of Samson's Ribs, lapped by the placid waters of Middlemere. The lake has yielded hundreds of bronze broadswords.

Was it here that the legend of the Lady of the Lake was born? I ponder. Was the sword Excalibur retrieved from its gravelly depths? Perhaps these votive offerings to the water spirits supplemented the weaponry of Arthur's ill-equipped native army.

Like Ambrosius Aurelianus, rallying the Celtic tribes in the south, Arthur's strength lay in using the Roman military tactics he had learned while serving in their cavalry legions. The Roman garrisons abandoned their colony, falling back to protect Rome from the barbarian hordes encircling it. Disbanding the Celtic auxiliary legions, they removed most ordinance with their retreat, destroying forts and military bases from Edinburgh to London. Arthur's impoverished army, left to defend the northland from the invaders, used the swiftness of mounted units and the grid of Roman roads to outflank and outmaneuver the Saxon foot soldiers.

Suddenly I see the historical parallels: the Celtic way of life still hanging on despite daily assaults by our Saxon overlords and us, the impoverished Celts, besieged in the vitrified fortress of our own wild culture. Safe within its certainties, we take nourishment from poetry, find refreshment in the deep streams of sweet music and, emboldened by our ancestral anthems, strike back with the sword of wit and the spear of wisdom at an enemy whose only fault lies in not understanding who we are.

I make a last effort and scramble up the rocks to the concrete pillar that marks the summit of Arthur's Seat. I stand, arms raised to the sun, a stiff sea breeze tugging at my hair.

"I AM THE ONCE AND FUTURE CELT!" I proclaim.

A violent vortex swirls my words into the crevices of the aged eminence and spits them away on the uncaring wind. I pay no heed. I have reached my goal, realized the nature of my calling, and surely now can pierce the veil. I lean into the wind, arms outstretched.

Giddy with vertiginous elation, I narrow my eyes to scan the view before me. At first nothing happens. Then the modern world begins to fade away in an atavistic trance. Dissolving through the centuries, the Georgian New Town vanishes into a vista of open tillage, and the great stone causeways of Leith docks abdicate their tenure to massive wooden galleys and sleek sailing skiffs. The square barrack buildings of Edinburgh Castle abandon their prominence to round, thatched huts, from whose roofholes long blue-gray plumes of smoke snake through the straw-strewn streets. Effused in amber light, children and dogs gambol, sending clouds of dust scudding toward rustic wattle ramparts. From their vantage point atop these bulwarks, plaid-clad warriors pace or stand in small groups, looking south and leaning heavily on long ash spears.

To the north, across the silvern expanse of the Forth estuary, the twin peaks of East and West Lomond form the breasts of mother earth, as from Burnt Island harbor, a swelling body of merchant ships, loaded deep with golden grain, leaves her fertile womb to replenish the granaries of Caledonia. On the thermals above the Ochil Hills, flights of wild eagles wheel and soar, guarding the passages to the northwest. South toward the Pentland Hills, sunlight flashing from shield and helm, comes a patrol of horsemen trotting homeward up the old Roman Dere Street. As the great iron-studded drawbridge slams shut behind the last of the riders, my vision fades and I am left alone and bereft, a human crucifix on an ancient hill.

For one all-too-brief moment, I have seen the world refracted through a dew drop—my world that dwells deep within my Celtic genes. Not for nothing are our people drawn to art, music, literature, and poetry; it is to create a balance for our fundamental spirituality, pagan or otherwise. These two lobes of the sacred trefoil hold in check our warlike nature and sense of honor. We are a three-leafed knot of light.

In my vision of the last great golden days of peace, before the sacking of Lothian by the Anglo-Saxons and the decimation, repression, and usurping of Celtic culture, I have finally understood who I am.

"I AM THE ONCE AND FUTURE CELT!" I again roar in triumph to the silent spirits!

Sublimely intoxicated, I wander about, hoping my chimera will re-manifest itself.

"Give me a sign . . . a token . . . some indication that I'm on the right track!" I plead to the elements, then check myself. "Thoir dhomh comhartha!" I demand, reasoning that the old gods would be better at understanding the Gaelic.

The golden orb of the late-afternoon sun springs abruptly from behind its cumulous concealment, causing me to look down sharpish.

By my left boot a queerly shaped stone lies half-interred in the compressed clay. I bend down and dig out a splendid flint arrowhead. With a sense of wonderment, I roll the aged artifact in my hand.

"Climb to the top of the high hill of the arrows," the Old Woman of the Roads had once told me.

No, this can't be it, I think.

Suddenly, with a buzz like an electric shock, I realize the place in which I'm standing is called, in the Gaelic tongue, Ar'saighead, the Height of the Arrows.

I have indeed found my token!

✦ Chapter 24 ✦

But mousie, thou art no thy lane
In proving foresight may be vain
The best laid schemes of mice and men,
Gang oft times a-gley.

Robert Burns

MY DESCENT OF THE MOUNTAIN IS A SLOW INCREMENT IN harmony with the setting sun. Elation floats my footsteps across town to the St. Vincent, where I hope to find friends to share in my exhilaration. Except for a few cloth-capped old men playing dominoes and a couple of students reading books, the Vinny is empty.

"Naw, sorry, son, I've no seen any of yer pals a' nicht," says Jimmy the barman.

I check the basement where we are staying. No sign of anyone there either, though something appears different since this morning. I light a fire in the gaping stone grate that once housed an iron cooking range, now long gone to the scrap dealers. The chimney draws well, and with all the building and demolition work, there is no shortage of firewood to burn. The crackling timbers spit sparks haphazardly, like tracer bullets, into the frigid room. Spasmodic, orange shadow dances play on the crumbling plaster walls. With the fire taking the chill off the air, I hear the St. Stephen's Church clock strike eight.

Where in the name of God are the lads? I wonder, checking my pockets for any loose change.

A mixture of curiosity and the price of a pint takes me across the road to the Baillie bar at the very end of the street, where we often go when the St. Vincent is full.

"Naw," says Yatz, leaning over the bar, "I haven't seen any of your friends. It's been a quiet night, except for that lot in the corner."

He points to a group of well-dressed girls gathered in various states of inebriation under a bunch of multicolored helium balloons.

"What's going on there?" I ask, taking a sup of my beer.

"It's either an office party or a hen night—I don't know."

"What's a hen night?"

"It's when a bunch of lassies go out and get drunk just before one of them gets married."

"Oh."

As if summoned by my question, one of the young ladies gets up from the table and walks toward me. She is dark-haired with coal-black eyes and very red lips. The girl stands hesitant in front of the three walnut doors leading off from the barroom.

"Are you looking for the ladies', miss?" I offer.

"I am, yes."

"It's that one there. They took the old signs down to put up new brass ones, but when the plaques came, they had no screw holes in them."

"Why didn't they put the old signs back up?"

"Because they'd varnished the doors."

"How silly," she laughs and disappears.

I look over to her pals, one of whom, covered in ribbons, is sliding majestically under the table.

My God, if she's the bride, it's going to be an awful sickly wedding, I say to myself.

The dark-haired girl comes back out from the loo.

"Do you know me?" she asks, smiling quizzically.

"No, miss, I don't."

"Why do you call me miss?"

"Because I don't know your name."

"Oh, I see. I thought maybe you knew me. I'm a school teacher and am used to being called Miss. My name's Leslie, by the way." She holds out her hand for me to shake.

"I'm Bill, but my friends call me Billy," I say, taking her hand and, in a fit of devilment, kissing it.

"Do you want a drink?" she asks.

"No, it's all right . . . I can't get you one back."

"No bother . . . I just got paid. Hey, mister, a pint of Guinness and a gin and tonic, please."

Yatz serves the young girl and while she's rummaging in her purse for change, he gives me "the look," querying if I fancy her.

I nod back, Too right I do.

"Come on, Leslie, we're off to Tiffany's for some dancing!" The posse of beauties is getting ready to leave.

"Okay, I'll be along in a while. I just got a fresh drink."

"Aw, come on!"

"No . . . I'll wander up in about five minutes. You go ahead."

She leans over and whispers in my ear.

"Do you dance?"

"No," I say, "I've got two left feet."

"I don't mind the dancing, but I hate that disco music they play. It gives me a headache," she confides.

Her mates totter over. One of them whispers in Leslie's ear. She shakes her head. Another one whispers and she shakes her head again. Then they leave without her, laughing and whooping into the night.

Leslie sits next to me on a bar stool.

"What do you do?" she asks.

"I'm a . . . a . . . freelance Druid."

"Oh, that sounds fun. What does it entail?"

"I don't know, I've only just started."

"Ah-ha . . . you're pulling my leg." She laughs. "Where do you live?"

"Erm . . . I . . . er . . . live in a derelict shop basement over the road."

"You're kidding me."

"No."

"Show me then, I want to see," she says, gulping her cocktail down in one go.

"Really?"

"Yes."

We walk out, arm in arm, into the foggy night. Fifty yards away, I open the iron gate at the top of the stone steps and guide her down into the dark, shadowy vault where the fire cinders provide the only lighting until I can find the candle.

I toss more wood onto the fire and coax the flames to life.

"This is so romantic," she sighs. "Where do you sleep?"

"We're sitting on it," I reply, picking up the corner of the sleeping bag so she may see.

"Don't you get cold?"

"Yes, freezing."

"I'm getting a chill just thinking about it." She shivers.

I pull a woolen horse blanket over our shoulders. She snuggles her dark curls into my chest.

"Have you ever wanted to run away with the gypsies, Billy?"

"No, I grew up with the gypsies. I wanted to run away with a team of chartered accountants!"

"You *are* silly—but nice," she says, kissing me long and hard. I'm overawed by this welcome turn of events. If this is what one climb up the magic hill does for you, I'll go up again tomorrow and the day after for that matter.

In the midst of such unanticipated pleasure, I sense anguish. Leslie's embraces and kisses are not the slow, caressing love that I had dreamed about. They are a desperate torrent of passion, hurried and hungry, a tongue-nipping, teeth-clattering frenzy that alarms me. In a flurry of limbs, the dark-haired girl kicks off her shoes and wriggles from her clothing, tearing at mine in the process. Never once does she let the feverish kisses stop until we are both naked in the flickering firelight.

She mounts me as if I'm a riderless horse, and saddled with the fury of her desire, I take off in the pursuit of pleasure.

In the flame-twitching glow of the embers, her unveiled body flits shapely in the shadows as across the Elysian fields of gasping gratification we gallop. My mind is roiling with mythic imaginings. I fancy we are back in the days of heroes and monsters. In a sudden flare of firelight,

Leslie is transfigured into a vision of the copper-skinned Ethiopian princess, Andromeda, and I shall be her rescuer, Perseus the wanderer. My thoughts take flight on winged sandals, carrying her with me across the constellations on my soaring journey. She is a meteor blazing across the sky, I am a signal rocket that bursts in a hundred flashing orbs of iridescent light, leaving only the stick to flutter slowly back to earth.

Leslie is a little girl again, lying sweet and breathless in the fire's glow, small tear-like beads of amber rolling from her brow. Pulling the blanket around her body, I wrap her in my arms, and we fall asleep together, the princess and the vagabond.

I had forgotten what it feels like to lie with a woman. What a hard world it is without the warm softness of the female body. The night passes in snapshots of fantasy and reality. My terror is that I may awaken to find, yet again, that this encounter was just another dream. The cold focus of morning holds the proof: Leslie still nestles in my arms.

"Hello," I say, as her eyes flicker open.

"Hi," she says, demurely gathering her clothes together and trying to untangle them.

"How are you feeling?"

"C . . . c . . . cold," she stammers.

"I'll light the fire, it'll warm you up."

"No, it's okay. Thanks all the same. I have to go."

"When can I see you again?"

"You can't," she says, pulling on her skirt.

"Why not?"

"Because."

"Because what?"

"Because I'm getting married tomorrow, that's what!"

She grabs her shoes and slips them on. At the door, she stops and turns.

"I'm sorry. Please don't tell anyone."

The last I see of Leslie is her blue high heels clicking up the steps and out of my life.

I don't know which has left me more stunned, her sudden arrival or her even swifter departure. The guilt machine starts to edge its gears forward. I'd have a hard time getting around this one at confession.

There's a name for this sort of thing, isn't there? I think to myself.

Fornication! accuses the little white figure with the halo on my left shoulder.

Sweetness! soothes the wee red-horned guy with the spiky stick to my right.

Lustfulness! charges the angel. Lewdness! Licentiousness! Lechery!

Sweetness, hisses the demon.

Yeah . . . sweeeetness! I smile to myself as I doze back off to sleep.

I am rudely awakened by Terry and Gordon standing by the fireplace, both having a good laugh at my expense.

"Got your oats then, last night, did you?" smirks Terry.

"Eh?"

"Don't come the innocent with us. It's written all over your face!" Gordie grins.

"I don't know what you mean."

"Who was here last night?"

"I'm telling you, Terry, no one," I squirm.

"Then whose dainty little footprints are these?" Gordie points to the dusty floorboards.

"They're mine," I chance.

"And I suppose these are yours, too?" A smirking Terry holds up a pair of tattered pantyhose.

"All right, you got me, but I'm saying no more about it, okay?"

"Sure, Billy, we'll wait till it comes out in paperback. What's it going to be called, *Lust in the Dust*?"

"Piss off!"

"Well, we're going over to Fat Annie's teashop for breakfast. If you want to come, wash yer face first," chortles Gordie.

"Why?"

"'Cause that shade of lipstick really isn't your color."

We sit in the small café drinking tea. I sense the lads have some other scheme at hand.

"What's going on, you two?"

"Well, while you were dipping yer wick, we found a new apartment. We started moving stuff up there yesterday when you went missing."

"Where is it?"

"At the top of Broughton Street, number sixty-nine," says Gordie. Terry starts smirking again. I ignore the obvious inference.

"How big is it? Is there room for all of us?"

"There's three bedrooms, a big kitchen, and a toilet."

"No bathroom?"

"Don't be daft."

"Three bedrooms? Does that mean we get one each?"

"No, there's already a guy called Kevin living there. I was at art school with him. So he's got one, me and Chris have the big room at the back, and you and Terry can share the wee room at the front."

"It's a legitimate place, isn't it? Proper rent book and everything?"

"Yep, it's all above board, owned by a Mr. Pandit," Gordie smiles.

"Great, that means I can sign on the sausage again, doesn't it?"

"It does, Billy boy, it does."

"Good! Can someone buy me breakfast then? I'm Hank Marvin!"

"All that shaggin', I suppose?" giggles Terry.

After a meal of tuna fish and brown rice, I carry boxes of Gordon's books up from the dusty cellar where I had spent the past few nights, and stack them on the pavement. Chris Dale arrives in a big blue van with "Northern Lights" painted on the side.

"Nice motor, Chris. Is it André's?"

"Yeah, he said we could use it to move house."

"That's decent of him."

"Yep. Come on and we'll get the last of it loaded and take a ride up to the new gaff."

"That's the last box," grunts Terry, sliding the carton onto the van.

"Terry!"

"What?"

"Take the lassie's tights off yer head!"

The new flat is on the top floor of a four-story tenement block not far from the schoolyard steps where I exercised Rufus.

"Jasus, this place has more steps than a lighthouse." I'm wheezing under the weight of books.

"Aye, it's quite a climb. You can see why they take oxygen up mountains," gasps Chris, hands on knees.

"Thank God we're too poor to have much gear," says Terry, panting up with the final box.

"Phew!" I throw myself down on the settee.

"You better get up to the dole office and sign on before they close. Here's a copy of the rent book with your name on it."

"Thanks, Gordie . . . I will . . . when I . . . get my . . . breath back."

"Aye, and tell them that you do something really weird or they might send you back to the *Gardy Loo* to puncture condoms. They're still advertising that job."

"I'm not surprised," I say, grabbing my coat.

Signing on the dole is a way of life in Scotland, but still carries a certain social stigma. Unemployed folk refer to it as being "on the broo" or, in rhyming slang, "the sausage roll." All of Britain is in the grips of the current recession. South of the border, the English are screaming blue murder. No one here pays them any heed. After all, Scotland has been in a recession for two hundred years.

To sign on for unemployment benefits, you need a legitimate address and now I have one. At the busy dole office I pass my paperwork to a bored-looking clerk. He sniffs at me and wearily looks at my claim.

"Ha! That's a new one on me! So, you're an ancient manuscript bookbinder, are you?"

"I was, yes, before I was made redundant."

"So, what's your preferred binding material, worked leather or velum?"

I guess he's testing my supposed credentials, but if he is, I've done my homework.

"Probably Levantine goatskin morocco, tanned with sumac, of course, although human skin is also rather nice. It's so tactile." I smile back innocently.

"Well, there's nothing of that nature on our list. So here, take this to the pay office."

He stamps my card and throws it across the desk.

"Fuckin' chancer!" he mumbles under his breath.

At the payout desk, I join the huddled masses, and before long a pleasant young girl counts out eight pounds and fifty pence into my eager hand. Folding the notes of my dole money into my long-empty pocketbook, I stroll like a king out into the sunshine.

Now I have all the power in the world and prove it by clapping my hands to scatter a garrulous group of pigeons pecking at some spilled barley on the cobbled street. They rise in a fluttering gray flock, soaring toward the stark, blackened ramparts of Edinburgh Castle, some two hundred feet above. The wind is from the sea. A zephyr of malty yeast wafts upon the salt air from the environs of the Scottish and Newcastle brewery down by Leith docks.

I am a happy boy. A happy boy with a mission! Now, with some means to live beyond, I'm on my way to buy some new clothes and then, since my long-slumbering passions have been recently rekindled, I'm going courting.

A young lassie stands motionless by the bus stop on Lothian Road. She looks vaguely familiar. She turns around and I see that it is indeed Delectable Diana, goddess of the hunt. She stands daydreaming in a fluffy white afghan coat. Her long auburn hair tumbles in luscious folds to her shoulders. Diana has the most soulful almond-shaped eyes that hint of exotic, faraway places, somewhere east of Samarkand. This is all the more surprising, because the last time I spoke to her, she told me she came from Leith.

Fate has set this scene, I'm sure of it. The mystic mountain is working its magic again. Since my epiphany on the sacred mount, I feel invincible. No woman would be strong enough to resist my newfound charms, especially not Diana, who's just been dumped by her boyfriend and is also suffering the indignities of being on the dole. Perfect—there's my opener! I'll ask if she's still receiving her unemployment money; we'll get chatting and then, she's as good as mine.

"Hello there, Diana. How are you doing?"

"Oh, hello, Billy, I didn't see you there. How's tricks?" She shades her lovely eyes from the slant of the setting sun. Her smile is as welcoming as the flowers of spring.

"Grand—and yourself? Are you still getting the sausage?" She takes two steps back, the smile fades, and her face begins to redden. I think she must have misheard me, so I repeat the question.

"The sausage. I know things have been a bit rough for you of late, but as long as you're still getting the sausage, eh?" I grin expectantly.

"What on earth has that got to do with you, Billy? You disgusting bugger, I never thought you were like that! Get oot my way!" She plows past me and hops onto the rear platform of the bus that has just pulled up. Before I can take stock of the situation, she sits down, glaring out the window at me.

"Diana, damn it all! I only asked if you were still getting the sausage."

She continues to glower at me from the rear seat of the bus. Maybe I had misjudged her. Perhaps she's a nutcase. What did she think I meant? Then the penny drops. Oh no, of course! She thought I meant *the* sausage.

"No, Diana, you've got me all wrong. I just meant th—"

The engine of the bus revs up, drowning out my voice. In my panic, I notice what looks like a little brown leaf flutter across the pavement and vanish up the leg of my bell-bottoms. As the bus pulls away, I realize that what I've taken to be a leaf stem is, in fact, a tail and the tail is attached to a small brown mouse, which is swiftly clawing its way into my private parts. A frenzied dance of unzipping and unbuckling ensues, exposing the nimble rodent among the family jewels. A quick flick of the wrist sends it packing. Trousers at half-mast, I beam a smile of deliverance as my tormentor scurries into an adjacent doorway.

"Diana . . . Diana!"

"Get away oot of it, ya durty wee bastard!" shrieks an elderly Edinborovian matron, as her umbrella crashes down on the top of my head.

"Ye want locked up, ya clarty wee purvert!" screams an old wifey, jabbing me in the ribs with a walking stick.

"It's a dirty flasher!"

"Ca' the polis!"

"Get a scissors!"

Amidst a rain of invective and blows, I get one last glimpse of the lovely Diana burying her florid face in her two trembling hands. Then, clutching my unzipped trousers together, I run like a hare from the howling mob.

→ Chapter 25 ←

Ceo draoidheachta i gcoim oidhche
[A fog of wizardry in the depths of the night]
Eoghain Ruaidh Ui Shuillebhain (1784)

"LOOK WHAT I FOUND ON ARTHUR'S SEAT YESTERDAY." I PLACE
the delicately chipped flint piece on the kitchen table.

"What is it?" asks Terry, picking it up.

"It's an arrowhead!"

Terry pulls a puzzled, anthropoid face so apelike that it would convince the most dim-witted Christian fundamentalist that Darwin was right.

"What's it for?"

"It's for—what d'ya mean, what's it for? It's an arrowhead, fer Christ sake. What's it for? It's for putting under your pillow to stop toothache, what d'ya think it's for? Dear God, give me strength!"

Terry shrugs his shoulders and hands it back. He picks up a book from one of Gordie's boxes.

"*Quietly Flows the Don*—is it any good?" He looks at the back cover.

"Oh yeah. Mikhail Sholokhov was brilliant. He wrote about life amongst the Russian Cossacks."

"Cossacks? I thought it was about Aberdeen," Terry says, grinning.

Terry is a constant source of amusement. Besides his fanciful way with the girls and legendary ability to get into scrapes, he has an inquiring mind and reads constantly. Facts and unrelated data stick to him like lint to a black velvet suit. He has that odd ability to look at a page and read the whole thing at a glance. I've often wondered if he was one of those strangely gifted people called idiot savants.

Terry sits at the table, plundering the Old Tome's book collection. With the bemused gorilla expression on his face again, he opens volume after volume, gleaning some bizarre truth or speculation from each. Having depleted the first carton of books, he disappears off to the toilet clutching a copy of *The Book of Incredible Facts*. This becomes Terry's bible for a while and while I try to arrange the bedroom, he spends the early part of the evening pelting me with abstract facts.

"Did you know that the coastline of Norway, if it was stretched out in one long line, would go right around the world?"

"Well, who'd have thought it."

"Did you know that the longest word in the English language that you can make up from the top line of a typewriter is *typewriter*?"

"Well, I do now."

"Did you know—wow! That's a freakout, that is!"

"What?"

"It says here that the Javanese Komodo dragon, which can grow to a length of ten feet and weigh up to three hundred pounds, has two penises! Wow!"

"That's handy—something extra for the weekend!"

Terry continues his quest through Gordon's bizarre book. Then, as decidedly, he gets bored with it and goes back to the kitchen for another.

"Ah! Here it is, this is what I was looking for." He carries a slim treatise titled *The Early Christian Church in Northumbria*.

Now I'm in for a real treat, I think. "What in the name of God has got you interested in the early Celtic church?"

"Ah, let me see . . ." He fingers through the work, nodding his head and humming approval, then he reads aloud for my benefit:

> *"Lindisfarne, or Holy Island, is the jewel in the crown of Northumberland. The hallowed island stands apart from the mainland at the end of a three mile tidal causeway. The land was granted to St. Aidan by Oswald, King of Northumbria, in the year 635 A.D. for the building of a wooden chapel. After leaving the sacred island of Iona, St. Aidan set up his mission*

*on this site to spread the gospel to the pagan Saxons. This
earned the region the name 'The Cradle of Christianity.' The
first monastery was destroyed by the marauding Vikings in
875 A.D. who took away the bejeweled covers of the Lindisfarne
Gospels. Luckily the pages were of no value to the illiterate
raiders and survived to be treasured as fine examples of early
Celtic Christian art' . . . dum-te-dum . . . 'The ruins of the
present priory date from the thirteenth century and a statue
of St. Aidan nearby commemorates his death in 651 A.D.
There is also an effigy of Grace Darling, who is buried in the
graveyard.'"*

Here Terry stops, looking even more puzzled than usual. "Who was Grace Darling? Was she his wife?" he asks.

"No, I've heard of her. She was a lighthouse keeper's daughter. Rowed out in a gale to help rescue a crew shipwrecked on the rocks in the middle of a terrible storm."

"When was that?"

"In the 1830s. I think the ship was the *Forfarshire*. Anyway, she became famous and that's why people say, 'You're a proper little darling!'"

"Well, fair play to her then. Let's see, what else have they got here?

*"'The present ruins are from the Benedictine Romanesque
period and were once the hermitage of St. Cuthbert, who
dwelt here many years, walling himself up in a garden, so
he might only see the heavens.'"*

"Why this sudden interest in Lindisfarne, Terry?"

"It's a Celtic holy place, right?"

"Yeah, I suppose so. Aidan was an Irish Celt."

"Well, don't think I'm daft or anything . . ."

"Perish the thought, Terry."

"No, seriously, I want to go on a pilgrimage, like they did in the olden days."

"What for?"

"It's not easy to explain . . . it's to do with the curse!"

"And are you going to tell me what that's all about?"

"I will . . . I will if you come to Lindisfarne with me. You will come, won't you?"

"Sure, Terry, but it's a bit far away. Why don't we go up Arthur's Seat? That's a real mystical place. Maybe you can tell me about it there."

"No, I'd feel more comfortable in a place like Holy Island. I'd rather like to see if I could get the curse lifted! Do you pray?"

"Yes, I do."

"But if you're a Druid, what do you pray to, Jesus, Mary, or what— God?"

"I pray to the universal spirit, which I imagine as being neither male nor female, but taking many forms."

"So, what do you think about evil and sin and such like?"

"Terry, as the archbishop of Canterbury once said, *'I'm agin it!'*"

Terry sits smiling to himself as if digesting our discourse; then his tangential mind kicks in.

"Bill, do you think the Scots swear a lot?"

"No more than most folk in the British Isles. Why do you ask?"

"Oh, nothing. It's just I heard this bloke cursing at his car engine the other day. He stands there in a great cloud of steam, looking under the bonnet, and then he says, 'Fuckin-fuck, the fucker's fucked!' and gives it a kick. It's kind of weird to hear a sentence made up almost entirely of one word, but making perfect sense; wouldn't you say?"

"Yeah, no kidding! *Fuck* isn't really a swear word, it's just an old Saxon word meaning 'to dig a hole in the ground.' The hole you make is called a cunnit, and the stick you dig with is called a bugger; as in the term 'as strong as a bugger,' which was the central lodge pole of a Saxon round house. So there's your English swear words, they're more to do with agriculture than sex."

"Well, bugger me!"

"Ah, now, Terry that's a different sort of buggerment. That word is coincidental and came from the Bogomil heresy in the tenth century."

"Who in hell's name were they?"

"They were an offshoot of the Bulgarian Christian Church, a sect who believed that Christ was the devil's younger brother and had entered Mary's body through her right ear, later exiting from her left ear in the form of a phantom. They reckoned Jesus never took real shape and that the crucifixion and resurrection were myths. They practiced some odd taboos, too. Eating meat was evil, because animals procreated by intercourse; drinking wine was evil, due to the devil planting the vine in the Garden of Eden, and having sex with your wife was evil, because it led to the reproduction of matter."

"What happened to them?"

"They died out."

"I'm not surprised, miserable buggers!"

"Anyway, the Bogomils thought that the devil, Satanael, they called him, created Adam and that God created Adam's soul. Then the devil stole the soul, but couldn't keep it in Adam's body because it kept falling out of his arsehole, so he plugged it up."

"What with?"

"What d'ya think? So as I was saying, the Bogomils were accused of sodomy by the pope and that gave rise to the now obsolete words *bulgary* and *bogomy,* which was later contracted to *buggery.*"

"What about *bog off*? Is that possibly connected?"

"It may well be, Terry."

"It's amazing what people can bring themselves to believe, no wine, no sex—dear God, life wouldn't be worth living. But, Billy, how do you know all these things?"

"How do you know the Komodo dragon has two penises?"

"Hmm, I see, two penises, eh? There's a thing!" Terry lies back on his bed, hands folded behind his head, whilst his mind roams the farmyard of his thoughts like a free-range hen.

"Have you ever noticed the amount of words the Scots have for dirt? It's like the Eskimos have all those different words for snow!"

"Like what? Give me an example."

"Well, like . . . erm . . . like *clarty,* that means filthy, and *boggin,* even more filthy, and *mawkit,* which means stinky. Then there's *baufing,* which is really stinky, and *mingin,* which is stinkier still."

"So what's your point?"

"No point, I was just saying. Do you believe in the Loch Ness monster?"

"Yes, sure, isn't he sighted every year?"

"When?"

"Just before the tourist season, I think. Why?"

"Do you believe that if you wish hard enough for something, it will come true?"

"I believe that faith can move mountains. Yes, I do."

"So do I—well, I try to be an optimist. I'd rather be that than one of those other type of folk, the opposite to an optimist. You know, it be-gins with a *P*—a miserable sort of bastard." Terry's voice is getting softer and slower; eyes shut and head back, he's on the verge of slumber.

"Begins with a *P*? Presbyterian?"

"Aye . . . *zzzz*."

The sound of early-morning traffic and the squealing of bus brakes herald in the morning. The smell of coffee drifts down the hallway, and following the aromatic scent trail, I have my first encounter with the flamboyant character known as Kevin the Wizard. He sits at the kitchen table drinking hideously strong coffee and nervously thumbing a pack of tarot cards. He's a bit of an odd one, dressed in the style not unlike the storybook magician Gandalf or those representations of Merlin found in Pre-Raphaelite paintings. A cloak of purple velvet drapes from his shoulders, almost obscuring the gold-trimmed, white monk's habit beneath, the hem of which in turn flutters above a pair of curly-toed red Moroccan sandals that the Caliph of Baghdad would be proud of.

"Hi, I'm Bill." I smile.

"The divine universal truth bids you welcome," Kevin says, in all seriousness.

"Oh, that's nice. This is my friend Terry."

"Yes, we've met. Shall I read your tarot?"

"No thanks, I haven't had breakfast yet."

He stares at me blankly as if not comprehending. Chris wanders in with Gordie in tow and makes for the coffee pot.

It's amusing how people react to Kevin. Gordie seems to think he's normal, Terry is convinced he's a fairy, whereas Chris takes an obvious delight in taking the mickey out of him.

"Hey, Kevin, have you ever noticed that crap newspapers have horo-scopes and quality papers don't?"

"No, what that's supposed to mean?"

"Intellectuals have no future!"

"I don't get it."

We all laugh and Kevin withdraws with a pouty face.

"You want to be careful, he might put a spell on you," I say.

"I wouldn't worry too much about that," says Gordon. "He can't remember anything from one minute to the next."

"What put him that way?"

"I don't think he heard the warning, 'Don't take the brown acid!'"

Each morning before the adventures of the day begin, we gather around the four-sided pine table that sits like a dolmen in the center of the square kitchen. Every evening, we return to our seats to share our tales of the day's doings and speculate on the morn. The bare boards of this piece of farmhouse furniture seldom see food, unless it comes from the fish-and-chip shop, although a fair number of empty wine bottles do crowd one corner of the room, like penguins in a blizzard. The great table is the sounding board for our daft stories and Kevin's mystical meanderings. Politics, poker games, the prophecies of Nostradamus, horse racing, Bede's ecclesiastical history of Britain, caving, and Kevin's daily tarot readings, all find a place here. The table hears all and says nothing. The one subject seldom discussed is sex. Not directly at least.

Kevin likes to interpret dreams, and part of the morning ritual becomes him holding a nocturnal debriefing. He finds a sexual theme in almost anything.

"I dreamed of cocks last night. What do you think that means, Kevin?"

"Oh, really? What sort of cocks?"

"Cock-a-doodle-doo cocks!" Terry says with an embarrassed smile.

"Let me see now . . ." Kevin sits back, eyes closed as if in prayer. "The cock is considered a sacred bird in Celtic mythology. A herald of the sun, his flame-red comb spiking skywards like the rays of the morning sunrise. He has the ability to drive away darkness and protect mankind from ghosts and other evil spirits. The cock is a powerful fertility symbol, so to dream of the cock is fortuitous."

Terry is pleased. Gordon takes up the job.

"I dreamt I was swimming with a shoal of eels. What d'you make of that?"

"Oh, Gordon, here the sexual connotations are obvious. Eels are queer wee animals who make their thousand-mile migrations to the spawning grounds of the Sargasso Sea to indulge in a mad, writhing melee of mass mating."

"What's that got to do with me?"

"I don't know, Gordon, it was your dream."

The room falls silent and I take this as a cue to put my tuppence worth into the proceedings.

"In Ireland it is reckoned that the devil is in the eel. I've seen fishermen kill them in a most curious way. They make a furrow in the dirt of the riverbank in the form of a cross. Then the eel is held belly up in the groove with the head at the crux of the cross. Within minutes the beast is as stiff as a poker and as dead as a doornail."

"Hmm," says Gordie, "that's like the old method of killing chickens. Years ago, folk used to draw a white chalk line across the kaleyard floor and hold the bird's beak down on the line for a few moments. The hen would get mesmerized by the white line and didn't move. Then they'd whack it across the neck with a hatchet."

"They should've used that chicken trick when they beheaded Mary, Queen of Scots. Apparently the executioner was so nervous, he hit her three times with the ax before he managed to cut her noggin off."

"Just so, Chris, just so," mumbles Gordie.

"Yeah, the poor wee chickens get a raw deal. Back in the winter of 1626, Sir Francis Bacon started stuffing chickens with snow to see what happened."

"What did happen, Terry?"

"He died of pneumonia."

Kevin has the coffee shakes and he's showing signs of stress. In trying to pour another cup, he spills great brown puddles of java all over the tabletop.

"Hey, Kevin? I dreamed I turned into an Irishman," says Chris.

"Oh, really?"

"No, O'Reilly!"

Kevin jumps up, glowering. Then, with a Zorroesque swirl of his cape, he storms off to his room in a red-faced blaze, slamming the kitchen door behind him.

"Touchy little wizard, isn't he?" Chris smiles with satisfaction.

He is, too. Kevin drinks so much coffee, he hardly sleeps. Long, moaning mantras can be heard issuing from his bedroom in the dead of night, curtailed only by Chris's cries of, "Shut the fuck up, you mad bastard!"

A lot of Kevin's time is spent trying to conjure up spells to keep him on the dole and out of the work force. This is his greatest success. Try as they may, the reemployment service cannot find a job for a necromancer, but they do offer him a position as a clown's assistant in the kindergarten service. He's black-affronted by this proposal and threatens the staff with a plague of boils. The high dudgeon in which he sweeps out of the dole office is somewhat dampened when his six-foot hazel wand becomes jammed in the revolving doors and the wind lifts his habit over his head while he bends to extricate it. Few onlookers had realized that wizards traditionally wore skimpy black lace panties.

When not engaged in making an eejit of himself, Kevin is an accomplished artist. He draws a cartoon strip each week about the goings-on in the Broughton Street apartment, and the finished work, complete with caricatures of all the people in the flat, appears on the food cupboard door each Friday evening. Kevin calls the strip "The Silly Wizards."

It's late at night, we sit in the kitchen. Chris is reading the *Daily Record* newspaper and Terry has a copy of *Cosmopolitan* that he nicked from the dentist.

"What's happening in the world, lads?" says Gordie.

Chris ruffles his tabloid and announces, "'Boots the Chemists was broken into last night. Everything was stolen except condoms and hair-oil . . . police are looking for a bald-headed Catholic!'"

"Don't you take anything seriously?" Kevin asks Chris.

"Only comedy," he answers.

Terry adds to the mix by reading from his glossy magazine: "'You can tell a lot about people by looking at their bathrooms.'"

"What would they tell about us? We haven't got one."

"They'd tell that you were a bunch of clarty wee bastards," says Gordie, snatching up a guitar and breaking into an old ragtime song.

Take it slow and easy, if you want to get along with me
Take it slow and easy, it's as easy as it can be
I'll give you one . . . two . . . three . . . four . . . five . . . six reasons
You double-crossed me, that's an act of treason
Take it slow and easy if you want to get along with me.

I pick along on Gordon's other guitar. The room fills with a rich blend of clawhammer picking and syncopated chord progressions until the words are exhausted and the music peters out.

"Hey now, that was cool," Gordon says, beaming.

The other lads stare and nod. Even Kevin is impressed.

"You guys sound great. You should form a band."

"There you go," says Gordon.

I smile.

→ Chapter 26 ←

Romeo, come forth . . . thou fearful man
Affliction is enamored of thy parts
And thou art wedded to calamity.
William Shakespeare

WITH MY SECOND WEEK'S DOLE MONEY IN MY POCKET, I LEAVE the unemployment office and stride purposely down Lothian Road to where the mouse ran up my trousers last week and nearly got me lynched in the process. Diana is nowhere to be seen, and, lucky for it, neither is the mouse. Across the busy street and through the doors of the St. Cuthbert's Co-operative Store to the men's wear department I march.

"Can I help you, sir?"

"You can. I want a pair of tight blue jeans with narrow bottoms, as snug around the ankles as you can get."

"There are these Levi's, sir, at three pounds, or these similar pair, at one pound fifty."

"I'll take the less expensive ones, they look identical."

"Oh, they are, sir." The clerk smiles and coughs nervously. He seems even more tense as I squeeze myself into a pair of skintight denims.

"Is that the new fashion, sir? I thought wide bottoms were still in?" the clerk inquires, looking baffled.

"Not for me they're not, never again! Throw those bell-bottoms in the garbage—they're not safe to walk the streets in. Ruined my chances of romance . . . bloody mice!" I look in the mirror. My legs look like two straws hanging out of a hayloft, but at least I'll be safe from the attentions of itinerant rodents.

"I'll take them!"

"Are you sure, sir? They're a bit tight."

"The tighter the better, mate. No one's nibbling on *my* cheese!"

"Well, really!" he says, blushing.

I step out into the fading afternoon light. Mice hold no terrors for me now, but I have taken to walking with a gunfighter's swagger, rather like Cowboy Coulson used to do. Bugger it! I don't care. I'd had my setback with Diana last week. Nevertheless, as the proverb says, "There's plenty of fish in the sea." Walking like a saddle-sore Texan, I reach the St. Vincent for happy hour.

Liz is in the bar. Ooooh! Long-legged, lithesome, lovely Liz had caught my eye before when she'd ventured into the back room with her girlfriends. Her flaxen hair falls long and straight, and she wears wee gold wire-rimmed spectacles. I've always been very taken by girls who wear glasses, but I've no idea why I find them so attractive.

Glasses or not, Liz is a sweetheart. She has a natural clumsiness that bestows a certain endearing quality on her. Like Terry, Liz seems to inhabit a world that's been made backward for her. Something as simple as a visit to the toilet would, like as not, see her return with the back of her skirt tucked into her drawers, and most of the time she gets more makeup on her glasses than on her face. Despite how God made her, she is bright, witty, and vivacious. When I ask her for a date, to my surprise, she accepts. Next Saturday we'll meet for a few drinks, then go to the Lyceum Theatre to see a production of Henrik Ibsen's *Peer Gynt*—very sophisticated!

I need a bath desperately. I'm mingin, and I need to get my clothes clean, too. This means starting off with a long walk to the public bathhouse, where for a small fee I get soap, shampoo, and a towel with half an hour to do my ablutions.

Next door to "the bathy" is the public laundry, or "the steamy," as the Scots call it. Here sinks and scrubbing boards are for hire, along with a ship's rigging of clotheslines in an indoor drying area. I can't use the laundry because I've nothing to change into, but at least I get a good soak in the bath. Wet haired and fragrant, I make my way back to the flat, where I will have to scrub my clothing in the kitchen sink.

The normally frowsty atmosphere of the attic apartment has taken on a new and tantalizing element: Gordie and Chris are making a huge pot of curry. The Liverpool lads chop, grind, and grate, until a spicy, ambrosial sauce is left to simmer for several hours, permeating the air with exotic aromas.

The downstairs neighbors call the landlord, thinking the sewers are backed up. Mr. Pandit duly arrives, but being from Pakistan, delights in the cooking smells and tells the neighbors that they are "uncultured infidels who can't tell curry from crap!"

Pandit the Bandit then invites himself to dinner and is very pleased at the lads' culinary expertise.

"Oh, just like home . . . very, very good, oh dear me, yes. You are such good boys, oh yes, wonderful boys, always full of surprises. Oh yes indeed!"

"We've another surprise for you, Mr. Pandit."

"Oh, lovely! What is that now, Mr. Chris?"

"We haven't got this month's rent money."

"What? You are bad boys! You will have me starving! What will you do then?"

"We could send you round some of our curry."

"Your curry is crap—*crap*! You make it in the piss pot! Bugger you and the Duke of Edinburgh!"

"Don't worry, we have your rent money, okay? Chris is only joking."

"Thank you, Mr. Gordon. You are a gentleman and you make jolly fine curry, too!"

Chris enjoys teasing the landlord as much as he does Kevin. This will become part of the monthly ritual along with a trip to the bathhouse and "the steamy."

We settle in quickly and in no time have made the house into a home, or rather, to be nearer the mark, turned a madhouse into a mental home.

Terry is peeling potatoes in the sink, while in the opposite corner, Gordie paints the number 69 on the heavy plastic lid of the steel garbage can, which sometimes doubles as a seat. He has just finished the job when Kevin's pal, Graham Jordan, wanders in and sits down on the dustbin to light a cigarette.

"Where's Kev?"

"He's at his girlfriend's."

"Ruthie's?"

"Aye."

"Okay, tell him I popped round," Graham says, walking out the door with 69 printed like a Pisces sign on the arse of his orange workman's trousers.

I count the days till Saturday and my rendezvous with Liz. It's good to be dating again. It gives me confidence. Suddenly I feel like one of the boys and find myself cockily saying "Hey!" to people, instead of the more subdued "Hello there."

With a steady girlfriend to entertain, a man needs employment, so I find myself a job as a freelance house-wiring electrician. It doesn't pay much, but it's cash and will help to eke out my dole money; also, being employed has a certain cachet with the ladies.

As the fateful night draws near, I have an attack of the butterflies and spill milk all down the front of my new jeans. I give them a rinse in the sink and most of the blue dye runs out, turning my white socks and T-shirt gray. I now regret throwing away my bell-bottoms at the clothing store. All I have left is my old trawling jeans, which, despite repeated washings, are still stiff and stink of cod liver oil.

The next night, I attempt to pull on my washed-out new jeans. Much to my dismay, they seem even tighter than before.

"I think my Levi's have shrunk. They're not supposed to do that, are they?"

"These aren't American Levi's. Look at the label—they're Leevi's made in Formosa," says Chris, trying to help me pull them up. "I hope you don't have as much trouble getting into her pants," he adds.

"Keep it clean—I've no room for passion in these things!" I wheeze, tugging up the zipper. Chris chuckles salaciously as I inch my way slowly past him, like a hermit crab too big for its shell.

Unable to take a deep breath for fear of bursting my breeks, and wearing a purple turtleneck sweater to hide my gray T-shirt, I teeter my way to the St. Vincent to meet Liz. The stars blink above the chimney-turreted rooftops, as I step with all the trepidation of an unsure sapper in an unmarked minefield. Down the long hill, I creep to the alehouse below in Stockbridge. On such a brisk spring night, I regret not having worn my underpants, but with them on, I can't do up my zip at all. Still, when you're going courting, it's rather sporting to be *au naturel*.

Liz waves as she catches my eye. I sidle up to the bar, trying to be cool, and call up two pints of Guinness. Liz has reserved a couple of bench seats by the old iron-based mahogany table in the recessed window. Very cozy! Painstakingly, I manage to sit my tight arse down on the chilly oak plank.

"Liz, you look lovely."

I smile, she smiles. Even in her smeary specs, Liz looks fine. Seizing my chance, I lean forward to kiss her. She leans forward too, and as our lips meet, her nervous hand knocks my drink off the table and into my lap.

"Oh my goodness—I'm sorry!" Liz jumps up, spilling her pint as well. It all runs across the table toward me. With a swiftness born of desperation, I struggle to my feet. Too late! I am saturated in Dublin's finest and look like I've wet myself.

"Oh, Billy, Billy, I'm so sorry . . . I'm so stupid."

Poor Liz, I feel more sorry for her than myself.

"It's okay, love, no harm done. It was my fault anyway. I'll just pop home and change. I'll be back in a minute."

I run for the door, dark brown stout running down the inside of my legs. I've never been a great one for jogging, but these are the longest two miles of my life. The chill night air brings steam from my crotch, and the drying process begins shrinking the cheap denim even more.

"Oh God, no!"

By the halfway point, the seams of my Taiwanese jeans are splitting and the pants are falling apart. In desperation, I try to run, but this aggravates the disintegration. Before long, my toodle is making an unscheduled appearance and I am forced to cup it in one hand and hold my arse end closed with the other.

"Please God, let there be no one at home."

Up the stairs I sprint and into the kitchen.

"Billy! By heck, lad, she's overkeen—tore the pants off you, did she?"

"Very funny, Chris, I don't think! Liz spilled my pint, that's all. Have you seen my old fishing jeans?"

"I threw them out—you told me to this morning!" says Terry.

"Give me your trousers?" I screech, tugging at his waistband.

"Fuck off!" he says, beating me back.

"Chris?"

"Oh no . . . no no no . . . I've got a date tonight, too!"

"Oh God! What will I do?"

"Here wear these—I get them free at work!" says Kevin's pal, Graham.

He delves into his work bag and throws me a pair of orange dungarees complete with straps and a bib, emblazoned with the logo of Edinburgh Corporation on the front and a large white zodiac sign smudged on the backside. The figure gazing back at me from the hallway mirror looks like a cross between a street cleaner and the flag of some banana republic.

"Orange pants and a purple sweater! I look like a clown. Well, I suppose they'll have to do. Thanks, man, I better go—Liz is still waiting for me down the pub." I dive out the door. Another heart-pounding dash along the chilly streets and I'm back where I had been an hour before. She is still there.

"Oh, Bill, you look very . . . erm . . . colorful. Come sit down—no, here, where it's nice and dry! I'm so sorry about what happened. I'm so accident prone. Here, I got you another pint!"

With exaggerated care she hands me the drink, like an assistant crook passing a stick of sweating gelignite to a safecracker. I take a firm grip on the glass, then relax. Maybe it will turn out fine after all. We'll go off to the show, then back to her place and out of these stupid-looking overalls and . . .

"Cheers!" Liz leans forward and clinks her glass against mine.

"Sláinte!" I smile back, gazing into her cornflower-blue eyes, coyly hiding behind their smudgy lenses. I feel a warm sensation in my heart . . . I feel a cold sensation in my bollocks! My glass has cracked down its full length and split in half, emptying its foaming contents into my crotch!

Despite my pleas, Liz runs out the door and I never see her again.

The ghastly orange dungarees do come in handy as I set out walking up the High Street to my first job as an electrical contractor. I have been hired to wire a fifteenth-century building at the top of the Royal Mile, just a pistol shot from the castle gates.

The medieval tenement of some six stories is a monument to the problems faced by its builders. In an ancient walled town, if you couldn't build out, the only solution was to build up. Some of these skyscrapers reached fourteen stories, and, although they were cramped close together, many collapsed under their own weight. They had other hidden dangers, too. Sewers in the Old Town ran down the middle of the street and piss pots were emptied out of upstairs windows, which was okay as long as the emptier gave the old French warning, "Gare d l'eau" (watch out for the water), before letting fly. Just last year, the Lord Provost received such a soaking from a bunch of reveling students during Charity Week.

The building that I will be working on is almost in ruins and is being turned into flats for trendies. The building has never been plumbed for gas, let alone electricity. It has seen nothing more modern than a candle or an oil lamp. Left on my own for most of the day in this decaying, window-gaping hulk, I take to exploring.

The top floor of this once prestigious town house has been home to thousands of pigeons over the past hundred years, and the entire upstairs is knee-deep in bird droppings. The former tenants had simply moved farther downstairs as each floor became too damp and drafty to live on. Finally, when the basement was no longer wind- and watertight, they sold up, leaving the place in an appalling state.

I'm told to start on the ground floor and work my way up as the other tradesmen make it safe to do so. It is destined to be a shitty job, and I soon realize why others have turned it down.

On lifting a floor board to run cables through the joists, I discover that the three to four feet of space between floors is crammed with ash, cinders, and old coal dust. This filler must have acted as sound and heat insulation, and I have to dig through it to run my cables. On my first session of shoveling, I discover a human skeleton, stained coffee-colored by the detritus about it. I uncover the pelvic area first; some judicial scraping produces a collapsed rib cage and eventually a gap-toothed skull. I walk down the hill to the central police station to make a report.

"You've found a what, sir?" the desk sergeant asks, detachedly pouring his tea from a large brown pot and examining the contents of a biscuit tin.

"It's a skeleton . . . a human skeleton, in the space under the floor boards."

"What's it doing there, sir—under the floorboards, as you say?"

"It's doing the bloody hokey-pokey, what d'ya think?"

He looks up from his teacup and for the first time takes me seriously.

"Oh, I better call the duty detective . . . er . . . I won't be a minute." He goes out of the office.

The detective seems like a nice bloke and we saunter up the hill in no great hurry.

"I think I know what this is," he says. "I've seen it before. In the olden days, when coffins and funerals were so expensive, if somebody died, the family would just lift the floor boards and bury the body in the packing between floors—a sort of do-it-yourself necropolis, well out of the clutches of Burke and Hare."

"Didn't that cause a stink?"

"No, I don't think so. The charcoal would absorb most of the stench, and I suppose those places didn't smell all that wonderful anyway."

"Aye, just my luck that I've got to dig through the buggers. I'm not looking forward to this caper."

The policeman inspects the remains and thinks it is a three-hundred-year-old family interment.

"If it *is* a murder, I don't think we'll catch the villain now," says the cop.

He leaves me and my newfound friend to our own devices. In the course of the restoration, I find more bones, some of which look like children and babies. The building manager says to leave them be and to say nothing about what we find to anyone.

One morning I unearth what I think is the skeleton of a dog.

"That's no a fowkin' dug," says a plumber, "that's a fowkin' big rat! Will ye no look at the teeth on the bastard—he could bite through a fowkin' pickax handle!"

He's right, the enormous rodent's incisors look like bolt cutters. Imagine *that* going up yer trouser leg!

One underfloor discovery is a little more pleasant. It is a delicate glass inkwell with a silver top, made in Edinburgh and assay marked for the year 1786. Sticking by my orders to say nothing about what I find, I take my prize to the antique shop and double my wages for the week.

I am glad when the job is halted due to financial problems. I don't like working knee-deep in human remains, it's as bad as being up to the waist in codfish. My next wiring contract is an attic flat up near Sandy Bell's bar. This place was at least plumbed for gaslight in the last century, so it's easier to work in. Access to the attic is gained either from inside the flat or by way of a trapdoor that opens onto the common staircase. Here again, the roof deadening is composed of fire ashes spread between the joists. It's incredibly dusty and soon my sinuses are killing me.

I am forced to invest in one of those pig mask–type respirators that riot cops wear. The black rubber mask covers my whole face. It has two glass eyeholes and a bright-red, circular dust trap in the center. The filter can be renewed when needed, and my air quality is much improved by it. Adorned in my now shit-encrusted orange dungarees and a green woolly hat pulled down over my hair and ears, I'm ready to do battle with the dusty environment. Work progresses apace and the job is near completion. One afternoon, while doing some finishing work in the attic, I hear a crash and a scream out on the stairs. Someone is moaning, and I can hear a sound like trickling liquid running down the staircase.

"Oh Jesus Christ, help me . . . oh my God . . . oh Jesus!" come the cries of despair from the stairwell.

In my mind's eye I picture some poor old soul bleeding from a fall, leg broken and jagged-edged bone protruding through the flesh. Surely that other noise is blood dripping down the stone steps. I push hard against the trap, but it's stuck. I give it a ram with my shoulder and it flies open with an ear-splitting bang. From the dimly lit staircase, a startled tramp stares in horror at the goggled-eyed, red-nosed monster appearing from the hole in the wall above his head.

"Argggh!" screams the old vagrant, scrambling to his feet and trying to cover his face with his hands. "Argggh, Jesus help me! ARRGHHH!"

"Are you all right, mate?" I try to shout, but the sound comes out of the sides of the rubber mask like a string of wet farts. All the tramp hears is, *"ARP YARP ALRP RAAP, MARP!"*

"Arggh!" Down and down the staircase the poor old vagabond flees in his attempt to escape the demon of the stairwell. Soon all is silent, except for my breathing and the steady *drip, drip* of a shattered bottle of Buckfast Sweet Wine plopping its contents into the darkness below.

Spitting dust and cobwebs, I retire across the road for a cold beer in Sandy Bell's. There is a great sound of fiddle and banjo emanating from the back room. It's Nuff the Scruff and Bloggs down from Aberdeen for the weekend.

"Hey, lads, how's it going?" I call over.

After their set, the boys fill me in on the latest news from up north.

"So, Johnny and the Clown and Jongleur met this bloke down at the Kirkgate bar who said he could sell them a gadget that turns the wheel in the electricity meter backwards so we could get free power."

"Oh, aye, I've heard of these things . . . very dangerous and highly illegal."

"Aye, true. Anyway, the boys rig this thing up between the supply meter and the fuse box and flick the main switch. *Boom!* The pair of them are engulfed in a fireball that singes most of their hair off and plunges the common stair into darkness. So what can they do? The meter is a pile of melted junk, the wallpaper is all blackened, and the house is full of smoke."

"What *did* they do?"

"Ah-ha! Our failed electricians were not fazed. When the engineers from Scottish Power eventually came hammering on the door, they had prepared the scene well and dressed the room like a movie set. A big pentagram was chalked on the wall below the meter and a ouija board put in the center of the table. Various cabalistic symbols and satanic devices were drawn on the walls, and a pack of tarot cards was scattered all over the room."

"Well, what good did that do?"

"The Clown and Jongleur told the investigators that the meter had blown up when, during a seance, they invited an evil spirit called Fergie to manifest itself."

"And the engineers believed this?"

"Oh, aye. One of them was a Free Presbyterian. He told them that they were very lucky not to be dragged away to the sulfurous pit of hell and that they should never do anything as foolish again. Then he got them to fall on their knees and beg forgiveness from the all-powerful Lord."

"And did they?"

"Oh yes . . . they might be daft, but they're not stupid!"

"So they got away with it, crafty sods?"

"They did, but the landlord wasn't very pleased with the electricity company's report, and we all got thrown out."

Nuff and Bloggs go back to their session, and I go back to finish off my wiring contract. I take special care when hooking up the main electricity meter.

Back in the more humble surroundings of Stockbridge, I begin to "check my lobsterpots." This peculiar Scottish ritual entails going around all of the pubs in the neighborhood to seek out cash jobs and other unofficial employment. It's a bit of a hit-and-miss affair, but more productive than panning for gold and much more fun than a trip to the government employment office. This day, it's as well that I pop into the Baillie for a quick pint. A lobster has been ensnared!

Big Robbie Coltrane hails me from the other side of the smoky room.

"Hey, Watkins, you old wanker!" He beckons me over to a quiet corner.

"Not so much of the 'old,' if you don't mind, Robbie! So how's the craic?"

"Ever widening, you bloody impostor. Come and sit down, I wish to talk with you."

"What's up?" sez I, settling into an old armchair at the corner table.

Robbie leans across the beer-stained table, darting looks over his shoulder like a fugitive on the run.

"Billy, my spies tell me that you are wiring apartments on the cheap these days. It's the talk of the Casbah. If the Fat Man was to pay you well, would you do me the great courtesy of wiring mine, my friend?" he elicits, in a skin-crawling Peter Lorre accent.

"Sure, you live just around the corner from the St. Vincent, don't you?"

"Yep, top floor, right. The flat was partially wired years ago with that old lead-encased cable, but the mortgage company says I have to get rid of it for some reason. Isn't it supposed to be dangerous?"

"Well, it wouldn't do you much good if you were to eat it, but electrically it's usually safe enough. I've just done an upstairs top and attic, so I reckon about twenty pounds in materials and thirty in labor should sort it and I could start Monday, if that's any good?"

"Fifty quid, eh? That's a deal then—great! The lowest estimate I got was eighty." Robbie goes to the bar to buy pints to settle the bargain. Minutes later, the contract is sealed *à la mode de Édimbourgeois,* with a clink of glasses and a sup of beer.

Robbie is a good lad with an impious wit and an incredible gift for mimicry. A conversation with him is a whirlwind pageant of multi-character voices switching back and forth with the narrative. The gossip and daily events in his life are recounted by such illuminaries as Charles Laughton, John Wayne, Jimmy Stewart, Adolf Hitler, Marlon Brando, and the man who gave the orange a bad name, the Reverend Ian Paisley. Each saga is enunciated with faultless precision, becoming an absurd journey into the surreal. Robbie, as Michael Caine, tells the tale of "ow me mowtacar bleedin' well broke down, an' I'm stuck in the middle of Lothian bleedin' Rowd, wiv a bleedin' great bus up me arse." An afternoon with Robbie has the twin prospects of your ribs bursting from laughing or ending up in the home for the terminally bewildered, as daft as a chocolate teapot. Robbie is a natural.

Work at the top flat in Calton Street starts with the removal of floorboards. No nasty surprises this time! If there were any bones hereabouts, the gas company had removed them when plumbing the place in the late 1800s.

The apartment is light and airy. Across the road, its twin building is absent, giving the appearance of a set of front teeth with one missing. This was due not to the oversight of the designers, so steeped in Georgian symmetry, but to a Luftwaffe bomb, one fateful November night in 1941.

The removal of the window skirting boards and wainscoting reveals a time capsule. The workmen who reglazed the shattered windows after the blitz had left behind their lunch wrappers, a couple of Wild Woodbine cigarette packets, a Swan Vestas matchbox, and a copy of the *Edinburgh Evening News,* complete with a front-page spread showing the air raid devastation of the night before. Matted and framed, the mementos made an inviting collage and looked well on the wall of the newly wired apartment.

"Of course," says Robbie at the housewarming party, "the French were your specialists in collage. I mean, Georges Braque's *Le Courrier* is a masterpiece."

"Do you like the French Impressionists?" asks a young debutante.

"Naw, they're all shite. I met one once and he couldn't even do Jimmy Cagney!"

→ Chapter 27 ←

Jack Orion was as good a fiddler
As ever fiddled on a string
He could make young women mad
With the tune his fiddle sang.

Traditional folk song

MOST OF THE SHOP BASEMENTS GORDIE AND TERRY HAVE been cleaning out and painting now require electrical installations. Chris is still working for André at Northern Lights, doing theater lighting, so we are able to get supplies and components at a trade discount. With this advantage, Chris and I decide to form our own electrical contracting company. We call it Down to Earth Electrics. Now I can sign off the dole.

Many of the paying jobs provide a surplus of materials that I can use on other contracts where barter is the more common method of payment. In exchange for supplying the mighty amp and volt, the Asgard Clothing Emporium kits me out in new jeans, shirts, and leather boots, the Chinese carryout gets an up-to-date wiring system, and I don't have to worry about being hungry for a long time.

What had been a line of dirty, derelict shop fronts is transformed into the fashionable St. Stephen's Street. One by one, the dark basement shops glow with electric light, and the whole area teems with a colorful tide of people buying antiques, silk scarves, old oil paintings, and cheesecloth dresses. One shop sells gramophone records, another watercolor miniatures, painted by a group of local women in a style that becomes known as the Stockbridge school. The next hawks military collectibles and has a window full of Nazi daggers. At the far end of the street, Donald's four-legged bird still stares from its glass case at the throng of bargain hunters that trek the sidewalks every day bar Sunday.

Cafés and pubs spring up along the once dilapidated curve of St. Stephen's Street, where people sit in the warm sunshine, chatting, weaving, or selling prehuman bowls to the increasing flood of tourists that make it downhill to the bohemian neighborhood of Stockbridge. A buzz of conversation rises from the bustle of trade, and the fragrance of coffee, leather, and exotic body oils floats above it all, infusing an atmosphere already imprinted with the sweet whiff of bhang. This aromatic mix, varied and cosmopolitan, smacks more of the labyrinthine marketplaces of old Tangier than the staid leafy suburbs of Edinburgh town.

Covered in enough dust to make a dozen Adams and Eves, Robbie Coltrane labors alongside me on the construction of the Antiquary tavern, where his mimicry and never-ending cheerfulness keep me laughing for the entire, grime-ridden contract. The Fiddle-de-Dee violin shop proves to be a good customer, and I receive a beautiful French violin made in the 1840s in part payment for my labors. The last shop we work on is the one where I had lain with the lovely Leslie. The very day I start work on it, I see her faded picture in the "Newlyweds" section of an old newspaper. The caption under the picture says she has married a doctor and moved to Glasgow, but I can still see sadness in her smile and hope she finds her happiness someday.

Standing at the end of the street, looking along the rows of bright stores, Gordon puts out his hand.

"Well, I think we've done a fantastic job, eh, lads?"

"Bloody right, we have," says Terry.

We all shake hands and are unemployed again.

"Come on, chaps, I'll treat you to a pint," I offer, descending into the Baillie bar.

"Hey, Billy, do you fancy playing at the Triangle on Saturday?" Gordie asks, wiping Guinness froth from his mustache.

"Aren't they a bit 'Puff the Magic Dragon?'"

"Not really. Some of the singers are a bit lightweight, but it's the audience that matters."

"Fine, let's do it."

"Maybe we should get Bob Thomas to play with us. He's a good all-round instrumentalist and we could do some jigs and reels."

"I don't really know him. Isn't he the president of the University Folk Club?"

"That's him—Bob the Knob, the Electric Scotsman, purveyor of guitars, banjos, mandolins, concertinas, and veterinary care for small furry animals."

"Why's he called 'Bob the Knob?'"

"Don't ask!"

At Gordie's invitation, Bob Thomas pops round to the flat the next evening for a sort of impromptu audition. At first sight, he cuts a strange figure. Even in a household as crazy as ours, Bob looks odd. He strides into the kitchen and immediately takes up a quarter of the available space. At six feet three and well built, he is impressive enough, but his Sherlock Holmes cape and deerstalker hat, combined with his blue eyes and prominent nose, give the illusion that "the great detective" is indeed among us. Bob's accent is that of the middle-class professional Scot, and his speech is spare and somewhat clipped. Though he may say little, his real eloquence radiates from his fingertips, which dance like spiders on an electric grid. As he plays, tangled, multinote runs and pinging harmonics rise effortlessly from the sound hole of his old Guild guitar. He performs the bewildering stampede of Doc Watson–style flattop picking, known as "Jackson Stomp," without even watching where his fingers are going. Then, by way of contrast, Bob lulls the ear with the slow choir of chords that make up the backbone of the tragic lullaby "Hush, Hush, Time to Be Leaving," each progression the canticle of displacement and forced immigration well known to the Highland Gael.

When at last the room falls silent, there is no need for a vote: Bob Thomas becomes the third member of the band.

On the following Saturday night, we play our first gig at the Triangle folk club, in the west end of Edinburgh, which is run by the Youth Hostel Association. The audience, being used to "Michael Row the

Boat Ashore" and "Kumbaya," seem unsure as to what they are witnessing:

Take it slow and easy . . .
If you want to get along with me . . .

Gordie croons, leaning back in the relaxed style of a jazz-era lounge lizard. To his right, Bob stands erect, a stone-faced colossus, picking each note from his long-necked mandola with brow-bending intensity, while I take to waltzing around the stage, playing my fiddle like a Hungarian gypsy in an expensive restaurant.

As the ragtime ditty comes to its three-note ending, the audience sits stunned. In the eternity of silence that fills the five seconds between the last notes of music and the first hand clap, we wait. Eventually, a ragged ripple of applause, sounding like a bunch of nudists sitting down quickly on cold marble steps, breaks out among the sixty or so folky fans in the hall, many of whom have started chatting or drifting off to the bar.

"Well, at least they didn't throw anything at us," says Gordie.

"The night is yet young," Bob breathes through clenched teeth.

"Okay, lads, let's take them up a notch," I propose, laughing.

Laying down the fiddle and tuning the bottom string of my guitar to low D, I swing into a rock-and-roll rhythm, belting nine sorts of be-jasus out of the guitar in the process. Disdainful faces in the crowd scoff at the driving sound, but when I start singing, they suddenly realize the song is an ancient one:

Our gallant ship the Ampithrite
She lay in Plymouth Sound
Blue Peter at her foremast head
For she was outward bound;
We were laying there for orders
To send us far from home
Our orders came for Rio,
And thence around Cape Horn.

Gordon and Bob haul close in on the harmony, their silver strings humming like the north wind in a trawler's antenna wires. The old seafaring song takes the listener through the rigors of daily life on the South American run, where storms and shipwrecks stand in the path of those wishing to venture to Chile, California, and beyond in those days before the Panama Canal. This song had always been a special favorite of mine, and the last verse ends with one of the finest lyrics ever written by an anonymous sailor:

> *And if ever I live to be paid off,*
> *I'll sit and I'll sing this song—*
> *God bless ye pretty Spanish girls*
> *That we met around Cape Horn.*

The song finally ties up at the end of its trip and the mixed applause proves that the folkies don't seem to know what to make of us at all.

Gordon takes the helm again. Sitting bent over his guitar, while Bob plays a fine accompaniment on the concertina, Gordie purrs the salty immigration song that I often sang on the old steamer *Isle of May:*

> *Oh the work is hard*
> *And the wages low.*
> *Amelia where you bound to?*
> *The Rocky Mountains is my home*
> *All across the Western Ocean.* . . .
>
> *There's Liverpool Pat,*
> *With his tarpaulin hat,*
> *Amelia where you bound to?*
> *And Yankee John the packet rat,*
> *All across the Western Ocean.*

I weave my fiddle tunes in and out of the reedy notes of the squeeze box. Gordon's voice echoes all the groans and creaks of a ship's timbers. Imperceptibly, his song takes on the rhythmic roll of a square-rigger tacking across the Atlantic on the uphill run to America. The audience is transformed into willing passengers for the duration of Gordon's vocal voyage, rising and falling on each pitch and swell until, with a cheer as hearty as those of the immigrants catching their first sight of the Statue of Liberty, the last notes fade and the crowd rise roaring to their feet. We take our bow and then stand like three mountain climbers on top of a newly conquered peak. Our smiles say it all: Silly Wizard has arrived!

We finish our set with a medley of instrumentals: "The St. Louis Tickle," "Jackson Stomp," and "Chief O'Neill's Favorite." After which, just to confuse everybody even more, I thank the audience in Gaelic.

To the more conservative minded, we are a scandal. To the radical youngsters, we're outrageous, but the vast majority of Trianglers adopt a "wait and see" attitude, which suits us because we'll be back.

I sum up the night by quoting Chris Dale: "They may love us, they may hate us, but they'll never forget us!"

Amen to that.

The Saturday evening sessions at the Triangle folk club bring forth a rich mix of musicians and singers. Some of the "Magic Dragonists" boycott the place in protest of our brand of Celtic music, but as someone said, "You know when you've got a good idea, 'cause all the fools are in confederacy against you."

Bugger 'em. My father once told me, "If a culture is going to survive, it requires innovation and especially an influx of youth." We do our best to encourage the up-and-coming musicians.

One night a gangly fair-haired laddie about twelve years old plucks at my sleeve at the end of the gig.

"Excuse me, sir, would you be so good as to teach me some fiddle tunes, please?" he asks politely.

"Aye, surely. What's your name?"

"I'm Johnny Cunningham and this is my wee brother. He plays the accordion."

"I play the tin whistle, too, mister," says the little boy, impishly nudging his big brother in the ribs and pulling a bad face.

"Good for you. What's your name?"

"Phil. I'm Phil Cunningham, fae Portobello," he answers, grinning mischievously.

"Well, lads, if you come around to number sixty-nine Broughton Street about noon tomorrow, we'll be having our Sunday afternoon session and you can learn what you want."

"I play classical style at school, but I'd love to play that Celtic stuff. I can read music, too, mister!" says Johnny, all excited.

"An' I can read music tae, mister—an' better than him!" says young Philip.

"Okay then. Take this copy of *O'Neill's Irish Melodies*. It's full of jigs and reels. Here, try learning this one—'The Ten-penny Bit.' It's a nice easy one to get started on."

The brothers, true to their word, call round the next day. They can both play "The Ten-penny Bit" and a couple more besides. In fact, the cheeky wee sods can play the bloody tune backward, sideways, and each-week-till-Wednesday. These clever little buggers are adepts, with a mind-boggling ability to play the holyjasus out of anything you give them. Before long, both are regular guests of the band and play weekly at the Triangle.

The club becomes a lightning rod for talent and a focal point of Celtic musicians in Edinburgh. Many fine players are drawn here. Most sit in with us, and for some it's their first stage appearance. Young Davy Arthur, on tenor banjo, likes to join us for a knockabout session; so does Dougie Maclean on fiddle and Alasdair Donaldson on flute. Often the rich voices of Maddy Taylor, Titch Frier, and Chris Prichard provide a background harmony that blends into a weave of sounds the likes of which have never been heard before. It is a hard road, bringing Celtic music back from the brink of oblivion, but a road shared is a road shortened, and Caledonia's hardy sons rise to the task.

The people at the Causey Stane bar like the first gig we play there and show their appreciation by not beating us up. The Ancient Antediluvian Order of Water Buffaloes pay us to play at their very posh club and don't beat us up either. We've got it made!

Over the next few months, Silly Wizard makes a lot of hullabaloo, a lot of friends, but sadly, not a lot of money. Never mind that—we're used to the wolf being at the door, but back at the flat, the wolf isn't at the door, he's in the kitchen sitting expectantly at the table.

"Hello, Mr. Pandit, what you doing here?"

"Oh, Mr. Gordon, I come earlier and say to Mr. Chris, 'Mr. Chris, I am going to raise the rent,' and he says, 'Thank the Jesus of Christ for that, because we can't!' What does this mean, Mister Gordon?"

"Okay, Mr. Pandit, we'll work something out—he's only pulling your leg."

"Pulling *my* leg? It's *his* leg wants the pulling! He is a bloody bugger!"

Electrical work in St. Stephen's Street is about to start up again. A new antique market is almost finished, and the various booths will require individual lighting. This will take a few weeks to get off the ground, and, in the meantime, I help Gordon and Terry on the construction side of it.

The talk of the street is the bizarre accident that has just taken place in one of the recently wired basements. The foreman on the job site fills us in on the details.

"That long-haired young chap who repairs musical instruments in the back room yonder, he was put unconscious from the fumes of some queer chemical stuff he was using. Poor bastard collapsed facedown on the work bench, spilling a pot o' glue in the process. Hours later he regains consciousness, but his beard and longy hair were stuck fast to the work top. He couldnae reach for any sharp tools to cut himsell free and they reckon he lost consciousness again. So he was there all week with his nose in they chemical shite till it all evaporated. That's when his mate found him. Stone mad they say, aye, he was turned stone mad!"

"Bugger his luck!" says Terry, sagaciously handing me a bucket of damp plaster rubble.

I trudge out into the daylight and empty the pail into the dumpster.

Aye, surely life can deal you a queer hand on occasions, I'm thinking.

I have to jump out of the way to avoid the great billow of dust raised by two other workers emptying a rubble-filled bin into the curbside dumpster. When the cloud settles, a round wooden face stares up at me through the detritus. White with dust and riddled with woodworm, the visage is that of a longhaired gentleman with a wee wispy beard. He looks a bit like Sir Walter Raleigh or Sir Francis Drake or one of those Elizabethan buggers. When I get my break, I clean him up a little and take him along to Bob and Tom's shop. Tom is just on the point of leaving when I enter.

"And who have we here, my friend? This is truly a momentous day for arboreal manifestations of divers kinds."

"I think it's a figurehead from an old sailing ship or something. He looks a fraction like Sir Francis Drake. What d'you think?"

"Methinks he more resembles the Bard of Avon."

"What makes you say that?"

"My boy, if he be a mere sailor he's worth about two pounds. However, if he be William Shakespeare, he be worth at least a fiver. It's up to you."

"Hello, Willy Wagglestaff!" I say, rinsing him under the cold-water tap. Tom finds a suitable wooden plinth for mounting the head, and the bust is placed in the window with a five-pound price tag. Good business all around.

The next day I notice the head has moved to the shop across the road and is now marked up to ten pounds. Tom counts out five one-pound notes into my hand and, like the gentleman he is, now that he knows me, refuses to take any commission.

Within the week, Shakespeare's head travels up and down the street akin to the severed head of Bran the Blessed, coursing the ley lines of ancient Britain. Each movement increases the bust's value by at least five pounds. After traversing all of the junk shops of St. Stephen's Street, the gnarled noggin is elevated to the posh emporiums to be found along the bourgeois environs of Thistle Street. Here the Bard continues his meteoric career as a priceless antiquity. He eventually is bought by an American dealer from Arizona and sadly vanishes from the pages of our history, no doubt to roam the streets of Tucson, like a Wild West outlaw with an ever increasing price on his head.

As Shakespeare himself wrote:

> *His head unmellowed, but his judgement ripe;*
> *And, in a word, far beyond his worth*
> *Comes all the praises that I now bestow,*
> *. . . complete in feature and in mind*
> *With all good grace to grace a gentleman.*

In the haven of the Broughton Street flat, Silly Wizard begins to live and breathe as an entity. Bob the Knob moves in permanently, and, to ease the lack of bedroom space, I knock down the brick wall between two adjacent cupboards and make a nice little bedroom out of it. The resulting chamber has two doors, no windows, and is just big enough for a double mattress, a style known in Scotland as a shaggin' palace.

The band evolve in the cramped confines of this fourth-floor asylum, but things are alleviated a little when Kevin blows his mind with one of his own spells. The silliest wizard of them all has attempted to conjure up a horse and put himself mental in the process. We try to send him home to his parents by putting him on a bus to London, but he eats his ticket. Eventually, we raise enough money for another bus ticket, but this time give it to the driver for safekeeping. Kevin the Wizard passes out of our lives and into obscurity. The last reported sighting of him was in London, where he was seen wandering around with his head shaved and his body painted purple, which seems to be the color of choice when you go nuts.

The remaining Silly Wizards take to experimenting musically, honing new edges along the tenets of the age-old music. Long, late nights around the pine table produce a vibrant, fresh sound that, we hope, will change the face and fortune of Celtic music forever. I am honored to be one of the yeast spores that have brought this fermentation into being, but the beer is only as good as the wort, and I'm fortunate to have landed among such ebullient company.

The gatherings in the kitchen grow ever larger. Johnny and Phil become regular weekend visitors as does Andy M. Stewart and his friend Mame Hadden, from the Perthshire band Pudduck's Wells. A blend of fine music, jokes, and unlikely tales makes sleep a daytime affair and we become increasingly nocturnal as jam sessions last till dawn.

As well as being wizards, we have become the Knights of the Square Table, and, just as our namesakes of old, each of us is searching for the Holy Grail in our own way.

✦ Chapter 28 ✦

Sad day for the order that sent them tae the Border
The English by guile, for once won the day,
Sad grief and mourning on every green and loaning,
The flowers of the forest are a' weed away.

Old Scottish lament

TERRY IS ITCHING FOR HIS PILGRIMAGE TO HOLY ISLAND AND I fulfill my promise to go with him. At the railway station we buy two tickets; one is a return, the other a one-way single.

The train runs south from Edinburgh to London, but by getting off at Berwick, we can hike the last few miles to Lindisfarne Island along the beach. We travel for a while in silence, me reflecting on passages from *The History of Lowland Scotland* and Terry lost in the maze of his own thoughts.

I glance out the window to where a pile of stones stands defiant on a distant headland. Jutting out on a wind-whipped promontory, above the cliffs of the North Berwick coastline, a stockade of ivy-wreathed ruins is all that remains of the once mighty Fast Castle, except the legend that a vast treasure awaits the lucky underground explorer.

"See that ruined castle over there? Gordie went there once, looking for a great buried chest of Jacobite gold."

"How'd he get on?"

"Divil a thing he found—an' he rummaged through the sea caves and stuck his head down every rabbit hole for miles around."

"What's the Gaelic word for *treasure*?"

"Oh, I suppose it's *stór,* as in storeroom, or *stór mo chroí,* treasure of my heart. Why?"

"No why. I was just wondering."

Off to seaward, the Bass Rock pokes an impudent finger at the mainland, just as it did in 1746 when a group of Jacobite prisoners on the island overpowered their English guards and declared the rock for Bonnie Prince Charlie. Supplied occasionally by French warships, the Bass Rock was the last place in the British Isles to hold out for the "king over the water." Now its sole population consists of millions of gannets, who couldn't give a bugger about who sits on the throne of Great Britain.

> *The sea oh, the sea, it's stór geal mo chroí*
> *Long may it roll between England and me*
> *It's a sure guarantee that some hour we'll be free*
> *Thank God we're surrounded by water.*

Our journey takes us past the towering mass of Berwick Law, an ancient volcanic plug surmounted by a prehistoric hill fort and crowned with an arch made from the jawbones of an enormous whale that washed ashore in the 1800s.

On to the castle and harbor of Dunbar, where Black Agnes, Countess of Dunbar and March, held out successfully against the besieging English army of Montague, Earl of Salisbury, in 1338. For nineteen weeks she antagonized her attackers by strutting the battlements in full view, using her white silk handkerchief to dust away the marks left on the tower masonry by projectiles hurled from the English siege engines. With the cold northern winter coming on and no chance of either the castle surrendering or the besiegers making a breakthrough, Montague gave up and retreated back to England, muttering:

> *Cam I earlie, cam I late,*
> *I founde Agnes at the gate.*

Agnes did well not to fall into enemy hands. One such unfortunate who did was the Countess of Buchan. It was this noble lady who placed the Scottish crown on Robert the Bruce's head as he sat on the Lia Fáil at the Palace of Scone. She was a MacDuff, and hers was the ancient right to crown kings. This, of course, angered the English, who on her capture, hung her for many years in an iron cage high on the walls of Berwick. Despite hot summers and freezing winters, she miraculously survived, fed secretly by passersby, and lived to ride in triumph with King Robert the Bruce after he crushed the army of Edward II at Bannockburn. If Scotland had hard men, it had tougher women.

The train glides past the gaily painted fishing boats bobbing in neat rows in Eyemouth harbor. I wonder how they are finding the downturn in the industry. I suppose the fact that they're tied up, and not out dropping nets, tells it all. The train sounds its whistle before entering a long tunnel, then spurs the last few miles into Berwick.

Berwick on Tweed was once the largest port in all of Scotland and the biggest town, too. Its medieval walls look impregnable, but sadly, this was not the case, and many times in its bloody history the town was sacked by the English. I have just been reading about this period in time, so without having to rack my brains too hard, I fill Terry in on the details.

"Edward the First, or Longshanks as they called him, ordered his troops to massacre the whole population of seventeen thousand men, women, and children and leave their bodies to rot in the streets."

"Why'd he do that?"

"To show the Scots who was boss."

"Dirty bastard!"

"No, it gets worse! Weeks later, Edward summoned the Scots lords and bishops to the town and, in the midst of all the stinking corpses, made them sign a treaty recognizing him as their sovereign. This paper he called 'The Ragman Roll,' which is where you get the word *rigmarole*. Anyway, the Scots gave in and signed, all but one. That gallant gentleman was William Wallace, a true Celtic hero."

"Yes, I've heard of him—beat the English a couple of times in battle, didn't he?"

"He did, until he was betrayed and taken to London for torture and execution. He was hung, drawn, and quartered, poor sod. After that, it was left to Robert the Bruce to finish the job at the Battle of Bannockburn in 1314.

'Scots, wha hae wi' Wallace bled
Scots, wham Bruce has aften led
Welcome tae yer gory bed, or to victory
Now's the day, and now's the hour,
See the front o' battle lour,
See approach proud Edward's power—
Chains and Slavery.'"

"Yeah, Bruce and Wallace were great men! Still at war with Russia, you know?"

"Who? What in the name of God are you talking about now?"

"Berwick on Tweed. It's still at war with Russia and has been since the Crimean War."

"Terry, have you been out in the sun too long? What are you on?"

"No, it's true! When the 'Articles of War' were drawn up by the Russkies they declared war on England, Ireland, Scotland, and Wales in separate articles."

"So?"

"Well, at that time, no one was sure if Berwick on Tweed was in Scotland, as it was then, or in England, as it is now, so they declared war on Berwick in a separate paragraph. When the armistice came, it only mentioned cessation of hostilities with England, Ireland, Scotland, and Wales, leaving Berwick on Tweed still at war with Russia."

"If I didn't know you better, I would be certain you're talking right out of your backside!"

"Bet you a fiver?"

"I haven't got a fiver."

"Bet you anyway."

We saunter through the streets where "the Hammer of the Scots," as Edward liked to call himself, had shown the world that being known as "the Flower of English Chivalry" was as hollow as his empty suit of armor.

"You know, Terry, Edward Longshanks hated the Scots so much that when he died he wanted his body boiled off his bones and his skeleton carried at the head of his army back into Scotland for one more round of savagery."

"Is that what happened?"

"No, his wimpy son didn't fancy it and had him buried in London."

"They used to like boiling people alive that time of day, ain't that right?"

"That's the truth, Terry. In Scotland they often sealed folk in lead coffins and then boiled them to death."

"Like what happened to the crab that time."

"Aw, shut up!"

On the south side of the town a long stone bridge spans the gray-green race of the salmon-rich Tweed. This was where the border used to be many years ago. Farther on into Northumberland, the misty outline of Holy Island can be seen way off in the distance. We elect to walk along the beach, as trying to hitchhike down the old Roman Great North Road, or Dere Street, as they called it, will take us too far inland, and the walk looks pleasant, too. First we have to cross the busy main railway line from England to Scotland. During a brief gap in the traffic, we scamper over the tracks and have the greatest difficulty scaling the fence the other side. Jagged iron palings and stringy curls of rusty barbed wire bar our way, but eventually we tear free and descend whooping like kiddies at the seaside to splash in the rock pools and tidal rivulets.

The wind is mellow and the tide at full ebb. It's heaven sauntering down the deserted shoreline. Only inquisitive seals and nosy seabirds record our passage as the pilgrimage proper begins.

"This is more like it, Terry—no tourists, no cars, nothing but the lonely sea and the sky."

"Yes, and it's hard to tell which is which."

He's right. There is no discernible line to show where the leaden sky meets the cold expanse of the great North Sea. The squat, elongated outlines of the distant Farne Islands resemble overladened barges making slow progress against a running tide; the ever attendant flocks of terns and guillemots form white plumes overhead.

Berwick is now far to our rear and Holy Island lies directly ahead of us as we trudge along the lifeless, mottled flats of pockmarked wet sand.

All across the barren tidal reach, huge poles of decaying wood thrust up from the sand to tower some twenty feet above us.

"What do you make of these totem pole things, Billy?"

"Well, unless the area is reserved for Vlad the Impaler, I'd guess they were put here in the Second World War to stop German planes landing on the flat beach."

"And what about those things?"

Terry points to the strings of huge concrete cubes, each the size of a garden shed, that run in long rows across the top of the sand dunes.

"They're called Churchill's Blocks and were laid all over the beaches of Britain to prevent tank attacks. See, there's an old gun emplacement over there."

"Let's go take a look."

We walk up the gentle slope of the beach to the reinforced concrete bunker. The gunless, gaping mouth of the pillbox grins above a beard of wild squitch grass. Inside the redoubt, the rusty traverse mountings of the coastal defense artillery piece are still fixed to the floor, and sketched on the wall above is a rather artistic cartoon of a screaming Hitler catching his famous lone testicle on a barbed wire entanglement with Holy Island depicted in the background. The open slit of the gun emplacement gives a panoramic view of the seascape before us. On the bleak horizon, a lone trawler plies the sea lane north, leaving a silver wake trailing across the gray canvas of the elements.

Terry enjoys me telling him the wee bit I know about the fortification of Britain during the early days of the war, when invasion was expected any minute. As we resume our pace across the strand, he takes up a cheery wartime song to the tune of "Colonel Bogey":

> "Hitler, he only had one ball
> Göring, had two, but very small
> Himmler had something similar
> But poor old Goebbels had no balls at all!"

Several twin rows of water-filled pools pit the surface of the damp sand, threading across the seashore, like the stitch holes of a giant sewing machine. Terry picks up a brass cylinder from one of these. It's the spent cartridge case of a machine-gun bullet. Each puddle contains the same, and, from the corroded detonator cap, we can read the words Kannon 20mm.

"Das Kraut, Wilhelm?"

"Das ist right, Terrence!"

A little farther on, we realize that the parallel lines of cannon shells are converging on a single spot. Here, almost buried in the dunes and covered in seagrass, is the remains of a coastal patrol boat. By the layout of her hull and the remains of the keel, I recognize the type of vessel: she was a Fairmile Class ML, similar to the *Comanche*.

"She's a wartime wreck, all right. I wonder why no one has stripped the phosphor-bronze screws and drive shafts off her? They'd be worth a pretty penny in the scrapyard."

"How would you get them away? It must be miles to the nearest road."

"I don't know, Terry. Maybe you could just drive a truck along the beach from Berwick, the same way we walked. It seems odd that nobody ever bothered."

"Maybe this has something to do with it?" Terry brushes the sand away from a half-buried stone obelisk, on which is inscribed

1939–1945

RIP.

"Poor bastards, we should say a prayer for them," I say.

"I only know one."

"Go on, then!"

> *"Our father, which art in Hendon*
> *Harlow be thy name. Thy Kingston come,*
> *Thy Wimbledon in Erith as it is in Enfield.*
> *Give us this day our daily Brent,*
> *And forgive us our Westminsters,*
> *As we forgive those that Westminster against us,*
> *And lead us not into Thames Ditton,*
> *But deliver us from Ealing,*
> *For thine is the Kingston, the Purley, and the Chorley*
> *For ever and ever, Amen."*

"What, in the name of the wee man, is that?"

"It's called the London Bus Driver's Prayer—good, isn't it?"

At the end of the three-mile spit of tidal sandbar, the sacred island rises like a green oasis in a wet desert. The scowling mass of Bamburgh Castle thrusts up behind it, a giant, seaborn granite mass turreted and defiant, guardian of the coastal ports of Northumbria.

"That castle looks like a bloody great wedding cake, eh, Billy?"

"It'll end in tiers, Terry!"

On rounding a headland, we are confronted with a bewildering array of barbed wire entanglements and concertinas of razor wire stretching clear to the water's edge and beyond.

"What the bloody hell's all this?"

I look for a way through the jagged labyrinth, while Terry takes himself off to scout the area behind the dunes and the tank traps.

"It is a bit less tangled up here. A lot of the fence posts have rusted through—ow, ya bastard! Ow!"

When I get up there, Terry has caught himself on the barbed wire and ripped his breeks. I am not surprised.

"Look out, or you'll end up like Hitler! Grab that old wooden board and lay it over the wire. Then we can shimmy over the tangle and use it to get over the next one."

Terry tugs hard at the board, which doesn't want to leave its rusty wire nest.

"It's stuck—give me a hand."

I help him pull the door-sized plank free of the jagged wire. Flakes of red and green paint curl up from its face. The sand falls away, revealing the startling secret beneath.

"Oh dear God!"

Ministry of Defence
Warning
Unexploded Mines—Keep Out

"Jesus, Terry, we've just walked through a minefield!"

"Life's like that!" says Terry, giving me his gorilla grin.

✦ Chapter 29 ✦

We twa have run about the braes
And pulled the gowans fine:
We've wandered many a weary foot
Since auld lang syne.

Robert Burns

Position: 55° N. 01° W.
Lindisfarne. Holy Island
Journey's end

THE TIDAL CAUSEWAY THAT KEPT ST. AIDAN, ST. CUTHBERT, and their devout acolytes isolated from the wicked secular world of Saxon Northumbria curls like a crooked sickle of sand out to the green rise of Holy Island.

Here the same antiaircraft tree posts follow the line of the pilgrim path to mark its course through the marsh on either side. Each has a herring gull or cormorant standing atop, as if emulating the columns of some muddy Apian Way. The white feathered forms act as wind vanes. With every major shift of the breeze, the seabirds rotate so's to be always beak to the blow. When we started our three-mile march across the sand spit the birds were facing north; now their keen eyes take in the view south.

"The tide is coming in, Terry, and the wind's picking up. We'd better get a move on!" I say, setting a striding pace.

"I'm trying to hurry up, but I've got sand in my shoes."

"Ye'll have seawater up your arse if you don't keep up."

My warning comes a little too late. Before we can clear the causeway, the running tide is swirling in icy eddies around our knees. Soaked and chilled, Terry and I struggle out of the water and up onto the grassy dunes where we lie out of the raw wind, like commandos under fire. Shivering, I collect sticks and driftwood to make a fire.

"Have you got any paper, Terry?"

He looks slightly embarrassed and produces the only paper he has, a copy of the King James Bible.

"Jasus, Terry! I can't light a fire with the Bible, not on Holy Island!"

"It's all I've got. I brought it along for the pilgrimage and anyway . . ."

He lets the soft cover fly open to show that the first part of the Pentateuch is missing!

"What the hell happened to Genesis and Exodus?"

"I smoked them," Terry sits in a self-conscious huddle.

"What d'ya mean? How do you smoke a Bible?"

"Well, they gave me the Bible when I got three months in Peterheid Prison, after a bar fight. Then I got into a fight in the prison and they put me in solitary confinement. Just to be pure bastards, they let me have my tobacco, but no cigarette papers. So I used the pages of the Bible to roll up the smokes. The paper's nice and thin, you see."

"What d'ya mean, 'The paper's nice and thin, you see?' Fer Christ sake, that's the HolyJasus Bible!"

Terry looks woefully guilty, like a puppy that's pissed on a rug. Suddenly I feel sorry for him.

"Well, in for a penny, in for a pound!"

Leviticus, Numbers, and Deuteronomy start the core of a fine blaze, and soon steam rises from our wet clothes.

"Do you think it's a sin to burn the Bible?"

"In this case, Terry, no, I don't. And anyway, the King James Version is as suspect as King Jamie himself. He had parts of the book translated out of context to suit his political ambitions. People called him 'the wisest fool in Christendom,' but I think he probably had brain damage from when he was a kid."

"How d'you work that out?"

"Well, his mother was Mary, Queen of Scots, right?"

"Right."

"And his father was either the fop Darnley, who got murdered, or her Italian secretary Rizzio, who also got murdered."

"Go on."

"Right, so she was a Catholic and got murdered by her Protestant cousin, Elizabeth the First. The baby James was brought up to become the Protestant king, James the Sixth of Scotland, and after the union of the crowns, James the First of England as well. But sweet baby James was an ugly little bollix, with a tongue so large that it wouldn't fit inside his closed mouth and lolled down his chin all the time. He had other hereditary deformities that made it hard for the wee boy to sit up straight."

"What's that got to do with anything?"

"Well, folks liked their kings to look like pop stars—you know, handsome, debonair—but this little kid was a mess. So they had the court carpenter make a special chair for the infant which worked on the principle of balance. If he didn't sit absolutely upright, the chair tipped over and smashed his face on the floor? *Now* do you see?"

"I do, but where does the Bible come into it?"

"Jamie grows up paranoid and always expecting something horrible to happen to him or to be murdered like the rest of his family. He sees plots to kill him everywhere, and when he takes ship to Denmark, to meet his bride-to-be, he runs into a squall and thinks that a coven of witches in North Berwick is responsible. Witch hunts are going on all over Europe at this time, so he introduces them to Scotland as an excuse to execute his political rivals on false charges of witchcraft."

"Crafty sod . . . so where's the Bible fit in?"

"Well, being king, he orders a new version to be written, overlaid with his own interpretations, like, 'Suffer ye not a witch to live,' which he added just to suit himself. So that Bible, blazing away there, accounted for the deaths of thousands of innocent people. What a bloody mess. Many's the poor soul who made herbal medicines for the sick ended up being burnt as a witch by these balmpots. So, I guess the Good Lord would not take it ill that two wet pilgrims dry out on such an ill-starred translation."

"Thanks, Bill. You've put my mind at rest. I've worried about that

Bible business for a long time. And well put too. I swear to God, you could sugarcoat shite!"

With the fire drawing nicely, I unpack my rucksack and boil some water for the tea. The last time I sat round a campfire like this was with Angus up in the Highlands, a long time ago.

"Hey, Terry, who played the part of Wishbone in the TV series *Rawhide*?"

"Erm . . . let me see . . . his name waaaas . . . Paul Brinnegar, I think."

"That's right—Paul bloody Brinnegar! How did I forget that?"

Terry's agile mind, now free from Bible-burning guilt, takes another detour from the commonplace.

"He's buried in a pauper's grave in the slums of Glasgow."

"Paul Brinnegar?"

"No! Sir Thomas Lipton . . . this guy with the sailor's hat—on the teabags."

He points at the figure on the red-and-yellow package.

"Wee Tommy Lipton was born in the slums of Glasgow. He went off to America and became a millionaire."

"Doing what?"

"Selling teabags."

"Teabags? I didn't know the Yanks drank tea."

"Aye, they do—they drink it cold with lemon in it."

"Dear God in heaven!"

"Anyway, so when he died, Old Tommy Teabag wanted to be buried back in the Gorballs, where he grew up."

"Fair play to him. So, why did he wear a sailor's cap?"

"He was a famous yachtsman years ago. He nearly won the America's Cup five times."

"He was more successful with the teacup, then."

"Aye. He wrote 'Wee Willie Winkie,' you know?"

"Naw!"

"He did!

> *'Wee Willie Winkie*
> *Runs through the town*
> *Upstairs, downstairs in his night-gown*

Prying at the windows, trying at the locks
All the children in their beds
It's past ten o'clock.'"

"Well, I never!"

"Have you got any biscuits, Bill? Tea's too wet without bikkies."

"Biscuits! What d'ya think this is, the Royal Garden Party?"

"What was King James to Charles the First?"

"Erm . . . James was his dad, I think. Why?"

"Well, when Charles gets booted off the throne by Parliament in 1648, they stick him and his fart catchers in Hampton Court Palace, where he carries on whooping it up. But the government gets fed up paying the bills, so they call him on it.

"'You're gonna have to cut back on your attendants,' they say.

"'Cut back?' says the king. 'I'm down to the bare bones of my arse already.'

"'Bollocks!' says Parliament. 'It says here that apart from all your other hangers-on, you've got sixty-three pastry cooks.'

"'Well, fuck me,' says the king. 'It comes to something when a chap can't have a biscuit when he feels like it!'"

"Ha-haa, Terry! Well here's one for you. Charles the First was only four feet ten inches tall. So, in 1649, when they cut his head off, he lost a foot! D'you get it?"

"No, but there was a nursery rhyme about him, too."

"Which one?"

"Humpty dumpty sat on a wall
Humpty dumpty had a great fall
All the king's horses and all the king's men
Couldn't put Humpty together again."

After a cup of char and a bite to eat, jeans now dry, we explore the island sanctuary. The roofless ruins of Lindisfarne Priory rise in round-topped Norman arches. The stonework is held together "Irish style" by packing flat slabs into the mortar layers to save on cement. Only the wind sings in these hallowed walls that once knew the chant of monks, the tolling of the Angelus bell, and the gentle intoning of whispered devotions. The tourist season is not yet begun, and the only vehicle we have seen leaving the island must have been the last one. The tide is now in and the causeway under several feet of water, cutting us off from the mainland.

Terry stands in the twilight nave of the old church.

"How many people d'you think have prayed here—thousands, eh?" he wonders.

"Maybe more."

Darkness grows, a great creeping gauntlet of iron-black obscurity sweeping in from the east to swallow up the dusk. The only illumination to be seen is the red eye of our campfire cinders as we wander back through the sand dunes. We have no tent, but as long as the rain keeps off, we'll be fine.

Terry grabs my arm.

"It feels good here, holy, like. Will you pray with me?"

"Yes."

"How do you do it?"

"You just talk, like you would to anyone."

"How do you know if your prayers are heard?"

"You'll feel better afterwards."

"So, how do you know if they've *not* been heard?"

"You *won't* feel better afterwards."

"It's as simple as that?"

"Yes."

"Do I kneel down?"

"If you want to."

"I do."

We kneel in the orange glow from the campfire, the two least likely specimens of anguished humanity ever to grace an ancient site of prayer.

For the next hour or so, Terry prays his heart out and makes me cry. I had long puzzled over the nature of his supposed family curse and now I know. The burden that he carries is more than I could bear, and the fortitude with which he faces it is more than I could muster. Eventually, he stops praying and stares at me.

"Have I said enough?"

"More than enough. Do you feel any better?"

"I feel kind of relieved, yes."

"Then your prayers are heard."

"Thanks for coming with me. I couldn't do this on my own."

"I think you should stop thinking of it as a curse and take the positive view, that one day science will find a cure."

"I'll try, but I'm sure that the witch that knew the cure was burnt long ago."

"Cheer up—let's have a drink!"

I take a bottle of red wine out of my rucksack.

"It's a present from Gordie," I say.

"Cool!" says Terry. "Can we have some bread with it, like the last supper?"

"Sure."

I delve into the rucksack and fish out a couple of morning rolls that I was saving for breakfast.

"Do that thing with bread and wine like Jesus used to do."

"What, Holy Communion?"

"Aye."

"Well, okay, if it makes you happy."

"Aye, it will."

"This is my body." I hand him a lump of bread. "This is my blood . . . do ye this in remembrance of me."

With eager eyes, Terry watches my every move, as I nibble on a morsel of bread and take a sip of wine. He even imitates my mistake of spilling wine down my chin and wiping it away.

"What did Jesus do then?"

"I think he said to the disciples, 'Love one another, as I have loved you.'"

"Love one another . . . yes, that's the message. What's that in Gaelic?"

"Grá céile, I guess, or Grá eile. Why?"

"Gra ella. It sounds a bit like *Grail*, don't it?"

"Grá . . . eile . . . Gra . . . il!" I mouth, rolling the sounds around my tongue. "Ye gods! Terry, you might be on to something there. It's possible the Holy Grail wasn't the cup used at the Last Supper. Perhaps it was just that—the love Jesus had with his followers! The love that binds friends together. Maybe we've been searching for something we already have, and we couldn't see it because it's right under our noses! Terry, you're a genius!"

"So that's what it means, eh? Love one another?"

"Why not?"

"What about the holy bit?"

"Well, Terry, if that isn't holy, what is?"

Terry lies back, chuckling to himself, and closes his eyes. Soon he is asleep. I am too excited to lie down just yet and walk to the flooded causeway to gaze back across to the mainland.

"Grá eile . . . grá eile," I say to the salty wind.

As I stand on the dark water's edge, the North Sea whispers the words of the old Cailleach in my ear: "A journey to the holy island which is, is not, and is again."

Now I understand. Lindisfarne is a promontory at the ebb of each tide and at high water is an island again. I wish I had asked the Old Woman of the Roads more, but as Tom Reid would say, "Wisdom is earned, not gifted."

Far out to sea, the red and green navigation lights of ships pass in the night. It's getting late. Retiring to the hollow of the sand dunes, I stretch out on my bedroll under a starless sky and fall asleep where only the sea, the wind, and the crackling fire dare to murmur.

Morning comes, cold and misty, pressing its chill fingers into my hair. After rising, I sit on the tufty grass, attending to the breakfast fire. Terry stirs. A long moan of "Teeeea!" issues from his sleeping bag.

"The tea's made. Get up or we'll miss the tide!"

Terry squeezes out of his down bag like spotty toothpaste emerging from a tube.

"God, you'd think sand would be soft to sleep on."

"It is till it gets compacted, then it's like an iron tractor seat."

"What's for breakfast?"

"Tea and . . . tea. We ate the rest last night."

"No bikkies?"

"Sorry, Your Majesty, no."

The long march across the sands reveals just how far the tide goes out.

"Blimey! The tide's out clear to Bergen."

"What's that nice place in Bergen . . . sells about a hundred different kinds of soused herring?"

"Madame Felle's? Shut up, Billy, I'm starving. I could eat a tramp's arse through his underpants!"

We trudge on until the causeway ends at a lane, which in turn, winds up to a crossroads on the Great North Road. Over a breakfast of bacon and eggs in a local truckers' café, we discuss our plans.

"So, Grail Finder, what are you going to do?" I ask Terry.

"I'm off down to Liverpool to take the boat for Ireland. My old pal Seán Hannon has gone back over and he says the fishing out of Killybegs is good craic. Maybe you'll fancy doing some trawling, Irish-style?"

"Naw, no more fishing for me, Terry . . . I hate fish!"

"Well, Bill, this is good-bye then." Terry stretches out his hand.

"Yeah, good-bye, old friend. I'll look you up in Ireland, to be sure."

He shakes my hand and I can see in his eyes that he can't resist a final parting joke.

"Why does an Irishman wear two condoms?"

"I don't know."

"To be sure, to be sure!" He giggles out the door.

The last I see of Terry is a small black dot leaping into a Charlie Alexander Fish Transportation truck that stops for him on the A1 south. A final wave in that direction and I walk on, hitchhiking back toward Berwick and the Scottish-English border beyond. It will be a long train ride back to Edinburgh on my own, but I don't mind. I've been left with plenty to think about.

✦ Chapter 30 ✦

Though the wind may shake the twig . . .
One needs a pick to get the root up!
Old Celtic proverb

THE TRIP TO HOLY ISLAND HAS CHANGED ME. I FEEL RENEWED, like a battery vibrant with volts. I'm also feeling a restless urge to release my current and be on the move again. It's been over two years since I was last at home with my folks. I wonder what they'll make of me when I return. "Let the lad win his spurs," my dad had said. I knew what he meant. In days long past, for a young squire to become a knight, he had to win his spurs by showing valor on the field of battle. I've never been in such an enterprise, but I have battled with the elements and survived hardships while others around me perished. I have lost old friends and found new ones and never taken pleasure in being miserable. An old Irish saying states, "It's impossible to be unhappy if you have a grateful heart." My twenty-one years on this planet may not have been a barrel of laughs, but they've been anything but dull and thankful I am for it. As the old tailor of Gougane Barra said, "Life's only an old blue bag, knock a squeeze out of it when you can." Ah, Ireland. I hope Terry does all right over in Ireland, especially with his tendency to get himself into a pickle. Seán Hannon will have his work cut out for him, I'm thinking, keeping Terry away from mischief and out of harm's way.

Trains are great for daydreaming on, with the world outside tumbling past. At Dunbar the person sitting opposite me gets up to leave, discarding a newspaper in the process. I haven't read the news for ages.

While I've been off gallivanting with Terry, the world has stolen a march on me.

The *Sunday Times* spells out a dismal picture of events over the water, where the troubles in Northern Ireland have taken a turn for the worst. The British army, sent there to safeguard the Catholic ghettos from armed Protestant mobs, now appears to be siding with the Loyalists and have begun attacking the very people they were sent to protect. What had started as a police action is fastly becoming a full-blown war. Worse still, the government has introduced the internment of Catholics without trial, and rumors of a new British interrogation technique known as "sensory deprivation" have made their way to journalists, who say it's tantamount to torture. The newly appointed army chief, General Tuzo, is a heavy artillery man and believes in using heavy-handed methods to keep Ulster under control. His new intelligence chief, Brigadier Kitson, is fond of quoting Oliver Cromwell's dictate that the "suppression of the Irish" and the "defence of the Protestant religion" are the two main reasons for the British army's existence, which doesn't seem very intelligent at all.

Of course it's all very well to make the bullets for other folk to fire; brass hats seldom do the dirty work themselves. One such unfortunate who did was Gunner Robert Curtis. The paper says Curtis was the first English soldier to die at the hand of an IRA sniper in fifty years. The article goes on to say that by a strange twist of fate, the man who shot him was killed shortly afterward during a shootout with the army in *Curtis* Street. It's peculiar how coincidences like that come about. I remember hearing that the first construction worker to be killed on the Hoover Dam was an Irish immigrant called Gallagher and that the last to die on the project was another Irishman called Gallagher, who, as it turns out were father and son.

I suppose many more young lads will die before this thing is through. When I was wee my mother asked me what I wanted to do when I grew up.

"I want to die for Ireland!" I said, standing to attention with an air rifle on my shoulder.

"Go'way an' chase yerself," she snapped. "We don't need any more poor buggers dying for Ireland. We need people to *live* for Ireland—and live well!"

My poor country, deafened by gunfire and the wrathful roaring of Free Presbyterian fundamentalist preacher, Dr. Ian Paisley, graduate of Bob Jones's Bible Belt university. Ye gods! He's enough to give an aspirin a headache.

I doze off to the rhythmic clacking of the railroad wheels, the soft horsehair seats being more comfortable than the hard sand of last night's slumbers. Yes, it would be nice to see my mam and dad, after all this time. Two years before the mast, eh? My God, it's been nearly *three* years since I was last at home, if I can call Birmingham home. I don't feel a part of that world anymore. It's like a shell I've outgrown.

When I awaken, I'm in Waverley Station, Edinburgh. Everything seems sublimely different. The city glows in the rays of the setting sun, infusing me with an inward glow that makes my steps light on the stone staircase winding up to the Broughton Street flat. Before I reach the door, I hear the music. The lads are just wrapping up their Sunday afternoon session and it sounds wonderful.

Inside the kitchen, the boys all want to know how the trip to Lindisfarne went and I tell them, but only so much. Terry had asked me not to divulge the secret of his curse to anyone, unless he subsequently succumbed to it. I decide not to mention finding a possible solution for the mystery of the Holy Grail either. As Terry said, each must seek the grail in his own way. It doesn't matter anyway. I can see the grail all around me. It is shining in the eyes of the musicians gathered in the dingy kitchen. Bob, Gordie, Mame, Andy, Phil, and Johnny are all jewels in an invisible chalice that holds the heady wine of sweet music. Hundreds of thousands are destined to sup from its brim.

Chris Dale knows. He takes one look at me and says, "You found what you were looking for, didn't you?"

I say nothing, but just smile and tap the side of my nose.

"Oh, by the way, Billy, you've got a letter from Birmingham," says Gordie, handing me a large manila envelope.

I recognize the copperplate handwriting. It's my father's. The envelope contains no note, just a finely sketched pen-and-ink likeness of a Celtic cross drawn by my dad. I realize that he copied the image from the postcard I'd sent telling them of the death of Angus. It says more than an elegy. The stark beauty burns an image into my soul, forever to be associated with the passing of my first Scottish friend. Even when I close my eyes, I still see the Druidic circle of eternity fused with the Christian cross; male and female symbols wedded together, decorated with never-ending knotwork spirals. I marvel at my father's restraint. He was well able to screed off a long, melancholy letter of condolence, but like the artist he was, he knew what would be the more lasting testament.

My spirit, renewed by my pilgrimage to Holy Island, is ravenous for adventure. The fortunes of the Gael will be restored, and I feel that even the sad escalation in the troubles in Ireland has a part to play in this. The game is afoot, and somehow I sense the beginnings of a great resurgence in our culture. Silly Wizard no longer needs me, but I'm proud to have been a cog in this machine that now runs as smooth as a Swiss timepiece. Though I helped build it, I am now content to wind the clock and stand back to hear it strike. Johnny and Phil will grow in my place, making fine, seamless music destined to woo the world. Of this, I am sure.

My future lies in being a catalyst to others, just as Bob and Tom have been for me. Our Celtic inheritance is on the long march back from oblivion and will survive to flourish in the Camelots of a million minds, in a thousand countries. "Tiocfaidh ár lá," our ancient motto proclaims: Our day will come. And when that day comes, like all of these friends gathered here, I will be able to say, "I have done my bit!"

At the end of the following week, I gather my meager belongings and prepare to leave. All I own is a rucksack, a sleeping bag, and a fiddle in its battered old case, where my dad's drawing lies pressed like a rare butterfly between the pages of *Kerr's Merry Irish Melodies*. I stack my stuff in the hall and ask Chris Dale if he'd like to take a walk with me.

"Where do you want to go?"

"I don't know, just around the town a wee bit, you know?"

"Sure."

We make a circuit of the incidental places where memories abound. The words of an immigration song I had adapted from an old poem by William Allingham echo through my mind:

I wander round this dear old town
In the early morning sun
If enemies along past I meet,
I'll pardon every one,
I hope that man- and womankind,
Will do the same by me,
My loving friends I'll bear in mind
As I cross that rolling sea.

"Well, at least with you gone, I can move into the shaggin' palace."

"I hope you have better luck than me. That old cupboard needs fumigating."

"Where are you heading to?"

"I'm going to visit my folks, then I don't know. Ireland maybe."

"Keep your head down, as the bishop said to the actress."

At the top of the schoolyard steps, a tooth-scarred tennis ball still sits green with mold in a drain, where poor dopey Rufus last dropped it. Passing through the mews to the Purple Onion, I wave to Jean-Pierre standing at the kitchen door.

"Ow eez your crabs?"

"Much better, thank you—I got some ointment!"

"Eh?"

We laugh past the Laughing Duck, down the hill, over the cracked circle of the bonfire site and down the steps into the St. Vincent bar, my refuge, business office, and university.

The band members have set up their instruments in the back room. Dick Ollett and Cameron Crosby, from Maritime Studios, are preparing to tape the proceedings. My old mentors, Bob and Tom, are there to wish me well on my travels.

"Happy trails, Billy."

"Caress a tree, my friend!"

Dainty Madame Doubtfire sits in her snug, blowing kisses to one and all and smiling like the Queen of the May. Chris and Robbie Coltrane are playing the one-armed bandit, jokes flying as fast as the wheels. Donald, of the prehuman bowl, corners an attractive, middle-aged woman. She must have money as he seems to be on the verge of proposing. Secondhand Stuart is putting the moves on the large-lunged singer, Maddy Taylor. His advances are not being reciprocated.

"Jesus, you! Would ya ever back off? You've got more hands than Big Ben!" she roars, in a voice that can shatter a beer mug at fifty paces.

All human life is here, including Jimmy the barman, whose knotted Neanderthal brow and nasally distorted speech give many the impression that they've just met the missing link.

Andy plucks the banjo, Mame gouges the bass, Gordie sings, Johnny fiddles, Bob strums, and young Phil squeezes the music pure from an accordion as big as himself. My soul rises on a tidal wave of joy. In the midst of the tumult, I stand steadfast, back to the bar, resting my elbows on the countertop like a Breton fisherman.

"Perfect!"

The next morning, while everyone else slumbers deep, I get the bus to Fairmile Head and begin hitchhiking south. A truck loaded down with Friesian cows stops for me and I clamber in. The driver doesn't say much because the noise of the diesel is too loud for conversation, but it gives me time to reflect.

Soon we are speeding into the East Lothian coastal flatlands where Arthur rallied the Welsh-speaking Votadini to the defense of Celtic Britain. A giant hump, like the back of a great blue whale, swells from the gray mists of the plain in steeply terraced defenses. It must be Traprain Law, from whose slopes the noble chieftain Cunedda sent his sons to Wales to fight the foreign invaders. All fell in that fray, except Meirion and his brother, Ceredigion, who survived to have the Welsh kingdoms of Merioneth and Cardigan named in their honor.

Deeper into the heart of Lothian the vehicle meanders. The land around sings out its history to me. Away in the distance nestles the town of Haddington, whose quiet respectability belies its fame as the birthplace of the woman-hating Protestant zealot, John Knox, and a hungry young gentleman, Alexander Bean, who later moved to a cave on the coast of Galloway and became better known as the cannibal Sawney!

From Edward I to George III, the English armies had marched up and down these roads. Their orders were usually the same: *"Burne*

Edinborough towne, when you have sackit it and gotten what you can of it.
Then sack Holyrood house and sack Leith and burne and subvert it and all
the rest, putting man, woman and child to fyre and sword without exception."

The route the armies took is marked by the line of burned-out abbeys they left in their wake. Melrose, Dryburgh, Kelso, and Mary, Queen of Scots' favorite abbey, Jedburgh, all lie in ruins. It's here I get dropped off by the cattle truck.

A few short-haul lifts and rides on farm tractors take me inland and upward. The thin, gray road threads its way up the towering, green slopes of the Cheviot Hills to where the grass gives way to wild tufts of purple mountain heather.

The sun is slowly declining as I reach the top of Carter Bar on the old Roman military road, now called the A68. On the line of the English border, at an altitude of fourteen hundred feet, a gigantic standing stone marks the frontier. Hewn from the ancient metamorphic rock, the igneous incisor, erect and audacious, bears the name Scotland chiseled deep into its veined, grainy heart.

Enthroned on a time-worn boulder, beneath the shadow of the granite tusk, I tarry for a while, gazing back at the magnificent, fascinating country that had both overwhelmed and intrigued me in the two years of my residency. Thanks to sister Scotland, I would never be the same. The oldest monarchy in Christendom, with her quaint Scots laws and picturesque speech, will long sing her song in my heart.

To the east, way out beyond the high peak of Cheviot Law, blink the white waves surrounding Holy Island. Here, Terry had finally divulged his secret: he carries the faulty gene that may imprison his everactive mind in a functionless body. Like his father and brother before him, he has a fifty-fifty chance of being cursed by the voiceless, pitiful atrophy known as Huntington's chorea.

"Half a chance is better than no chance at all," I told him. He just smiled.

I say a prayer for him in this high place. The wind blows it to the west.

"Will ye no come back again?" pipes the skylark soaring aloft in the gilded gloaming.

"Aye, I will," I say to the sky.

Struggling to my feet, I cross the border, feeling my real adventure is about to begin. Just time for one last look: God's ain beautiful country.

I wonder what the Roman legions thought when they arrived at this far-flung point of their avaricious empire. "Ne Plus Ultra" perhaps? Nothing lies beyond? Or did they believe, as Angus did, that King Solomon's mines lay hidden somewhere in this strange land of Caledonia.

I march downhill into England through the phantom files of legionary cohorts marching north. What are these Roman ghosts looking for? Twenty thousand have fallen to Pictish spear and lance, yet still they come. Where else in their enormous empire will they construct such massive walls as those of Antoninus and Hadrian? What drives them? Pride or greed? What axiom do they carry in their hearts as they march into Scotland? "Veni, vidi, vici"? I came, I saw, I conquered? What slogan cries defiant from the heart of the motherland—"Nemo me impune lacessit"? No one attacks me with impunity? What shall the battered legions say when they return from their fruitless quest in this unconquerable country? "Caledonia non hospita fastidiosis est"?

Yeah, I guess it's just that: Scotland is not for the squeamish.

Postscript

DURING 1996, IN A DESPERATELY CYNICAL ATTEMPT TO BRIBE the Scottish electorate, British Conservative prime minister John Major returned "the Stone of Destiny" to Scotland. It was accepted with dignity and placed, not in its original home at Scone Abbey, but in Edinburgh Castle. Whether the people of Alba knew it was a fake or not, I cannot say, but in the subsequent election, no one voted Conservative.

In July 1999, the Scottish Parliament sat in Edinburgh for the first time in three hundred years. At last, Scottish affairs are back in the hands of Scotland's people.

Alba gu Brath!

Some of the Songs
Alluded to in the Text

Leave Her Johnny (Sea Chantey)

I thought I heard the Old Man say.
LEAVE HER JOHNNY, LEAVE HER,
It's one more pull and then belay,
AND IT'S TIME FOR US TO LEAVE HER,
LEAVE HER JOHNNY, LEAVE HER,
The sails are furled, our work is done
And it's time for us to leave her.

It's growl you may, but go ye must,
LEAVE HER, JOHNNY, LEAVE HER,
No matter if ye're last or fust,
FOR IT'S TIME FOR US TO LEAVE HER,
LEAVE HER JOHNNY, LEAVE HER,
Our work is done, we'll rest or rust,
AND IT'S TIME FOR US TO LEAVE HER.

The Rounding of Cape Horn

Our gallant ship the Ampithrite, she lay in Plymouth Sound
Blue peter at her foremast head, for she was outward bound,
We were lying there for orders to send us far from home
Our orders came for Rio, and thence around Cape Horn.

When we arrived in Rio, we made way for heavy gales,
We lengthened all our rigging rope and strengthened all our sails.
From ship to ship they cheered us, as we did sail along,
And wished us pleasant weather, for the rounding of Cape Horn.

In cruising off Magellan, it blew exceeding hard,
In stormy sea two Gallant tars fell from the topsel yard.
In angry seas the ropes we threw, from their poor hands were torn
We were forced to leave them for the sharks, that prowl around Cape
Horn.

When we were round the Horn, me boys, we had three glorious days,
And very soon our killick dropped into Valparaíso Bay,
The pretty girls came round in flocks, I solemnly declare,
They're far before those London girls, with their long and curly hair.

For they love a jolly sailor when he spends his money free.
They'll laugh and sing and merry-merry be, and have a jovial spree.
And when your money is all gone, they won't on you impose.
They're far before those Plymouth girls, who will pawn and sell your
clothes.

So farewell to Valparaíso and it's farewell for a while.
Likewise to all you Spanish girls, along the coast of Chile,
And if ever I live to be paid off, I'll sit and I'll sing me song—
God bless you pretty Spanish girls that we met around Cape Horn.

Across the Western Ocean (Hauling Shantey)

Oh the work is hard and the wages low.
Amelia where you bound to?
The Rocky Mountains is my home
All across the western ocean.

The land of promise soon you'll see,
Amelia where you bound to?
I'm bound across that western sea,
For to join the Irish army.

To Liverpool I'll make my way,
Amelia where you bound to?
To Liverpool that Yankee school,
All across the western ocean.

There's Liverpool Pat, with his tarpaulin hat,
Amelia where you bound to?
And Yankee John the packet rat.
All across the western ocean.

Beware these packet ships I pray,
Amelia where you bound to?
For they steal your food and yer clothes all away.
All across the western ocean.

The Skye Boat Song
(After the Battle of Culloden, 1746)

Speed bonny boat, like a bird on the wing. Onward! the sailors cry.
Carry the lad, born to be king, over the sea to Skye.
Loud the winds howl, high the seas run. Thunderclaps rend the air.
Baffled our foe, stand on the shore, follow they will not dare.

Speed bonny boat, like a bird on a wing. Onward! the sailors cry.
Carry the lad, born to be king, over the sea to Skye.
Many's the lad, fought on that day, well could the broadsword wield.
When the night came, silently, lay dead on Culloden's field.

Speed bonny boat, like a bird on a wing. Onward! the sailors cry.
Carry the lad, born to be king, over the sea to Skye.
Burnt are our homes, exile and death, scattered our loyal men.
Slow sinks the sun, down on the heath, never to rise again.

Speed bonny boat, like a bird on a wing. Onward! the sailors cry.
Carry the lad, born to be king, over the sea to Skye.
Over the sea to Skye.

Scots Wha Hae
(Battle of Bannockburn, 1314)

Scots, wha hae wi' Wallace Bled,
Scots, wham Bruce has oftimes led
Welcome tae yer gory bed,
Or to victorie!
Now's the day and now's the hour,
See the front o' battle lour,
See approach proud Edward's power,
Chains and slavery!

Wha will be a traitor knave?
Wha can fill a coward's grave?
Wha sae base as bee a slave?
Let him turn and flee!

Wha for Scotland's King and Law
Freedom's sword will strongly draw
Freeman stand or freeman fa',
Let him follow me!

By Oppression's woes and pains
By our sons in servile chains
We will drain our dearest veins,
But they shall be fee!

Lay the proud usurper low!
Tyrants fall in every foe!
Liberty's in every blow!
Let us do or dei!

The Flowers of the Forest
(Battle of Flodden Field, 1514)

I've heard them lilting, at oor ewe milking,
And I've heard them lilting afore light o' day.
Now they are mourning, a long time lamenting.
The flowers of the forest. Are a' weed away.

Sad day for the order, that sent them tae the Border.
The English, by guile, for once won the day.
Sad grief and moaning, on every green and loaning
The flowers of the forest are a' weed away.

The flowers of the forest. That fought tae the foremost.
The flowers of the forest, are a' weed away.

The Haughs of Cromdale
(Battle of Alford, 1645)

As I cam in by Auchendoon, a wee an' fair bit frae the toun
Unto the Heilands I was boon, tae view the Haughs of Cromdale.
I met a man in tartan trews and speired at him, "What is the news?"
Quoth he . . . "The Heiland army rues, the day we marched on
    Cromdale . . .

"For, we were at bed, sir, every man, when the English host upon us
    cam.
A bloody battle then began, upon the Haughs of Cromdale.
The English horse they were so rude, they bathed the boots in
    Heiland blood, But our brave Clans they boldly stood upon the
    Haughs of Cromdale.

"But alas, we could no longer stay, and o'er the hills we cam away
And sourly did lament the day, that e'er we marched to Cromdale.
Just then the great Montrose did say . . . 'Young Heiland lad show me
    the way and I'll go o'er the hills this day, to view the Haughs of
    Cromdale.'

"'But alas, my Lord, yer no so strong. Ye barely have two thousand
    men,
There's twenty thousand on the plain, stand rank and file on
    Cromdale.'
To this the great Montrose did say . . . 'If you direct the nearest way,
    Then I'll go o'er the hills this day and tak the Haughs of
    Cromdale.'

"They were at dinner, every man, when the great Montrose upon
    them cam.
Anither battle then began, aboon the Haughs of Cromdale.
The Grant, MacKinnon and Montrose, they charged upon our
    English foes
And beat them doon with Heiland blows, upon the Haughs of
    Cromdale.

"MacDonald he returned again, the Camerons did their standard join,
And the Mackintosh threw a bloody game, upon the Haughs of
    Cromdale.
Of twenty thousand Cromwell's men, five hundred fled to Aberdeen.
The rest of them lie on the plain. Rank and file on Cromdale."